# SOCIAL CONSTRUCTIONS OF NATIONALISM IN THE MIDDLE EAST

SUNY series in Middle Eastern Studies
Shahrough Akhavi

# SOCIAL CONSTRUCTIONS OF NATIONALISM IN THE MIDDLE EAST

*edited by*

## FATMA MÜGE GÖÇEK

State University
of New York
Press

Published by
State University of New York Press, Albany

© 2002  State University of New York

For information, address State University of New York Press,
90 State Street, Suite 700, Albany, NY 12207

Production by Susan Geraghty
Marketing by Michael Campochiaro

**Library of Congress Cataloging-in-Publication Data**

Social constructions of nationalism in the Middle East / [edited by] Fatma Müge Göçek.
        p.  cm. — (SUNY series in Middle Eastern studies)
    Includes bibliographical references and index.
    ISBN 0-7914-5197-6 (alk. paper) — ISBN 0-7914-5198-4 (pbk. : alk. paper)
        1. Nationalism—Middle East. I. Göçek, Fatma Müge. II. Series.

DS63.5 .S63 2001
320.54′0956—dc21
                                                                            2001020144

10  9  8  7  6  5  4  3  2  1

# CONTENTS

PART III    Cultural Representation

# ABOUT THE CONTRIBUTORS

**Fatma Müge Göçek** teaches in the Department of Sociology and the Women's Studies Program at the University of Michigan.

**Şükrü Hanioğlu** teaches in the Department of Near Eastern Studies at Princeton University.

**James L. Gelvin** teaches in the Department of History at the University of California, Los Angeles.

**Miriam Cooke** teaches in the Department of Asian and African Languages and Literature at Duke University.

**Julie M. Peteet** teaches in the Department of Anthropology at the University of Louisville.

**Suad Joseph** teaches in the Department of Anthropology at University of California, Santa Barbara.

**Shiva Balaghi** teaches in the Program in Near Eastern Studies at New York University.

**Walter Armbrust** teaches in the Center for Arab Studies at Georgetown University.

**Mandana E. Limbert** is a postdoctoral fellow at the Program in Near Eastern Studies at New York University.

# CHAPTER 1

# Introduction:
# *Narrative, Gender,*
# *and Cultural Representation*
# *in the Constructions of*
# *Nationalism in the Middle East*

## Fatma Müge Göçek

"The story of nationalism is necessarily a story of betrayal," Partha Chatterjee tells us, since nationalism "confers freedom only by imposing new controls, defines a cultural identity for the nation only by excluding many from its fold, and grants the dignity of citizenship to some because others could not be allowed to speak for themselves."[1] This contradictory essence runs through most of the literature on nationalism as scholars debate its definition, differential impact, and disparate transformation. The chapters in this volume step back from these debates to focus instead on the social construction of nationalism. They emphasize the process through which nationalism is constituted through the constant negotiation of its boundaries by including some groups, meanings, and practices and excluding others. The chapters cluster specifically around three sites of boundary negotiation in the construction of nationalism in the Middle East: narrative, gender, and cultural representation. These sites especially help illuminate both the silences nationalism rests upon and the new voices it creates.

## NATIONALISM AND ITS CONTRADICTIONS

An examination of the current debates on nationalism, ranging from its specific origins to the nature of its present manifestations reveals a fun-

1

damental dichotomy between the political and cultural. While some scholars emphasize the political dimension of nationalism in terms of its legitimation of the bureaucratic state organization,[2] others stress the cultural dimension in terms of it emotional, ethnic, quasi-religious aspects.[3] The epistemological roots of this political/cultural dichotomy are traced to Kant and to Herder's alternate conceptions of the nation:[4] Kant depicts the nation as a political community comprising individuals signifying their will in determining the form of government, whereas Herder perceives the nation as a natural solidarity comprising unique cultural characteristics. The debate on the specific historical location of the origin of the nation builds upon this dichotomy: scholars such as Ernest Gellner[5] emphasize the political dimension trace the emergence of the nation to the seventeenth-century conceptions of statehood, while others such as Anthony Smith,[6] stressing the cultural dimension, trace back the idea of nation and national loyalty to antiquity.

The shift from theory to praxis whereby scholars attempt to identify and categorize national constructions replicates the political/cultural dichotomy. The focus on the nature of political institutions leads Michael Mann[7] to identify two factors accounting for the different forms nations take: the lack of fit between the boundaries of a nation and the existing state, and the forms of popular mobilization from the top down or the reverse. The disparate political forms of nationalism between France and England on the one side and the rest of Europe on the other leads John Hall[8] to bring forward another factor lodged in history: as nationalism is disseminated by design by French armies during the Napoleonic era, it gets transformed as the Prussian state adopts it defensively "as a revolution from above" in order to survive its impact, as the Czechs mobilize from below to develop "risorgimento nationalism," and later as the German national socialists produce "integral nationalism" in their attempts to unite a new society at the expense of the minorities. Leah Greenfeld[9] draws upon the political framework as she categorizes nationalisms into three types as individualist/civic (as in England), collectivistic/civic (as in France) and collectivistic/ethnic (as in Russia and Germany). In contrast to the emphasis of the political perspective on structures and forms of mass mobilization, the cultural perspective emphasizes the emergence of different visions of nationalism. Miroslav Hroch[10] emphasizes the significance of ideas in the development of nationalism among smaller European nations; the initial phase comprises the scholarly activity of a small group of intellectuals developing the idea of the nation, which leads to conscious national agitation for emancipation by a growing number of patriots, which in turn generates mass nationalist activity. The delineation of the difference between France and England on the one side and the rest of Europe on the other also emerges in the cultural perspective: Hans Kohn[11] argues that the French nationalism set the parameters of nationalism with its cosmopolitan outlook, universalism, and acceptance of civilization along the standards of the Enlightenment—German nationalism "deviated" from this positive model by assuming an ethnic and cultural character with an anti-Enlightenment and romantic stand.

The cultural/political dichotomy disappears as both camps move away from France and England toward Germany, Russia and the rest of the world. Both view these emergent nationalisms as "deviations" that often hegemonize and terrorize people, thus introducing a new dichotomy between the "Western" model and its "non-Western" imitations. Eli Kedourie[12] identifies colonialism and the Western education of indigenous intellectuals as the two predominant factors determining the contours of Third-World nationalism. New states in Latin America, John Hall[13] argues, are created on an entirely different conception of nationalism based on "desire and fear blessed by opportunity." The transformation of the political\cultural dichotomy into a Western\non-Western one become complete when Partha Chatterjee[14] argues that the anti-colonial nationalism in the non-Western world divides the world of institutions and social practices into two domains, the material domain of the "outside," of a West-dominated science and technology, and the "inner" spiritual domain bearing the "essential" marks of cultural identity where the modern conception of nation is forged. The inconsistency produced by this divide leads non-Western nationalism to failure:[15] the nationalist project cannot maintain its distinctive identity and also adjust it to the requirements of progress.

How does one surmount the political/cultural and Western/non-Western dichotomies in the analysis of nationalism? Bruce Kapferer[16] suggests that each nationalism be treated as a distinct case without being compared to others: such an approach would alleviate the problem of the evaluation and interpretation of one nationalism by the norms and practices of another. Another more practical suggestion is to seek analytically for frameworks that overcome the dichotomies. Ron Suny[17] recommends, for instance, that political process and meaning creation be analyzed simultaneously since "the generation of shared meanings, feelings and perceived interests cannot be derived directly from social processes or structures . . . but is mediated and comprehended through the discourses of nationalism as they reach intellectuals, activists and ordinary people." This approach also follows upon the work of Benedict Anderson,[18] who focuses on the imagined and constructed nature of nationalism as contemporary political processes interact with technological and cultural developments to produce new visions of political community. The essays in this edited volume build upon this last approach as they focus on the process through which Middle Eastern nationalism is constructed. This focus on the process of construction introduces a fluidity to the analysis that does indeed largely succeed in escaping existing divides.

## A NEW FOCUS ON THE
## SOCIAL CONSTRUCTION OF NATIONALISM

This volume delves into the social construction of nationalism in the Middle East by arguing that the boundaries of nationalism take shape through a practice of constant negotiation that includes some groups, meanings, and practices and excludes others. The essays in the volume identify narrative, gender, and cultural representation as the three sites around which boundary negotiation becomes significant.

The work of Max Weber[19] on social closure and its subsequent interpretations by Frank Parkin[20] and others forms the theoretical foundation of this constructionist approach. Max Weber first alerts scholars to the falsely assumed cultural and ethnic homogeneity in the conceptualizations of the modern nation-state and then proceeds to unravel this false assumption of homogeneity by pointing out internal cleavages based on religion, ethnicity, or linguistic, racial, and cultural differentiation. These internal cleavages become obscured through the process of social closure whereby dominant groups exclude some and usurp others to erase signs of difference. Frank Parkin[21] studies this process of exclusion and usurpation in more detail, arguing that the process occurs simultaneously since the exclusion process inadvertently reveals the criteria of inclusion and usurpation. In addition to production relations, public and private property and education emerge as the two most significant exclusionary devices in contemporary society through which dominant groups exclude others. We argue here that nationalism is constructed through a similar process of social closure whereby a social group assumes the cloak of the "nation" to contest, negotiate, and determine which groups, meanings, and practices ought to define the imagined community of the nation. As this group identifies certain shared characteristics of what comprises a nation, as it creates common myths, employs specific cultural symbols, passes particular laws, it concomitantly starts to form social boundaries around the imagined community that include some elements and exclude others.

In the context of the Middle East, narrative, gender, and cultural representation emerge as the three significant sites where the boundaries of nationalism are negotiated through a process of inclusion and exclusion. The site of narrative discloses the experiences that unite social groups into political communities—the stories of the past and the present are told and retold to include the historical memories of certain social groups, to privilege certain symbols and myths, and to overlook others. The site of gender similarly reveals that nationalist projects consistently favor the standpoint of men and privilege the masculine and that they do so with the firm support of the state. The site of cultural representation explores the venues of fiction, theater, film, and television through which nationalism generates and reproduces meaning, favoring some interpretations over others. In all these sites, the emerging boundaries are continuously tested and contested by all members of society both within and outside the imagined communities. This process of contestation both reproduces existing conceptions of nationalism and, at the same time, creates ambiguities that could potentially challenge them.

The edited volume also takes a methodological position. Unlike the works on nationalism that often present in-depth case analyses or bring together nationalisms of specific geographical regions, it focuses on themes that crosscut existing boundaries. In doing so, it follows the example of Rashid Khalidi's edited volume *The Origins of Arab Nationalism* (1992), which brings together analyses on Arab nationalism in Lebanon, Syria, Egypt, and the Hejaz. Our edited volume similarly focuses on themes that connect Arab, Turkish, Persian, and other nationalisms. Our contributors also crosscut academic divides as they come from a multiplicity of disciplines, ranging from literature, history, anthropology, and political science to sociology. Their essays employ a wide range of sources from official correspondence, theater, literary narratives, demonstrations, films, and television programs.

## OUTLINE OF THE VOLUME

A more detailed discussion of the themes and essays in comprising the volume demonstrates these points in more detail.[22]

### Part 1: Narrative

"The narration of the nation," Homi Bhabha argues,[23] contains "thresholds of meanings that must be crossed, erased, and translated in the process of cultural production." Indeed, the ambiguity of the boundaries of the nation becomes apparent in narration as social groups continually contest and renegotiate their interpretations of the past, present, and future. The nationalist narrative often emerges as a simple, strong story painted in wide, bold brush strokes, one that frequently suppresses alternative sequences and erases sites of resistance. "Dissenting and marginal voices," Partha Chatterjee[24] tells us, "are appropriated with varying degrees of risk and success."

Narrative is significant in constructing a shared experience around which social groups build solidarity. As events of the past are recited, as leaders and heroes are identified, as certain values and norms are emphasized at the expense of others, certain ethnic, religious, and racial groups emerge triumphant over others to define the boundaries of nationalism. The essays in part 1 all focus on constructions of narratives that privilege the experiences of certain social groups over others. While Fatma Müge Göçek studies the emergence of narratives of nationalism by Greeks, Armenians, Turks, and Arabs in the Ottoman Empire, Şükrü Hanioğlu focuses on the historical events that enabled Young Turks to form Turkish nationalism at the expense of Ottomanism. James L. Gelvin's essay illuminates how the separate demonstrations of the elite and masses in Syria created disparate narratives and thus multiple Arab nationalisms.

According to Göçek, three elements interacted to from the narrative of Greek, Armenian, Turkish, and Arab nationalisms: structures of war, commerce, and reforms; visions of history, literature, and education; and organization of philanthropic associations, secret societies, and political parties. While all four nationalisms shared these elements, their diverse locations within the Ottoman social structure accounted for the disparate political outcomes: the Greeks and Turks formed their own nation-states, the Armenians failed to sustain theirs within the empire, and the Arabs fractured into many political units.

Hanioğlu focuses on the transition form Ottomanism to Turkish nationalism; he argues that the failure of appeals to groups to join Ottomanism, the inability of the Ottoman state to socialize its subjects into citizens, and outrage against the policy of Great Powers and subsequent Ottoman defeats enabled Turkish nationalists to create a narrative that promised a new vision. The Japanese victory against the Russians, which demonstrated to the Ottomans the possibility of success of non-European races over European ones, was especially significant in the emergence of this racially based new vision.

Gelvin analyzes one form of collective ceremony, the demonstration, under British rule and the Faysal administration in Syria to illustrate how different types of demonstrations demarcated the boundaries of different imagined communities. The government-planned demonstrations fronted by the elites emphasized vertical relations of patronage, contained short speeches in French and English, and briefly utilized popular participation as a backdrop. Mass demonstrations, however, emphasized a political community with horizontal relations of power, highlighted popular participation, contained impassioned long impromptu speeches, and thus concretized the will of the nation. The different narratives produced by these two disparate experiences thus produced multiple Arab nationalisms.

*Part 2: Gender*

Even though women are very prominent in nationalist imagery, not only has nationalism never granted women and men equal access to resources of the nation-state, but it also continuously favored a distinctly homoso-cial form of bonding. The nation-state remains "a repository of male hopes, male aspirations, and male privilege."[25] The image of the nation as woman frames women as chaste, dutiful, daughterly, or maternal, thereby symbolically both limiting and absorbing women into the body politic.[26] Even though nationalism acknowledges women's reproductive role, the cultural reproduction of the national spirit still remains a male act, as men imbue eternal life upon the nation through "culture, heroic deeds and qualities of the spirit."[27] Women become further eroticized and exoticized in colonial discourse to justify imperial domination in the name of a civilization where the European male springs to action to pro-tect the oppressed indigenous female.[28] The anticolonial nationalist dis-course that emerges in opposition to this portrayal reacts in turn by withdrawing women into the private sphere; nationalism situates "the women's question in an inner domain of sovereignty, far removed from the arena of political contest with the colonial state."[29] In nationalist struggles, the discourse is thus about women but often not by them; the location of women in the inner domain precludes any possibility of effective reform in altering their political exclusion.

The site of gender thus becomes significant in identifying a funda-mental boundary around which the imagined communities exclude women as social actors. Even though women actively participate in all stages of nationalist endeavors, their contribution is often decontextual-ized and idealized in the narratives and their participation often curbed or demobilized in the ensuing public institutions. The essays in part 2 all problematize gender within the context of nationalism to explode this patriarchal interpretation; in order to uncover women's agency, the first essay explores women's literary narratives, and the latter two decon-struct the role of the state. Miriam Cooke studies women's literary nar-ratives in Lebanon to develop a humanistic nationalism where women develop outside the boundaries of the state as social agents. In focusing on the intersection between gender and the state in the context of nationalism, Julie M. Peteet examines the Palestinian resistance move-ment to illustrate the gradual emergence of the state control of gender and sexuality, while Suad Joseph demonstrates how in Lebanon gender and patriarchy weave through the public/private and state/civil society distinctions to render them meaningless.

Cooke's focus on women's literary constructions as a response to the failure of nationalist projects and state nationalism leads her to an alternate formulation of women-centered imagined communities and political selfhood. It is in this context that Cooke discovers the form of humanist nationalism generated by women, one rooted in an individual, nurturing relationship with Lebanon that is dynamic, reciprocal, and quasimaternal—one that induces self-generation rather than destruction. After exploring new sources of knowledge on nationalism to reveal and challenge the boundaries of state nationalism that exclude women, Cooke constructs instead an inclusionary humanistic nationalism.

Peteet's analysis focuses on the process through which the gendering of political practice takes place in Palestinian nationalism. Based on her ethnographic research, she argues that political structures control sexuality and gender identity through two processes; while the militarization of society and the concomitant gender ambiguity facilitate control over definitions of legitimate sexualities, the replacement of the family by the committees enables the hierarchization of forms of gender identity and participation in political struggle. As a consequence, political structures start to determine who is to be included in the movement at what level, given their sexual proclivities and gender identity. Suad Joseph argues that local gender systems, especially patriarchy, operate as central threads in the cloth of cultures that weave through all social and structural divides in Lebanon. She uses gender as the main agent of boundary formation as opposed to the existing one premised on the state/civil society divide. This formulation leads Joseph, like Cooke, to advocate for a democracy based on the elimination of gendered forms of domination.

## Part 3: Cultural Representation

"Every nation," Hegel states in The Positivity of the Christian Religion,[30] "has its own imagery, its gods, angels, devils or saints who live in the nation's traditions . . . [and whose] history, recollection of . . . deeds is linked with public festivals, national games, with many of the state's domestic institutions or foreign affairs, with well-known houses and districts with public memorials and temples." Even though Hegel then continues to predict the demise of these cultural symbols with the world-historical progress of nations, they nevertheless form a site in creating meaning structures for the nation-state. Indeed, in nineteenth-century Europe, rites and festivals, myths and symbols draw people into active participation in the national mystique, and national monuments in stone and mortar anchor them in national consciousness.[31] These cultural processes become especially significant in the Third World as the only sites that escape the material domination of the West in science and technology "to protect, preserve and strengthen the inner core, the distinctive spiritual essence of the national culture."[32] Nation-states in the Middle East seek similar reassurances as they delve into the historical past to create public events that culturally reaffirm their existence.[33] For instance, the Turkish republic excavates pre-Islamic Hittite sites in its attempt to extend the Turkish presence in Anatolia to antiquity while Syria reconstructs a second-century Roman theater to instigate its rule as the extension of ancient civilizations; Iran seeks for roots in pre-Islamic Akhaemenian Persia, and Egypt's pharaonic past becomes a source of national self-assertion. These sites of cultural representation also become globally transportable with the current developments in communication; citizens living abroad recreate their imagined nation and its imagined past through broadcasts.

The site of cultural representation is significant in displaying a multitude of media such as theater, film, television, posters, or novels that become contested sites of meaning for constructions of nationalism; the state and civil society vie for control of these sites to affirm the legitimacy of the social groups controlling them. The essays in part 3 all focus on how cultural representations set the boundaries of the imagined communities by selectively giving meaning to the experiences and interpretations of certain social groups. Shiva Balaghi focuses on the creation of a new form of theater in Iran that fostered the emergence of a specific nationalist vision; Walter Armbrust's comparison of films by a popular producer in Egypt with state-sponsored posters conveys two different interpretations of the modernist ideology underlying the Egyptian nationalist project. Mandana E. Limbert similarly compares two disparate visions of the Iranian nation presented in the Persian-language television programs in the United States as proroyalist/secular images clash with those of the Islamic Republic.

Balaghi analyzes how the new cultural medium of the theater identified Iran's internal woes, generated new visions of Iran and Europe on stage, and gradually set a national agenda to remedy the perceived weaknesses. The Iranian theater also revealed European political ambitions in that it provided a new window for the Orientalists through which they could identify Iranian disorder and justify European intervention to remedy it. Armbrust focuses on another more recent cultural medium, the film, in the context of Egypt; he illustrates two disparate visions of the Egyptian nationalist project by comparing the popular films of 'Adil Imam with to the Ministry of Culture's official poster of Egypt's hundred years of enlightenment. While the poster projects an imagined sense of historical continuity where Egyptians successfully accomplish the modernist vision embedded in the nationalist project, the films of 'Adil Imam criticize such a pristine and positive image of Egyptian modernity—the protagonists of all the films believe in the system at first but are then either corrupted, imprisoned, or ostracized by it.

Mandana Limbert identifies another site of such contestation as she analyzes Persian-language television programs produced in the United States by the proroyalists who support the return of the Pahlavis, the secularists who espouse a Western-style democracy, and the government organizations of the Islamic Republic of Iran who are currently in power in Iran. Even though all three claim to be the legitimate representatives of the Iranian national identity, the political priorities, lifestyles, and moral principles they advocate for their imagined communities vastly differ from one another.

## BIBLIOGRAPHY

Alter, Peter. 1989. *Nationalism*. London: Edward Arnold.

Anderson, Benedict. 1983. *Imagined* Communities: Reflections on the Origin and Spread of Nationalism. London: Verso.

Balakrishnan, Gopal. 1995. "The National Imagination." *New Left Review* 211: 56–69.

Baram, Amitzia. 1990. "Territorial Nationalism in the Middle East." *Middle Eastern Studies* 26: 425–48.

Bhabha, Homi. 1990. "Introduction: Narrating the Nation." Pp. 1–7 in *Nation and Narration*. London: Routledge.

Breuilly, John. 1993. *Nationalism and the State*. Chicago: University of Chicago Press.

Brubaker, Rogers. 1992. *Citizenship and Nationhood in France and Germany*. Cambridge, MA: Harvard University Press.

Chatterjee, Partha. 1993. *The Nation and Its Fragments: Colonial and Postcolonial Histories*. Princeton, NJ: Princeton University Press.

———. 1986. *Nationalist Thought and the Colonial World: A Derivative Discourse?* London: Zed Books.

Connor, Walter. 1994. *Ethnonationalism: The Quest for Understanding*. Princeton, NJ: Princeton University Press.

Eley, Geoff. 1981. "Nationalism and Social History." *Social History* 6/1: 83–107.

Gellner, Ernest. 1994. *Encounters with Nationalism*. Oxford: Blackwell.

———. 1987. *Culture, Identity and Politics*. Cambridge: Cambridge University Press.

———. 1983. *Nations and Nationalism*. Oxford: Blackwell.

Giddens, Anthony. 1985. *The Nation-State and Violence*. Cambridge: Polity.

Hall, John. 1993. "Nationalisms, Classified and Explained." *Daedalus* 122/3: 1–28.

Hobsbawm, Eric. 1990. *Nations and Nationalism since the 1780s: Programme, Myth, Reality*. Cambridge: Cambridge University Press.

Hroch, Miroslav. 1985. *Social Preconditions of National Revival in Europe: A Comparative Analysis of Social Composition of Patriotic Groups among the Smaller European Nations*. Cambridge: Cambridge University Press.

Kapferer, Bruce. 1988. *Legends of People, Myths of State*. Washington, DC: Smithsonian Institution Press.

Kedourie, Elie. 1966. *Nationalism*. London: Hutchinson.

———, ed. 1971. *Nationalism in Asia and Africa*. London: Weidenfeld and Nicholson.

Khalidi, Rashid. 1992. *The Origins of Arab Nationalism*. New York: Columbia University Pres.

Kohn, Hans. 1967. *Prelude to Nation-States: The French and German Experience, 1789–1815*. New Jersey: D. Van Nostrand.

Mann, Michael. 1995. "A Political Theory of Nationalism and Its Excesses." Pp. 44–64 in *Notions of Nationalism*, Sukumar Periwal, ed. Budapest: Central European University Press.

McClintock, Ann. 1991. "No Longer in a Future Heaven: Women and Nationalism in South Africa." *Transitions* 51.

Mosse, George. 1975. *The Nationalization of the Masses: Political Symbolism and Mass Movements in Germany from the Napoleonic Wars to the Third Reich*. Ithaca: Cornell University Press.

———. 1985. *Nationalism and Sexuality: Middle-Class Morality and Sexual Norms in Modern Europe*. Madison: University of Wisconsin Press.

Parker, Andrew, M. Russo, D. Sommer, and P. Yaeger. 1992. "Introduction." Pp. 1–18 in *Nationalisms and Sexualities*. New York: Routledge.

Parkin, Frank. 1979. *Marxism and Class Theory: A Bourgeois Critique*. London: Tavistock.

Rex, John. 1986. *Race and Ethnicity Open*. Stratford: University Press.

Seton-Watson, Hugh. 1977. *Nations and States: An Enquiry into the Origins of Nations and the Politics of Nationalism*. Boulder: Westview.

Smith, Anthony. 1995. *Nations and Nationalism in a Global Era*. New York: Polity.

———. 1988. "The Myth of the Modern Nation and the Myths of Nations." *Ethnic and Racial Studies* 11/1: 1–26.

———. 1986. *Ethnic Origins of Nations*. New York: Oxford University Press.

———. 1983. *Theories of Nationalism*. New York: Holmes and Meier.

Suny, Ronald Grigor. 1993. *Looking toward Ararat: Armenia in Modern History*. Bloomington: Indiana University Press.

Taylor, Charles. 1989. *Sources of the Self: The Making of Modern Identity*. Cambridge, MA: Harvard University Press.

Tilly, Charles. 1975. "Reflections on the History of European State-Making. Pp. 3–83 in *The Formation of National States in Western Europe*. Princeton: Princeton University Press.

Tivey, Leonard. 1981. "Introduction." Pp. 1–12 in *The Nation-State: The Formation of Modern Politics*, L. Tivey, ed. Oxford: Martin Robertson.

Verdery, Katherine. 1994. "From Parent-State to Family Patriarchs: Gender and Nation in Contemporary Eastern Europe." *East European Politics and Societies* 8/2: 225–55.

Weber, Max. 1967. *Economy and Society.* Berkeley: University of California Press.

## NOTES

1. Chatterjee 1993, p. 154.
2. See, for instance, Breuilly 1993; Gellner 1983; Giddens 1985; and Hobsbawm 1990.
3. See, for instance, Anderson 1983; Seton-Watson 1977; Smith 1986; and Tivey 1981.
4. Refer to Kedourie 1966 for an extensive discussion.
5. See especially Ernest Gellner 1983.
6. Refer especially to Smith 1986.
7. See, for instance Mann 1995, p. 46.
8. Refer, for instance, to Hall 1993.
9. See, in particular, Greenfeld 1992, p. 11.
10. See, for instance, Hroch 1985.
11. See, in particular, Kohn 1967.
12. See Kedourie 1971.
13. See, in particular, Hall 1993, p. 9.
14. Refer to Chatterjee 1993, in particular.
15. Refer to Chatterjee 1986, in particular.
16. See Kapferer 1988.
17. See in particular Suny 1993, p. 17.
18. See Anderson 1983 in particular.
19. Refer to Weber 1967 for an extensive discussion of his conceptualization.
20. See, in particular, Parkin 1979.
21. See ibid., p. 45.
22. Please note that the Arabic transcriptions vary across the essays. The particular transcription employed in each essay reflects the preference of the author of the essay.
23. Bhabha 1990, p. 4.
24. Chatterjee 1993, p. 156.
25. McClintock 1991, p. 122.
26. See in particular Mosse 1985, p. 67.
27. Verdery 1994, p. 242.
28. See, in particular, Enloe 1989, p. 44.
29. Chatterjee 1993, p. 117.
30. Refer to the citation in Balakrishnan 1995, p. 59.
31. See, for instance, Mosse 1975, p. 2.
32. Chatterjee 1993, pp. 120–21.
33. See Baram 1990.

# PART I

# *Narrative*

# CHAPTER 2

# The Decline of the Ottoman Empire and the Emergence of Greek, Armenian, Turkish, and Arab Nationalisms

## Fatma Müge Göçek

In the late nineteenth century, a Muslim army physician commented on how the attempts to salvage the empire led ironically to its demise by generating disparate identities, including his own Turkish one. He stated:[1]

> We saw that a Circassian club had opened in our neighborhood. Then an Albanian association was formed. Soon after, an Arab philanthropic society appeared! . . . Circassians wanted their freedom, as did the Albanians. The members of all these clubs were graduates of our own schools. . . . Hence the Bulgarian . . . Albanian . . . Arab independence movements were all manned by those reared and educated in our country, our schools . . . I am dying for the Turkish cause, but I am carrying this cause like a secret bowl in me. I do not tell about it to anyone. For I know that if we do that, our action will legitimate the explication of the inner thoughts of the others. And that would mean the fragmentation, the extinction of the empire.

In spite of the precautions of the physician, the ensuing polarization generated Greek, Armenian, Turkish, and Arab[2] nationalisms. This chapter focuses on the emergence of these nationalisms through time and in comparison to one another. It argues that structures, visions, and organizations interact to construct nationalisms. Specifically, political structures combine with visions of history within the context of specific organizations to produce Greek, Armenian, Turkish, and Arab nationalisms.

While the historical phenomena of war, commerce, and reform movements determine the structure of nationalisms, the new visions of history, literature, and education gave meaning to them. The political mobilization during these phenomena and around these visions occurred as a consequence of the new organizational forms of philanthropic associations, secret societies, and political parties. It was thus the interaction of these three elements of structures, visions, and organizations within the historical context of Ottoman decline that determined the specific forms and trajectories of emergent nationalisms.

Although these nationalisms have been studied separately, there are no existing surveys that problematize and comparatively analyze their disparate destinies. Yet a comparative analysis of the social construction of these four nationalisms might illuminate why nationalisms acquire a particular shape, trajectory, and outcome. Among the four nationalisms, Greek nationalism was the first to become established with ample European support of its independence in the early nineteenth century; the Armenian nationalist movement, which developed almost a century later, faced a harsher, polarized, and more nationalistic Ottoman state that totally destroyed it. The Arab nationalist movement, which emerged in early twentieth century and gained momentum during and after the First World War, led, with Western help, to the secession of the Arab provinces from the empire. Escalating military defeats and social polarization enabled Turkish nationalism to gradually triumph over Ottomanism, culminating in the foundation of a Turkish nation-state on the ruins of the empire.

## MULTIPLE DIMENSIONS OF NATIONALISM
## AND THE OTTOMAN CONTEXT

The current literature on nationalism articulates the structural, cultural and organizational dimensions employed here. Scholars who trace the historical formation of nationalism[3] often emphasize the institutions and organizational framework through which nationalisms become publicly visible. Tracing the roots of the word *nation* to the Latin root *nasci* "to be born," implying the idea of a people of common breed or place of origin, Leonard Tivey[4] focuses, for instance, on how the state employs educational institutions, a system of citizenship to create such imagined unity, and uniformity of origin. Peter Alter[5] traces the emergence of the nation-states to the Congress of Vienna and emphasizes how nations create their own definition through the Western European historical transformation. Anthony Smith focuses instead on the spread[6] of nationalism "from its French and English heartlands" to seeds planted in Germany, Hungary, and Italy, which then, in turn, serve as models for the nationalisms of Serbia, Greece and others. In studying nationalism among the smaller European nations, Miroslav Hroch[7] focuses on the social actors and the processes through which nationalism mobilizes society; he emphasizes the significance of the interaction between the urban strata, especially the new social groups of the bourgeoisie and the professionals with new material interests, with the countryside.

Scholars who focus on the meaning systems that generate and interpret nationalism emphasize especially the role of culture in producing the spectrum of nationalisms.[8] Ernest Gellner identifies[9] homogeneity, literacy, and anonymity as the traits of nationalism where men profess political loyalty to a culture, often transmitted through education. The sense of solidarity, common culture, and national consciousness often defines the elements that gradually bind a community of people into a nation.[10] Anthony Smith delves[11] into the construction of nationalism and highlights ethnicity as the significant category through which communities generate "common myths of descent, shared historical memories, a common culture, an association with a recognized territory and a sense of solidarity." Geoff Eley[12] problematizes the ahistoricity often embedded in the formulation of nationalism[13] when he reconceptualizes nationality as a "complex, uneven unpredictable process forged from an interaction of cultural coalescence and specific political intervention." Benedict Anderson's work focuses on the imagined nature of this newly created political community, "imagined as both inherently limited and sovereign . . . as a cultural artefact of a particular kind,"[14] that spreads out to Asia and Africa where its constructed nature becomes even more apparent. Even though the organizational elements within which these nationalisms take shape are not extensively discussed in and of themselves, all the scholars also take notice of the philanthropic and secret societies and political parties that help reproduce nationalisms.

Structure, cultural processes, and organizational forms interact within a historical framework to produce different constructions of nationalisms. The nationalisms produced in the Ottoman Empire do indeed follow such a pattern. The Ottoman Empire, founded in the late-thirteenth-century in Asia Minor, was ruling over parts of the Balkans, Crimea, Asia Minor, the Fertile Crescent, and North Africa in the eighteenth and part of the nineteenth centuries and gradually disintegrated in the course of the late nineteenth and early twentieth centuries as Greek, Armenian, Turkish, and Arab nationalisms emerged from within. The empire ended officially in 1922 as it was replaced by the Turkish Republic.

What was the effect of the Ottoman social structure on how the four nationalisms emerged? The Ottoman social structure[15] was theoretically based on the personal delegation of authority by the sultan. Those who administered the sultan's delegated authority were the "rulers" who dispensed justice, governed the provinces, recruited soldiers, and collected taxes. In return for carrying out these services, the officials received grants and revenues, did not pay taxes, wore distinct clothing, carried arms, and had an exclusive educational and legal system. The rest of society without the sultan's delegated authority made up the "ruled" who had no access to the sultan's authority or thereby to any of the privileges associated with it. They were subdivided along the lines of religion and settlement into Muslim and non-Muslim, town people and peasants, and sedentary and nomadic people, each with different tax obligations. The significant divide among the Greek and Armenian nationalisms on the one side and the Turkish and Arab nationalisms on the other emerged from the fact that religion was the fixed requirement for joining the ranks of the rulers—being a Muslim was the most important requirement in reaching the highest echelons of the Ottoman social structure. Such a divide categorically placed the non-Muslims of the empire among the ruled—only under exceptional circumstances and through display of skills could a select number of Ottoman minorities join the ranks of the rulers.

The Ottoman social structural location of the non-Muslim religious minorities within the ruled informed the organizational basis of the subsequent Greek and Armenian nationalisms. The Ottoman minorities had protected legal status as a religious community; each was granted some internal autonomy and had to pay special protection and military exemption in return.[16] This internal autonomy often comprised the right to designate communal administrators to oversee communal property, to adjudicate conflict within the community, and to represent the community to the Ottoman state at large. The Ottoman religious minorities[17] mainly comprised the Greeks, Armenians, Jews, and Arab Christians[18] in the provinces. All Orthodox Christians, including the Greeks, Serbs, Bulgarians, Melkites, Rumanians and Albanians were placed under the authority of the Greek patriarch, and the non-Orthodox Christian subjects,[19] comprising the Armenian, Ethiopian, Syrian Jacobite, Georgian, Chaldean, and Coptic communities, came under the jurisdiction of the Armenian patriarch.[20] Hence Greeks and Armenians became the two ethnoreligious categories in the empire as the religious elements identifying these minority groups combined with cultural ones: sumptuary and legal codes, codes on the use of space carefully defined and reflected this basic separation. The restrictions placed upon the minorities prevented them from developing social ties with the Muslims through marriage, inheritance, or attending same places of worship or bathhouses. Such restrictions, whether present in theory or in practice, delineated and maintained the boundaries of minorities as a separate social group[21] and led them instead to develop social ties with other non-Muslims who were either members of other Ottoman minorities or with foreign residents who were often connected to European powers.

The Ottoman social structure affected the developing Greek and Armenian nationalisms in a manner quite different from the Turkish and Arab ones. Turks and Arabs were predominantly Muslim and therefore united as one within the large community of believers, a community that overlooked ethnic, racial, and other divides from within the congregation. They in theory appeared as actors equally eligible for recruitment as the officials of the empire. It was this unity, one that did not exist with the Ottoman Greeks and Armenians, that gave their nationalist movements a different slant. The Ottoman ethnoreligious divide certainly inhibited the mobilization of nineteenth- and twentieth-century emergent nationalisms around a common vision. Still, one factor that united the experiences of actors in all four nationalisms was that in each case those social actors who initially drew power from the sultan lost out.

## PATTERNS OF EMERGENT NATIONALISMS IN THE OTTOMAN EMPIRE

The communication revolution that occurred with the establishment of the newspapers, the development of the telegraph and the railroad system, and the linkage of ports and hinterland escalated the impact of the interaction of the structural, cultural, and organizational elements that shaped the emergent nationalisms in the Ottoman Empire. Social and political interactions within and across social groups occurred at a much accelerated pace and promptly transformed existing arrangements.

### Structures of War, Commerce, and Reform

The wars involving the Ottoman Empire in the nineteenth and early twentieth centuries stemmed mostly from the "Eastern question," referring to the quandaries faced by England, France, Austria, Germany, and Russia, in locating the Ottoman Empire within their realignment of political and economic spheres of influence throughout the world. Many wars were fought among the European powers, Russia, and the Ottoman Empire to delineate the boundaries of this realignment. As economic influence interacted with political might, European powers intervened more in the future course of the Ottoman Empire. The European need for both raw material and new markets led to increased European economic penetration and the subsequent weakening of Ottoman trade and production. Another European intervention was its support of social reforms; France and England urged social reforms onto the Ottoman Empire to overcome its increasing political, economic, and social weaknesses. It was within this context of war, commerce, and reform that the course of Greek, Armenian, Turkish, and Arab nationalisms started to take shape.

**War, Foreign Policy, and Population Movements**    The late nineteenth century was a period of significant political conflicts and ensuing population movements. As wars polarized states and social groups within them, and as population movements and foreign policies advocated social realignments along lines of shared language, religion, and ethnicities, the potential conditions of nationalism, of shared characteristics across a social expanse started to emerge. The Ottoman wars of the nineteenth century evolved around the Eastern question; the Russian Empire was the main adversary of the European powers often taking sides as befitting their political interests. The rapid succession of wars with Russia in 1877–78, Greece in 1897, Italy in 1911, and the two Balkan wars of 1912 and 1913, in addition to rebellions[22] sapped the strength, morale, and manpower of the Ottoman army. Also, the Ottoman Empire had to hand Cyprus over to British administration and, in 1881–82, had to accept the imposition of the French protectorate over Tunisia and the British occupation over Egypt.

What effect did these wars have upon emergent Ottoman nationalisms? Polarization within the Ottoman Greek and Armenian communities escalated, and communal divides started to emerge between those siding with the Ottoman state against those preferring foreign protection; those opposing the Ottoman state often actively volunteered in wars to fight against the Ottomans. During the Crimean War between the Ottomans and Russians, for instance, a Greek volunteer region was sworn in to assist in the Russian defense of Sebastopol.[23] Similarly,[24] in the Russian-Ottoman War of 1877–78, several thousand Armenian men in Constantinople volunteered to serve in the Ottoman army of the eastern front, while the Armenians of the Russian Empire volunteered on the other side.[25] The effects of these wars were different in the case of the Ottoman Turks and Arabs; the continuous Ottoman defeats and the internal rebellions consolidated the power of the ethnic Turkish and militaristic elements within the government as the Young Turk ideology of Ottomanism was gradually replaced by pan-Turkism—the cultural and economic policy of Turkification quickly intensified throughout the empire.[26] The severe Ottoman defeats especially against Italy and against the Balkan states strengthened the belief among the Ottoman Arabs that the empire might no longer be powerful enough to control the non-

Turkish regions of the empire; the Ottoman losses against Russia especially alarmed the Ottoman Arabs and alerted them to the possibility
that Western powers, especially France, might occupy Syria.[27]

The main European foreign policy concern was to contain the rising
challenge of the Russian, German, and Austro-Hungarian Empires. This
military need was compounded with an economic one as the various
powers tried to parcel out the raw materials and new markets located
outside of Europe. The Ottoman Empire was thus faced with a political
and economic context that was continually shifting. Different communities in the empire came to terms with these shifts in different ways. The
Ottoman Greeks managed to forge a small independent Greek kingdom
in 1830 partially as a consequence of this policy impasse. The Ottoman
Armenians instead attempted to mobilize European political support for
additional communal reforms.[28] For instance, in the 1878 Treaty of San
Stephano that the Ottomans had to sign with the victorious Russians,
the Armenians persuaded the Russian government to insert article 16
whereby the Ottomans were obliged to promise immediate reform in the
Armenian provinces.[29] The Armenian patriarch also presented the Great
Powers with a program of administrative autonomy within the Ottoman
Empire after this war.[30]

The Russian foreign policy of encouraging the settlement of
Ottoman Christian populations on its lands was the most successful in
terms of propagating Greek and Armenian nationalisms. This measure,
coupled with the effect of population movements as a consequence of
Ottoman defeats, constructed and consolidated new homogenized
Greek and Armenian identities. These Russian attempts started as early
as the eighteenth century; on 19 April 1795, for instance, the Russian
empress, Catherine II, sent a decree to the Russian ambassador at Constantinople translated to modern Greek, to be disseminated among the
Ottoman Greeks declaring "the provision of permanent quarters on the
outskirts of Odessa for those Greeks and Albanians who had taken
refuge in South Russia following their service with the Russian forces
during the war with the Ottoman empire, and invited persons from the
Aegean islands and elsewhere who might want to settle in the town
itself."[31] Similarly, after the Russian-Ottoman war of 1828–29, there
was an outward movement of the Ottoman Greek population to Russia
countered by the inward movement of the Russian Muslim population.[32]

The Russian invitation and Ottoman hostility also lured many
Ottoman Armenians. In 1779, Catherine II invited Armenians from
Crimea, then still outside the empire, to settle in Nakhichevan near the
mouth of the Don. The colony was granted a charter settlement that was
then extended to the colonies in Karasubazar, Staryi Kim, and Grig-
oropol; many founders of ethnic nationalism such as Mikael Nalban-

dian emerged from these Armenian settlements.[33] Similarly, in 1829, at
least one hundred thousand Ottoman Armenians migrated to Russia—
eventually there were half as many Armenians in Russia as in the
Ottoman Empire.[34] At the conclusion of the 1829 Russian-Ottoman
War, more than two hundred thousand Armenians arrived in Erevan
and Nakhichevan from Beyazid and Kars.[35]

As the Ottoman Greeks and Armenians moved away from the
empire, and as the Russian expanded at the expense of the Ottomans,
the Ottoman Turks acquired, for the first time, a demographic majority
in the empire—a development that fostered Turkish nationalism. Before
1876, no nationality[36] had been a majority in the Ottoman Empire, and
most groups were, in addition, widely dispersed and mixed throughout,
a factor that had helped sustain the multinational character of the
empire. This started to change in the late eighteenth century, however.
The first wave of Turkish Muslim immigration into the Ottoman
Empire came from the Crimea as Russia annexed it in 1783, and shortly
thereafter from the Volga-Ural area. The second wave came from the
Caucasus, where most immigrants were Circassians and Turkish-speak-
ing Nogays. The Russian advances into Central Asia in the 1860s and
the ensuing appeals for help by the Turkish khanates in Turkestan certainly increased sentiments about Turkish identity in the Ottoman
Empire.[37] After 1878, many Muslims[38] from the regions north of the
Black Sea, the Kuban, the Crimea, the Caucasus, and Transcaucasia
moved into the Ottoman Empire as these lands were gradually lost to
Russia. The contestation of Ottoman territories by Serbia, Greece, and
Bulgaria also prompted a migration of Turks and Muslims to the
empire.[39] The total number of these Turkish immigrations to Rumelia
and Anatolia[40] might have reached 2 million in number.

**Commerce, Foreign Protection, and Trade Networks**  Changing commercial patterns between Europe and the Ottoman Empire, the ability
of the European powers to ensure foreign protection to Ottoman
minorities who conducted business with them, and the trade networks
that the minority merchants established were significant factors in generating the resources for the development of all four Ottoman nationalisms. The Ottoman Turks and Muslim Arabs did not benefit from the
changing patterns of commerce as much as the Greeks and Armenians;
in the case of the Ottoman Turks, the commercial successes of the
Ottoman minorities generated enmity and fostered Turkish nationalism.

The European demand for Balkan food and raw materials and the
availability of cheap manufactured European goods transformed commercial relations in the eighteenth century both within Europe and outside. In the Ottoman Empire, these changing conditions altered the agri-

cultural trade relations, as well as the relations with the state; preben-
dalism emerged, production for an international market ensued, and the
Ottoman state started to lose control over the production and exchange
process.[41] One significant indication of this Ottoman loss of control was
the foreign protection[42] the European powers were now able to offer
Ottoman subjects who had commercial transactions with them. The
Ottoman subjects they selected for these privileged positions were often
their coreligionists, namely Ottoman Greeks and Armenians who also
cultivated their ethnic and family ties and networks in Europe. It was
especially in the Greek and Armenian diaspora communities that the
first seeds of national identity were planted.

The Ottoman Greeks benefitted from the opening of trading rights
in Habsburg domains to Ottoman subjects in 1699 with the Treaty of
Carlowitz to establish banks and commercial houses in Vienna; they also
profited from the decline of Venice and Genoa as levantine traders.[43] The
opening up of the Black Sea trade to the Russians by the Treaty of
Küçük Kaynarca of 1774, the convention of Aynalıkavak of 1779, and
the Russian-Ottoman commercial treaty of 1783 gave a substantial
boost to the Greek merchants; many undertook much of the commerce
under the Russian flag[44] since it facilitated their passage through the
straits as the Ottomans were treaty-bound to admit all Russian ships.[45]
The Greek merchant community of Odessa, which both used the Russian trade privileges and had access through networks and language
skills access to Ottoman trade, prospered especially during 1801–5. The
French revolutionary wars and the Continental blockade in 1806 and
the frequent Russian-Ottoman wars made Greeks the principal carriers
of southern Russian produce to Western Europe and the Ottoman
Empire, mostly in contrabandal form. At the end of the Napoleonic
Wars, the Greek merchant marine[46] was estimated at a thousand ships;
the profit margin was consistently more than 100 percent.

The diaspora Greek merchant communities then started to form
their own organizations; for instance, the one in Odessa[47] established,
with other European merchants, the first commercial insurance company, its own commercial association by 1808, and its own bank and
insurance firm by 1817.[48] Substantial Greek diaspora communities were
to be found in Italy, in particular in Venice, Trieste, and Livorno, and in
other parts of the Mediterranean; in the late eighteenth century, Greek
merchants established a mercantile network in the eastern Mediterranean, the Balkans, and as far afield as India; in the nineteenth century,
migration occurred to Egypt and southern Russia. These merchants provided a subvention for the publication of translations, especially of a secular nature, financed schools, colleges, and libraries in their native towns
and islands, and sponsored the education abroad of promising young

Greeks.[49] The concentration of financial, organizational, and human resources in these diaspora communities,[50] and the changing trade patterns prepared the ground for the Greek independence movement. It was especially the decline in commercial income after 1850 whereby the average profit fell to 15 percent that marginalized many merchants in these communities who in turn became more willing to join or support secret societies espousing for alternate visions.[51]

The Ottoman Armenians who had been active in trade and agricultural production in Asia Minor and the Fertile Crescent also benefitted, like the Greeks, from the changing trade patterns and the Safavid decline in the East. They were also active in the West; Armenian merchants founded many commercial establishments in most European ports including Marseilles and Amsterdam; in Amsterdam alone, there were some 60 such establishments by 1660.[52] Their position improved even more in the nineteenth century as they became intendants of customhouses, bankers to local pashas, purveyors of luxury goods, minters of coins and practitioners of long-distance trade.[53] The overwhelming majority of the Ottoman Armenian population in the major cities consisted of artisans and merchants whose increased affluence led to their challenge against the power structure within the Ottoman Armenian community. After their first participation in the election of a new catholicos in 1725, this group of merchants and artisans actively supported educational institutions and demanded equal representation in communal affairs. These activities led to new conceptions of self-rule and to the eventual establishment of the Armenian constitution.[54]

The most significant merchant diaspora communities that also affected the course of development of the Armenian national movement were located in India and Russia. The Armenian diaspora community of Madras was composed primarily of wealthy merchants trading in Europe and the Far East who were, like their Greek counterparts, very active in philanthropy.[55] In addition to subsidizing and producing many literary activities, they helped establish, for instance, a press and a paper factory in Echmiadzin in 1774, an Armenian school in Europe; they also promoted secular education.[56] In 1773, the Madras group published a detailed constitution for the proposed independent[57] Armenia. The Armenians in Russia were also a significant community that grew populous along the borders with the Ottoman Empire as the Russians evicted them from the Crimea and settled them in the southern Caucasus in Tostov-on-Don, in an Armenian colony, New Nakhichevan. In 1769, these Armenians presented, without success,[58] a plan to Empress Catherine II on how to free Armenia and recreate an Armenian state. Yet detailed visions of an independent Armenian state continued to be elaborated upon until the establishment of the Armenian Republic within the Soviet Union.

The Unionists who were in power in the Ottoman Empire in the early twentieth century resented the Greco-Armenian domination[59] in Ottoman trade and wanted to raise the Muslims to at least the same level of prosperity. The vast debt[60] to Europe that the Ottoman Empire had immersed itself in during the nineteenth and twentieth centuries also accentuated the resentment against the Greco-Armenian domination. Ottoman borrowing, which had begun in 1854, led in 1881 to Ottoman insolvency and the establishment of the Ottoman Public Debt Administration through which European powers administered and took over the Ottoman domestic revenues. After the Europeans, Ottoman minorities held most positions of responsibility in the Public Debt Administration. It was this economic intervention coupled with minority domination that provided support to the Turkish nationalist faction in the Ottoman government. Another factor that enhanced this radicalization was the trade boycotts that the Ottomans engaged in against the Austrians and Greeks. Austrian goods were boycotted in 1908 upon the Austrian annexation of Bosnia-Hercegovina; similarly, a general boycott of Greek commerce was undertaken during the 1909 declaration by Crete to unite with Greece.[61] These boycotts led the Unionists to conclude that only a national economy and a Turkish bourgeoisie could withstand foreign intervention and domination. In resettling the hundreds of thousands of refugees who had fled the Balkans, the Ottoman government did indeed activate this policy as it consciously placed Turks in jobs monopolized by the Greeks.[62] The increasing economic disadvantages felt by the Muslim elements in the empire, coupled with the attempts to generate a Turkish national bourgeoisie, thus accelerated the emergence of a Turkish national movement.[63]

In the Arab provinces of the Ottoman Empire, the move from locally manufactured goods to purchases of food and raw materials in exchange for European manufactured goods altered the nature of the trade. As more and more agricultural regions were linked to the world market, mostly the Arab Christians[64] in the local population learned international trade and finance and also often entered foreign protection.[65] Christians of Aleppo profited from the great prosperity of the city's trade in the seventeenth and eighteenth centuries; the later emigrations of Arab Christians to Livorno, the center of the Levant trade, and to Egypt, where the persecuted Greek Catholics settled, also extended and maintained trade networks. Once again, the prospering Arab Christian community engaged in sponsoring literary activities, printing newspapers, and, in general, started to articulate the consciousness of an Arab culture and civilization that looked beyond the Muslim-Christian divide.

**Ottoman Reforms, Ottomanism, and Communal Tensions** The Ottoman attempt to contain the separation of especially the non-Muslim populations of the empire led to a series of reforms[66] that were based on Western conceptions of human rights and guaranteed the security of life, honor, and property to all Ottoman subjects regardless of religious affiliation; the communal definition of identity was thus replaced by one based on individual rights. In addition to these fundamental rights,[67] the Ottoman reforms also introduced Western-style transformations through the establishment of governmental institutions such as ministries, military reforms, and technological innovations such as telegraphs and railroad networks in an attempt to catch up with the rising West.

These reforms generated social polarization in the sphere of Western-style political representation, however. In the case of the Greeks, Armenians, and later the Arabs, the inability of the Ottoman government to secure them equal political representation with the Turks led to disputes, discontent, and eventual alienation. The inherent stratification among the minorities of, in that order, the Ottoman Greeks, Armenians, and Jews was also overturned by the reforms.[68] Different minority communities, especially the Greeks, were upset by this loss of prestige and often stated that they would prefer the dominance of Muslims to the new equality with Ottoman Armenians and Jews. The introduction of Western-style institutions, technology, and media produced among Greeks, Armenians, Turks, and Arabs a new Ottoman citizen who believed in individual rights, was knowledgeable about the Western political conceptions through which to acquire them, and was also willing and able to formulate alternate social systems if the present ones failed to work.

Problems with the political representation of non-Muslims in public institutions demonstrate the magnitude of the structural resistance to Ottoman reforms. In the case of the newly founded Ottoman assembly, for instance, minority representation still remained corporate as Ottoman officials assigned minorities or reassessed the presence of minorities in public life according to their population proportions.[69] Similarly, in 1845, when the sultan asked for representatives from all provinces to be sent to the capital for advice, "all members were reimbursed for their expenses, the Christians at only half the rate of the Muslims."[70] The promised equality that did not easily translate into practice led the non-Muslims to pay more for military exemption, and they could not attain government posts to the same degree as Muslims.[71] The 1908 elections held in the empire after the accession of the Young Turks to power raised the hope of the minorities in finally achieving political equality. Non-Muslim communities, with their long tradition of communal elections, were much better prepared to participate and "could therefore expect to elect candidates far out of proportion to the size of their population merely through the process of mobilization and voter turnout."[72] Still, at the polls, a large number of minorities were not allowed to vote because they could not establish their Ottoman citizenship—indeed, many were foreign subjects or had been unregistered in an attempt to evade taxation. The Greek and Armenian leaders at the capital joined forces to protest the elections, without any success.[73]

Ottoman reforms also prompted greater distinctions between the secular and spiritual spheres within minority communities as they restricted[74] the absolute control of the Greek and Armenian patriarchs and instead enhanced secularization and increased mass participation in communal affairs.[75] This shift faced the active resistance of the religious leadership and the communal elites who derived their power from their association with the Ottoman sultan. Yet the growing influence of the entrepreneurial elites and the secular intelligentsia challenged more and more successfully the traditionalist ideological position of the Orthodox patriarchate.[76]

An additional source of challenge to the Greek Orthodox hierarchy in the empire was the establishment of patriarchates in the Russian Empire and the Greek kingdom, measures that challenged the sole patriarchal leadership of Constantinople in communal matters.[77] This challenge forced the leadership to reject the parochial, ethnic tendencies and appeal instead to the universalist religious loyalties of all Orthodox Christians. The bureaucratic caste of Phanariots,[78] who had a lucrative monopoly of political power and its economic perquisites in the Danubian principalities of Wallachia and Moldavia, were also wedded to the status quo and joined the religious leadership in resisting the reforms.[79] The real hold of the Phanariots on the church was political and financial—political because of the sultan's delegation of authority, and financial because the church, chronically in debt, used the Phanariots as its bankers, and all ecclesiastical offices were sold for ready cash.[80] The power of these two groups nevertheless started to erode with the increased wealth of the merchants and the continuous political challenges provided by the newly founded Greek state.

The exclusive hold of the Armenian Apostolic church also came under a number of challenges, both without and within: Catholic and Protestant missionaries continued their activities, often successfully, among the Armenians, and, within the church, the Romanizing influences necessitated the constant renegotiation of religious boundaries. The internal religious disputes, which had continued since the advent of Catholicism,[81] resulted in 1830 in the establishment of an Ottoman Catholic community separate from the patriarchate; communal tensions increased as some leaders such as the Düzians gave considerable assistance to the Catholic Armenians, while others such as Amira Bezjian supported the Armenian church.[82] The papal Armenian clergy were also divided into two factions, the party of Collegians based in Rome and named after the College of Propaganda in that city, and the Mkhit'arists headquartered at the convent of St. Lazarus in Venice, which adhered to the traditions of the national church much more. Many meetings took place in Constantinople to overcome these divides, but without success.[83] This period also coincided with the emergence of Protestantism in 1831 which led to new conflicts and disturbances, resulting in the emergence of an Ottoman Protestant community in 1847.[84]

The intracommunal tension was significant in the case of the Ottoman Armenians as well. The Armenian community had, similar to the Phanariots, the amiras who were high government functionaries, businessmen, and bankers mostly engaged in the finance of the Ottoman Empire;[85] their wealth and power in the government also translated to positions of power in the community as their opinions were sought on the selection of the patriarch, and they financed[86] religious, educational, and charitable causes.[87] It was the abolition of Ottoman tax-farming that limited the economic power of the banker amiras and thereby undermined their communal power as they no longer could underwrite many of the communal expenses. What ensued was an increase in the power of the artisans, although the power conflict between the two groups continued throughout the century.[88] The urban-rural divide compounded by class also introduced additional tensions to political representation within the Armenian community: the Constantinople Armenians, who comprised less than 10 percent of the Ottoman Armenian population, were powerful in opposing the revolutionary movement. They had five-sevenths of total representation in the communal assembly,[89] as opposed to the meager two-sevenths representation of the Ottoman provinces, which contained over 90 percent of the Armenian population.[90] The inability of the Ottoman state to accommodate Armenian demands and the internal tensions led to the Zeitun rebellion on 1862, which became the first in a series of insurrections against the Ottoman state. The Sasun rebellion of 1894 and the second Zeitun rebellion of 1895 further polarized the Armenians and the Ottoman state and led to Ottoman persecutions in retaliation.[91]

The effects of the reforms on the Ottoman Muslims were largely negative. The Ottoman Muslims interpreted the rights promised to the minorities as a loss of their privileged position in the empire. In many Ottoman provinces, ranging from Manisa, Denizli, Nazilli, Diyarbakır, Harput, Mardin, Maraş, and Varna to Golos, tensions between the Muslims and minorities escalated, often leading to skirmishes, especially during and after religious holidays and ceremonies or over commercial transactions across groups. This strife in turn created divisions among the Muslims as some wanted to unite around the banner of Islamism, while others supported Ottomanism, which assumed that all divisions in the empire could be overcome by strict adherence to the reforms. The strife among the opposing factions of Islamists and Ottomanists and the continuing rebellions within the empire of both Muslims and others sapped the strength of both parties. As a consequence, the leadership role of the Turkish element[92] in the empire became more and more pronounced.[93]

The other effect of the Ottoman reforms was the creation of the first generation of young military officers, officials, and intellectuals who were all trained in the new Western-style institutions that the reforms had instigated. These officers challenged the status quo with their newly acquired knowledge; they replaced the legitimacy of experience attained through serving in regiments (*alaylı*) with knowledge acquired through schooling on military affairs (*mektepli*).[94] Even though most indeed lacked training and experience, the officers firmly believed that their knowledge would naturally overcome this weakness; they defined their identity in terms of Turkish language and history.[95] Even though the Ottoman state continued to advocate a policy of Ottomanism to unite the disparate elements of the empire, many officials such as the grand vezir, Ali Pasha, in 1867 believed that "the Ottoman Turks were best fitted to govern the empire."[96] When these officers did indeed take over after 1908, they transformed the largely cultural nationalism into a political one, thereby weighing in on the ethnic Turkish nationalist elements among the ruling cadre.

The negative reaction of the Ottoman Muslims to the reforms also extended to the Arab provinces of the empire as these produced anti-Christian riots in Aleppo in 1850, Nablus in 1856, and Damascus in 1860.[97] The increase in Christian prosperity, social and cultural ascendancy, and their new freedom to ring church bells, carry crosses, and erect new Christian establishments increased the hostilities. During the same period, during the reign of Sultan Abdülhamid II, there was an attempt made to give Arabs equal standing in the Ottoman structure of rule, an attempt that was discontinued by the Union and Progress Committee that deposed the sultan. Abdülhamid II selected Arabs such as Abu al-Sayyadi and Zafir al-Madani to serve as his advisors; in addition, the administrative structure of the empire was altered to make Arab provinces provinces of the first order,[98] enabling administrators appointed there to draw higher salaries.[99]

When the Union and Progress Committee reestablished constitutional rule in the empire in 1908, later deposed the Ottoman sultan,

Abdülhamid II, in 1909, and reinstigated reforms, the Ottoman Arabs still shared high hopes in the possible union in progress within the empire. These instances were also coupled with the Arab realization of the futility of equal representation in Ottoman politics with the Ottoman Turks. Even though the Young Turk movement officially had the policy of equality of treatment among all Ottoman ethnoreligious groups, the confidential correspondence demonstrated this not to be the case: the Young Turks often used derogatory phrases for the Arabs to whom they saw themselves as bringing civilization and protection against Western imperialism.[100] This was also reflected in their decisions concerning the Ottoman Arabs. During the elections, the number of Arab delegates selected for the Ottoman assembly was much lower than their population proportion dictated; the ensuing the high-level administrative appointments of the empire also went disproportionately to ethnic Turks.[101]

The administrative centralization of the Arab provinces was probably the most significant reform that fostered Arab consciousness. The appointment in the Arab provinces of Turkish higher officials unacquainted with Arabic and the use of Turkish as the language of government in the law courts and principal public services instigated protests.[102] One additional expression of this discontent was a student protest in Beirut over the appointment of "a man from Anatolia" as professor of Arabic at the state preparatory school as the students wanted a Syrian to be appointed to the position.[103] Eventually the differences between the Syrian-Arab notables who were becoming more and more independent through agricultural production and trade and the members of the Committee of Union and Progress at the capital became too vast to be contained within the existing political structure.

## Visions of History, Literature, and Education

The transformations through war, commerce, and reform certainly set the parameters within which nationalisms emerged. Yet it was the new interpretations offered by historical visions, literary interpretations, and educational innovations that endowed the structural transformations with meaning. As history and religion created new visions of the future, as literature and linguistics generated new realms of meanings, and as education and the print media reproduced entire sets of alternate images of society, the Greek, Armenian, Turkish, and Arab nationalisms acquired a boundless spirit that recaptured the past, present, and future.

The official Ottoman visions of history, literature, and education aimed to preserve the empire by focusing on Ottomanism, which hoped to save the multinational empire by granting rights to all its decisions without distinction on basis of religion or race. There were some minorities[104] and Ottoman officials who believed in and advocated Ottomanism, mostly because of the implied and largely imagined secularism within. The idea of Ottomanism gained ascendancy in the empire after the 1908 revolution; in July 1908, all the ethnic and religious communities greeted the restoration of the constitution with great enthusiasm as Muslims and Christians fraternized in the streets.[105] Yet this policy could not sustain itself against escalating Ottoman defeats that polarized the social groups and eventually gave way to the emergent nationalisms.[106]

**Historical Repertoires and Religious Interpretations**    History intertwined with religion reinterpreted the past and recast the future, thereby shifting the existing boundaries of meaning. In the recovery of the past, the Greek nationalist movement had two alternate visions, one grounded on Byzantinism promoted at the capital, and the other based on Hellenism advanced at the peninsula.[107] The Phanariots and the upper Greek clergy of the patriarchate both residing in Constantinople aspired for the restoration of the Byzantine Empire. Imagining a Christian, preferably Orthodox-dominated multinational and theocratic regime based on Turkish-Hellenic participation, they promoted Greek-Ottoman cooperation. This gradualist approach of conquest from within gained credibility with the 1897 Greek defeat by the Ottomans and also accounted for the initial interaction of the Ottoman Greeks with the liberal elements in the Committee of Union and Progress.[108] The Unionists had taken the initiative for the contact specifically to ask for their cooperation for the establishment of a constitutional regime.[109] Yet, as the Unionists became more radicalized especially after the Balkan wars in 1912, and as the Greeks of the peninsula followed their own path, these Ottoman Greeks of the capital lost ground.

The predominant myth created in the Balkan lands was based on a Hellenic past that could both potentially unite ethnic communities in the Balkans and at the same time provide an alternate source of legitimation to the movement in the Balkans, one independent from the Phanariots in Constantinople. The Hellenes[110] included all the descendants of classical Greeks,[111] all those who had culturally experienced a Greek past, including, besides the Greeks, the Rumanians, Bulgarians, Albanians, and Serbs. This development was followed by the emergence of the *megali idea*, the grandiose vision of restoring the former Byzantine empire emerged once more, but this time under the leadership of the Hellenes.[112] Yet such a vision was dispelled during the nineteenth century as all groups formed their own visions—the Greeks had underestimated the strength of ethnic divides.[113] The Russian interest in the area also weaved, at times, new possible saviors[114] into the existing myths of the past; particular among them was "the legend of the *xanthon genos*, a fair-haired race of liberators from the north," who widely became identified with the Russians.[115] This identification was also fostered by the idea of a Christian crusade to restore Byzantium, which had sustained the Greek hopes for centuries.[116] The Russian empress, Catherine the Great, even contemplated a restored Byzantine Empire, which included the Slav as well as the Greek Orthodox populations of the Ottoman Empire and centered on Constantinople with her Greek-speaking grandson Constantine as the emperor. Yet this vision too shattered as the European forces diligently checked Russian advances. Hence, in the end, the Greeks established their own kingdom with British support.

The Armenians similarly sought for saviors to bring back the Armenian kingdom during the fourteenth, fifteenth, and sixteenth centuries. These attempts were often led by Catholic missionaries. When King Louis XIV of France contemplated the idea of a new crusade to the East to liberate the Holy Land and all territories once ruled by the Latin princes, his agents and missionaries tried to coax the Armenians that salvation would come from the Franks.[117] When the next attempt, in 1678 to seek aid for Armenia from the pope and France, proved fruitless, the delegation sought help in Dusseldorf from Prince Johann-Wilhelm of the Palatinate by promising him the Armenian throne; this attempt too eventually failed.[118] The Armenians next started putting their faith in a geographically proximate, swiftly rising Russia, and indeed it was in this context that the Armenian republic was formed after the First World War within the new Soviet state.

The reinterpretation of history was especially significant in the emergence of Turkish nationalism. Traditional Ottoman histories did not at all mention the history of Turks before their adoption of Islam but traced instead the genealogy to a tribe of Kayı Khan, a branch of Oğuz Turks, descendants in turn of Japhet, son of Noah.[119] Yet a change in these perceptions occurred in the mid-nineteenth century when Ahmed Cevdet Pasha argued that the Arabs and Turks were the two great nations to rule the Islamic world. Later, more and more studies[120] were conducted into the history of the Turks before their tenth-century conversion into Islam. Süleyman Pasha, a general and minister of military schools, attempted to introduce Turkism[121] by writing a history of the Turks based, for the first time, on Chinese sources—an attempt he undertook after saying that "the need for histories could not be met by translations, because all history books written in Europe were full of calumnies either of our religion or of our nationality."[122] He made the Ottomans aware that the Hiung-nu of Chinese history were the first forefathers of the Turks. At the same time, traveler and Orientalist Arminian Hermann Vambery contended that all Turkic groups belonged to one race, subdivided according to physical traits and customs.[123] The disastrous drought of 1872 followed by another drought alerted the Ottomans to the significance of a homeland, of Anatolia, the land on which the Ottoman Empire was founded, to their "homeland brothers who raise most of our soldiers and most of our laborers."[124] This was followed by the claim that all Anatolians were racially of Turkish stock, going back to before the entrance of Ottomans. An immediate Turkish homeland was thus established with Anatolians as true bearers of an uncorrupted Turkish culture. These historical links with the pre-Islamic past that unified all the Turks ultimately led the Ottoman general Enver Pasha on an ill-fated campaign[125] after the First World War to establish on the ashes of the Ottoman Empire a Turkish one along the silk trade route from Adrianople to China, with its capital in Samarkand. This vision was arrested by Soviet Russia in 1922 when Enver died in battle. What was left instead was an amended form of Turkish nationalism that was geographically limited to Anatolia.

In their task to educate both the Turks and the Europeans about the great Turkish history, the new generation of Ottoman Turkish historians started to compare the roles of Arabs and Turks in Islamic history, where many pointed out that "those who fought to protect Islam for seven or eight hundred years were not Arabs but Turks."[126] The first communal leader to call on the Arabs to secede from the Ottoman Empire was the exiled Maronite leader Yusuf Karam, who wrote to Amir 'Abd al-Qadir al-Jaza'iri during the 1877–78 Ottoman-Russian War about the necessity of Arab independence and suggested an Arab confederation where each unit was to be headed by an independent amir.[127] This was followed by the correlation of Arabism with early Islam by thinkers such as Muhammad 'Abduh and his disciple Rashid Rıda.[128] Similarly, many others emphasized the theme of Islamic regeneration[129] in works that were secretly and very widely distributed throughout Syria. Another theme that developed in the movement was the illegitimacy of despotic rule to criticize Ottoman rule over Arab lands; in addition, some advocated[130] the abolition of the Ottoman sultan's title to the caliphate and the setting up of a Quraishi-born Arab (i.e., one of belonging to the same tribe of the Prophet) as caliph in Mecca.[131] Still others attempted to bring in constitutional rule to the empire based on the Islamic concept of the necessity for deliberative consultation (*shura*). Some lodged Arab distinctness in Arab culture, and others, in the Islamic Arabic religion. The large number of Arab Christians focused on the contributions of Arab civilization and culture independently of religion.[132] It was within this Muslim-Christian tension that Arab nationalism developed and later splintered due to competing European interests in the region.

The new nationalist visions often entered a tenuous relationship with those who had traditionally had control over meaning creation: the religious establishment and its clergy. Often, while the upper clergy attempted to maintain the status quo, the lower clergy provided direct or indirect support to independence movements. Still, the movement did indeed cost the lives of higher clergy;[133] a number of bishops and Phanariot grandees were also executed.[134] Many of the more independent bishops and priests in the Balkans were enlisted in the secret societies of the Greek independence movement; on Mount Athos, during the first decade of the Greek war, about half the monks left to serve in the uprising in various ways that were officially denied them.[135] After the creation of the Greek state, the bishops started to avoid the Greek patriarchate in Constantinople and even omitted mentioning his name in their liturgy; the church in Greece separated from the patriarchate in Constantinople in 1833.[136] The Greek revolution also capitalized on religious symbols to mobilize the masses;[137] the Greek flag emerged when the Metropolitan Germanos of Old Patras raised a banner with the cross on it at the monastery of Ayia Lavra.[138]

The newly emerging rituals of the Armenian liberation movement similarly drew upon former religious ones. Those devoted to the liberation movement, called it, for instance, the Holy Task (*Soorb Gords*), referred to the volunteers as disciples, and duplicated the baptism of Christ in inducting members. On the eve of battle, the volunteers took communion and heard speeches on the glories of martyrdom.[139] As there were originally no leaders accepted by all, the first leadership of the Armenian movement also came from the church.[140] In the Armenian case, it was the attempts of the Armenian Catholic priest Mkhit'ar Sepasdat'si (1676–1749),[141] who founded the Mkhit'arist order in Constantinople in 1701, that produced an Armenian literary awakening, one that would spark the historical visions of an Armenian past and prepare the grounds for a consistent effort to accomplish such a future. Priest Mkhit'ar stated that in achieving such an enlightenment, he "would sacrifice neither his nation to his religion nor his religion to his nation."[142] Yet the Armenian case also displayed the first tension between the religious and the secular because of the influence of socialism where anticlerical, secular nationalists often blamed the church for the disorganized state the Armenian community was in.[143]

The role of religion in the Turkish and Arab nationalisms was much more tenuous. The dervishes from Central Asia who had retained tekkes in Constantinople were significant in developing the conception of a Turkish culture; the sheikh of one such place, Buharalı Süleyman Efendi, published in 1882 a book on the Chagatay language and Ottoman Turkish, introducing Ottomans to the literary language of the eastern

Turks and claiming it to be the linguistic origin of Ottoman Turkish. Another member published a Chagatay dictionary.[144] Yet the Young Turk movement ultimately developed in opposition to Sultan Abdül-hamid II who had advocated Islamism and therefore assumed, along with other factors such as the inherent dominance of Ottoman Turks in the movement, an antireligious and eventually pro-Turkish stand. Religion again played a tenuous role in the case of Arab nationalism because of the large active population of Arab Christians. The actual connection between Islam and Arabs was therefore problematized; Shakib Arslan, for instance, stressed the bond of Islam and rejected both the partisan bond of nationalism and the idea that Arabs have a special status in Islam.[145]

**Literary Interpretations and Linguistic Remappings**   Even though the Greek language was the commercial lingua franca of most of the Balkan merchants, and in the fifty years before the Greek War of Independence, any person residing in the Balkans who wanted an education had to study at a Greek school, the Greek language and literature were still unable to unite all the Balkan peoples.[146] Instead, it was the European recreation of their Hellenic past that endowed the Greek language and literature with a sense of distinctness and emancipatory power deriving from the past. Indeed, a person living in Europe, Adamantios Korais, first edited and translated the authors of ancient Greece to form a library of twenty-six volumes to demonstrate the vitality of the Hellenic spirit; he was also the first scholar to use modern Greek as a literary language.[147] Still, in the 1830s, when the Austrian historian J. P. Fallmayer contested on linguistic grounds that the Greeks were the lineal descendants of the ancient, he caused an uproar among the new Greek intelligentsia.[148] Even though the Greek language eventually generated a sense of ethnic identity, it also had to come to terms with the tension between the ancient and modern Greek.[149]

Literature and linguistic innovations created a sense of unity among the Armenians during the nineteenth and early twentieth centuries.[150] The Armenian debate on language[151] that generated the Armenian literary Renaissance entailed the use of classical Armenian (*grabar*) of the church,[152] which was unintelligible to the common people as opposed to the vernacular spoken by the people (*ashkharabar*). The Armenian Renaissance[153] that occurred between 1843 and 1915 revived the vernacular into a vehicle of literary expression, and with the publication of many journals, the vernacular[154] indeed surpassed[155] the classical language and became the linguistic medium of the national movement. It was the activities of the Armenian Catholic Mkhit'arist order in Venice and Vienna that had provided the foundation of this literary renaissance;

the Mkhit'arists had been the first ones to deliver both to Europe and to the Armenians themselves the long-lost knowledge of an Armenian past.[156] Supplementing the work done by church leaders in publishing religious tracts, the Mkhit'arists had translated, and continued to translate, many inaccessible manuscripts to easily readable volumes on history, linguistics, lexicography, numismatics, and theology; they had also published a grammar of modern Armenian to familiarize the Armenians with the laws of their own vernacular.[157] From the publication of Armenian classics, the Mkhit'arists had moved on to the translation of Greek and Latin masterpieces, also introducing Armenian readers to many non-Armenian languages through grammars and bilingual and trilingual dictionaries. In addition, many playwrights among them emphasized dramas glorifying religion, human virtues, and patriotism.[158] Translations of the works of modern Italian, English, and French authors by others followed.[159]

Even though these translations into Armenian did create a sense of literature, it was with the production of original works that the Armenians interpreted the new meanings with which they were now surrounded. Some scholars distanced themselves from translations by becoming critical[160] of the excessive European influence.[161] Even though only four Armenian novels were written until 1864, others started soon thereafter experimenting with different literary genres, including the epic, romantic drama, short story, and novel; these forms also created a very vibrant Armenian theater.[162] Because of the increasing body of literature in Turkish with Armenian script in the midnineteenth century, many Ottoman officials, including Reshid Pasha, learned the Armenian alphabet to follow this literature.[163] In the body of literature that thus started to emerge, Armenian nationalism fluctuated between love of fatherland (*hayrenasirutiun*), which had a distinctly defined land and advanced the people as the dominant force in liberating this land, and love of nation (*azgasirutiun*), which was much more abstract and timeless.[164] It was the love of the nation that was forever instilled through everlasting images; the pictures and poems of Mikael Nalbandian, which were secretly circulated among the Armenians, captured the passion behind this love, especially in his poem entitled "Liberty":[165]

> Then the words that first I spoke
> Were not "father, mother, dear,"
> "Liberty!" the accents broke
> In my infant utterance clear.[166]

Through the combination of a linguistic revival of the vernacular and a new literary narrative, the Armenian national movement was able to develop new images of emancipation. Yet these images, though very vivid, did not always contain specifically marked territories of the fatherland and often remained abstract.

In the context of Turkish nationalism, the word for nation, *vatan*, shifted in meaning in the last years of the eighteenth century after the French revolution from its original meaning of one's place of birth to evoking sentimental attachment and ethnic pride in a tangible and visible place.[167] It was once more a total linguistic transformation that commenced with the dissection of the Ottoman language into its Turkish, Persian, and Arabic parts and culminated with the attempts to recapture the pure Turkish component. In late nineteenth century, Ahmet Vefik Pasha, an Ottoman statesman, translated *Şecere-i Türki* (The genealogies of Turks) into Istanbul Turkish and compiled a Turkish lexicon entitled *Lehçe-i Osmani* (The Ottoman dialect); he also proved that the Turkish spoken in the empire was a dialect of Turkish of which there were other dialects throughout the world.[168] Süleyman Pasha identified the Ottoman tongue as being composed of three languages, namely Turkish, Arabic, and Persian, and wrote a book specifically on Turkish grammar[169] entitled *Sarf-ı Türki* (grammar of the Turks). He stated explicitly[170] that "it is incorrect to speak of Ottoman literature, just as it is wrong to call our language the Ottoman language and our nation the Ottoman nation. The term Ottoman is only the name of our state, while the name of our nation is Turk. Consequently, our language is the Turkish language and our literature is Turkish literature." In language and literature, the separation between Ottoman and Turkish thus commenced. It was in this context that a campaign for the purification of the Turkish language began, an attempt to eliminate all words derived from Arabic and Persian roots and replace them with ancient Turkish rootwords or with new words created out of Turkish roots and new particles. [171]

The treatises on Turkish nationalism originated both in the works of European Orientalists and among the scholars of the Turkish diaspora community from Russia.[172] Leon Cahun's *Introduction a l'histoire de l'Asie: Turcs et Mongols des origines a 1405* (Introduction to the history of Asia: The origins of Turks and Mongols in 1405) published in 1896 was translated into Turkish by Necip Asım Bey; with his appendix on Turks, the book aroused interest on Turkism in all quarters.[173] In it, Cahun claimed a theory of a Turanian race as the forerunner of civilization in Europe. An earlier publication, Joseph de Guignes's *Histoire generale des Huns, des Turcs, des Mongoles, et autres Tartares occidentaux* (The general history of the Huns, Turks, Mongols, and other Western Tartars), emphasized the role of the Turks in Asia before their conversion to Islam. Another significant book was published in 1869 by

Mustafa Celaleddin Pasha,[174] entitled *Les Turcs anciens et modernes* (Turks old and new), where he articulated the Turkish contributions to civilization and stressed their racial origins. Within the Turkish diaspora community in Russia, Mirza Fethali Ahundov wrote plays in Azerbaijani Turkish and developed nationalist themes. İsmail Gasprinsky, the publisher of a prominent Crimean newspaper *Tercüman* advocated unity in language, thought, and action and promoted a union for all the Turkic groups in Russia under the spiritual guidance of Ottoman Turkey.[175] Hüseynizade Ali Bey, a recent Azeri immigrant from Baku, taught the principles of Turkism at the Ottoman Military Medical School and advocated the unification of all Turks.[176] Related to him was Yusuf Akçura, who considered Ottomanism, rejected it because it minimized the rights of Turks, criticized pan-Islamism for antagonizing non-Muslim groups in the Ottoman Empire, and lauded Turkism for offering the only opportunity for union.[177] Through these intellectuals, the Ottoman Turks started to acquire a new sense of their national identity.

Writings on Turkish nationalism in both prose and poetry began to appear in the Ottoman Empire soon thereafter. Namık Kemal,[178] a literary figure, formed the vision and kindled the passion for the Turkish fatherland; his composition of the first Turkish drama *Vatan Yahud Silistre* glorified patriotism and death for the sake of the fatherland.[179] Ziya Gökalp, one of the intellectual founders of Turkish nationalism, transferred to the nation all the divine qualities and replaced the belief in God with the belief in nation so that nationalism actually became a religion.[180] He advocated that Turks accept only the material achievements and scientific methods from Western civilization, and from Islam, only religious beliefs, without its political, legal, and social traditions, stating that "we are of the Turkish nation (*millet*), of the Islamic religious community (*ümmet*), and of Western civilization (*medeniyet*)."[181] Yet the combination of these factors ultimately gave an advantage to the westernized Muslim Turks of the empire over the other social groups, excluded the Ottoman religious minorities, and created an ethnically based Turkish nationalism.

The employment of the term *qawm*, "a people," to refer to the Arabs, leading to the emergence of the concept of *qawmiya* for Arab nationalism, can be traced to the works of al-Zahrawi. He was also able to employ the Arabic language as a symbol in locating the boundaries of these people by pointing out that 50 to 60 million people whose lands were "all contiguous and separated by no body of water other than the Suez Canal" spoke Arabic and thereby formed a natural group.[182] Visions of Arab patriotism were further developed through the works of scholars such as Rifa'a al-Tahtawi, Muhammad 'Abduh and 'Abd Allah al-Nadim.[183] In composing a patriotic poem, Tahtawi linguistically reinterpreted the love of the homeland in the Prophetic tradition "Love of the homeland is an article of faith" into the recurring refrain "Love of the homelands is an article of faith," referring now to a physical space populated by Arabs united by a shared language, a sovereign, a system of government, and the guidance of sacred law.[184] 'Abduh expounded on the role of the homeland as the foundation of political life; the homeland now became a social space where one traced one's descent, had one's rights protected and obligations known, and kept secure life, family, and property. 'Abd Allah al-Nadim developed the idea of the bond of homeland (*al-jami'a al-wataniya*) to appeal for unity and a brotherhood of patriotism among the various religious communities by identifying all as sons of the land. Hence *homeland* acquired more and more a new meaning and an imagined space.

The idea of homeland (*watan*) developed into patriotism (*wataniya*) among the writings of Arab intellectuals in the second half of the nineteenth century, such as those of Butrus al-Bustani and Ibrahim al-Yaziji.[185] When lecturing in Beirut in 1859 on Arabic literature, Bustani[186] differentiated the Arabs from non-Arabs by using the term *Sons of Arabs* (*Abna al-Arab*) and compared their current unsatisfactory performance in philosophy, science, and arts with those of their glorious ancestors. The past glory of the Arabs was also captured by the poems of Ibrahim al-Yaziji, who in two separate odes stated:[187]

> O Arab folk so noble: Hail!
> O'er your abodes clouds prevail.
>
> Awaken, O Arabs, and leave slumber aside,
> As danger's flood washes your knees in its tide!

The discussion of past glories now became reinterpreted in new literary genres. The rediscovery and publication of Arab classics by Western Orientalists aided this revival of Arabic literature as did mission schools. Groups of writers gathered in this milieu to rediscover the past, reinterpret it according to the changing conditions of the future, and create new Arabic literary forms such as the poetic drama, the novel, and the romantic autobiography.[188] Together with this literature flourished visions of a renewed Arab civilization that would once more unite its inhabitants as it had done in the past.

**Educational Innovations and the Print Media**   The establishment of Western-style education was also significant in the creation of new visions. The nineteenth[189] century was significant in terms of the foreign missions[190] and minority and state-sponsored schools, all of which introduced Western-style education to Ottoman society. The English and

American Protestants were especially active in bringing the "pure doctrine" of Christianity to predominantly the Ottoman Christians through establishing many philanthropic and educational missions.[191] The Ottoman state and minority schools also offered Western-style education, thereby breaking the monopoly of the religious institutions over education. The new Western-style knowledge brought with it Enlightenment concepts and notions of citizenship and provided the Ottomans with conceptual tools to create new meanings.

The most enlightened and liberal sections of the Greek nationalists[192] comprised members of the medical, legal, and literary professions, all of whom shared a Western-style education and the Enlightenment vision embedded within it. Most were trained at the University of Athens, founded soon after liberation in 1837, which aimed to re-Hellenize the entire Greek world and attracted students throughout the Balkans; it defined Greek as the mother of wisdom that, through the civilizing mission of Greek culture and language, would wake all the Balkans from their "deep slumber of ignorance."[193] The textbooks employed in Greek education also aimed to create a national identity; Greek educators employed[194] the textbook O Gerosthatis by Melas where the main character, after and in spite of extensive travels in Europe, retains his classical Greek knowledge and his faith and ultimately brings back wisdom to the Greek youth, saying, in his last breath to a school instructor that "the principal and ultimate purpose of all your efforts and all your teachings should be the education of the Greek youth according to the way of Christ and for the benefit of the motherland." Still, the emergence of Western-style education became very significant in the declining fortunes of the church as the motherland replaced religion. As national revival gathered momentum, the church identified more with educational obscurantism and political reaction and conducted heresy trials, the burning of offending books, and opposition to the increasing emphasis on the natural sciences and Greece's classical heritage. Even though one patriarch questioned "what benefit the youth derived from learning numbers, algebra and a myriad such things, if in speech they were barbaric, if they had no idea of religion, and if their morals were degenerate,"[195] the Enlightenment philosophy and science triumphed over morals, and the new Western-style education persevered. The Greek state then established schools embedded with this new vision for the Ottoman Greeks still in the empire.

The circulation and reproduction of these new ideas occurred through the print media. Greek printing escalated in the nineteenth century[196] as some 1,300 titles appeared during the first two decades.[197] Even though 180 out of the 228 publications in Greek between 1700 and 1730 were concerned with religious issues, from 1780 through 1790, the publication of religious and secular themes was at par, 157 religious to 153 secular themes.[198] Many translations, literary journals, newspapers, and pamphlets were printed during the same period. Hence there was an escalation of print media both in quantity and in terms of the coverage of secular issues. For instance, in 1797, a printing house printed Rhigas's revolutionary manifesto, "which contained a proclamation, a declaration of the rights of man, a Greek constitution, and a martial hymn calling on the Balkan Christians to fight for liberty."[199] Similarly, a literary journal, *Mercure savant*, was published in Vienna in 1811 devoted to Greek interests, and it was widely read throughout Europe.[200] Through such media, the visions of the Greek nation multiplied throughout time and space.

Many Ottoman Armenians sent their children to Europe for education, first for religious education and, after the eighteenth century, for studying liberal arts and professions. Here, they came under the influence of the Mikhit'arists who established schools throughout Europe. In 1846, for instance, the Muradian school of the Mikhit'arists transferred its forty students from Padua to Paris; many of the students actively participated in French political demonstrations. The Mkhit'arist students in Venice similarly attained a patriotic sentiment from those like Manzoni, Mazzini, and Garibaldi.[201] In the empire, it was the activities of the Armenian community and missionaries that provided Western-style education to the Ottoman Armenians. With this education came the conception of a national identity; for instance, the 1884 novel by Krikor Zohrab entitled *A Vanished Generation* criticized the abysmal ignorance of things Armenian by students attending foreign schools and stated that, in the case of a French boarding school for girls, "every little stream, mountain, and valley, the most obscure hamlet [in France] were known to this Armenian girl, who was ignorant of, and did not wish to know, about her native Ararat."[202] Zohrab advocated using the knowledge and experience of the Europeans, but within the framework set by Armenian culture and history. As early as 1846, the Armenian newspaper in Constantinople, *Hayastan*, stated:[203] "Wake up, Armenian nation, from your death-inviting slumber of ignorance; remember your past glory, mourn your present state of wretchedness and heed the example of other enlightened nations: take care of your schools, learn other useful languages and liberal sciences (professions) . . . only then can you reach the goal of happiness." The role of the Armenian church in this process was filled with conflict. Armenian communal administration divided into the spiritual and civil in 1847 whereby the civil council, consisting of twenty lay members,[204] looked after secular education, communal property, and justice, and the spiritual council was concerned with dogma, ordination of clergy, and religious education.[205] The threat

of the Catholic and Protestant missionaries generated and sustained the
Armenian patriarchs' interest in publishing old Armenian polemic literature to sustain the community's interest in orthodoxy and to combat
the Catholic and Protestant discourse.[206] Still, the scientific knowledge
and the professional training offered by Western-style education gradually eclipsed the role of the church in the Armenian case as well.

The Armenian print media diffused these new visions. Armenian
journalism[207] in the Ottoman Empire proceeded with the establishment
of an Armenian section in Armeno-Turkish called "Lroy Gir Meci
Terut'ean Osmanean" in 1832 in the first official newspaper of the
Ottoman Empire, Le Moniteur Ottoman.[208] Utujian published his Mas-
sis (Ararat) for a long run between 1853 and 1908; there were also the
journals Aravelian Mamoul (The Orient express), Portz (Essay), and
Hairenik (Fatherland) published around the same time. These journals
mostly aimed to bring the old and the new together without provoking
radical social changes. They provided a public forum for the discussion
of politics, history, economics, and philosophy.[209] All Armenian literary
activities in the empire had a very strong utilitarian bent: they were all
geared to aid the nation, and art for art's sake was considered a luxury.[210] It was outside the empire that the nationalist passion developed
through the print media. The four periodicals of the Mikhit'arists in
Europe were also intended to keep the Armenians abreast of world
developments.[211] Similarly, the Armenian students in St. Petersburg and
Moscow admired the sacrifices of the Balkan peoples to establish political independence from the Ottoman Empire and printed and distributed
brochures on the Greek and Bulgarian revolutions. Revolution after the
Balkan example seemed the most expedient road to freedom.[212]

The Ottoman sultan introduced Western-style schools into the
empire to train a new cadre with skills and expertise to take on the military challenges of Europe. Yet the Enlightenment knowledge taught at
these schools created new visions and led the new cadre to develop alle-
giances not to the sultan but instead to the abstract notion of the nation.
As the ideology of Ottomanism failed, the conception of the nation
became more and more defined along ethnic lines as the Turkish nation.
The debate over the language of instruction signified this transformation:
even though French had been the teaching medium, in the midnineteenth
century attempts to replace French with Turkish gained dominance.[213]
The publication of Turkish grammar books and dictionaries followed.
Next came the debate in the purification of the Turkish language and the
role of Arabic words within it.[214] The emerging nationalists advocated a
pure Turkish language, one solely based on Turkic roots.

The next debate to follow concerned the possibility of abandoning
the Arabic script in favor of the Latin one. The Turkish language did

indeed become a rallying point around which Turkish nationalism solidified. By 1876, the newly drawn constitution stated for the first time in Ottoman history that Turkish was the official language of the state and made its knowledge a requirement for the members of parliament and officials.[215] What followed was the educational policy adopted by the Committee of Union and Progress in 1911 to employ the Turkish language in all the schools of the empire, with the aim to "denationalize all the non-Turkish communities and instill patriotism among the Turks."[216] The Ottomans indeed recognized the significance of language, especially as it was employed in the educational system to reproduce new meanings and new visions, ones that now put the non-Turks of the empire at a disadvantage.

The many scientific journals established at the time with the explicit aim of following the Western technological developments in addition to those that explicitly debated historical and cultural issues[217] helped set the ideological parameters of Turkish nationalism. The new visionaries were certainly secular and Western oriented; science, technology, and progress emerged as the new ideals, followed by the increased spread of biological materialism and scientific objectivity, and loyalty to the state and rationality in administration became the new maxims.[218] Positivism and realism brought, after the 1860s, a new world view, a new vision based on a scientific analysis of social relations.[219] Among the many publications of the Turkish nationalists such as *Büyük Duygu* (The great sentiment), *Türk İli* (The land of the Turks) and *Turan* (the mythical homeland of the Turks), the most significant was that of the *Türk Yurdu* (Homeland of the Turks) in 1911, a weekly periodical that set itself as an objective "to create an ideal acceptable to all the Turks, defend the political and economic interests of the Turkish elements in the Ottoman empire, and strive for the progress and strengthening of the Turkish national spirit among the Ottoman Turks."[220] Its call for solidarity gradually converted to an appeal for action, slowly endowing the new rational and secular cadres with a sense of historical and cultural mission.

It was after the Egyptian occupation of Syria that Western-style education became a significant source of social change as French Jesuits and American Presbyterians competed for influence by establishing schools.[221] Once the Ottomans resumed rule, the Ottoman sultan, in an attempt to gain loyalties across generations, encouraged the local Arab notables to send their sons to be educated at the capital and founded[222] many Western-style schools in Syria, including the lower elementary (*sıbyaniye*), secondary (*sultaniye*), and military preparatory schools. In all these schools, even though the language of instruction was Turkish with some French, with Arabic receiving only scant attention, many of the graduates, especially those trained at the capital, became very active in the Arab movement. The missionary schools, unlike the Ottoman state schools, accorded Arabic a privileged position in the curriculum; indeed it was among the graduates of the Syrian Protestant College— founded in Beirut in 1866, the first of its kind, with Arabic as the language of instruction—and the Jesuit Universite Saint-Joseph—established in 1865—that the main cadre of the Arab national movement formed.[223] Hence the expansion of Western-style education awakened and intensified, this time, the Arab national consciousness. Secular teachers at these institutions as well as the graduates who were taught public administration, civil law, and military science created new visions of the future of the Arab world.

This escalating interest in education brought with it an increase in the number of Arabic printing presses as the schools needed manuals for instruction. In compiling these works and thus indirectly reviving Arab literature, the schools also secured the services of scholars such as Nasif Yaziji and Butrus Bustani, who started the first[224] political newspaper, *Clarion of Syria*, in the Arab world and started spreading Enlightenment ideas of tolerance and patriotism.[225] Butrus Bustani also published *al-Jinan*, a political and literary review,[226] which used, for the first time, the motto "Patriotism is an article of faith." The independent political newspaper and the literary and scientific periodical were the two new types of publications[227] that appeared in Arabic in the 1870s.[228] It was especially after the suspension of the Ottoman constitution in 1877 that Arab demands for reforms started to be circulated through the print media. One of the earliest Arabic papers in Beirut, *Lisan-ul-Hal*, published by Khalil Sarkis, contained many articles on these reforms.[229] After 1908, the print media played a significant role in fostering a Syrian public opinion in favor of Arabism. The most influential among these was *al-Muqtabas* (The quoter), edited by Muhammad Kurd 'Ali a former supporter of the Committee of Union and Progress and a member of the Arab Revival Society.[230] From 1909 through 1914, in spite of strict Ottoman censorship, about sixty new newspapers were established in Beirut and about forty in Baghdad. Although these were short-lived, they nevertheless generated a lively forum for the discussion of new political scenarios.[231]

In all, visions of history and literature played a very significant role in creating and determining new meanings and their boundaries, which were then reproduced through the educational system. It was the combination of structural conditions with the new universe of meaning that generated the nationalisms in the Ottoman Empire. Yet this combination of structure and meaning had to be combined with a third factor, that of organization, in setting the parameters for the final course the nationalisms undertook.

## Organizations for Political Change

The structures of war, commerce, and reforms thus interacted with visions of history, literature, and commerce to give meaning to the Greek, Armenian, Turkish, and Arab nationalisms; yet both needed a third and crucial factor in determining the trajectories these nationalisms took: an organizational base. It was through the establishment of philanthropic associations, secret societies, and political parties that people became mobilized and transformed into nationally conscious citizens.

**Philanthropic Associations**   These associations, often established in the Enlightenment spirit to improve social conditions, were significant in mobilizing people and resources and in identifying their target population in terms of certain "national" characteristics. In the case of the Greek national movement, philanthropic associations first formed in Europe around the conception of a Greek civilization that had been the cradle of the current European one. The philhellenic movement, which encaptured this sentiment of a consuming love for Greece, a sentiment nourished and strengthened by romanticism, emerged in the second and third decades of the nineteenth century. Even though the philhellenes were at first much more interested in the historical sites and literature than the Greek nationalist movement,[232] the arrival of Lord Byron and his poetry led them to start to perceive the Greeks as people and Greece as a land. As a consequence, in the 1820s, European *philhellenic societies* were established in Madrid, Stuttgart, Munich, Darmstadt, Zurich, Berne, Genoa, Paris, and Marseilles to raise money for the Greek war of independence against the Ottomans and for the relief[233] of its victims.[234] Their efforts continued the work started by an earlier[235] organization, the London Greek Committee, which was established in 1823 when twenty-five friends of Greece issued an appeal to the known philhellenes; this committee grew in size to eighty-five before the end of the year. Among its members were many peers and other nobility, professionals, poets, clergy, and literary people; the list included a future prime minister, a past and a future lord chancellor, and the former lord mayor of London.[236] The London Greek Committee ordered two sailing ships from America. It had to sell the first to finance the second, the *Hope*, which was renamed the *Hellas* and became the flagship of the Greek fleet.[237] Yet the rest of their efforts were ineffectual and did little financially to further the Greek cause, except to light and create a vision in Europe for an independent Greece. The philanthropic activities of the Ottoman Greeks remained largely confined to the capital; the Constantinople Literary Society provided an intellectual leavening to the Greek community as it coordinated educational activities and provided a cultural model for the dispersed centers of Hellenism.[238]

The most significant philanthropic society in the Armenian national movement was also formed abroad in Paris in 1849 by "the Young Armenians," named after the Young Ottomans, who had come into contact with the Western world and subsequently wanted to transform their community. Many had studied in Paris, acquainted themselves with European political systems and progressive ideas, and had come to appreciate the French Revolution, the positivism of August Comte, and the ideas of Lamartine, Victor Hugo, and Alfred de Musset among others. As a consequence, they formed the Ararat Society (*Araratean Enkerut'iwn*) as a nonsectarian and nonpolitical organization with the aim "to bring progress to the Armenian nation and to provide for all its needs."[239] The Ottoman Armenians also formed many educational societies within the boundaries of the empire; the most outstanding among these was the United Societies, which came into existence in 1880 by the union of three organizations (*Ararathian, Tebrotzasiratz Arevelian,* and *Cilician*), all of which were active in opening schools in the provinces. Another educational society, the Altruistic Society (*Andznever*) was established in Constantinople in the 1860s; defining literacy as a solution to poverty, the members of this organization aimed to teach the Armenian language to the migrant Armenian workers at the capital. The Benevolent Union, founded[240] in Constantinople in 1860, similarly attempted to improve the financial and social conditions of the nation through education and agricultural innovations; it set up a model farm in Cilicia, for instance, to educate Armenian farmers in scientific agriculture.[241]

The philanthropic associations founded by the Ottoman Turks were also external in origin. The first such independent Ottoman association was to be the "Beşiktaş group," which was founded in 1826 and named after the İstanbul neighborhood where most of the members resided. The members, who were mostly Ottoman state officials and religious scholars, met regularly with the explicit purpose of "learning and teaching among all those individuals longing for science and education."[242] Later, it was the Turks from outside the empire who had migrated during the last decades of the nineteenth century that founded in the capital the associations of Tatar immigrants, students originating from Russia or the Crimea, and the Bukharan Benevolent Society. These eventually widened their membership base by addressing significant cultural and historical issues on the ethnic origins of the Turks. One of the associations founded in 1908 soon after the Young Turk revolution was the Association of Turks (*Türk Derneği*), which aimed "to study and impart all the written works and activities, past and present, of the Turkish peoples in archeology, history, linguistics, literature, ethnography, ethnology, sociology, civilization, and the old and new geography of Turkish lands."[243]

Meanwhile, many societies such as the Ottoman Medical Society (*Cemiyet-i Tıbbiye-i Osmaniye*) and Ottoman Scientific Society (*Cemiyet-i İlmiye-i Osmaniye*) undertook the task of finding Turkish equivalents for modern scientific and technical terms. The efforts mounted in constructing the Turkish identity escalated after the Balkan Wars; three such new philanthropic organizations espousing Turkish nationalism were the Homeland of the Turks (*Türk Yurdu*) established in 1911; the Hearth of the Turks (*Türk Ocağı*), which was a semisecret club set by medical and other students; and the Turkish Association for Knowledge (*Türk Bilgi Derneği*), formed in 1913 under the patronage of the Young Turks' Committee of Union and Progress.[244] All of these societies published profusely and gradually developed a body of knowledge on which rested the social and historical origins of Turkish nationalism.

The Arab philanthropic organizations that generated the Arab national movement were mainly formed in the provinces of the empire, often with missionary support. The first one, founded by Yaziji and Bustani in 1847 in Beirut with Protestant encouragement was the Society of Refinement (*Jam'iyat al-tahdhib*); it was established to discuss topics ranging from language and literature to patriotism and the revival of past glories. Arab Christians formed the majority of its members.[245] The Jesuits followed suit by supporting the establishment in 1850 of the Oriental Society (*Jam'iyat al-sharqiya*) along similar lines.[246] The Syrian Scientific Society (*Jam'iyat al-'ilmiya al-suriya*) was also founded in 1852 with the aim to disseminate knowledge in the sciences and arts, especially in terms of the historical contribution of the Arabs to these fields;[247] it explicitly overlooked religious and political issues in an attempt to overcome sectarian differences. Such activities took a political bent as the twentieth century commenced and spread to Europe. In Najib Azuri,[248] a Christian Arab, had founded in 1904 a society known as League of the Arab Nation (*Ligue de la Patrie Arabe*), which declared as its aim the freedom of Syria and Iraq from Ottoman domination and attempted to incite Arabs to achieving this aim.[249]

The first Arab society founded at the capital was the Ottoman Arab Fraternity (*al-Ikha' al-'Arabi al-'Uthmani*); it explicitly attempted to actualize an Ottoman democracy[250] that the Committee of Union and Progress had envisioned when it came to power in 1908. In 1909, another such society, the Literary Club (*al-Muntada al-Adabi*) was founded in Constantinople by officials, scholars, and students equipped with a library and a hostel. In the ensuing general elections to the Ottoman assembly, when the Turks were grossly overrepresented at the expense of all other ethnoreligious groups, including the Arabs, all the Arab organizations of the empire started protests. Another society established in 1907 in Cairo was the Society of the Ottoman Council (*Jam'iyyat al-Shura al-'Uthmaniyya*) with the equal participation of Arabs, Turks, Albanians, Kurds, and Armenians, both Muslim and Christian; the aim of the society was to unite all the nationalities of the empire and establish a constitutional regime.[251]

Branches were set throughout the Arab countries as well. Even though the Committee of Union and Progress invited them to join their organization at the capital, the council in Egypt turned the offer down and argued that, unlike the CUP, they were including in practice as well in theory all nationalities and not restricting upper echelons to Turks. The Beirut Reform Society (*Jam'iyat Bayrut al-Islahiya*), which was established in the era of broadening calls for reform after the failure of the Ottoman forces in the Balkan War and the fall of the Unionist government, advocated reliance on internal strength of the homeland within the general context of the empire. During the same period, in 1913, the Basra Reform Society was formed, patterned after the one in Beirut. Because of the ensuing unrest, all such organizations were banned eight months later.[252]

**Secret Societies**    The nationalist reactions against French domination during the Napoleonic era and the failed expectations of many social groups after the Congress of Vienna in 1815 had led to the emergence of secret societies in Europe. The structure of these societies were based on patterns borrowed from Freemasonry. They were very significant organizations in resisting existing state control by withholding information through close networks. Masonic lodges were established in Corfu in 1811 by Count Romas, with other similar lodges in the Ionian Islands, Lefkas, Paris, and Moscow during the same period.[253]

The first Greek secret society that laid the organizational groundwork for the Greek nationalist movement was the Friendly Society (*Philiki Etairia*) founded in Odessa in 1814 with the explicit aim to liberate the motherland through armed revolt; among the membership, more than half were merchants.[254] Secret words and complicated codes were a part of every function; orders from the governing body always came in code signed with a seal bearing sixteen compartments containing sixteen initials. These messages were brought to the other members[255] through networks of well-paid agents known as apostles who spread the Gospel throughout Ottoman territory. Even though the element of secrecy and of imagined leadership by Alexander I, the emperor of Russia, strengthened the society,[256] it disintegrated when the Greek revolt began as many clan-based loyalties and local ties came to play.

Many secret societies formed among the Ottoman Armenians after their escalating persecution in the 1860s. The uprisings in Zeitun, Van, and Erzurum and the escalating Kurdish aggression led to the establishment in 1872 of the Union of Salvation (*Miuthiun I Perkuthiun*)[257] among the Ottoman Armenians of the Van province for self-protection. Similarly, in 1880, two years after another Ottoman aggression, a group formed in Erzurum, the Defenders of the Fatherland. The 1878 persecutions in Van resulted in the formation of three Armenian revolutionary groups,[258] the Armenagan, which provided general education for the public, trained an Armenian self-defense unit, and aimed to win the right for self-rule through revolution; the Black Cross Society (*Sev Khatch Kazmakerputhiun*),[259] where a group of young Armenians vowed to protect their unarmed compatriots by the use of armed force; and the Protectors of the Fatherland[260] (*Pashtpan Haireniats*), which, approved by the Armenian patriarch in Constantinople,[261] armed the inhabitants for defense against future attacks by Turks, Kurds, and Circassians.[262] Even though these secret societies, mostly formed in the eastern provinces in Erzurum and Van, mobilized the Ottoman Armenians around the national cause of self-preservation, the weak connections with the Armenians at the capital and the vigilant control of the Ottoman state often curbed their impact.

The first clandestine opposition organization in the empire was the Patriotic Alliance (*İttifak-ı Hürriyet*), which was established during the summer of 1865; it changed its name to the Young Ottoman Society[263] in 1867. All who joined had ideas of constitutionalism and popular representation and wanted to transform Ottoman rule into a constitutional one. Facing increasing persecution by the Ottoman government, many of its members started to escape to Europe in the late 1860s. Later, with the accession of Abdülhamid II and the abolition of the constitution and the assembly, many constitutionalists, including three members of the royal family, Damad Celaleddin Pasha, the sultan's brother-in-law, and his two sons, Sabaheddin and Lütfullah, also fled to Europe. The first secret society, founded by the Ottoman military cadets in 1889, which was also the most significant one in that it assumed legitimacy and political power within two decades, was the Committee of Union and Progress (*İttihat ve Terakki Cemiyeti*). Mobilizing adherents among the junior military and civilian bureaucrats, dissident intellectuals in exile, and the emergent middle class, the secret society initially aimed for a policy of Ottomanism to keep the empire together where all social groups would be equal.

It soon became evident that this pluralist policy did not take ground in practice; first Muslims, then Ottoman Turks were favored over other groups. The members circulated a confidential correspondence in 1897 stating "our aim is great union. For that reason you may allow Christians to become members of the Committee. But do not give the secret numbers of the Committee correspondence to them! Only show them the published materials of the committee."[264] The committee became further radicalized in its policies during the early twentieth century: in its 1911 convention, it decided to strive for the universal advancement of the Turkish language, sent agents to Albania, Afghanistan, and Azerbaijan, and established branches in the Caucasus and Turkestan. Similarly, in the 1913 convention, it decided to pursue the cultural and economic policy of Turkification.[265]

The first mention of a possible secret society in Syria took place in 1879 when the British ambassador had a conversation with the Ottoman governor of Syria, Midhat Pasha, and asked him if there were truly a great Arab conspiracy with branches in Aleppo, Mosul, Baghdad, Medina, and Mecca. The response[266] was in the affirmative that indeed an Arab state headed by Amir 'Abd al-Qadir al-Jaza'iri was contemplated, but no action had been yet taken. This amir had established a philanthropic society, the Society of Good Intentions (*Jam'iyyat al-Maqasid al-Khayriyya*), to invest money received from the government and rich local notables to establish schools for the education of Arab youth and to found a printing house to publish textbooks in Arabic. Even when the Ottoman state abolished this society for its alleged separationist[267] activities, the members continued to meet in secret circles to study Arabic history, language, and literature and to spread Arabism among the youth. Another similar secret society in Beirut was formed by twelve Christian graduates of the Syrian Protestant College of Beirut advocating an independent Arab state.[268] In recruiting members and mobilizing against the Ottomans, these graduates united with the Muslims through the cultural ties they all shared in Arabism. Within a couple of years, they started distributing placards[269] throughout Syrian towns, which described the magnificent past of the Arabs and demanded autonomy for Syria. The newly appointed Hamdi Pasha pressured the secret society to stop its activities. Another significant organization, Comite Turco-Syrien, became public a few years after its inception with participants and activities ranging from Europe, to the Ottoman capital, to Syria. Reformist in nature, the organization was eventually absorbed into the Committee of Union and Progress.[270]

The most significant secret society for Arab nationalism formed at the Ottoman capital was the Society of the Arab Revival (*al-Nahda al-'Arabiyya*). Formed in 1906 by Arab students,[271] the aim of the society was "making the intellectual Arab youth aware of their Arabism and to encourage them to cooperate in improving Ottoman society, whose righteousness was dependent on that of Arab society from the Taurus mountains to Bab al-Mandib." Even though the society became legal after the Young Turks assumed power, the escalating Turkification of the government led first to a name change, to the Society of the Syrian Revival, which localized the ambitions of the group, and later to a gradual disintegration under Ottoman censorship, which resulted in the departure of many members to secret societies.

Two secret societies were significant in the emergence of Arab nationalism. The one formed in 1909, entitled al-Qahtaniya after one of the legendary ancestors of the Arab race, aimed to transform the Ottoman Empire into a dual monarchy, a Turco-Arab empire fashioned after the Austro-Hungarian federal model.[272] Recruiting from among the members of the Ottoman Arab Brotherhood (*al-Ikha al-'Arabi al-'Uthmani*), which was founded after the proclamation of the Ottoman constitution, this new secret society included many high-ranking Arab officers in the Ottoman army. Still, its activities ceased after a year when they were betrayed to the Ottoman administration.[273] In its stead formed the Covenant (*al-'Ahd*), which, aiming to establish an Arab Kingdom within a wider Ottoman Empire, explicitly recruited soldiers and formed branches throughout Syria. Many members[274] of this association formed the seeds of the first Arab nationalists in Syria and became the first generation leaders of the post-World War I Arab states. The other association, the Young Arab Society (*Jam'iyat al-'Arabiya al-Fatat*), was founded[275] in Paris in 1911 by seven young Arab Muslims all studying at the French capital—their objective was liberation from Turkish or any other alien domination and the placement of the Arab nation in the ranks of living nations.

The most significant activity of the Arab societies organized abroad was the Arab Congress of Paris held in 18–23 June 1913, which formed a general platform for the Arab demands of the Ottoman Empire.[276] Even though the manifest aim was to confirm the social and political solidarity of the Arab nation uniting both Christians and Muslims and to profess loyalty and allegiance to the Ottoman Empire, the Ottomans attempted to sow dissension among the participants and offered 'Abd al-Hamid Zahrawi, the president of the Paris Congress, a seat in the prestigious Ottoman senate, a position he accepted after breaking with his allies.[277] These secret societies started to strive for independence after World War I; most members of the Syrian elite started to identify with Arabism after the 1918 occupation of the European and Sharifian[278] troops of the Syrian provinces, a development that they rightfully identified as the final defeat of the Ottoman Empire.

**Political Parties**    Political parties were significant as the organizational form for the total mobilization of the populace around the national cause. In the case of the Greek nationalist movement, secret societies immediately transformed into political parties within the newly independent Greece and therefore decreased the incentive among the Ottoman Greek organizations to have political parties, as there already were some in the newly independent Greek state. The Armenian, Turkish, and Arab nationalisms, however, did indeed witness the formation of political parties to further their national cause.

The two major Armenian political parties,[279] both initially founded outside the boundaries of the Ottoman Empire but soon embarked upon political activities within, were the *Hnchak* (Bell) Party,[280] founded in Geneva in 1887, and the *Dashnaksutiun* (Armenian Revolutionary Federation),[281] established in Tiflis in 1890. The Hnchaks, whose immediate objective was the political and national independence of Ottoman Armenia, chose Constantinople as the center of their organization and activity and recruited seven hundred members within seven months: most of these members were professionals working in foreign consulates and maritime companies. In 1890, they organized the demonstration of Kum Kapu to force the sultan into carrying out the promised reforms and to gain the support of the European powers. Hoping to synchronize their efforts, they joined in 1891 the Oriental Federation, which was composed of Macedonian, Albanian, Cretan, and Greek revolutionaries; they also placed placards throughout the empire to mobilize others against government oppression.

In a protest against the Ottoman sultan's refusal to decree reforms, the Hnchaks also staged a demonstration in Bab-ı Ali, the center of Ottoman government in Constantinople in 1895. The demonstration led to much bloodshed but also alerted the European powers to the Armenian demands and forced the Ottoman sultan, Abdülhamid II, to sign the Armenian reform program. A split occurred within the Hnchak Party in 1896 over whether socialism was compatible with Armenian nationalism and over what tactics to follow in achieving independence. Although the Hnchaks were also interested in national liberation, they placed class interests over national interests, unlike the Dashnaks who placed the interests of the Armenian nation above all. Ultimately, it was the Dashnak Party formed in Russian Armenia that rose to predominance.

The Dashnaksutiun party was formed in reaction to the closing of Armenian schools by the Tsar's edict and the Guilizar incident where an Armenian peasant girl was raped by a Kurdish chief.[282] Even though the headquarters of the Dashnak Party was to be Trabzon, Tiflis nevertheless remained the operating center. It was then that Sarkis Googoonian, a young student, approached the party and volunteered to cross the border to the Ottoman Empire with 125 comrades to protect the Ottoman Armenians against persecution. Even though the mission got underway, it was the Russian border patrols who attacked and arrested them before crossing the border, and the attempt went no further.[283] The other major accomplishment of the party was the seizure of the Ottoman bank in Constantinople by twenty-six revolutionaries on 26 August 1896 to force the Ottoman government to carry out reforms in the provinces that would protect Armenian lives. After the intervention of the Russian consul, the revolutionaries were given a safe passage to Europe.[284]

The party also produced the first significant fighting units of the Armenians, the first volunteer fighters who would defend Armenian rights by killing the enemy or die fighting initially in the Ottoman Empire and later, at the beginning of the twentieth century, in Russia against forceful Russification. They also attempted in 1905, with other organizations, the assassination of Sultan Abdülhamid, without success, and joined the dissenting[285] elements against Hamidian rule. Indeed, when the sultan was deposed in 1908, whereby the Dashnaksutiun "laid down its arms and joined wholeheartedly in parliamentary cooperation."[286] Of the twelve Armenian deputies to the newly elected Ottoman parliament, six were members of the party, and the Dashnaksutiun soon thereafter became the central political power of the Armenian community.[287] The aim of the party now was to realize autonomy with peaceful coexistence; indeed the official committee of the Dashnaksutiun made another public announcement with the Committee of Union and Progress, stating that "the two organizations declare that they are in harmony concerning the increasing of the provincial rights which will guarantee the general progress of the Ottoman fatherland."[288] Yet the promised self-rule in the provinces did not materialize; the radicalization of politics, the return of the Ottoman government to oppression, and the continued and even harsher persecution of the Armenians in the Ottoman Empire soon put an end to all these endeavors.

The most significant political party in the empire was that established by the formerly secret society of the Committee of Union and Progress.[289] Upon assuming power in 1908, the Unionists fell quickly into disarray for two reasons; they had not defined future aims other than the restoration of the constitution and were therefore suddenly faced with power struggles among the factions, especially over the appointments of the ministers of war and marine that effectively controlled the armed forces. The other reason was external: the crises of the Bulgarian independence, the Austrian annexation of Bosnia and Hercegovina, and the decision of Crete to join Greece all came in October 1908 and effectively destroyed the chance of the Unionists to formulate adequate policies.

In addition, the tension over the division of power between the committee, which just claimed to be the guardian of the constitution, and the Ottoman sultan led to many additional tensions, among them the establishment in 1908 of the Liberal Union (*Osmanlı Ahrar Fırkası*) as an opposition party. The membership of the Liberal Union came largely from the prosperous and conservative elements and wanted decentralization in government, with a laissez-faire economic system and virtual autonomy for ethnic groups—a policy that won them the support of the non-Turkish elements of the empire. Another political organization that formed was the Muhammedan Union (*İttihad-ı Muhammedi*), which championed Islamic orthodoxy, argued that national union must be based on the ideal of Islam, and opposed modernization that displaced the Sheriat. The political conundrum between the Unionists, Liberals, and traditionalists was resolved with the march in 1909 of the army in Macedonia to the capital as the Action Army (*Hareket Ordusu*); ultimately, the Unionists eliminated the other parties as their political control of the Unionists over the army proved too strong to be overcome. And their adoption of the policy of Turkification strengthened the stronghold of Turkish nationalist groups at the expense of others.

Arabism did not necessarily mean Arab nationalism but instead support for the Entente Liberal Party (*Hürriyet ve İtilaf*), which advocated administrative decentralization, some local autonomy, respect for the empire's nationalities, and protection of democratic freedoms.[290] Still, the significant political party among the Ottoman Arabs was the Ottoman Decentralization Party (*al-Hizb al-Lamarkaziya al-Idariya al-'Uthmani*), which was founded in Cairo in 1912 with the aim to advocate decentralization both among the rulers of Turkey and the Arabs; the motto of the party was "Religion is for God, homeland is for all."[291] The party surmised that the Ottoman Empire could be better defended against European attacks if it were decentralized and each province organized in self-defense—a stand that was in direct opposition with the Unionist vision, which saw the solution in increased centralization. The party nevertheless asked for wider administrative authority and for Arabic as the official language of the province and as one of the official languages of the Ottoman Parliament. The Arab National Congress in Paris in 1913 reiterated these demands as they called for the introduction of reforms, proportionate representation in the administration, and the recognition of Arabic as an official language of equal stature with Turkish.[292]

Even though the Unionists attempted to recruit Ottoman Arabs into their ranks by promising Arabic instruction in schools and Arab representation in the Senate, they were not able to keep these promises.[293] Instead, most of the Arab officials in high administrative positions both at the capital and the provinces were purged between 1908 and 1914.[294] Within this context, the escalating Turkification policies of the Unionists further intensified the political transition[295] from the Arab decentralization movement to independence; it was the Ottoman Empire's entry in World War I that ultimately launched the Arab independence movement. On the eve of the war, Cemal Pasha, who took over the command of the Fourth Army in the Syrian province and started his rule with a policy of tolerance and clemency emphasizing the commonalities of the Arabs and Turks, soon ordered executions and deportations toward Arab leaders in an attempt to contain them and to prevent their collaboration with foreign powers[296] against the empire.

After World War I, as Ottoman forces were driven out of Syria in October 1918, the Allies took over and established three administrations, the British in Palestine, the French in Lebanon and along the Northern coast, and the Arabs in the interior from Aleppo in the north to Aqaba in the south; Britain and France ultimately divided the country between them, partitioning the Ottoman province of Syria into four entities, Syria, Lebanon, Palestine, and Transjordan.[297] The result of the opposition in Syria to the European and Sharifian[298] occupation was the formation in 1919 of the National Party (*al-Hizb al-watani*), which asked for full Syrian independence within its national boundaries.[299]

## CONCLUSION

The combination of war, commerce, and reforms that transformed existing social relations thus interacted with new visions painted by history, literature, and education and, under the parameters set by the existing organizations of philanthropic and secret societies and political parties, determined the patterns the nationalisms within the Ottoman Empire took. There was also an element of continuity among the different nationalisms, as ideas and social practices germinated, diffused, and transformed from one context to another; as one scholar points out, "one nationalism begat a competing nationalism. One nationality's claims to a better position stimulated rival claims by its neighbors."[300]

Empires often lacked the tools with which to contain these nationalisms; they were founded on principles of social power that privileged lineage and proximity to the center and built on carefully defined and segmented social groups whose boundaries were carefully guarded. When the Enlightenment ideas of citizenry that strove at least for political equality (even though initially restricted only to urban males with property) diffused from the United States, France, and Haiti to the rest of the world, the empires had a difficult time containing these principles and what they implied. The privileging of lineage and proximity to the center hindered the principle of political citizenry based on equal access to resources throughout the land; the segmented social groups had taken roots in the societal structure to such a degree that the empires could not, in spite of many attempts, transform these groups they had tried so hard to contain into the imagined community of a federal political entity. Even though such a federal entity might have theoretically prevented the emergence of nationalist movements, the increased political conflict over territorial control resulting in frequent wars radicalized the existing movements foreclosed that possibility.

⸱Ultimately, what determined the form and trajectory of the Greek, Armenian, Turkish, and Arab nationalisms? This comparative analysis reveals two significant insights. One is that the form all these Middle Eastern nationalisms took contained many similarities in structure, meaning, and organization. The epistemological shadow of the nation-state on historical scholarship has obfuscated this commonality in form and has instead treated each nationalism as unique, thereby highlighting difference at the expense of similarity. Once analyzed within a comparative context, not only do similarities among Middle Eastern nationalisms become evident, but one also starts to observe patterns between the Middle Eastern nationalisms and those occurring elsewhere. Indeed, the observation of one scholar,[301] made in the context of Western Europe, becomes relevant to the Middle East as well when he states that "the emergence of nineteenth century nationalities was no natural or logical development from a series of objective and empirically observable characteristics of human populations, like a common territory, language or religion," but "bore a far more arbitrary and less predictable relationship to existing patterns of social organization."

The question of a comparative analysis of the trajectories of these Middle Eastern nationalisms is harder to analyze, since the concept of trajectory contains within it the element of historical process, of transformation, which in turn entails many interactions. Still, however, the comparative analysis of Greek, Armenian, Turkish, and Arab nationalisms reveals the significance of the historical context that patterns these interactions. This article has argued that the interaction of three historically contextualized patterns determine the trajectory of each Middle Eastern nationalism: (i) the structures of war, commerce, and reform; (ii) the meanings set by history, literature, and education; and (iii) the organizational framework provided by philanthropic and secret societies and political parties.

## SELECT BIBLIOGRAPHY

Abu-Manneh, Butrus. 1980. "The Christians between Muslim and Syrian Nationalism: The Ideas of Butrus al-Bustani." *International Journal of Middle Eastern Studies* 11: 287–304.

Adalian, Rouben Paul. 1992. *From Humanism to Rationalism: Armenian Scholarship in the Nineteenth Century*. Atlanta: Scholars Press.

Aharonian, Kersam. 1989. *A Historical Survey of the Armenian Case*. Watertown, MA: Baikar.

Ahmad, Feroz. 1982. "Unionist Relations with the Greek, Armenian and Jewish Communities of the Ottoman Empire, 1908–14." Pp. 401–32 in volume 2 of *Christians and Jews in the Ottoman Empire: Functioning of a Plural Society*. B. Braude and B. Lewis, eds. New York: Holmes and Meier.

―――. 1969. *The Young Turks: The Committee of Union and Progress in Turkish Politics 1908–14*. London: Oxford University Press.

―――. 1968. "The Young Turk Revolution." *The Middle East* 3/3: 19–36.

―――. 1966. "Great Britain's Relations with the Young Turks, 1908–14." *Middle Eastern Studies* 2/4: 302–29.

Akçuraoğlu, Yusuf. 1990. *Türkçülük ve Dış Türkler* (Turkism and Turks outside Turkey). Istanbul: Toker.

Akşin, Sina. 1987. *Jön Türkler ve İttihat Terakki* (Young Turks and the Union and Progress Committee). Istanbul: Remzi.

Alexandris, Alexis. 1983. *The Greek Minority of Istanbul and Greek-Turkish Relations 1918–1974*. Athens: Center for Asia Minor Studies.

Alter, Peter. 1989. *Nationalism*. London: Edward Arnold.

Anderson, Benedict. 1983. *Imagined Communities: Reflections on the Origin and Spread of Nationalism*. New York: Verso. 1991 edition.

Antonius, George. 1969. *The Arab Awakening: The Story of the Arab National Movement*. Beirut: Librairie du Liban.

Arai, Masami. 1992. *Turkish Nationalism in the Young Turk Era*. Leiden: Brill.

Arpee, Leon. 1909. *The Armenian Awakening: A History of the Armenian Church, 1820–1860*. Chicago: University of Chicago Press.

Artinian, Vartan. 1989. *The Armenian Constitutional System in the Ottoman Empire 1839–63: A study of its historical development*. Istanbul.

―――. 1981. "The Role of the Amiras in the Ottoman Empire." *The Armenian Review* 34: 189–94.

―――. 1975. "The Formation of Catholic and Protestant Millets in the Ottoman Empire." *The Armenian Review* 28 (Spring): 3–15.

Atamian, Sarkis. 1955. *The Armenian Community: The Historical Development of a Social and Ideological Conflict*. New York: Philosophical Library.

Augustinos, Gerasimos. 1992. *The Greeks of Asia Minor: Confession, Community, and Ethnicity in the Nineteenth Century*. Kent, OH: Kent State University Press.

Balaghi, Shiva. 1994. "Theories of Nationalism: Creating New Spaces in Old Debates." Working Paper, the University of Michigan.

Bardakjian, Kevork. 1982. "The Rise of the Armenian Patriarchate of Constantinople." Pp. 89–100 in *Christians and Jews of the Ottoman Empire*, B. Braude and B. Lewis, eds., vol. 1. New York: Holmes and Meier.

―――. 1981. "Armenia and Armenians through the Eyes of English Travelers of the Nineteenth Century." In *The Armenian Image in History and Literature*, R. G. Hovannisian, ed. Malibu: Undena Publications.

———. 1976. *The Mekhitarist Contributions to Armenian Culture and Scholarship*. Massachusetts: Harvard College Library.

Barsoumian, Hagop. 1982. "Dual Role of the Armenian Amira Class within the Ottoman Government and the Armenian Millet, 1750–1850." In *Christians and Jews of the Ottoman Empire*, B. Braude and B. Lewis, eds., vol. 1. New York: Holmes and Meier.

———. 1979. "Economic Role of the Armenian Amira Class in the Ottoman Empire." *The Armenian Review* 31: 310–16.

Bournoutian, George A. 1983. "The Armenian Church and the Political Formation of Eastern Armenia." *The Armenian Review* 36 (Autumn): 7–17.

Brass, Paul. 1985. "Ethnic Groups and the State." In *Ethnic Groups and the State*, P. Brass, ed. New Jersey.

Braude, B., and B. Lewis. 1982. "Introduction." In *Christians and Jews of the Ottoman Empire*, B. Braude and B. Lewis, eds., vol. 1. New York: Holmes and Meier.

Braude, Benjamin. 1982. "Foundation Myths of the Millet System." In *Christians and Jews of the Ottoman Empire*, B. Braude and B. Lewis, eds., vol. 1. New York: Holmes and Meier.

Brubaker, Rogers. 1992. *Citizenship and Nationhood in France and Germany*. Cambridge, MA: Harvard University Press.

Caprielian, Ara. 1975. "Attempts at Armenia's Political Liberation, 18th–19th Centuries." *The Armenian Review* 28 (Summer): 147–57.

Çark, Y.G. 1953. *Türk Devleti Hizmetinde Ermeniler, 1453–1953*. Istanbul: Yeni Matbaa.

Carr, Edward. 1983. "States and Nationalism: the Nations in European History." In *States and Societies*, Held, David et al., eds. New York: New York University Press.

Chatterjee, Partha. 1993. *Nationalist Thought and the Colonial World: A Derivative Discourse*. Minneapolis: University of Minnesota Press.

Clogg, Richard. 1992. *A Concise History of Greece*. Cambridge: Cambridge University Press.

———. 1982. "The Greek Millet in the Ottoman Empire." In *Christians and Jews of the Ottoman Empire*, B. Braude and B. Lewis, eds., vol. 1. New York: Holmes and Meier.

———. 1981. "The Greek Mercantile Bourgeoisie: 'Progressive' or 'Reactionary'?" In *Balkan Society in the Age of Greek Independence*, R. Clogg, ed. London: Macmillan.

———. 1973. "Aspects of the Movement for Greek Independence." In *The Struggle for Greek Independence: Essays to Mark the 150th Anniversary of the Greek Independence*, R. Clogg, ed. London: Archon.

Dakin, Douglas. 1973. *The Greek Struggle for Independence 1821–1833*. London: B. T. Batsford.

———. 1973b. "The Formation of the Greek State, 1821–33." In *The Struggle for Greek Independence*, R. Clogg, ed. London: Archon Books.

———. 1972. *The Unification of Greece 1770–1923*. London: Ernest Benn.

———. 1955. *British and American Philhellenes during the War of Greek Independence 1821–33*. Thessaloniki.

Davison, Roderic. 1982. "The Millets as Agents of Change in the 19th century Ottoman Empire." In *Christians and Jews of the Ottoman Empire*, B. Braude and B. Lewis, eds., vol. 1. New York: Holmes and Meier.

——. 1977. "Nationalism as an Ottoman Problem and the Ottoman Response." In *Nationalism in a Non-national State: The Dissolution of the Ottoman Empire*, W. W. Haddad and W. Ochsenwald, eds. Columbus: Ohio State University Press.

——. 1968. "The Advent of the Principle of Representation in the Government of the Ottoman Empire." In *Beginnings of Modernization in the Middle East: The 19th Century*, W. R. Polk and R. Chambers, eds. Chicago: University of Chicago Press.

——. 1963. *Reform in the Ottoman Empire 1856–1876*. Princeton: Princeton University Press.

Dawn, Ernest. 1991. "The Origins of Arab Nationalism." In *The Origins of Arab Nationalism*, R. Khalidi et al., eds. New York: Columbia University Press.

——. 1973. *From Ottomanism to Arabism: Essays on the Origins of Arab Nationalism*. Urbana: University of Illinois Press.

Deringil, Selim. 1994. "The Ottoman Empire and Russian Muslims: Brothers or Rivals?" *Central Asian Survey* 13, no. 3, 409–16.

Devlet, Nadir. 1987. "Yusuf Akçura'nın Hayatı, 1876–1935 (Yusuf Akçura's Life)." In *Yusuf Akçura Sempozyumu*. Ankara: Türk Kültürünü Araştırma Enstitüsü.

Dimaras, Alexis. 1973. "The Other British Philhellenes." In *The Struggle for Greek Independence*, R. Clogg, ed. London: Archon Books.

Duri, A. A. 1987. *The Historical Formation of the Arab Nation: A Study in Identity and Consciousness*. London: Croom Helm.

Eley, Geoff. 1981. "Nationalism and Social History." *Social History* 6, no. 1: 83–107.

Enloe, Cynthia. 1989. *Bananas, Beaches and Bases: Making Feminist Sense of International Politics*. London: Pandora.

Etmekjian, James. 1979. "The Utilitarian Nature of the Western Armenian Renaissance." *The Armenian Review* 31: 303–9.

——. 1972. "The Tanzimat Reforms and Their Effect on the Armenians in Turkey." *The Armenian Review* 25 (Spring): 10–23.

——. 1964. *The French Influence on the Western Armenian Renaissance 1843–1915*. New York: Twayne Publishers.

Etmekjian, Lilian. 1976a. "The Reform Movement in Turkey: Background." *The Armenian Review* 29 (Autumn): 281–92.

——. 1976b. "The Armenian National Assembly of Turkey and Reform." *The Armenian Review* 29 (Spring): 38–52.

——. 1976c. "Armenian Cultural and Political Contributions to Reform in Turkey." *The Armenian Review* Summer 29: 167–191.

Fallers, Lloyd. 1974. "Turkey: Nation-state out of Polyglot Empire." In *The Anthropology of the Nation-State*. Chicago: Aldine.

Farah, Ceasar. 1977. "Censorship and Freedom of Expression in Ottoman Syria and Egypt." In *Nationalism in a Non-national State: The Dissolution of the*

*Ottoman Empire*, W. W. Haddad and W. Ochsenwald, eds. Columbus: Ohio State University Press.

Frangos, George D. 1973. "The *Philiki Etairia*: A Premature National Coalition." In *The Struggle for Greek Independence*, R. Clogg, ed. London: Archon Books.

Frazee, Charles. 1969. *The Orthodox Church and Independent Greece 1821-52*. Cambridge: Cambridge University Press.

Gellner, Ernest. 1983. *Nations and Nationalism*. London: Blackwell.

Georgeon, François. 1986. *Türk Milliyetçiliğinin Kökenleri ve Yusuf Akçura 1876-1935* (Origins of Turkish nationalism and Yusuf Akçura). Ankara: Yurt.

Gillis, John. 1994. "Memory and Identity: The History of a Relationship." In *Commemorations: The politics of national identity* J. Gillis, ed. Princeton, NJ: Princeton University Press.

Göçek, Fatma Müge. 1996. *The Rise of the Bourgeoisie, Demise of Empire: Ottoman Westernization and Social Change*. New York: Oxford University Press.

Goode, Alexander. 1970. "A Brief Account of the Mechitaristican Society: Text of a Rare Study Dated 1835." *The Armenian Review* 23: 28-44.

Gökalp, Ziya. 1981. *Türk Devletinin Tekamülü* (The evolution of the Turkish state). Ankara: Kültür Bakanlığı.

——. 1968. *The Principles of Turkism*. Leiden: Brill.

Göyünç, Nejat. 1983. *Osmanlı İdaresinde Ermeniler* (Armenians under Ottoman rule). Istanbul: Gültepe.

Greenfeld, Liah. 1992. *Nationalism: Five Roads to Modernity*. Cambridge: Harvard University Press.

Gülsoy, Ufuk. 1991. "1856 Adalet Fermanına Tepkiler ve Maraş Olayları" (Reactions to the 1856 Imperial Rescript and the Maraş incidents)." In *B. Kütükoğluna Armağan*. Istanbul: Edebiyat Fakültesi Basımevi.

Haddad, Mahmoud. 1994. "The Rise of Arab Nationalism Reconsidered." *International Journal of Middle East Studies* 26: 201-22.

——. 1991. "Iraq before World War I: A Case of Anti-European Arab Ottomanism." In *The Origins of Arab Nationalism*, R. Khalidi et al., eds. New York: Columbia University Press.

Haddad, Robert. 1970. *Syrian Christians in Muslim Society: An Interpretation*. Princeton: Princeton University Press.

Haddad, William W. 1977. "Nationalism in the Ottoman Empire." In *Nationalism in a Non-national State: The Dissolution of the Ottoman Empire*, W. W. Haddad and W. Ochsenwald, eds. Columbus: Ohio State University Press.

Hanioğlu, Şükrü. 1995. *The Young Turks in Opposition*. New York: Oxford University Press.

——. 1991. "The Young Turks and the Arabs before the Revolution of 1908." In *The Origins of Arab Nationalism*, R. Khalidi et al., eds. New York: Columbia University Press.

——. 1985. *İttihat ve Terakki Cemiyeti ve Jön Türklük 1889-1902* (Young Turks and the Committee for Union and Progress). Istanbul: İletişim.

Heusen, Robert. 1987. "In Search of Armenian Nobility: Five Armenian Families of the Ottoman Empire." *Journal of the Society for Armenian Studies* 3: 93–117.

Heyd, Uriel. 1950. *Foundations of Turkish Nationalism: The Life and Teachings of Ziya Gökalp.* London: Luzac.

Hobsbawm, Eric. 1990. *Nations and Nationalism since 1780: Programme, Myth, Reality.* New York: Cambridge University Press.

Hourani, Albert. 1983. *Arabic Thought in the Liberal Age 1798–1939* Cambridge: Cambridge University Press.

———. 1968. "Ottoman Reform and the Politics of Notables." In *Beginnings of Modernization in the Middle East: The 19th Century,* W. R. Polk and R. Chambers, eds. Chicago: University of Chicago Press.

———. 1957. "The Changing Face of the Fertile Crescent in the 18th Century." *Studia Islamica* 8: 91–122.

———. 1946. *Syria and Lebanon: A Political Essay.* London: Oxford University Press.

Hovannisian, Richard G. 1967. *Armenia on the Road to Independence 1918.* Berkeley: University of California Press.

Hroch, Miroslav. 1985. *Social Preconditions of National Revival in Europe: A Comparative Analysis of Social Composition of Patriotic Groups among the Smaller European Nations.* Cambridge: Cambridge University Press.

İhsanoğlu, Ekmeleddin. 1987. "19. yüzyıl başlarında—Tanzimat öncesi—kültür ve eğitim hayatı ve Beşiktaş Cemiyet-i İlmiyesi olarak bilinen ulema grubunun buradaki yeri (The location of the group of religious scholars known as the Beşiktaş scientific society within pre-Tanzimat cultural and educational life)." In *Osmanlı İlmi ve Mesleki Cemiyetleri,* E. İhsanoğlu, ed. Istanbul: Edebiyat Fakültesi.

Kakridis, John Th. 1963. "The Ancient Greeks and the Greek of the War of Independence." *Balkan Studies* 4: 251–64.

Kamenka, Eugene. 1976. "Political Nationalism—The Evolution of the Idea." In *Nationalism: The Nature and Evolution of an Idea.* New York: St. Martin's Press.

Karal, Enver Ziya. 1982. "Non-Muslim Representatives in the First Constitutional Assembly, 1876–7." In *Christians and Jews of the Ottoman Empire,* B. Braude and B. Lewis, eds., vol. 1. New York: Holmes and Meier.

Karidis, Viron. 1981. "A Greek Mercantile *paroikia*: Odessa 1774–1829." In *Balkan Society in the Age of Greek Independence,* R. Clogg, ed. London: Macmillan.

Karpat, Kemal. 1985. "The Ethnicity Problem in a Multi-Ethnic Anational Islamic State: Continuity and Recasting of Ethnic Identity in the Ottoman State." In *Ethnic Groups and the State,* P. Brass, ed. New Jersey: Barnes and Noble Books.

Khalidi, Rashid. 1991a. "The Origins of Arab Nationalism." In *The Origins of Arab Nationalism,* R. Khalidi et al., eds. New York: Columbia University Press.

———. 1991b. "Ottomanism and Arabism in Syria before 1914: A Reassessment." In *The Origins of Arab Nationalism,* R. Khalidi et al., eds. New York: Columbia University Press.

────. 1977. "Arab Nationalism in Syria: The Formative Years, 1908–1914."
In *Nationalism in a Non-national State: The Dissolution of the Ottoman
Empire*, W. W. Haddad and W. Ochsenwald, eds. Columbus: Ohio State
University Press.

Khoury, Philip S. 1987. *Syria and the French Mandate: The Politics of Arab
Nationalism, 1920–1945*. New Jersey: Princeton University Press.

────. 1983. *Urban Notables and Arab Nationalism: The Politics of Damascus 1860–1920*. Cambridge: Cambridge University Press.

Koliopoulos, John. 1987. *Brigands without a Cause: Brigandage and Irredentism in Modern Greece 1821–1912*. Oxford: Clarendon Press.

Koumarianou, Catherine. 1973. "The Contribution of the Intelligentsia towards
the Greek Independence Movement, 1798–1821." In *The Struggle for Greek
Independence*, R. Clogg, ed. London: Archon Books.

Kuran, Ercümend. 1968. "The Impact of Nationalism on the Turkish Elite in the
Nineteenth Century." In *Beginnings of Modernization in the Middle East:
The Nineteenth Century*, W. Polk and R. Chambers, eds. Chicago: Univer-
sity of Chicago Press.

Kushner, David. 1977. *The Rise of Turkish Nationalism 1876–1908*. London:
Frank Cass.

Kutvirt, Thomas Otakar. 1984. "The Development of the Mission to the Armenians in Constantinople through 1846." *The Armenian Review* 37 (Winter):
31–62.

Landau, Jacob. 1981. *Pan-Turkism in Turkey: A Study of Irredentism*. London:
C. Hurst.

Lewis, Bernard. 1988. *The Political Language of Islam*. Chicago: University of
Chicago Press.

Libaridian, Gerard. 1983. "Nation and Fatherland in Nineteenth Century
Armenian Political Thought." *The Armenian Review* 36 (Autumn): 71–90.

────. 1981. "The Changing Armenian Self-Image in the Ottoman Empire:
*Rayahs* and Revolutionaries." In *The Armenian Image in History and Literature*, R. G. Hovannisian, ed. Malibu: Undena Publications.

Lowenthal, David. 1994. "Identity, Heritage and History." In *Commemorations: The Politics of National Identity*, J. Gillis, ed. Princeton: Princeton
University Press.

Mackridge, Peter. 1981. "The Greek Intelligentsia 1780–1830: A Balkan Perspective." In *Balkan Society in the Age of Greek Independence*, R. Clogg, ed.
London: Macmillan.

Mango, Cyril. 1973. "The Phanariots and the Byzantine Tradition." In *The
Struggle for Greek Independence*, R. Clogg, ed. London: Archon Books.

Mann, Michael. 1986. "The Autonomous Power of the State, Its Origins,
Mechanisms and Results." In *States in History*, John Hall, ed. Oxford: Blackwell.

Ma'oz, Moshe. 1982. "Communal Conflicts in Ottoman Syria during the
Reform Era." In *Christians and Jews of the Ottoman Empire*, B. Braude and
B. Lewis, eds., vol. 2. New York: Holmes and Meier.

────. 1968. *Ottoman Reform in Syria and Palestine 1840–1861: The Impact
of the Tanzimat on Politics and Society*. Oxford: Clarendon Press.

————. 1968b. "The Impact of Modernization on Syrian Politics and Society during the Early *Tanzimat* Period." In *Beginnings of Modernization in the Middle East: The Nineteenth Century.* W. Polk and R. Chambers, eds. Chicago: University of Chicago Press.

Mardin, Şerif. 1983. *Jön Türklerin Siyasi Fikirleri 1895–1908* (The political ideas of the Young Turks). Istanbul: İletişim.

————. 1962. *The Genesis of Young Ottoman Thought: A Study in the Modernization of Turkish Ideas.* Princeton: Princeton University Press.

————. 1960. "The Mind of the Turkish Reformer 1700–1900." *Western Humanities Review* 14, no. 4: 413–36.

Megrian, Leon D. 1973. "Mikayel Nalbandyan: A Study in the Rise of Ethnic Radicalism in the 19th Century in Russia." *The Armenian Review* 26 (Autumn): 9–22.

Mousa, Suleiman. 1977. "The Rise of Arab Nationalism and the Emergence of Transjordan." In *Nationalism in a Non-national State: The Dissolution of the Ottoman Empire*, W. W. Haddad and W. Ochsenwald, eds. Columbus: Ohio State University Press.

Muslih, Muhammad. 1991. "The Rise of Local Nationalism in the Arab East." In *The Origins of Arab Nationalism*, R. Khalidi et al., eds. New York: Columbia University Press.

Nalbandian, Louise. 1963. *The Armenian Revolutionary Movement: The Development of Armenian Political Parties through the Nineteenth Century.* Berkeley: University of California Press.

Nicolopoulos, John. 1985. "From Agathangelos to Megale Idea: Russia and the Emergence of Greek Nationalism." *Balkan Studies* 26, no. 1: 41–56.

Nur, Rıza. 1992. *Hayat ve Hatıratum* (My Life and Memoirs). İstanbul: Ötüken.

Ochsenwald, William. 1991. "Ironic Origins: Arab Nationalism in the Hijaz, 1882–1914." In *The Origins of Arab Nationalism*, R. Khalidi et al., eds. New York: Columbia University Press.

Ortaylı, İlber. 1983. "The Problem of Nationalities in the Ottoman Empire following the Second Siege of Vienna." In *Das Osmanische Reich und Europa 1683 bis 1789.* Wien.

Oshagan, Vahe. 1983a. "Modernization in Western Armenian Literature." *The Armenian Review* 36 (Spring): 62–75.

————. 1983b. "Cultural and Literary Awakening of Western Armenians, 1789–1915." *The Armenian Review* 36 (Autumn): 57–70.

————. 1980. "Some Notes on German Influence on Western Armenian Literature in the Nineteenth Century." *The Armenian Review* 33: 48–64.

Panayotopoulos, A. J. 1980a. "Early Relations between the Greeks and the Young Turks." *Balkan Studies* 21, no. 1: 87–95.

————. 1980b. "The "Great Idea" and the Vision of Eastern Federation: A Propos of the Views of I. Dragoumis and A. Souliotis-Nicolaidis." *Balkan Studies* 21, no. 2: 331–65.

Papadapoulos, Theodore. 1990. *Studies and Documents Relating to the History of the Greek Church and People under Turkish Domination.* Hampshire, GBR: Variorum.

Parla, Taha. 1985. *The Social and Political Thought of Ziya Gökalp 1876–1924.* Leiden: E. J. Brill.

Polk, W., and R. Chambers. 1968. "Introduction." In *Beginnings of Modernization in the Middle East: The 19th Century,* W. R. Polk and R. Chambers, eds. Chicago: University of Chicago Press.

Saab, Hassan. 1958. *The Arab Federalists of the Ottoman Empire.* Amsterdam: Djambatan.

Sarkiss, Harry Jewell. 1973. "The Armenian Renaissance 1500–1863." *The Armenian Review* (Autumn 1973): 43–57.

———. 1937. "The Armenian Renaissance." *Journal of Modern History* 9, no. 4: 433–48.

Seikaly, Samir. 1991. "Shukri al-Asali: A Case Study of a Political Activist." In *The Origins of Arab Nationalism,* R. Khalidi et al., eds. New York: Columbia University Press.

Seton-Watson, Hugh. 1986. "State, Nation and Religion: Some General Reflections." In Joseph Alpher, ed. *Nationalism and Modernity: A Mediterranean Perspective.* New York: Praeger.

———. 1977. *Nations and States: An Enquiry into the Origins of Nations and the Politics of Nationalism.* Boulder: Westview.

Shamir, Shimon. 1968. "The Modernization of Syria: Problems and Solutions in the Early Period of Abdülhamid." In *Beginnings of Modernization in the Middle East: The Nineteenth Century,* W. Polk and R. Chambers, eds. Chicago: University of Chicago Press.

Sherrard, Philip. 1973. "Church, State and the Greek War of Independence." In *The Struggle for Greek Independence,* R. Clogg, ed. London: Archon Books.

Shmavonian, Sarkis. 1983. "Mikayel nalbandian and Non-Territorial Armenian Nationalism." *The Armenian Review* 36 (Autumn): 35–56.

Simon, Reeva S. 1991. "The Education of an Iraqi Ottoman Army Officer." In *The Origins of Arab Nationalism,* R. Khalidi et al., eds. New York: Columbia University Press.

Smith, Anthony. 1994. "The Problem of National Identity: Ancient, Medieval and Modern?" *Ethnic and Racial Studies* 17, no. 3: 375–99.

———. 1988. "The Myth of the "Modern Nation" and the Myths of Nations." *Ethnic and Racial Studies* 11, no. 1: 1–26.

———. 1987. *The Ethnic Origins of Nations.* New York: Basil Blackwell.

———. 1986. "State-Making and Nation-Building." In *States in History,* John A. Hall, ed. Oxford: Blackwell.

———. 1983. *Theories of Nationalism.* New York: Holmes and Meier.

———. 1979. *Nationalism in the Twentieth Century.* New York: New York University Press.

Suny, Ronald Grigor. 1993. *Looking toward Ararat: Armenia in Modern History.* Bloomington: Indiana University Press.

———. 1985. "Some Notes on the National Character, Religion and Way of Life of the Armenians." Working Paper, Ann Arbor, MI.

———. 1983. "The Formation of the Armenian Patriotic Intelligentsia in Russia: the First Generations." *The Armenian Review* 778 (Autumn) 36: 18–34.

———. 1979. "Populism, Nationalism and Marxism: The Origins of Revolutionary Parties among the Armenians of the Caucasus." *The Armenian Review* 32: 134–51.

Tarabein, Ahmed. 1991. "Abd al-Hamid al-Zahrawi: The Career and Thought of an Arab Nationalist." In *The Origins of Arab Nationalism*, R. Khalidi et al., eds. New York: Columbia University Press.

Tatsios, Theodore George. 1984. *The Megali Idea and the Greek-Turkish War of 1897: The Impact of the Cretan Problem on Greek Irredentism, 1866–1897*. Boulder: East European Monographs.

Tauber, Elizabeth. 1993. *The Emergence of Arab Movements*. London: Frank Cass.

Ter Minassian, Anaide. 1984. *Nationalism and Socialism in the Armenian Revolutionary Movement (1887–1912)*. Cambridge: The Zoryan Institute.

Tibawi, Abd al-Latif. 1969. *A Modern History of Syria including Lebanon and Palestine*. Macmillan: London.

Tibi, Bassam. 1981. *Arab Nationalism: A Critical Inquiry*. Macmillan: London.

Tilly, Charles. 1975. "Reflections on the History of European State-Making." In *The Formation of National States in Western Europe*, C. Tilly, ed. Princeton: Princeton University Press.

Tivey, Leonard. 1981. "Introduction." In *The Nation-State: The Formation of Modern Politics*, L. Tivey, ed. Oxford: Martin Robertson.

Toprak, Zafer. 1982. *Türkiye'de "Milli İktisat," 1908–18* (The "national economy" in Turkey, 1908–18). İstanbul: Yurt.

Walker, Christopher. 1979. "From Sasun to the Ottoman Bank: Turkish Armenians in the mid-1890s." *The Armenian Review* 31: 228–64.

Wilson, Mary C. 1991. "The Hashemites, the Arab Revolt and Arab Nationalism." In *The Origins of Arab Nationalism*, R. Khalidi et al., eds. New York: Columbia University Press.

Woodhouse, C. 1973. "Kapodistrias and the *Philiki Etairia*, 1814–21." In *The Struggle for Greek Independence*, R. Clogg, ed. London: Archon Books.

———. 1969. *The Philhellenes*. London: Hodder and Stoughton.

Woodhouse, Christopher M. 1981. "The 'Untoward Event': The Battle of Navarino 20 October 1827." In *Balkan Society in the Age of Greek Independence*, R. Clogg, ed. London: Macmillan.

Yannoulopoulos, Yannis. 1981. "Greek Society on the Eve of Independence." In *Balkan Society in the Age of Greek Independence*, R. Clogg, ed. London: Macmillan.

Yapp, Malcom E. 1987. *The Making of the Modern Middle East, 1792–1923*. London: Longman.

Zeine, Zeine N. 1973. *The Emergence of Arab Nationalism*. Delmar, NY: Caravan Bookstt

## NOTES

1. See Nur 1992, pp. 268, 330.

2. Even though Egypt was also significant in the emergence of Arab nationalism, it was unique because of the relative independence of the khedive

from the Ottoman state; this chapter focuses instead on Arab nationalism that emerges in the Ottoman province of Syria, as it is more indicative of the social forces in Ottoman society that led to the formation of the movement. For further information on Egyptian nationalism, see especially Saab 1958, p. 209.

3. See, for instance, Tilly 1975; Tivey 1981; Carr 1983; Smith 1983, 1986, 1988, 1994; Hroch 1985; Mann 1986; Alter 1989; Hobsbawm 1990; and Brubaker 1992 for a survey of the literature.

4. See Tivey 1981, pp. 4–5.

5. See Alter 1989, pp. 60, 96.

6. See Smith 1983, p. 28. Smith further identifies four historical patterns to state and nation formation; (i) the Western model whereby the state and nation emerge together as dynastic-territorial states are built around an ethnic core that forms ties with other ethnic groups; (ii) the immigrant model where small groups form a state and absorb waves of new immigrants, as, for example, in the United States; (iii) the ethnic model where the ethnic group exists in varying degrees of completeness and self-consciousness prior to the advent of nationalism, which transforms these groups into nations with their own territories, economies, legal rights, and education systems, as in Greece for instance; and (iv) the colonial model where a modern state imposes from above a national identity on many ethnic communities and categories, as in the instance of Kenya. See Smith 1986, pp. 241–42.

7. Hroch 1985, pp. 8–9, 129–31.

8. See, for instance, Kamenka 1976; Seton-Watson 1977; Eley 1981; Gellner 1982, 1983; Anderson 1983; Smith 1987; Chatterjee 1993; Balaghi 1994; and Gillis 1994.

9. See Greenfeld 1992.

10. See, for instance, Seton-Watson 1977, p. 15.

11. The quotation is from Smith 1986, p. 245. He then analyzes nationalism as a "political myth" whereby a community creates an imagined national past. Indeed, it is the *ethnie*, "the collective cultural units and sentiments of previous eras " that creates the sense of ethnic origin of nations. Such an ethnie forms and reproduces itself through sedentarization and nostalgia, organized religion, and inter-state warfare." See Smith 1987, pp. 13, 32–41, and 1988, p. 1.

12. See Eley 1981, p. 91.

13. The transition from ethnicity to nationality occurs through the interaction of the global political and ideological situation, the inflexibility of dominant nationalities and their states, and the changing composition of the intelligentsia. See Eley 1981, p. 99.

14. Refer to Anderson 1991, p. 13.

15. See Göçek 1996 for a more detailed analysis of the Ottoman social structure and specifically the location of religious minorities and other social groups within it.

16. See Braude and Lewis 1982, p. 5.

17. Sociologically, a "minority" is a social group that does not equally share in the societal power structure. Hence a group can be numerically large, such as Blacks in South Africa or women, but still not share in the power struc-

ture equally. The Ottoman term for religious minorities is *zimmi* or *dhimmi*.

18. This book, focusing on the central lands of the empire rather than the Arab provinces, studies the Ottoman Greeks, Armenians, and Jews more than the Arab Christians. Yet the Arab Christians were a significant social force in the provinces, particularly in the nineteenth century. For an extensive analysis of Arab Christians, see studies such as those of Bakhit 1972, Braude and Lewis 1973, Cohen 1984 and 1973, Fawaz 1983, Hourani 1957, Hunter 1984, Masters 1988, Owen 1981, and Rafeq 1966 and 1977.

19. The Ottoman Armenians who had originally been under the jurisdiction of the Greek patriarch had their own patriarchate established in 1461 whereby the Armenian patriarch had all the rights and responsibilities of the Greek one. Thenceforth, all Christians professing the diophysitic doctrine remained under the jurisdiction of the Greek patriarch and the monophysitic doctrine under the Armenian patriarch. See Etmekjian 1964, p. 83.

20. See Artinian 1975, p. 3.

21. The minorities could escape these restrictions through one channel: conversion. Ottoman religious minorities sometimes converted to Islam either to enjoy the social rights of the Muslims or sometimes to marry a Muslim.

22. The rebellion in Greece of Ali Pasha of Ioannina was very significant in diverting the attention of the Ottoman state away from the local Greek mobilization for independence. During 1821–25, Sultan Mahmud II sent Muhammad Ali to crush the Greek rebellion, an intervention that the Syrian Arabs also encountered in 1831–40, this time without Ottoman consent. Although the Egyptian occupation was short-lived, it nevertheless opened the road to the Arab resurrection; during the occupation, for instance, the Amir Bashir of Lebanon emphasized the possibility of an Arab empire to mobilize support for the Egyptian army. See Dakin 1973a, pp. 57, 67; Clogg 1973, p. 5; Antonius 1969, pp. 26, 30, 35, and Duri 1987, p. 145.

23. See Clogg 1992, p. 60.

24. After the emergence of Bonaparte, in 1800, an Armenian priest, Hakovb Tjerpetian Shahaniants, suggested that the Armenians make contact with Napoleon's armies in Egypt or Syria as they were moving toward Cilicia. It was rumored that Napoleon was interested in Armenians as possible agents in furthering his interests of invading India through the Caucasus: indeed, he attempted in 1803 to take the Christians of Syria and Armenia under his protection. See Nalbandian 1963, pp. 37–38.

25. Ter Minassian 1984, p. 16, and Etmekjian 1976b, p. 48.

26. In addition, the diplomacy of the Balkan wars convinced the Young Turks that Europe would no longer intervene to maintain the integrity of the Ottoman Empire if the Ottomans could not do so themselves. See Ahmad 1966, p. 321.

27. See especially Duri 1987, p. 164.

28. In 1827, the Tengerian brothers in Constantinople announced to the Ottoman sultan that the eastern Armenians who were fighting during the 1826–28 war between Russia and Persia on the side of the Russians were soon planning to engage in hostilities against the Ottoman sultan—at a time when the Greek war of independence was in progress. The Tengerian brothers used this

occasion to ask the Ottoman sultan to grant the Ottoman Armenian community additional privileges, especially the papal Armenians the right to establish their own community. Yet the plan backfired, as the Ottomans banished all the papal Armenians, including the Tengerian family, especially after the Ottoman defeat at Navarino, which turned the Ottomans against all European powers. See Arpee 1909, pp. 55–56.

29. According to the article, the Russians would have the power to monitor the reforms. At the Congress of Berlin, England and France saw this clause as an expansion of Russian power and changed it to article 61, one that had much less accountability for the Ottomans, which resulted in many Ottoman persecutions against the Armenians after Russian withdrawal. See Aharonian 1989, pp. 34–37, and Etmekjian 1964, p. 131.

30. Article 61 of the 1878 Berlin Treaty repeated but watered down the promise of article 16 of the Treaty of San Stefano, but none was ever carried out. See Ter Minassian 1984, pp. 4–5.

31. See Karidis 1981, p. 112.

32. See Augustinos 1992, p. 30.

33. See Megrian 1973, p. 9, and Shmavonian 1983, pp. 36–37.

34. See Atamian 1955, p. 70.

35. See Bournoutian 1983: 14.

36. The Ottoman Turks comprised 35 percent of the population, with the others following, in descending order, Arabs (13.8 percent), Rumanians (11.4 percent), Bulgarians (7.8 percent), Serb-Croatians (7 percent), Armenians (6.5 percent), Greeks (5.5 percent), Albanians (3.1 percent), Kurds (2.6 percent), and Circassians (2.6 percent). See Davison 1977, pp. 29–30.

37. Modest military assistance was sent to Kashgar in 1875, but later appeals were not answered. See Kushner 1977, p. 11.

38. A significant factor in this migration was that of the flight of intellectuals from the Turkish provinces of the Russian Empire, mainly the Crimea, Central Asia, and the Volga region, including those most affected by the nationalist movements in Russia. See Kushner 1977, pp. 11–12.

39. See Ahmad 1982, p. 416.

40. While most originally settled in Rumelia, the Ottoman Empire encouraged them to move to Anatolia by offering them under the 1857 refugee code land and exemptions from taxes and conscription for twelve years compared to six if they settled in Rumelia. For further information, see Yapp 1987, pp. 121–22.

41. See ibid., p. 59.

42. At its inception, this protection was limited to Ottoman minorities who were locally recruited for service to Western powers "as vice-consuls, interpreters, commercial agents and more menial employs." Yet the scope eventually expanded to cover thousands. Non-Muslim merchants started accepting foreign citizenship more and more frequently until 1869 when the Ottoman citizenship law was introduced. See Davison 1982, p. 32 and Ahmad 1982, p. 404.

43. See Dakin 1973a, p. 21.

44. The Greeks acquired the right to fly under the Russian flag and the protection of Russian consuls in 1779. See Dakin 1973, p. 21.

45. See Karidis 1981, p. 124.

46. By 1813, there were 615 Greek ships amounting to 155,500 tonnes and 38,00 seamen involved in the trade of the region, a factor that aided the independence war. See Yapp 1987, p. 57.

47. The revolt in the principalities in 1821, the commencement of the Greek War of Independence in 1821–27 and the Ottoman-Russian War of 1828–29 brought further population growth to the Greek diaspora community of Odessa. See Karidis 1981, p. 117.

48. See ibid., p. 127.

49. For further information, see Clogg 1981, pp. 98–99; 1992, pp. 4, 27.

50. As in the case of the community of Sibiu (Hermannstadt) in Transylvania, these diaspora communities often had their own Greek church, priest to conduct the rituals, a teacher and a school house for education. The Greek merchant company elected a president and a council that often ran the town; hence they were miniature national societies. See Frangos 1973, pp. 91–92.

51. See Clogg 1981, pp. 94, 104, and Frangos 1973, p. 93.

52. See Etmekjian 1964, p. 60.

53. See Braude and Lewis 1982, p. 21.

54. See Artinian 1989, pp. 7–8, 27–29, 81–91, and 1981, p. 193.

55. See Nalbandian 1963, pp. 34–36.

56. See Etmekjian 1964, pp. 69–71.

57. Within the Madras community, Joseph Emin called for the liberation of Armenia, Shameer Shameerian suggested and financed the use of printed works to spread the idea of political freedom, and both believed that King Heraclius II of Georgia should lead the independence movement but with a republican state and constitution as the result. For further information, see Caprielian 1975, pp. 151–52.

58. Because Armenia was not considered strategically vital to Russia, the creation of an independent Armenia was not in the interest of imperial Russia. See Capraelian 1975, pp. 153–55.

59. The actual capital investment in the Ottoman Empire in 1914 demonstrates this domination: the Ottoman Greeks controlled 50 percent of such investment, Armenians 20 percent, Ottoman Turks 15 percent, foreign nationals 10 percent, and Jews 5 percent (Alexandris 1983, p. 32).

60. By 1914 the Middle East owed Europe about 500 million English pounds, about half of which was accounted for by governments. See Yapp 1987, p. 31.

61. See Ahmad 1982, p. 427.

62. See ibid., pp. 414, 417.

63. For further information on this emergence, see Toprak 1982.

64. In Lebanon, the Christian community was likewise enriched by increased silk cultivation. See Hourani 1957, p. 104.

65. See Yapp 1987, p. 132; Hourani 1957, p. 117; 1968, pp. 60–61.

66. The centralization policy of Sultan Mahmud II (1808–39) restored government authority and ensured the effectiveness of these reforms. This centralization policy drew very much upon the French concept of nation, attempted to unify the empire around the government in Constantinople. See Arai 1992, p. 2.

67. The 1839 Noble Rescript of the Rose Chamber, the 1856 Imperial Rescript, and the 1876 Ottoman constitution accompanied by the establishment of the first Ottoman parliament in 1877 spelled out these reforms. The sultan declared in 1830, for instance, that "his affection and sense of justice for all of his (Muslim, Christian, and Jewish) subjects was strong and indeed they were all his children." See Karal 1982, pp. 388, 389–95. The 1839 rescript stated that "the Muslim and other peoples (*ahali-i islam ve milel-i saire*) who are among the subjects of our imperial sultanate shall be the object of our favors without exception." See Ma'oz 1968, p. 22.

68. See Gülsoy 1991, p. 446.

69. See Davison 1968, p. 104.

70. See Augustinos 1992, p. 60.

71. One must note that individual minorities did indeed penetrate the system often and acquired positions of power, but they were the exception rather than the rule.

72. See Ahmad 1982, p. 407.

73. See ibid., p. 408.

74. After the 1856 proclamation, as an assembly composed of seven metropolitans and twenty-one lay members (ten from the capital and eleven from provinces) met at the capital to determine the structure of new communal representation, six archbishops resigned in protest. Still, a permanent mixed council of four bishops and eight lay members was successfully established. See Alexandris 1983, p. 33.

75. See Augustinos 1992, p. 189, and Gülsoy 1991, p. 445.

76. See Alexandris 1983, pp. 32–33.

77. See ibid., p. 37.

78. The Phanariots were originally drawn from families of Greek or Hellenized Romanian and Albanian origin. From the eighteenth century onwards, the princes governing Wallachia and Moldavia were selected from among Phanariots, who slowly started to cultivate a myth of aristocratic Byzantine ancestry. Hence, the Phanariots, "not by virtue for their descent, but by the virtue of their position in the Ottoman empire, the sources of their wealth, and their close identification with the church, represented a Byzantine tradition that was basically anti-national." See Mango 1973, pp. 44, 59.

79. Clogg 1982, p. 192; 1992, pp. 21, 29; Mango 1973, p. 42.

80. See Mango 1973, p. 48.

81. It was the lack of legal protection that challenged the existence of the Catholic Armenians the most. To secede from one community to join one not officially recognized by the government equaled renunciation of all civil rights and privileges and exposed the offender to the grim consequences of being outlaws. See Artinian 1989, p. 33.

82. See Etmekjian 1964, p.163.

83. See Artinian 1989, p. 39, and 1975, p. 6, and also Arpee 1909, pp. 43, 51.

84. See Etmekjian 1964, p. 86, and Nalbandian 1963, p. 42.

85. Two brothers, the Düzians, were appointed superintendents of the Ottoman imperial bank, while another, Amira Bezjian, became the sultan's con-

fidante and financial advisor. Mahmud II raised him to the rank of a member of the imperial court and gave him the privilege of sharing in the deliberations of the imperial divan; within the Armenian community, he also presided over the patriarch's advisory board and supported many educational, philanthropic, and religious enterprises. Others reached prominent positions later on. See Arpee 1909, p. 53, and Etmekjian 1964, p. 82.

86. For instance, the three architects of the Hovhannes Serverian, Garabed Balian, and Boghos Odian had sent Nahabed Rusinian, one of the most radical and dedicated participants in the Western Armenian Renaissance, to Paris, where, between 1840 and 1851, he studied and became acquainted with social and political issues. Upon his return, he worked indefatigably "for the national welfare, serving on many committees, participating as a member on the national administration, and translating French literary pieces." See Etmekjian 1964, p. 106.

87. For more information, see Barsoumian 1979.

88. See Artinian 1989, pp. 53–57.

89. The debates within the assembly were nevertheless significant in the negotiation of the boundaries of the complaints the Armenians should report to the Ottoman government. As always, the boundaries between criticism and the implication of the desire for autonomy were unclear and, indeed in 1876, a Turkish newspaper, *Basiret* (insight), publicly accused the Armenians of disloyalty. Soon thereafter the meetings of the Armenian assembly were closed to the public. See Etmekjian 1976a, pp. 288–89, and 1976b, pp. 39–41, 46.

90. See Artinian 1989, p. 94, and Atamian 1955, p. 118.

91. See Nalbandian 1963, pp. 127–28, and Hovannisian 1967.

92. Cemal Pasha, for instance, stated "speaking for myself, I am primarily an Ottoman, but I do not forget that I am a Turk, and nothing can shake my belief that the Turkish Race is the foundation stone of the Ottoman empire . . . in its origins the Ottoman empire is a Turkish creation. The quotation is in Landau 1981, p. 50."

93. See Gökalp 1968, p. 8, and Heyd 1950, p. 71.

94. See Akşin 1987, pp. 11–13.

95. See Ahmad 1968, p. 21, and 1969, p. 17.

96. See Etmekjian 1972, p. 16.

97. See Ma'oz 1968, p. 49 and 1982, pp. 96–105.

98. The Ottoman redrawing of Syria in 1887 into the provinces of Aleppo, Beirut, and Syria in an attempt to standardize rule and have governor generals appointed by and directly responsible to the capital increased unrest, one that was constantly stirred up by the European powers. The division of Lebanon into two separate districts along ethnoreligious lines into Christian and Druze polarized matters even further. See Antonius 1969, pp. 56 and 65–66.

99. For more information, refer to Hanioğlu 1995.

100. See Hanioğlu 1991, pp. 31–32.

101. This Turkification was more a result of political changes in the Ottoman ruling cadre—since the inner circle was mostly Turkish, when political replacements were necessary to solidify power over the administration, the positions became filled more and more by Turks at the expense of Arabs. See Khalidi 1991a, p. x.

102. See Antonius 1969, p. 87, and Khoury 1983, p. 17.

103. See Khalidi 1977, pp. 215–16.

104. Moiz Cohen, who later assumed the name Munis Tekinalp, believed in both Ottoman and Turkish nationalism. Committed to Turkish language and culture and to the fusion of minorities into the larger Turkish nation, Cohen attempted to further Turkify the empire. There were still others such as James Sanua, a Jew active in Egyptian nationalism, and Michel Aflak, a Christian in Syria, who served similar functions. See Landau 1981, pp. 3–7, 15.

105. See Ahmad 1982, p. 401.

106. A significant opposing force that also started to emerge was Islamism; this ideology argued that Islam needed to retain its position of influence on politics and society in the empire and thus form a significant link among the Muslim nations within and outside the borders. It also failed to sustain itself against emerging ethnic nationalisms.

107. See Smith 1986, p. 249.

108. See Alexandris 1983, pp. 37–41.

109. See Panayotopoulos 1980a, pp. 87–95.

110. Before the War of Independence, the term denoted "a mythical people of superhuman strength and stature who were imagined to have lived in Greece in the dim and distant past." It was only in the 1820s that it came again into current use. The quotation is from Dakin 1973a, p. 22; see also Kakridis 1963, p. 251.

111. During the war of Independence in 1821, the Greeks issued an appeal to the European courts, stating, "Greece, our mother, was the lamp that illuminated you; on this ground she reckons on your active philanthropy. Arms, money, and counsel, are what she expects from you." The quotation is cited in Dakin 1973a, p. 59, and 1973b, p. 162.

112. For further information, refer to Clogg 1992, p. 60, Tatsios 1984, Dakin 1973a, p. 316, and Panayotopoulos 1980b, p. 335.

113. See Frazee 1969, p. 15, Clogg 1973, p. 27, and Dakin 1955, pp. 10–11.

114. The French annexation of the Ionian islands by the Treaty of Campo Formia in 1797 had briefly raised among the Greeks hopes of Bonaparte as a savior; yet this interest gradually waned. See Clogg 1973, p. 26.

115. See Clogg 1992, p. 17.

116. See Nicolopoulos 1985, p. 42.

117. Indeed, among several plans put forth was a book entitled *La Turquie Chretienne sous la Protection de Louis le Grand, protecteur unique du christianisme en Orient* (Christian Turks under the protection of Louis XIV, the singular protector of Christianity in the East). See Etmekjian 1964, pp. 57–60.

118. The delegation was headed by Catholicos Hagop, and a layperson, Israel Ori, conducted the negotiations from the princes of Karabagh. With the German prince's support, Ori set out in 1698 to enlist the aid of Leopold of Austria and Peter the Great of Russia but died in Astrakhan in 1711 as Peter the Great's special ambassador to the Persian shah. The War of Spanish Succession and the Russian war with Sweden had prevented the development of this course of action. See Caprielian 1975, p. 149, and Etmekjian 1964, pp. 62–63.

119. See Kushner 1977, pp. 27–28.

120. Ottoman history textbooks reflected this change; even though one in 1877 did not mention the Turkish ancestry, another written a decade later did speak of the Turks, Chinese, and Indians as the three great nations of Asia. See Kushner 1977, p. 29.

121. One needs to distinguish, however, Turkism, a movement "to unite, physically, culturally or both, all peoples of proven or alleged Turkic origins, living both within and outside the frontiers of the Ottoman empire," and Turanism, which has as its chief objective "rapprochement and ultimately union among all peoples whose origins are purported to extend back to Turan, an undefined . . . area in the steppes of Central Asia." See Landau 1981, p. 1.

122. See Gökalp 1968, pp. 3–4.

123. See Landau 1981, p. 2.

124. See Kushner 1977, p. 51.

125. In 1918, when the war concluded, Enver ordered all Turkish officers be left in command of Azerbaijan and Northern Caucasus troops and that Azerbaijan be cleared of all Russians and Armenians to ensure Turkic-Turkish territorial continuity. In 1919, the propaganda to save Turkestan continued throughout Central Asia, calling upon all Muslims and Turks to secure the continuation of the Ottoman Empire. The arrival of Enver himself in Central Asia in 1921 and his assumption of the title of emir of Turkestan was the culmination of the Turkish movement. See Landau 1981, pp. 51–55.

126. See Kushner 1977, p. 34.

127. See Tauber 1993, p. 246.

128. Rida stated "Have we said . . . 'Is it possible to restore the glory of the East through the strength of Islam?' Yes! a thousand times yes!" The quotation is in Dawn 1973, p. 134; see also Duri 1987, p. 186.

129. 'Abdul-Rahman Kawakebi, for instance, wrote a work entitled *Umm al-Qura* (a name in the Qur'an as one of the designations of Mecca), about an imagined symposium on the destiny of Islam by twenty-two fictitious characters convened in Mecca for the pilgrimage who then decided to found a society for the regeneration of Islam. Most of the book entailed a verbatim report of the imagined proceedings. See Antonius 1969, p. 96.

130. The book was entitled *Tabai el-Istibdad* (the attributes of despotism). This book was a translation of V. Alfieri's *Della Tiranide* which had first been translated into Ottoman Turkish by Abdullah Cevdet in 1897 and then into Arabic by Kawakabi. See Hanioğlu 1995 for a more detailed discussion.

131. See Saab 1958, p. 204.

132. Many Christian Arabs such as Ibrahim al-Yaziji, Adib Ishaq, Nadrah Matran, and Ahmad Faris Ishyaq who actually converted to Islam identified themselves with the civilization of the East and with Arabism. See Dawn 1973, pp. 140–43. In the context of Egypt, the son of the ruler Muhammad 'Ali, who was a Muslim but not an Arab (but instead a Turk), claimed fictitious Arab identity by association, stating that he "came to Egypt as a child and his blood had since been colored completely Arab by the Egyptian sun." See Hourani 1983, p. 261, and Antonius 1969, p. 28.

133. One case in point was that of the ecumenical patriarch Grigoros V who was hanged on April 1821 at one of the gates of the patriarchate in Con-

stantinople for failing to guide and guarantee the loyalty of his flock. When the Russian tsar protested the action, the Ottoman sultan stated that the patriarch was punished as an individual rebel and traitor, as the head of the nation, and not as a dignitary of the church—hence the sultan declared he was fighting rebellion, not the Orthodox Church. The patriarch's corpse, then dragged to the Golden Horn, was picked up by the Greek crew of a Russian ship and taken to Odessa. Fifty years later, in 1871, the body was returned to Greece, and in 1921, on the hundredth anniversary of his martyrdom, he was proclaimed a saint.

134. See Clogg 1992, pp. 36–37, Dakin 1973, p. 60, and Frazee 1969, pp. 27–39.

135. It is interesting to note, however, that the Latin Catholics, fearing what may happen to them in a Greek state dominated by the Orthodox, maintained a neutral position and paid their dues to the sultan during the first years of the war. Similarly, when efforts were made to get the former Greek patriarch, Gregorius, now exiled on Mount Athos, to join, although he refused to take an oath that agreed to absolute obedience to a mysterious leader, he did nothing to discourage the society's activities. See Frazee 1969, pp. 41–42.

136. See Frazee 1969, pp. 12–13, 44, and Sherrard 1973, p. 183.

137. For instance, crosses were put on Ottoman mosques, the monks of Megaspelaion led the army in the hymn of the Trisaryon, and priests baptized some Muslim children as a reprisal for the Muslims having circumcised some Greek boys. Also, in the first year of conflict, Greek bishops were often called upon to take the lead in both military and civil affairs. See Frazee 1969, pp. 19–21.

138. See Frazee 1969, pp. 19–21.

139. See Libaridian 1981, pp. 164–65.

140. The role played by the various patriarchs of Constantinople, the Caucasian Nerses Ashtaraketsi, and Khrimian Hairik were especially noteworthy. See Suny 1993, p. 20.

141. After starting his religious order in Constantinople in 1701, Mkhit'ar moved to Morea, which was under Venetian rule in 1703 when the persecution of the Armenian Catholics in the Ottoman Empire escalated. After establishing a monastery in Modon in 1712, threatened by the impending occupation of Morea by the Ottomans, Mkhit'ar moved to Venice and leased the island of St. Lazarus in 1717. Mkhit'ar received only Armenian youth into his monastery; he did not distinguish rich or poor but chose the youngest.

142. The quotation is from Etmekjian 1964, p. 72. See also Nalbandian 1963, pp. 30–40; Goode 1970, pp. 29–39; Arpee 1909, pp.17–20; Adalian 1992, pp. 11–15; and Bardakjian 1976.

143. The novelist Hagop Melik-Hagopian (1835–88), known as Raffi, noted: "O fathers! O forefathers! I drink this glass, but not as a toast to your remains. Had you built fortresses instead of monasteries with which your country is full; had you bought guns and ammunition instead of squandering fortunes on holy urns; had you burned gunpowder instead of perfumy incense at the holy altars, our country would have been more fortunate than she is today. . . . From these very monasteries the doom of our country was sealed." The quotation is in Atamian 1955, pp. 78–79.

144. See Kushner 1977, p. 13.

145. See Duri 1987, pp. 204–5.

146. See Clogg 1982, p. 188, and Mackridge 1981, p. 66.

147. See Frazee 1969, p. 10.

148. See Clogg 1992, p. 2.

149. See Augustinos 1992, pp. 170–71.

150. At the beginning of the nineteenth century, "Armenians were still a people fragmented by geography, social class, even by language and religious affiliation." See Suny 1983, p. 24.

151. Armenians also had two major literary languages, eastern and western Armenian, in addition to many dialects and local variants.

152. Since the Bible, which was translated into classical Armenian in the first half of the fifth century, had been inaccessible to the common people, the priests who had to conduct the services fully controlled religious knowledge. See Arpee 1909, p. 13.

153. The exact dates were marked by the date of the publication of the Mkhit'arist publication *Polyhistory* in 1843 and 1915. See Etmekjian 1964, pp. 73–74, 98–99.

154. The romantic interest in the folk (*azgayin*) literature in the midnineteenth century had started to flourish among students at the University of Dorpat. See Shmavonian 1983, pp. 35–39.

155. The tension between classical Armenian and the vernacular was settled in favor of the latter when in 1866 Aydinian, a Viennese Mkhit'arist, published his grammar of the vernacular after laboring over it for twenty years. See Bardakjian 1976, pp. 9–10.

156. In an interesting twist, Lord Byron, who participated in the Greek Independence movement, presented himself in 1816 at the St. Lazaro convent of the Mkhit'arists to study the mysteries of the East; he learned enough Armenian to compose poetry. See Adalian 1992, p. 19.

157. See Oshagan 1983a, p. 63, and Adalian 1992, pp. 11, 61.

158. See Bardakjian 1976, pp. 11–12.

159. See Etmekjian 1964, pp. 154–55.

160. Many Armenians were critical of the degree of French influence; in 1874, Mamourian complained that Armenian "political, religious, moral, literary, educational, commercial, and artistic life are at a standstill, stagnating." In 1885, Eghia Demirdjibashian wrote that "a large and valuable portion of the Armenian nation, its eyes and its hands, its heart and its brain, its body and soul live for France." The quotations are in Oshagan 1983a, p. 70.

161. See Oshagan 1983b, p. 68.

162. The foundations of this theater had been laid the by the Mkhit'arist translations of classical Armenian literature and first emerged in Venice at the Mkhit'arist monastery in 1753. See Etmekjian 1964, p. 198.

163. See Etmekjian 1976c, p. 175.

164. For further information, see Libaridian 1983.

165. The poem can be found in Atamian 1955, p. 80.

166. The other stanzas are:

"Liberty!" The voice of Doom
Echoed to me from above,
"Wilt thou swear until the tomb
Liberty to serve and love?"

Till I die, or meet my doom,
On the shameful gallows tree.
Till the portals of the tomb,
I will shout forth "Liberty!"

167. See Lewis 1988, pp. 40–41.

168. See Gökalp 1968, p. 3.

169. The first systematic grammar of Turkish had been published in Europe in 1832. See Kushner 1977, p. 9.

170. See Gökalp 1968, pp. 4–5.

171. See ibid., pp. 6–7.

172. It was the Russification policy of Alexander II that pushed the Turkish intelligentsia to the Ottoman Empire. See Georgeon 1986, p. 15.

173. See Landau 1981, p. 29.

174. It is interesting to note that the former name of Mustafa Celaleddin Pasha, who was of Polish origin, was Constantin Borcezki; he immigrated to the Ottoman Empire in 1848.

175. See Landau 1981, p. 10, and Kushner 1977, pp. 11–13.

176. See Gökalp 1968, p. 5.

177. See Landau 1981, p. 14, and Devlet 1987, p. 23.

178. Namık Kemal also put the word *la Liberte* beside the title of his newspaper *Hürriyet* (Freedom), tried to introduce the concept of consultation (*meşveret*) into Ottoman politics, and searched for the equality of man before Islamic law.

179. See Arai 1992, p. 1.

180. Gökalp's definition of a nation was "a society consisting of people who speak the same language, have had the same education and are united in their religious, moral and aesthetic ideals—in short, those who have a common culture and religion." The quotation is in Heyd 1950, p. 63; see also Heyd 1950, p. 57. In another instance, he stated that nationality was based solely on upbringing—an argument that potentially could unite the disparate elements of an empire. See Parla 1985, p. 10.

181. See Parla 1985, p. 25.

182. See Duri 1987, p. 195.

183. See Hourani 1962, pp. 69–82; Dawn 1973, p. 123; 1991, p. 4; and Duri 1987, pp. 156–57.

184. Tahtawi had spent 1826 through 1831 in France, and it was there that he developed his conception of patriotism.

185. See Saab 1958, pp. 201–2; Hourani 1962, pp. 99–102; Dawn 1973, pp. 138–39; Abu-Manneh 1980, pp. 287–304; and Duri 1987, pp. 188–89.

186. He also signed his addresses as "he who loves his country" (*muhibb al-watan*).

187. The odes are cited in Duri 1987, p. 162.

188. See Hourani 1954, p. 36.

189. The first Protestant missionary societies entering the Ottoman Empire were the Church Missionary Society of the Church of England in 1815 and the American Board of Commissioners for Foreign Missions in 1818. See Arpee 1909, p. 93.

190. The missionary schools established throughout the Ottoman Empire were training grounds for new cohorts trained within the Enlightenment vision of Western secularist thought. See Mackridge 1981, p. 65. Legally, in the eyes of the Ottoman state, the missionaries were denationalized and therefore without the protection of states, unless the treaty between the Ottoman Empire and the pertinent state contained a clause specifically recognizing missionary endeavors as a legitimate pursuit worthy of protection. The American missionaries suffered from this clause. See Kutvirt 1984, p. 46.

191. See Augustinos 1992, pp. 114–15.

192. See ibid., p. 198.

193. See Clogg 1973, p. 20, and 1992, p. 50.

194. See Augustinos 1992, pp. 171–72.

195. See Clogg 1973, p. 18.

196. Many Greek books in the eighteenth and nineteenth centuries were printed in Venice, Vienna, Leipzig, Bucharest, Jassy and later Constantinople, Corfu, Chios, and Ayvalık.

197. From 1700 through 1725 there were a total of 107 books (80 religion, 10 grammar, and 17 miscellaneous); from 1776 through 1800 the total had reached 749, and the proportions had also changed (395 religion, 104 grammar, and 250 miscellaneous). Better still, the Greek publications from 1800 through 1820 easily surpassed 1,300. See Koumarianou 1973, pp. 70, 83. One significant category was books published for a specifically merchant readership, including a commercial encyclopedia. See Clogg 1981, pp. 96–97.

198. See Dakin 1973, p. 23.

199. See ibid., p. 28.

200. See Frazee 1969, p. 10.

201. See Etmekjian 1964, pp. 94–96.

202. See ibid., p. 172.

203. See Libaridian 1983, p. 76.

204. It was the new Armenian middle class, comprising professionals, literati, and small manufacturers who began the process of secularization and democratization of Armenian institutions. See Libaridian 1983 p. 75.

205. See Artinian 1989, p. 73.

206. See Etmekjian 1964, p. 69.

207. The first Armenian periodical appeared in Madras, India, in 1794 published by a priest. See Etmekjian 1964, p. 136. The first Armenian journal in Russia, *Govgas* (Caucasus) appeared in 1846 but was closed a year later for political reasons; the other journal, *Ararat*, was an Armenian translation of its counterpart. Yet the most significant journal was *Hiusisapile* (Aureola), which, as the title indicated, saw Russia as the northern sun around which Armenian hopes for salvation glimmered. Rather than an independent Armenia, it argued for the benevolent protection of Russia. See Atamian 1955, pp. 73–74.

208. See Artinian 1989, p. 68.

209. See Nalbandian 1963, pp. 52–53, 57, and Atamian 1955, p. 83.

210. See Etmekjian 1964, p. 140.

211. See Bardakjian 1976, p. 19.

212. See Nalbandian 1963, p. 141.

213. The evolution of Turcology in the latter part of the nineteenth century was also significant in leading native scholars to rediscover "their past history, the riches of their language and the beauty of their literature." See Landau 1981, p. 29.

214. This development also led to the differentiation of Arabic as a literary language versus Arabic as a religious language, leading to the separation of language and religion. See Kushner 1977, pp. 67–68.

215. See Kushner 1977, pp. 77, 93, for a more detailed discussion of the significance of language.

216. See Landau 1981, p. 47.

217. The Ottoman censorship on political matters also led to the flourishing of historical and cultural issues in the newspapers, to many debates that often disguised the political controversy embedded within them. For instance, a discussion of the influence of Arabic literature and history on the Ottomans often veiled the larger question of the future trajectory of the Ottoman Empire. See Kushner 1977, p. 15.

218. See Hanioğlu 1985, pp. 21, 57.

219. See Mardin 1983, p. 50.

220. See Landau 1981, p. 43.

221. See Antonius 1969, pp. 36–37.

222. From the early 1860s, the monopolization of the religious establishment over the educational system ended as state secondary schools were founded. See Khoury 1983, p. 29.

223. See especially Antonius 1969, p. 80; Zeine 1973, p. 40; and Mousa 1977, p. 240.

224. The first nonofficial political publication was *Mirat al-Ahwal*, by Rizq Allah Hassun of Aleppo in 1854, followed in 1858 by Kahlil al-Khuri's *Hadiqat al-Akhbar*. In 1860, Butrus al-Bustani's *Nafir Suriya* followed. See Farah 1977, p. 154.

225. See Antonius 1969, pp. 42, 48–50, and Dawn 1973, p. 132.

226. Ibrahim Yazeji, a member and son of Nasif, composed a poem in this review in the form of an ode to patriotism, singing of the glories of Arab literature, the achievements of the Arab race, and of a future they needed to construct away from sectarian dissensions and Ottoman misgovernment.

227. The Arab publications abroad also included *'Atarid* and *Birjis Baris* in 1858, published respectively in Marseilles and Paris. See Farah 1977, p. 154.

228. See Hourani 1962, p. 245.

229. See Zeine 1973, p. 50.

230. See Khoury 1983, p. 60.

231. See Hourani 1962, p. 281.

232. They "loved the Greece of their dreams: the land, the language, the antiquities, but not the people." See Woodhouse 1969, p. 39.

233. See Clogg 1992, p. 37, Dakin 1973, p. 108, and Woodhouse 1969, pp. 73–75. There was also a belief in Benthamite doctrine whereby "given printing

presses, schools, post offices, hospitals, model prisons and scientific instruments, it was assumed that the political and moral situation of Greece would improve as rapidly as the military," as stated in Dakin 1973, p. 114.

234. See Clogg 1992, p. 37; Dakin 1973, p. 108; and Woodhouse 1969, pp. 73–75.

235. There were also three even earlier though somewhat ineffectual organizations; one was the Greek-Speaking Guest House founded in 1807 in Paris by Choiseul-Gouffier aimed to organize a Greek rising; the second was the Phoenix, which was reputedly established in Russia by Alexander Mavrokordatos during his exile to found a Greek state. See Dakin 1973, p. 41. The third was the Philomuse Society, founded by Ionnis Kapodistrias, the Russian minister in Vienna and the future president of Greece, to "organize a group of men who would provide funds for Greek students to attend German and Italian universities and provide for a national revival through education." Frazee 1969, p. 11; also see Dakin 1973, p. 41.

236. See Dimaras 1973, p. 205, and Woodhouse 1969, pp. 71–75.

237. See Woodhouse 1969, p. 133.

238. See Augustinos 1992, p. 180.

239. See Artinian 1989, pp. 64–65.

240. Some members of the Benevolent Union proceeded in 1862 to form a Masonic Lodge (Haik-Orion) as a branch of the Odd Fellows Lodge of England. The leader, Serovbe Aznavur, predicted that the fraternal, benevolent manner of the lodge could unite the Muslims, Christians, and Jews. A similar Masonic Ser Lodge was established in 1866 in Constantinople with the explicit aim of bringing solidarity and brotherhood among the Armenians. See Nalbandian 1963, p. 75.

241. See Libaridian 1983, p. 77, and Nalbandian 1963, pp. 51–52; 71–72.

242. See İhsanoğlu 1987, pp. 49–50.

243. The quotation is in Landau 1981, pp. 38–39; see also Landau 1981, p. 34, and Arai 1992, p. 48.

244. See Kushner 1977, p. 57; Arai 1992, p. 71; Landau 1981, pp. 39–40; and Kuran 1968, pp. 109–17.

245. See Antonius 1969, pp. 51–53.

246. Another such society, the Literary Authority (Al-'Umda al-adabiya), attempted to cross sectarian lines and disseminate Arab literary works. See Duri 1987, p. 161.

247. In 1867, this society was recognized as a branch of the Ottoman Scientific Society. This society was termed, by one scholar, the "first outward manifestation of a collective national consciousness." The quotation is from Antonius 1969, p. 54; see also Duri 1987, 161.

248. Azuri also published a book in French entitled *Le Reveil de la Nation* (The awakening of the nation) in 1904 and a monthly review *l'Independance Arab* (Arab independence) in 1907.

249. See Saab 1958, p. 207, and Antonius 1969, p. 98.

250. A significant development that had preceded this one was the foundation in the provinces in 1905 of the Ottoman Shura Society (*Jam'iyat al-shura al-'uthmaniya*) by Rıda and Rafıq al-'Azm to oppose the despotism of the

Ottoman sultan and to restore the constitution based on the Islamic concept of deliberative consultation (*shura*).

251. See Tauber 1993, pp. 51–52.

252. See Antonius 1969, pp. 104–8, and Duri 1987, pp. 222–24, 280, 286.

253. See Woodhouse 1973, p. 106; Dakin 1973, p. 41; Frazee 1969, p. 11.

254. See Clogg 1981, p. 103; 1992, p. 32; Dakin 1973, pp. 41, 44–45; Frangos 1973, pp. 87–103; and Frazee 1969, pp. 11–13.

255. Every member who was initiated "promised on his knees unconditional obedience to his superiors, even if he had to kill members of his own family." Frazee 1969, p. 12; see also Dakin 1973, pp. 44–45.

256. The society failed to recruit members in the substantial and older Greek merchant communities of London, Paris, Marseilles, and Amsterdam—fourteen were recruited in Italy. Since their development "fell halfway between more advanced organizations like the Italian Carbonari and the Russian Decembrists and those that Eric Hobsbawm called 'primitive rebels,'" they failed to sustain themselves through time. Also, even though the society had a vision of liberation, it had no blueprint of what might follow afterward. See Frangos 1973, p. 95.

257. This union had relations with the Russian government and the Russian Armenian organizations of the Goodwill Society (*Barenepatak Enkeruthiun*) and the Devotion to the Fatherland Bureau (*Kontora Haireniats Siro*). Russian Armenians, under the influence of Russian revolutionary populism (*narodnichestvo*), similarly started to form secret circles in the 1880s to discuss the liberation of those Armenians across the Arax River in the Ottoman Empire. See Nalbandian 1963, pp. 80–82 and Suny 1979, p. 134.

258. Its leader, Mekertitch Portugalian, believed that "freedom could not be achieved without bloodshed, as evinced by the experiences of other Ottoman subjects such as the Greeks." Nalbandian 1963, p. 94.

259. Its members were sworn to secrecy, and those who broke their oath were marked with a "Black Cross" and immediately put to death (Nalbandian 1963, 84).

260. Its activities were discontinued two years later, however, when the Ottoman government discovered and sentenced 75 members to long jail terms. Gradually, most were released through the efforts of the patriarch. See Nalbandian 1963, pp. 85–89.

261. Even though the Protestant Armenians also established a secret society in 1836, the Evangelical Union, the Armenian patriarch soon started a campaign against them and issued a patriarchal bull forbidding them from any publications. See Kutvirt 1984, p. 45, and Arpee 1909, p. 99.

262. See Etmekjian 1964, p. 132; Nalbandian 1963, pp. 82, 90–103; Atamian 1955, pp. 92–93; and Ter Minassian 1984, p. 5.

263. The Young Ottomans, as they were called, fashioned themselves after the Young France, Spain, and Italy, which had fought against the restoration. See Mardin 1962, pp. 10–11.

264. Quoted in Hanioğlu 1991, p. 43.

265. See Landau 1981, pp. 49–50.

266. It might have been in Midhat Pasha's interest to exaggerate the threat in order to get the Ottoman sultan to increase the pasha's authority; it was pos-

sibly a combination of the activities of both societies along with the passive encouragement of the pasha that produced these placards. The sultan's suspicions about the pasha's ambitions led to his reappointment to Smyrna. See Duri 1987, pp. 167–71, and Tauber 1993, pp. 13, 18–19, 43.

267. Their aim was not secession but instead the establishment of a decentralized regime in which the rights of the Arabs in government would be assured and Arabic considered an official language in the Arab provinces of the empire. See Tauber 1993, p. 45.

268. It was the preaching of Elias Habbalin, a Maronite who taught French at the college and was very much influenced by French revolutionary ideas, that led to the formation of the society. See Tauber 1993, pp. 15–17; Antonius 1969, pp. 80–84; Zeine 1973, pp. 47, 55–59.

269. In these placards "headed by a picture of a sword, they called for all to take their fate in their own hands" and also "expressed their readiness to sacrifice themselves for their homeland." In late December 1880, two additional placards emerged that now had two swords and were addressed to the "sons of the fatherland" (*watan*). See Tauber 1993, p. 17.

270. See Hanioğlu 1995, pp. 44–49.

271. The elected leader, Muhibb al-Din, had been attending a Western-style school in Damascus when he was caught with forbidden books in his possession, among them works of the Turkish patriot Namık Kemal, and forced to transfer to Beirut from where he proceeded to the Ottoman capital; his lodges were used by Arab students as a meeting place to read forbidden material. The society defined Arabism as the noblest element in Islamic society because of the initial entrusting of Allah to the Arabs to carry the Islamic message and now gave the Arab youth the responsibility of Islamic renewal. See Hourani 1962, pp. 275; Tauber 1993, p. 46; Khoury 1983, pp. 64; Duri 1987, pp. 220–21; the quotation is in Tauber 1993, p. 47.

272. See Hourani 1962, p. 285; Antonius 1969, pp. 110–11; Tauber 1993, pp. 248–49: Zeine 1973, pp. 82–83.

273. See Saab 1958, p. 226; Dawn 1973, pp. 148–49; Khoury 1983, pp. 64–65; and Duri 1987, p. 222.

274. A complete list of the pre-1914 members of the Ottoman Decentralization Society, al-Fatat, and al-'Ahd is a complete roster of the members of the Arab nationalist societies before 1914; they contained both upper-class and middle-class elements among their ranks. While the most common occupation among the Arab nationalists was the army officer, pro-Ottomans often held administrative government positions. See Dawn 1973, pp. 152, 165–69; see also Antonius 1969, pp. 119; Saab 1958, pp. 240–55; Duri 1987, pp. 224–25.

275. The aims of this society were clearly defined as indicated in its manifesto, which stated that the Arabs "wished to detach themselves from the worm-eaten Ottoman trunk . . . to form themselves into a new Arab empire extending to its natural frontiers, from the valleys of Tigris and Euphrates to the Isthmus of Suez, and from the Mediterranean to the Sea of Oman . . . governed by the constitutional and liberal monarchy of an Arabian Sultan." The quotation is in Saab 1958, pp. 207–8; see also Tauber 1993, p. 248, and Antonius 1969, p. 111. It was this organization that selected in March 1914 the col-

ors of the Arab flag—white, black, and green. See Mousa 1977, p. 243.

276. See Saab 1958, p. 233; Khoury 1983, p. 65; 1987, p. 29; Duri 1987, p. 288; Zeine 1973, p. 92; and Tibi 1981, pp. 110–13.

277. See Khoury 1983, p. 66.

278. Because the Ottomans had suppressed Arabist political activities in Syria, the Arab revolt that erupted occurred in the Hijaz, led by non-Syrian Arabs rather than the Syrian Arabists. Yet the short-lived rule of Faysal in Syria (October 1918–July 1920) very much alienated the Damascus notables who were staunch opponents of the Hashemite family from whom Faysal had descended. Faysal tried to replace them in government with young lower-class military and civilian recruits. It was this opposition that also built the Syrian-Arab nationalist movement in that those forces who wanted an Arab kingdom under an Arab caliph such as the Sharif of Mecca clashed with those who wanted an independent Syria. See Khoury 1983, pp. 75–76, 78–80, and Hourani 1962, p. 289.

279. In the 1880s in Saint Petersburg and Moscow, there were numerous small organizations imbued with the ideals of the Greek emancipatory movement; it was through these organizations, among which was the Patriots Union, that the seeds of the Armenian political parties were sown.

280. The name *Hnchak* was taken from a political journal, and the intellectual orientation was "influenced to a great degree by the tenets of the social democratic revolutionary ideals promulgated by the early Marxists and proto-Marxists." Atamian 1955, p. 94; see also Nalbandian 1964, pp. 104–31, 151–78; 1963, pp. 108, 117–29; Walker 1979, p. 242.

281. Suny 1993, p. 24, and Ter Minassian 1984, p. 9.

282. It was the formation of the Young Armenia group in Tiflis that led to the emergence of the Dashnaksutiun—it sought the political and economic freedom of Ottoman Armenia. See Nalbandian 1963, pp. 132–39, 151–78; Atamian 1955, p. 102; Ter Minassian 1984, p. 11.

283. The expeditionary force and its flag bore the letters M.H., symbolizing Mother Armenia (*Mayr Hayastan*) or Union of Patriots (*Miuthiun Hairenaserneri*); it carried a flag sewn by the young Armenian women of Kars. The flag also had five stars surrounding the number 61 (symbolizing five of the Armenian provinces and article 61 of the Treaty of Berlin) on one side, and the slogan of the times Revenge! Revenge! (*Vrezh! Vrezh!*) and a skull on the other. See Nalbandian 1963, pp. 145–48, 158, and Atamian 1955, p. 106.

284. See Walker 1979, p. 253; Nalbandian 1963, pp. 176–78; and Atamian 1955, pp. 107–8.

285. It is interesting to note that in 1907 they agreed to and signed a proclamation with the Young Turks to depose the sultan, make radical changes in the existing form of government, and establish a system of representative government for all minorities. The signatories of the proclamation summarize the dissenting elements in the Ottoman Empire: they were the Community of Union and Progress, Ottoman Union for Privat Initiative and Decentralization (*Teşebbüs-i Şahsi ve Adem-i Merkeziyet*), Armenian Revolutionary Federation (*Dashnaksoutyun*), the Ottoman Union Committee of Egypt, the Jewish Committee of Egypt publishing the journal *La-Vara*, the editorial staff of *Khilafat-*

*Hilafet* (an Ottoman-Arabic journal), the editorial staff of *Armenia* (an Armenian journal published in Marseilles), the editorial staff of *Rasmig* (a Varna-based Armenian journal), and the editorial staff of *Hairenik* (American organ of the Dashanksoutyun).

286. The quotation is from Nalbandian 1963, p. 172.

287. The last significant Armenian party to be established in the Ottoman Empire, in Alexandria, Egypt, was the *Ramgavar* (Armenian Constitutional Democratic Party), which officially proclaimed to cease being a revolutionary group and started to work for maintaining Ottoman unity in a constitutional setting. Yet, as such, it was not fully differentiated from the Dashnaks and, in addition, did not have representation in the Ottoman parliament. See Atamian 1955, pp. 165–68.

288. Atamian 1955, p. 161.

289. See, for instance, Ahmad 1968, pp. 22, 28, 34, and 1969, p. 21.

290. See Khalidi 1991, p. 62.

291. For a more extensive discussion, see Antonius 1969, p. 109; Khoury 1983, p. 36; Duri 1987, p. 277; Mousa 1977, p. 243; and Saab 1958, p. 229.

292. See Tibi 1981, pp. 110–12.

293. Indeed, in the first elections after CUP victory, of the 250 parliamentary members elected, only 60 were Arabs while 140 were Turks. Arabs were systematically excluded from governmental positions. See Tauber 1993, p. 56.

294. See Haddad 1994, pp. 205–6, 211.

295. The shift can be observed through the Young Arab Society's placard, "The Three Outcries": the first called for administrative autonomy after the Italian attack on Tripoli; the second directed to the sons of Arabs everywhere after the Ottoman promulgation of the Law on Provinces in 1913 to support the reform movement; and the final third, addressing the sons of the nation following the First Arab Congress, openly stated the increasing doubts about Ottoman reforms. See Duri 1987, pp. 294–98.

296. Indeed, the Allied Powers actively encouraged Arab opposition to Ottoman rule and fostered ambitions of independence. See Zeine 1973, pp. 109–15.

297. See Mousa 1977, pp. 251–54.

298. The role of the Sharifian occupation in the development of Arab nationalism has long been debated; some see their adoption of Arabism over Ottomanism as a political move to achieve more control over inner fractions. Even though Faysal was declared constitutional monarch of Syria on 8 March 1920, he had to leave office four months later as the French forces occupied Damascus. See Dawn 1973, pp. 1–53.

299. See Khoury 1983, p. 90.

300. See Suny 1993, p. 27.

301. See Eley 1981, p. 90.

# CHAPTER 3

# Turkish Nationalism and the Young Turks, 1889–1908

## Şükrü Hanioğlu

The origins of nationalisms in the Ottoman Empire need to be traced back to the social structure of the empire itself. The Ottoman state administrated its subjects of various ethnic groups and different faiths with a method known as a *millet* system. Beginning with the midfifteenth century, four major millets existed within the empire. The Greek orthodox millet, the Armenian millet, the Jewish millet, and finally the Muslim millet. The highest-ranking religious clergy among the first three millets were also responsible for tax collection and other secular duties in their respective communities. Later, additional millets were recognized by the Ottoman administration.

Following the French Revolution and the spread of nationalism in Europe, this millet system became obsolete, since the members of various millets began to identify themselves not only as Greek Orthodox but as Bulgarian, Rumanian, Albanian, Serbian, and so on. The efforts exerted by Ottoman modernizing statesmen to reform the millet system yielded unsatisfactory results and allowed laymen who were more nationalistic than the clergy to assume control over their community affairs.[1]

Upon their failure to reform the millet system, the Tanzimat statesmen formally adopted a new and secular ideology for the empire: Ottomanism. This program dictated that all religious and ethnic groups in the empire were first and foremost Ottomans, irrespective of their distinct identities. However, the imperial administration lacked the ability to socialize every subject into an Ottoman citizen. A centralized educational system was lacking through which the values of Ottomanism could be inculcated. Rather than serving as agents of Ottomanization, religious schools for the various ethnic groups evolved into centers promoting ethnic separatism. There existed a high level of illiteracy in the Ottoman Empire. Furthermore, limited circulation of newspapers and journals made print media an unlikely instrument for Ottoman political socialization. Ironically, although the state endeavored to Ottomanize its subjects, the symbols used to evoke a supranational culture were Turkish. Thus, even non-Turkish Muslim Ottomans who had acquired important state posts and who had admired Tanzimat statesmen decried this policy as a Turcification process. İsmail Kemal Bey, who had worked under Midhat Pasha, a prominent reforming statesman wrote:

> The strong measures adopted by the Sublime Porte against the Albanians, while their object was the very praiseworthy one of general reforms in the Empire, nevertheless concealed the perpetual desire of Turkish chauvinists to bring about the unification of all the races in the Empire. Looking back on these events from the time when I am now writing, it would almost seem to have been the beginning of the political programme of the Young Turks, with this difference, that they were directed with Reshid Pasha, the author of the *Tanzimat* and a group of men of great talent and patriotism who made their appearance at this time and who would have done honour to any country in the world.[2]

The official ideology, then, made little headway with the non-Turkish groups in the empire and could attract only those groups who were already happy with the existing Ottoman order, such as Greek Phanariots; small minorities in various regions preferring the Ottoman rule to the prospect of becoming a minority in a small nation-state, such as Jews and Kutzo-Vlachs; and businessmen of various ethnic communities who needed the large Ottoman market to carry out their commercial and trade activities.

The failure of Ottomanization also prompted the Turks to focus inwardly on their own identity. But this quest for self-understanding was not thought of in nationalistic terms. The fact is, Turkish intellectuals were dedicated primarily to saving the empire and believed that efforts toward Turkish nationalism would further provoke secessionist ethnic movements in the empire. Besides, except for the minuscule number of Christians, almost all the Turks were Muslims. For all practical purposes, the existence of the homogeneity of religion did not favor the emergence of nationalism as a new force of integration as it had, for example, among the Arabs and Albanians. Islam itself was an obstacle since it viewed the believers—irrespective of ethnic[3] origin—as constituting a single political community.

The ideas of Turkish nationalism that emerged during the Young Turk era are of great importance. It may be recalled that the opposition that gathered momentum after the closure of the Ottoman Parliament against the despotic regime of Abdülhamid II is commonly known as the "Young Turk" movement. Because of the various bans introduced on political ideas and their propagation within the empire, the ideas put forth by the Young Turks who lived mainly outside of the empire may be seen as a reflection of the evolution of Turkish nationalism. Following the Young Turks' seizure of power in the Revolution of 1908, and especially after the Balkan Wars of 1912–13, Turkish nationalism became one of the most important ideological currents in the Ottoman Empire.

It is interesting to note that none of the founders of the first nucleus of the main Young Turk organization, the Committee of Union and Progress, in the Royal Medical Academy was of Turkish origin, and they represented the important Muslim groups in which a strong sense of nationalism was yet to develop—Albanians, Kurds, and Circassians. These ethnic groups also relied on Ottoman protection against Christian groups promoted by the Great Powers' diplomacy—Greeks, Serbs, and Armenians. The participation of many Turk and pro-Ottoman Arabs in the Young Turk movement made the movement a defender of the Muslims of the Ottoman Empire.

Thus, in the beginning, the Young Turks advocated Ottomanism. Even the identities of the five columnists of the French Supplement of the official organ of the Committee of Union and Progress were a strong expression of Ottomanism. The columnists were a Turk, Ahmed Rıza Bey; an Ottoman Greek, Aristidi Efendi; a Catholic Arab, who was also a deputy in the first Ottoman parliament, Khalīl Ghanīm Efendi; an Armenian, Pierre Anméghian; and a Jew from Salonica, Albert Fua, who used the pen name *Un ami de la Turquie*. They wanted to create an impression of Ottoman unity on the readers. The articles emphasized that all Ottomans were equal and invited them to common action: "We have tried, within the limits of law, to defend the rights and the interests of all Ottomans. We have never treated Armenians and Greeks differently from Turks. We consider those who inflict harm on the people for their own enrichment and those who raise the banner of independence and break away from us, irrespective of their nationality and religion, to be enemies of Ottoman interests."[4]

However, the Young Turks received favorable reactions only from groups who were in minority in the nationalist movements of various ethnic groups in the Ottoman Empire. In the case of Arabs, for example, some Arab intellectuals who claimed that "Turks exercise injustice, severity and harshness whereas Arabs sacrifice their blood in *Jihād*" also made it clear that "the injustice of the pashas is more beneficial for [the Arabs] than a takeover of their [land] by foreigners."[5] As a result, they allied themselves with the Young Turks. Yet a strong national consciousness of Arabism prevailed among the Arab members who advocated the promotion of an Ottomanist policy. They wrote: "How easy for the Turks in their early conquests to give up their language for the beautiful Arab language [in] religious and civil [matters], to embrace sublime Arab poetry and elevated Arab science . . . and glorious history. Until then they [the Turks] had no complete language, no glorious poetry, no science, no tradition, and no epic tales other than war stories, which are like a stroke of a pen on the pages of history."[6]

However, they were at pains to remain within the borders of the official ideology, Ottomanism. A very good example is furnished by an intermediary group of Syrians who published the journal *Enîn-i Mazlûm* (Moan of the oppressed) in both Arabic and Turkish. Their leader was a Catholic Arab from Antioch, Emin Bey, who attacked the separatist Syrian group Sūriya al-fātat (Young Syria) inviting them to work with the Young Turks fighting against the regime of Abdülhamid II.[7] Furthermore, translations from the works of Tunalı Hilmi Bey, a foremost name in promoting Ottomanism among the Young Turks, were published in that journal to invite the Arabs to unite with the Turks under the banner of Ottomanism.[8] In the case of the Albanians, a similar group emerged which promoted the union of Albanians and Turks as Ottomans.[9] Those who opposed such an alliance and advocated Albanian nationalism, however, gradually seized power within the Albanian movement.[10] The Young Turks also appealed to non-Muslim Ottomans for common action but received favorable replies only from those ethnic groups fighting against strong nationalist groups backed by the Great Powers. The Kutzo-Vlach community of the Ottoman Empire is a striking example of this.[11] These groups that heeded the call of Ottomanism were a *quantité négligiable* in the Ottoman Empire, thus their support did little to realize the goal of uniting Ottoman communities under the standard of Ottomanism. At best, intellectual and political leaders of various ethnic groups viewed Ottomanism, despite its Turkish character, as a useful weapon to be used against rival national groups. However, they had no interest in creating a hyphenated nationalism, such as Greek-Ottoman or Macedonian-Ottoman.

During the debates about Ottomanization, the Young Turks did not comprehend that Ottoman patriotism jarred many non-Turkish Ottoman intellectuals because of its exclusive use of Turkish symbols. For instance, in the Tunalı Hilmi's detailed plans for socializing Ottomans, the symbols used were all Turkish, such that Yusuf Akçura later called these writings the earliest fruits of Turkish nationalism.[12] In modern times, this can be compared with the employment of Javanese symbols in inventing a Pan-Indenosian symbology, which annoyed the non-Javanese.[13] Even the favorable responses by certain groups were given halfheartedly and then only for securing the Turks' backing against stronger groups.

When appeals to the other opponents of Abdülhamid II's regime failed to instigate a common movement, the Young Turks, although remaining within the boundaries of Ottoman ideology, began to emphasize the importance of the Turkish element within the Empire. For example, they argued that, while the empire was comprised of various nationalities, it was natural that the Turks, being the most numerous, should rule: "Among the developed nations and even those which are not developed, the right to rule is in the hands of that nation which constitutes the largest community in a society. Why should Turkey be an exception to this rule."[14]

Here are more laudatory remarks made about the Turks: "What remains are the Turks who are also underdressed, underfed and are suffering. This nation which is obedient, patient, easy going and mild mannered, is branded by some as leprous and lazy. As one of our great men has remarked, the Turks are in fact, like a bullet in a gun. They have a difficult time getting out, but once they are out, they will go as far as they can."[15]

This tendency toward Turkish consciousness coincided with the constitutional and parliamentary debates of the late nineteenth and early twentieth centuries. When Ottomanism was the dominant ideology among the Young Turks, the leaders of the movement favored the establishment of bureaucratic institutions to limit the power of the sultan. Murad Bey, the leader of Committee of Union and Progress in 1896, required only the establishment of an *assemblée délibérante*, consisting of statesmen and representatives of various religious communities.[16] He also asked for a responsible government in the Sublime Porte to replace palace rule, falling short of calling for the reinstatement of the Ottoman Constitution of 1876 and reopening of Parliament.[17] But the emergence of Turkish nationalism and the accompanying efforts to prevent intervention by the Great Powers into the Ottoman domestic politics changed this approach. Ahmed Rıza Bey and his followers considered Murad Bey's bureaucratic reform to be a continuation of the reform program of the Tanzimat statesmen and thought that reinstatement of the Ottoman Constitution would prevent the Great Powers from intervening in Ottoman domestic politics. As the Albanian opponents of Ahmed Rıza Bey pointed out, by using the Constitution as a tool, he and his friends were intending to solve all the ethnic problems of the empire:

L'idée fixe d'Ahmed Riza c'est de se croire 'philosophe' et de le répéter sans cesse. Le système philosophique de ce Turc se réduit a cette phrase: 'Le souverain bien, c'est la Constitution.' Si la Turquie à une Constitution, plus de question arménienne, albanaise etc. La prospérité, le bonheur, la tranquillité partout. La Constitution, c'est la panacée même . . . A[h]med Riza s'imagine que la Constitution sufirra-telle une baguette magique—à changer l'état esprit turc.[18]

The obsession of Ahmed Riza is that he thinks of himself as a "philoso-pher" and repeats that constantly. The philosophy of that Turk could be reduced to the phrase: 'Constitution is the best ruler.' If Turkey had a Constitution, more the question of the Armenian, Albanian etc. Pros-perity happiness and peace for all. The Constitution, that is the panacea of all. Ahmed Riza imagines that the Constitution will be a magic wand—to change the state of the Turkish spirit.

Ahmed Rıza Bey and his comrades defended their policy during the first congress of Ottoman opposition held in Paris in 1902. They opposed a prospective decision to secure the assistance of the Great Powers (i.e., Great Britain) in bringing down the sultan, alleging that all previous foreign interventions favored the Christians and a new one would certainly lead to dissolution of the empire. They asked all oppo-nents of the regime to unite around the Ottoman Constitution of 1876.[19] The Armenian delegation, which was a joint one of Dashnaktsutiun and Verakazmial (Reformed Hintchags), however, opposed this idea.[20] It announced that it "would never wish to see the six provinces of Anato-lia subjected to the Ottoman Constitution."[21] Furthermore, Sisyan Efendi claimed that the delegation "did not consider the Constitution as the only tool for their national liberation" and required the convention to accept the article 61 of the Berlin Congress of 1878 and the Great Powers' memorandum of May 11, 1895 as resolutions of the Congress,[22] but these demands were rejected by the convention.

Ahmed Rıza Bey advocated his own approach to constitutionalism at the Anglo-Armenian meeting of 1902. He adamantly opposed every form of autonomy for any part of the empire, exhorting Ottomans to unite around the Constitution. He alleged that "the autonomy bestowed on Crete had caused the flight of forty thousand Muslims."[23]

Following the Congress of Ottoman Opposition, Ahmed Rıza Bey and his clique of friends broke away from the main organization, build-ing the Committee of Progress and Union, and launched their own pub-lications. Although they had been a minority at the Congress, they were soon highly organized and asserted control over the Young Turk move-ment. The official publications of the committee were *Şûra-yı Ümmet* and *Mechveret Supplément Français*, but a number of members con-tributed to these periodicals concomitant with writing another Cairo-based journal, *Türk*. In all three journals, nationalism was praised in general. In an article Lajos Kossuth was presented as an example to follow,[24] and surprisingly, in another article, Pavlus Melas, who had been killed by the Ottoman troops while conducting Greek guerilla activity in Macedonia, was hailed. The guerilla activities of the non-Turkish groups in Macedonia was an oft-denounced event in the Young Turk journals. However, they claimed that although Melas had been fighting against the Ottomans, since he was fighting for "a nationalist idea," he must be considered as "a hero who sacrificed his life for his nation."[25] Besides praising nationalism in general, articles preaching a separate Turkish nationalism appeared with increasing frequency, and their nationalist focus reflected the outrage felt about political and economic interference by the European Great Powers into the Ottoman Empire: "Our courts cannot pronounce a verdict against Russian subjects! Mr. Maksimov slaps our privates. Greek bishops function as Russian consuls. We cannot collect taxes from Greek subjects. When a [Greek] prostitute falls in love with a fireman and wants to convert to Islam to marry him, the dragoman of the Russian consulate intervenes and scolds the mufti."[26]

A highly critical attitude toward Christian Ottoman populations for exhibiting separatist tendencies was the second characteristic of their approach:

> If there are among the Turks those who are hesitant to extend the right of citizenship to Christians, there are grounds for such hesitation. If a Christian happens to be a member of the Greek community, he looks toward Athens, if of the Bulgarian to Sofia, and if he is an Armenian, he dreams about the establishment of an independent Armenia. Attempting to wrest from us a piece of our homeland, it was the Greeks who rebelled yesterday, and now the Bulgarians and the Armenians are engaged in armed rebellion. Turks are witnesses to all this, and naturally are saddened and feel that the Christians have hurt them.[27]

Gradually, an attitude of viewing the world in terms of Turkishness appeared. An element of this approach was the emphasis on race. As early as 1904, Yusuf Akçura pointed out that one of the choices before the Ottoman Empire would be the pursuit of a Turkish nationalism based on race.[28] As a matter of fact, the nationalist wing of the Young Turks required the Ottomans to follow the advice given to the Japanese by Herbert Spencer, who invoked them to eschew marriages with Europeans in order to preserve their racial purity.[29] The Japanese victory over Russia in 1904–05 freed the hands of the Young Turks to use the racial theories, which they had wanted to do for many years, but they had restrained themselves because of low characteristics attributed to the Turks in Social Darwinist racial theories.[30]

Interestingly enough, the Young Turk movement in its inception had no singular allegiance to any political doctrine. As a prominent member of the movement pointed out in a letter to Edouard Herriot, the Young Turks claimed to have been founded on "science."[31] *Science* was a term Young Turks most often used when referring to *materialism*. The biological materialist theories of Büchner, Vogt, Moleschott, and especially Haeckel's work on morphology, which focuses on theories of biological superiority, and Le Bon's works on phrenology deeply influenced the Ottoman intellectuals.

Inspired by the Japanese victory over the Russians, the Young Turks wrote: "Some Europeans and some Ottomans who imitate whatever they see without understanding, regard us a race in the lower part of the racial hierarchy. Let's say it in plain Turkish: They view Turks as second-class human beings. Japanese people, being of the stock of the yellow race, are obliterating this slander against nature with the progress in their country and with their cannons and rifles in Manchuria."[32]

The final element of this newly emergent Turkish nationalism was a willingness to engage in debates about race with other Muslim populations of the empire:

One day in the future, history, the eternal mirror of the truth of events, will precisely show that one nation that has been unjustly confronted with the entire world's enmity is the Turks. Now we conclusively know, not because we are Turks, but because we closely observe and perceive the actuality, that no injustice can be imagined similar to that of the West's disrespectful enmity toward the Turks. Is it not unjust to ignore the distinct native talents of a nation which has developed from a small tribe into a magnificent state, a nation which, starting from a remote corner of Asia, Söğüd, reached a shining center of Europe, Vienna, by relying on the sword? During that very era and on the very same continent, there lived many other nations, both Muslim and non-Muslim. Why is it that others were unable to exhibit the same level of miraculous native talent? If the British were in the position in which the Turks find themselves today, we are confident that they would be in a similar condition. The Turk has acquired all present harmful habits that he has from the East; and it is in the East that he has encountered all causes for his weakness and decline. Because of his innate strength, he has been able for six centuries to resist calamities which others could not have resisted for a hundred years. If he had entered Europe through the north instead of the south, and if he had settled in the west like his Hungarian brethren rather than settling in the east, then unquestionably today he would have outstanding governance, authority, prosperity, and independence. The Europeans err on the following point: They confuse Turks, who since the earliest days of their national existence have never experienced slavery and subjugation and have perpetually lived free and in a domineering position, with the impotent nations of the East, who have heretofore been oppressed under the yoke of degradation.[33]

Also the Turkist wing of the Young Turk movement published articles in both *Şûra-yı Ümmet* and *Türk* about relations among Turks and non-Turkish Muslim groups in the empire, such as Arabs. In these articles, they described Turks as a superior race, while criticizing the separatist activities of Arabs and other non-Turkish Moslems:

> It is the Arabs who see themselves as the natural candidates for assuming the caliphate. Arguing that the prophet comes from their lineage, that the Holy *Qur'ān* is written in their language, and invoking the Arab civilization that flourished after [they had accepted] Islam, they hold that to possess the caliphate is their true right. Above all they envy the Ottoman Turks, who had adopted Islam six or seven centuries ago, and never accept that they have produced caliphs. . . . In my opinion all these causes are without foundation, all these claims are baseless, and all these remarks are unjust. The *shari'a*, intellect, and logic all dictate that the caliphate ought to be in the hands of that nation among the Muslims which is the most civilized, the strongest, and the most capable of withstanding attacks and encroachments from outside. If so, let us take a look at all of them: Can we identify any nation other than the Ottomans [Turks] who possess these characteristics? Never. . . . That the Christian world, even the Americans, have pestered the Turks and sought endless excuses to inflict harm on the Turks can be explained by the fact that Turks are the greatest and strongest pillar of Islam. For this reason all the blows aimed at Islam because of [Christian] fanaticism fall on Turkish heads. The responsibilities of the caliphate are not being discharged properly and as required. Sure enough. If there is someone who can do a better job, let him come forward. He should, however, prove himself in deeds, not in words. In such a case the Ottomans [Turks] are ready to turn over the holy relics immediately, and to retire to their own corner of leisure. But the government [you say] is preventing the Yemenis, the Syrians and the Iraqis from acting freely. But here are Moroccans, et cetera, et cetera. Do they not have a free hand?[34]

Another example is even more extreme:

> The Arab gang . . . try to deceive the reasonable Arabs who are willing to admit that the Arabs do not have among them men able to match the Turkish officers and governors, and that the Turks are superior to the other Muslims in the arts of war, administration, and law enforcement. . . . The present policy of the Arab gang is . . . to annihilate the power of the Turk in the Islamic lands. Essentially, this is the course that the nations who struggle to separate themselves from Ottoman

> rule adopt. The principal zeal of the Greek, Armenian, and Bulgarian revolutionary committees is directed at presenting the Turks as evil. In many articles published mostly by Syrians in Egypt and in Africa, the impotence of the Turk and the necessity of a restoration of the caliphate to the hands of the Arab is expounded. Friends residing at various locations in Arabia inform us that the authority of the Turk has been gradually diminishing. . . . If the Turks were only willing to look with open and worldly eyes to the Holy Kaabah rather than with eyes half open and half closed five times a day, they would see the truth and understand why they turn their heads to the left and right and look around [during the prayers].[35]

By late 1907, however, the leaders of the main Young Turk organization understood the difficulty in carrying out a revolution in the Ottoman Empire through promoting a strong Turkist ideology. This should be viewed as a tactical stroke on their part and not as their abandoning of Turkism. Contrary to accepted views, even before the Young Turk Revolution of 1908, a strong nationalist sentiment existed among Young Turks. Despite this fact, however, as "Empire-Savers" the leaders of the main Young Turk organization, the Committee of Union and Progress sidelined their Turkist ideology into the background out of political opportunism. In the opinion of these leaders and many Ottoman intellectuals of Turkish descent, Ottomanism was a useful shield to prop up the decadent Ottoman Empire.

The Young Turk leaders' replacement of their Turkist ideology with a new Ottomanist ideology beginning in 1907 helped them to carry out their revolution in 1908. The new Ottomanism crystallized after the Young Turk revolution of 1908, however, made very little headway. The opponents of the Committee of Union and Progress viewed this Ottomanism which aimed at the unification of various Ottoman elements in a melting pot as a "Turkification" progress because of the "dominant" role attributed to the Turks in it.[36] The non-Turkish groups which could viably harbor centrifugal ambitions did not wish to accept such an Ottomanism in which Turks would play a dominant role. The Committee of Union and Progress viewed opposition against its version of Ottomanism as a separatist activity. This difference over Ottomanism precipitated a bitter struggle between the Committee of Union and Progress and various organizations representing different ethnic groups in the Ottoman Empire, most of whom claimed to be Ottomanist, despite their defense of disparate theses. It is not coincidental that only Jews and Kutzo Vlachs, who were simply in no position to entertain separatist ideas, had representatives in the Young Turk movement after the revolution of 1908. Allegedly good relations between the Young Turks and the stronger ethnic elements of the empire deteriorated soon after the revolution.

Clear references revealing the Turkist proclivities of its leaders can only be found in the secret documents of the Committee of Union and Progress after 1907. Although the Committee of Union and Progress sidelined its Turkism after this date, the Turkism promoted by Young Turk intellectuals between 1902 and 1907 undoubtedly prepared the ground for the burgeoning intellectual Turkish nationalism after 1908.

## BIBLIOGRAPHY

"Aharar-i Osmaniye Kongresi ve Cemiyet-i İttihadiye-i Osmaniye." 1317 [1902]. *Muvazene*, no. 224 (27 February [11 March]): 2–4.

Akçura, Yusuf. 1904. "Üç Tarz-ı Siyaset." *Türk*, no. 24 (14 April): 1–2ff.

"L'Albanie et les Turcs." 1896. *La Libre Parole* (26 December).

Blind, Karl. 1902. "The Prorogued Turkish Parliament." *The North American Review* 175, no. 548 (July): 45.

"[Bois de] Boulogne Ormaninda Bir Rum ile Muhavere." 1903. *Şûra-yı Ümmet*, no. 41 (7 November): 3.

"Compte rendu du Congrès." 1902. *Mechveret Supplément Français*, no. 126 (15 February): 2–4.

"Contre les Jeunes-Turcs." 1897. *Albania*, no. 1 (30 December): 130.

Darwin, Francis, ed. 1882. *The Life and Letters of Charles Darwin*. London.

Davison, Roderic. 1963. *Reform in the Ottoman Empire*. Princeton: Princeton University Press.

Demir, Kan. 1932. *Jön Türklerin Zindan Hatıraları 1848–1903: Bir Devrin Siyasî ve Fikrî Tarihi*. Istanbul.

di Tiro, Tengku Hasan M. 1986. "Indonesian Nationalism: A Western Invention to Contain Islam in the Dutch East Indies." In *The Impace of Nationalism on the Muslim World*, M. Ghayasuddin, ed. London.

"Ebülhüda ve Avanesi." 1904. *Şûra-yı Ümmet*, no. 61 (10 October): 2.

Ghānim, Khalīl. 1895. "al-qānūn āsāsī." *Kashf al Niqāb*, no. 18 (10 January): 1–2.

Hagopian, J. Michael. "Hyphenated Nationalism: The Spirit of the Revolutionary Movement in Asia Minor and the Caucasus, 1896–1910." Unpublished Ph.D. Thesis, Department of Government, Harvard, 1942.

Hanioglu, Sukru. 1995. *Young Turks in Opposition*. New York.

———. *Young Turks toward Revolution*. Forthcoming.

Hilmi, Tunalı. 1898. *Makedonya: Mazi-Hâl-İstikbâl*. Cairo.

"Hutbe: Danışan Dağları Aşdı, Danışmayan Düz Ovada Yoldan Şaşdı." 1899. *Enîn-i Mazlûm*, no. 12 (7 August): 92ff.

"İbret." 1904. *Şûra-hı Ümmet*, no. 66 (22 December): 4.

[Konitza, Faïk Bey]. 1901. "Les Jeunes-Turcs et leur panacée." *Albania* F, no. 10 (15 October): 165.

Mağmumî, Şerafeddin. 1903. "Düşündüm Ki." *Türk*, no. 7 (17 December): 1–2.

M. A. "Osmanlı İttihadı."

"Makalât-i Siyasiye: Ermeni Kongresi." 1902. *Şûra-yı Ümmet*, no. 10 (20 August): 2.

"Makale-i Mahsusa: Kossuth." 1902. *Şûra-yı Ümmet*, no. 14 (18 October): 3–4.

"Makam-ı Akdes Cenâb-ı Hilâfetpenâhî'ye." 1897. *Osmanlı*, no. 1 (1 December): 2–3.

"Mawdū' ta'ammul ilā ikhwāninā al-suriyyin." 1896. *Turkiyyā al-fatāt*, no. 3 (10 January): 1.

"Me'yus Olmalı Mıyız[?]." 1904. *Şûra-yı Ümmet*, no. 62 (24 October): 1.

Mourad. 1895. *Le Palais de Yıldız et la Sublime Porte: La Véritable mal d'Orient.* Paris.

"Mülâhaza: Yeni Osmanlılar Kongresi." 1902. *İntikam*, no. 50 (10 March): 1–3.

Murad, Toptanzade. 1898. "Vatandaşlar." *Arnavudluk*, 1 July.

"Musahabe: Spencer'in Japonlara Vasiyetnâmesi." 1904. *Türk*, no. 23 ([7] April): 4.

"Paris'de Osmanlı Hürriyetperverân Kongresi." 1902. *Osmanlı*, no. 104 (16 April): 6.

Peyfuss, Max Demeter. 1972. *Die aromunische Frage: Ihre Entwicklung von den Ursprüngen bis zum Bukharest (1913) und die Haltung Österreich-Ungarns.* Vienna.

Rıza, Ahmed. 1896. "Hükümetsizlik." *Meşveret*, no. 17 (23 August) 108: 1.

Sarkisian, E. K. 1972. *Politika osmanskogo pravitel'stva v Zapadnoi Armenii i derzhavy v poslednei chetverti XIX i nachale XX vv.* Erevan.

"Scherbina'nin Vefatı." 1903. *Şûra-yı Ümmet*, no. 28 (13 May): 3.

Story, Somerville, ed. 1920. *The Memoirs of Ismail Kemal Bey.* London.

"Sūriya al-fatāt." 1899. *Enîn-i Mazlûm*, no. 6 (15 May): 48.

"Türk." 1903. *Türk*, no. 1 (5 October): 1.

"Yangın Var. Cankurtaran Yok Mu?" 1897. *Mizan*, no. 12 (22 March): 2.

Yusuf, Akçuraoğlu. 1928. *Türk Yılı 1928.* Istanbul.

## NOTES

1. For the efforts of the Ottoman statesmen to reform the Ottoman non-Muslim millets, see Davison, *Reform in the Ottoman Empire*, pp. 114–35.

2. Story, ed., *The Memoirs of Ismail Kemal Bey*, pp. 11–12.

3. For more information see my *Young Turks in Opposition.*

4. Rıza 1896, p. 1. The journal used the positivist calendar.

5. Ghānim 1895, pp. 1–2.

6. "Mawdū' ta'ammul ilā ikhwāninā al-sūrīyyin" 1896, p. 1.

7. See "Sūriya al-fatāt" 1899, p. 48.

8. See "Hutbe: Danışan Dağları Aşdı, Danışmayan Düz Ovada Yoldan Şaşdı" 1899, 92ff.

9. See Murad 1898, p. 1.

10. For good examples concerning the ideas of the members of this group, see "L'Albanie et les Turcs" 1896 and "Contre les Jeunes-Turcs" 1897, p. 130.

11. For the appeals made by the Young Turks to Kutzo-Vlachs, see Hilmi 1316 [1898], p. 14. Following the Young Turk revolution, cordial relations

were established between the Young Turks and the Kutzo-Vlachs. See Peyfuss 1972, pp. 110–11.

12. See Yusuf 1928, pp. 394–95.

13. See di Tiro 1986, pp. 65–67.

14. M. A., "Osmanlı İttihadı," *Meşveret* 1896, no. 5, February 1, 108, p. 1.

15. "Makam-ı Akdes Cenâb-ı Hilâfetpenâhî'ye," 1897, pp. 2–3.

16. Mourad, 1895, p. 43.

17. "Yangın Var! Cankurtaran Yok mu?" 1897, p. 2.

18. [Faïk Bey Konitza], 1901, p. 165.

19. "Paris'de Osmanlı Hürriyetperverân Kongresi" 1902, pp. 4–6; "Mülâhaza: Yeni Osmanlılar Kongresi" 1902, pp. 1–3; "Compte rendu du Congrès" 1902, pp. 2–4; "Ahrar-ı Osmaniye Kongresi ve Cemiyet-i İttihadiye-i Osmaniye" 1317 [1902], pp. 2–4.

20. See Hagopian 1942, pp. 217–21. Dcf. Sarkisian 1972, p. 231.

21. Blind 1902, p. 45.

22. "Paris'de Osmanlı Hürriyetperverân Kongresi" 1902, p. 6.

23. "Makalât-ı Siyasiye: Ermeni Kongresi" 1902, p. 2.

24. "Makale-i Mahsusa: Kossuth" 1902, pp. 3–4.

25. "İbret" 1904, p. 4.

26. "Shcherbina'nın Vefatı" 1903, p. 3.

27. "[Bois de] Boulogne Ormanında Bir Rum ile Muhavere" 1903, p. 3.

28. Akçura 1904, pp. 1–2ff.

29. "Musahabe: Spencer'in Japonlara Vasiyetnâmesi" 1904, p. 4.

30. Even Darwin himself regarded Turks as such. See his letter to W. Graham dated July 3, 1881: "Remember the risk of the nations of Europe ran, not so many centuries ago of being overwhelmed by the Turks, and how ridiculous such an idea now is! The more civilized, so-called Caucasian races have beaten the Turkish hollow in the struggle for existence." Francis Darwin, ed., vol. 1, p. 316.

31. Demir 1932, p. 106.

32. "Me'yus Olmalı Mıyız[?]" 1904, p. 1.

33. "Türk," p. 1.

34. Mağmumî 1903, pp. 1–2.

35. "Ebülhüda ve Avanesi" 1904, p. 2.

36. For more information, see my forthcoming book, *Young Turks toward Revolution.*

# CHAPTER 4

# *(Re)Presenting Nations: Demonstrations and Nationalisms in Premandate Syria*

## James L. Gelvin

As suggested in the introduction and in the preceding chapters of this book, and as will be reiterated in subsequent chapters, the introduction of new methodological strategies (ranging from world systems and neo-Marxist approaches to postmodern and postcolonial critiques) and the proliferation of interdisciplinary and comparative studies have transformed the study of nationalism during the past quarter century.[1] Not only have suppositions previously accepted as certainties been called into question, but essential categories, including "nation," "nationalism," and "national identity," have been subjected to renewed scrutiny and/or subsumed to heretofore unconventional analytical frameworks. One aspect of the contemporaneous discussion of nationalism is of particular relevance for this study: the tendency on the part of an increasing number of scholars to challenge the pretensions of dominant nationalisms that represent themselves as the inevitable and singular historically inscribed expressions of national destiny. Once this line of inquiry commenced, the rediscovery of less successful and frequently neglected alternative constructions of nation—such as those held by groups subordinated on account of social status, gender, class, ethnic or religious affiliation, and/or geographic placement—became a virtual cottage industry, and social scientists and historians increasingly made the hegemonizing process itself, as well as resistances to this process, focal points of examination.

This chapter—an examination of demonstrations organized in Syria by rival nationalist factions during the immediate post-Ottoman period—conforms to this revisionist agenda. Because demonstrations, like all collective ceremonies, both *contain* symbols and *act* themselves as symbols, and because demonstrations simultaneously serve a celebratory and inculcatory purpose, they function as polysemic representations that reflect the attributes of a particular community not only as it actually is, but as ritual planners wish it to be perceived. A synchronic comparison of officially sanctioned demonstrations staged by the Arab government and its allies, on the one hand, and those sponsored by a Syriawide network of popular nationalist committees, on the other, thus provides evidence from which historians might ascertain the disparate manner in which the two principal blocs within the nationalist field defined the national community, demarcated its boundaries, and narrated its progress through history.

## NATIONALISM AND POLITICS IN POST-OTTOMAN SYRIA

As in other parts of the late colonial world, conditions necessary for the appearance of nationalisms in the Arab Middle East were already in place before the advent of the twentieth century. During the mid-to-late nineteenth century, the accelerating rate of integration of the Ottoman Empire into the periphery of the world capitalist system, along with Ottoman attempts at administrative revitalization, transformed the empire, although in ways that were uneven and often unforeseen. As a result of these twin processes, market relations increasingly circumscribed or determined the organization of social and economic life for the inhabitants of an ever-widening expanse of the empire; the boundaries linking city and countryside became more permeable; local bonds of loyalty were loosened and frequently replaced by new, wider (sometimes quasinational) bonds of loyalty; and urbanization and the proliferation of institutions that encouraged the exchange of information (newspapers, coffeehouses) contributed to the emergence and expansion of a modern "public sphere" in which ideologies could be contested. Nationalisms in the Arab Middle East, like nationalisms elsewhere, could emerge because they were coherent with and germane to the new social realities that confronted the inhabitants of the region in the wake of these processes.

The use of the term *nationalisms* rather than *Arab nationalism* in this context is necessary and deliberate. Had the Arab provinces of the Ottoman Empire been homogeneous, had the effects of expanding market relations and the efficacy of Ottoman administrative reforms been uniform and coincident, and had the redistribution of economic, political, and social power within the empire been equable or perceived as such, historians might be justified in assuming a unitary ideological response to changing conditions. This, however, was not the case: the twin processes affected different regions, strata, and ethnic/religious communities in different ways, not only dividing late-nineteenth-/early-twentieth-century Middle Eastern society vertically along geographic/ethnic/religious lines (inducing such ideological responses as "Syrianism" and "Phoenicianism"), but dividing it horizontally as well, in effect pitting those who successfully navigated the new social, economic, and political landscape against those who did not. Thus, while in general all but the most isolated inhabitants of the Ottoman Empire shared a set of normative assumptions correspondent with conditions generated by the nineteenth-century transformation—assumptions necessary for the widespread diffusion of nationalist ideologies—the transformation simultaneously had a countervailing divisive effect as well. By the turn of the century an emergent stratum of "Westernizing elites" had come to inhabit a social and symbolic community that differed dramatically from the community inhabited by declining elites and nonelites. As a result, both the form and the content of their nationalisms also differed.

The dismemberment of the Ottoman Empire in the wake of the First World War eliminated the overarching structure that had loosely linked these two cultural communities within a single political framework. In the place of this structure, the victorious entente powers authorized the establishment of a temporary Arab government in inland Syria under the authority of Amir Faysal b. Husayn, son of the sharif of Mecca and leader of the celebrated Arab Revolt. Because the Arab government was weak and its legitimacy uncertain, the twenty-two-month interregnum that separated the end of the war and the French occupation of Damascus in July 1920 became a period in which the two cultural communities—and their contrasting visions for the Syrian future—vied directly against each other. In an attempt to achieve both political dominance and cultural hegemony within Syria, each of these communities structured itself through institutions and represented itself through paradigmatic activities that embodied its characteristic conceptions of the proper arrangement of society.

On one side of the social/cultural divide stood those affiliated with the Arab government and allied political and cultural societies (such as the Arab Club, which frequently organized demonstrations and disseminated propaganda in conjunction with the government). This cohort actually consisted of two groups that might be described as "outsiders" to traditional Syrian society. The first consisted of military men, the sharifians and their retainers, and so on, who had come to Damascus from other places—the Hijaz, Palestine, and Iraq—with the Arab army or in the wake of the Ottoman withdrawal from Syria. Asserting a right to political authority based upon their participation in or support for the Arab Revolt, their dominance of the Arab government naturally alienated many native-born notables who had customarily controlled local politics. A second, overlapping group of outsiders was drawn from the so-called middle strata, a relatively new social category in the Arab Middle East that included professionals, trained military officers, intellectuals, and bureaucrats. These were the self-styled *mutanawwirun* ("enlightened ones")—members of the middle strata who were conscious of themselves as an autonomous social category. They, too, were dissatisfied with existing social and political arrangements, believing that, regardless of their wartime activities, education or vocation qualified them to play a special role in postwar Syria. Each of these groups possessed attributes that complemented those of the other: while the immigrants provided the *mutanawwirun* with a legitimating narrative (the myth of the Arab Revolt) and access to power, financial resources, and the world stage (through their close relations with the British, which secured for the *mutanawwirun* a place at the Paris peace conference), the immigrants needed the *mutanawwirun* to link them to indigenous social and political structures, construct and direct unfamiliar institutions that were necessary for the proper functioning of a modern state, and articulate a comprehensive nationalist program.

For the most part, then, the *mutanawwirun* set the agenda and formulated the discursive field utilized by the Arab government and its allies. Because this group originated as the result of the expansion of market relations and calculated efforts at institutional rationalization along European lines, the specific categories and constellation of categories used by individuals within this group to organize their world and to order their society naturally cohered with and frequently duplicated those enjoined by the dominant culture within the European métropole. As a result, many of the institutions constructed by this group on behalf of the Arab government, and much of its discourse, would not have appeared foreign to the average European or North American bourgeois.

Integral to the beliefs held by the *mutanawwirun* was the association of nationalism with a Comtean notion of progress and technocratic pragmatism. For them, the concept of progress provided the paramount rationale for their activities: the national movement, under their leadership, would deliver to the population of Syria the material benefits associated with civilization and, through the appropriation of the cultural supports upon which continued progress depended, align Syria with the community of "civilized" nations and Syrians with the universal project of modernity.

One means by which both the immigrants and the *mutanawwirun* sought to achieve such an alignment was through the promotion in Syria of a civic model of the nation—a model in which the bonds of common citizenship and shared legal practice and political ideals, rather than presumptive primordial bonds such as those of ethnicity or religion, would unite the members of the nation. Attractive for both pragmatic and ideological reasons (the variegated composition of the Syrian population, the strictures imposed by the international community, the assumption that with the advent of modernity "religiosity [has become] over time a weaker influence in building social and political nations."[2]), theirs was a conception of nation building particularly apposite to Syria, a nation lacking historic precedent, which, they believed, might be created by a self-conscious political elite acting within a context delimited by political contingency and diplomatic constraints and imposed upon a population that, according to Amir Faysal, "like children . . . does not understand the meaning of nationalism, freedom or independence."[3]

Two designs for the structuring of a civic nation circulated among the nationalist elites. According to the first, espoused by the sharifians and their retainers who were especially anxious to preserve their paramount status within the future polity, Amir Faysal and the Arab government would provide the common bond to unite the independent, vertically differentiated communities, sects, and religions residing in the territory. Thus, according to military governor and sharifian ally ʿAli Rida al-Rikabi,

> The Arab government has been vigilant in preserving peace, maintaining law, and organizing the administration with a spirit of unity, concord, harmony, and cooperation among peoples of all sects, religions, and nationalities so that there will be no difference in rights. . . . The mutual ties between the government and the people are indissoluble because they are guaranteed by the hand of Faysal. The relationship of the government to the people is that of a compassionate mother to her son, and the people should act toward the government with faithfulness and devotion.[4]

Promotion of this protocorporativist model of authority naturally coincided with the promotion of sharifian legitimacy, and to this end the Arab government and its allies distributed written texts, authorized speeches and Friday sermons, and sponsored theatrical performances and ceremonies (including demonstrations) in which the celebration of the Arab Revolt, pledges of devotion to Amir Faysal, and the enumeration of the "crimes" of the previous regime played a central symbolic role.

The other image of Syrian society, cultivated assiduously by the *mutanawwirun*, stratified Syria into two hierarchically ranked sorts. On the first level stood the *mutanawwirun*, who, like Auguste Comte's *savants*, were responsible for guiding society and educating the masses so that Syria might aspire to the level of the civilized (*mutamaddin*) nations of Europe and North America. "The great mass of the nation is not confined to the educated, the notables, and the merchants of the cities who read the daily newspapers, follow international and domestic politics, and are concerned with scientific discoveries and technological innovation," wrote one prominent journalist on the pages of the government gazette.

> Rather, the great mass of the nation is composed of working people, those who dwell in villages and mountains, those who are devoted to breaking the soil and sowing it. It is to these that the educated must devote their zeal, to enlighten their hearts and advance their talents and intellectual abilities.[5]

For the *mutanawwirun*, ameliorative activities such as those recommended in the article were not only intrinsically meritorious but would act as an "announcement to the world that [Syria is] a nation worthy of life and independence."[6] In other words, the domestic activities prescribed by and for the *mutanawwirun* would complement their diplomatic strategy—a strategy suggested by the juridical foundation for the mandates system, article 22 of the Charter of the League of Nations. Thus, Syria would attain independence when Syrians demonstrated to the entente powers that they had reached a level of civilization that entitled them to independence.

As will be seen below, a desire on the part of the nationalist elites to display to foreign governments the advancement of the Syrian population provided much of the impetus motivating them to stage massive demonstrations on the streets of Damascus and other cities. Although willing to mobilize the Syrian population, however, the *mutanawwirun* never synthesized a discourse or political program compelling to nonelites. Syrian society for the *mutanawwirun* remained a dichotomous society, a society in which the cultured and educated were strictly differentiated from the base and vulgar. Such a world view not only envisioned a society that was hierarchically ranked—a society that pitted the "better sort" against their social inferiors—but it also stigmatized and alienated a vast majority of the population. The inability or unwillingness on the part of nationalist elites to integrate the "great mass of the nation" into their nationalist vision—to consummate a "passive revolution" as Partha Chatterjee, following Antonio Gramsci, calls it[7]—relinquished the nationalist field to others who not only rejected the modernist and eurogenic conceits of the *mutanawwirun* but who made such conceits the axial divide separating their nationalism from the nationalism promoted by the *mutanawwirun* and the Arab government.

By the Autumn of 1919, with the increasing immiserization of the Syrian population, the collapse of internal security, and the conspicuous failure of the aforementioned diplomatic strategy all but depleting the meager reserves of legitimacy previously husbanded by the Arab government and its allies, a very different nationalist movement emerged in Syria to contest the authority of the nationalist elites. Composed primarily of displaced former elites and nonelites who had experienced (or who believed themselves to have experienced) deleterious effects from Western economic penetration, the spread of market relations within the region, the expansion of state capabilities, and/or the disruption of customary local relationships of power, this movement found its institutional expression in an interlocking network of popular committees, including the Damascus-based Higher National Committee (*al-lajna al-wataniyya al-ʿulya*, branch committees of the Higher National Committees (*al-lijan al-wataniyya al-farʿiyya*), and local committees of national defense (*lijan al-difaʿ al-watani*).

The structure of the popular committees reflected the changes that had occurred in Syrian society during the previous three-quarters of a century. Combining emergent horizontal and associational bonds with more familiar vertical ties of patronage, the popular committees organized constituents into a multitiered, pyramidal network that linked neighborhoods, cities, and regions within a national structure. As the authority and capabilities of the Arab government continued to deteriorate, councils of elected representatives on each tier increasingly shouldered responsibility for a variety of functions normally assumed by governments or their representatives—the policing of local quarters, the provisioning of cities, the distribution of poor relief, and, most important, the organization of a loosely connected national network of militias to defend Syria from foreign (French) aggression. In sum, the popular committees provided a framework not only for the involvement of nonelites alongside their social betters in civic affairs but also for their integration as active participants into a nationwide political movement.

Like their rivals, the popular committees secured sanction for their activities from a distinctive rendering of the national narrative. As might be expected, however, the conception of Syria championed by the popular committees was very different from that promoted by their rivals. For the supporters of the popular committees, Syria was not a patchwork of vertically differentiated communities to be melded into a modern state by a strong government, nor were Syrians in need of guidance from Western-oriented *savants*. Indeed, texts distributed by the popular committees heaped scorn on both the pretensions of the *mutanawwirun* and on their habit of mimicking Western dogmas, such as the cult of progress. "The French in Syria do not care whether their territory is destroyed or not, whether its economic life comes to a standstill or not, whether the population lives or dies, nor whether villages are wiped out or are populous," one editorialist sympathetic to the popular committees wrote caustically. "They only care that the authorities in them should possess the sources of wealth and turn the free population into slaves in the name of progress, and that only the Syrians feel the effects of all this upon them."[8] Instead of the universal standards of civilization and modernity embraced as national goals by the *mutanawwirun*, the popular committees addressed the traditionalist yearnings felt by the those whom they sympathetically referred to as *mankubun* (the wretched) by accentuating and glorifying the unique Syrian legacy and by invoking images of a timeless and egalitarian Syrian past.[9]

According to spokesmen for the popular committees, Syrians were not united merely through the ties of common citizenship; rather, the ties that bound Syrians to each other were both organic and rooted in the soil that "has soaked up the blood of our grandfathers and fathers."[10] Syrians were, according to a widely echoed trope, family, and like the members of a family, they shared not only a common ancestry and common historical experiences but also a common responsibility for the well-being of their kindred. "Is it not the duty of the rich to construct hospitals for the poor of the nation, as well as eating places and schools for the education of their children, since they are all vital members of the nation, not dissevered limbs begging on the roads?" wrote a prominent *'alim* who had participated in one of the founding meetings of the Higher National Committee. Intimating that the Syrian nation was capable of self-organization without the meddling of a government of outsiders and parvenus, the same writer encouraged "people of good will of every quarter [of Damascus] to form associations whose purpose is the collection of alms from the rich to be given to the poor, and for all endeavors aimed at creating harmony among the individuals of the nation."[11]

Unlike the Arab government and the *mutanawwirun*, then, the popular committees did not claim to be architects of a modern Syrian nation; rather, they claimed to be the embodiment of a historic Syrian nation and custodian of its national will. "Public action for the nation cannot succeed if the individuals of the nation are not prepared for it," the Charter of the Higher National Committee began.

> The requirement (for public action) is mutual assistance, which is necessary to foster it. Thus were the circumstances when the matter of patriotic formations arose in the capital of Syria. The need for them was felt in homes of every neighborhood and in the heart of every individual. Thus, the people rushed to realize this undertaking on every front, and the people of (each) district did their part without collusion,

compelled by the feeling of patriotic duty. This glorious creation, which was given the name "Higher National Committee" and the branch committees, arose from the totality of their labors.[12]

As this and previously cited written texts should make clear, the characterization of the function of the nationalist movement and the contours of the Syrian nation/polity tendered by the popular committees differed starkly from that tendered by the Arab government and its allies. Accordingly, while both communities mounted demonstrations, each community used the demonstrations it mounted both to exemplify and to display—to inculcate and embody—a community-specific conception of nation and society. As I shall demonstrate below, demonstrations sponsored by the Arab government portrayed an arrangement of political relationships that was fundamentally vertical, a division between (subject/active) rulers and the (object/passive) ruled, and the primacy of the state and its representatives over their charges in their civilizing and mediatory roles. In contrast, the demonstrations organized by the popular committees portrayed the national community as comprehensive and essential, relationships of power as primarily horizontal, and the nation as both separate from and dominant over the institutions of state.

## Government-Sanctioned Demonstrations

In its attempts to display to the outside world that Syrians were prepared for and united in their desire for independence, the Arab government and its allies sponsored two types of demonstrations: petition demonstrations, in which the central drama consisted of the presentation of a list of demands directly or indirectly to representatives of the entente powers, and celebratory demonstrations, during which the Arab government and/or associated political organizations, such as the Arab Club, assembled the population so that they might display their devotion to the government, Amir Faysal, or both.

A generic blueprint for both types of demonstrations appeared in an unusual article which was published on the front page of the official government gazette, *al-ʿAsima*, on the eve of the arrival in Damascus of the King-Crane Commission. Although intended otherwise, the commission was an exclusively American venture sent to the Middle East "to elucidate the state of opinion and the soil to be worked on by any mandatory."[13] The article, entitled "A True Vision," was written in the form of a prophetic parable, which outlined the brilliant future of independence and progress awaiting Syrians if only they could convince the commission—and through the commission the entente powers—that they could behave in a "civilized" manner.

The article began with a description of the author at his desk, contemplating the news of demonstrations held in Egypt to show popular support for Egyptian independence: "We hardly see such good order in the demonstrations of the most advanced Western nations," the writer supposedly proclaims to himself. "I said to myself, 'By God! They unjustly accuse the East and its people of savagery, immaturity, and an inability to imitate the civilization of the West. What is more indicative of their readiness [for independence] than this admirably ordered and perfect demonstration?'"

Lulled into sleep, the author dreams of meeting a soothsayer who takes him on a tour of the future—a tour that includes a glimpse of the upcoming visit of the commission to Damascus.

In the dream, "the sons of the nation," supervised by their *savants* (*mufakkirun*), "held an orderly demonstration showing their national sentiments and desires in a way that would demonstrate to the delegation that the nation was worthy of independence." Syrians of all religious and sectarian affiliations (as the author is scrupulous to point out) participated in the demonstration, placing on their forearms or shirts bindings printed with the slogan We demand complete independence. So ubiquitous was the slogan that "one could not walk down the street without seeing the signs on every building and wall." Nevertheless, despite the fact that all Damascenes displayed the slogan and attended the demonstration, their participation was passive. "The demonstration that the people put on was perfect—quiet, without tumult, no speeches—yet through its silence the demonstration announced [to the commission] the advancement of the people." The commission, impressed by the "wisdom, advancement, and worthiness for complete independence," returned to Paris to recommend that Syrians be allowed their independence. "The matter was decided accordingly."

As will be seen shortly, while most demonstrations organized by the government fit the pattern outlined in "A True Vision," the author could not help but to omit mention of one indispensable aspect of these demonstrations: the Arab government did not stage demonstrations solely to impress the entente powers; rather, the government sponsored demonstrations to sway the beliefs of the participants and the attendant crowds as well. Often, the Arab government began this process even before the first demonstrators gathered. In those demonstrations in which the central drama was the presentation of petitions to the representatives of foreign powers, for example, the circulation of petitions and the gathering of signatures contributed to this end. Because the petition campaigns were centrally coordinated by the Arab government, often in conjunction with a small group of allied political and cultural associations, the petitions circulated in a given campaign contained many of the same demands couched in virtually identical language. Moreover, in addition to disseminating government-approved demands, the petitions followed a standardized formula, which reinforced notions of social stratification endorsed by the government and their *mutanawwirun* allies: the first sentence of each petition stated the district or town in which the petition had been circulated ("We, the undersigned residents of ———"), then, before listing the demands, enumerated the categories into which the Arab government divided residents of the area (such as "members of all creeds," "members of all sects," "members of all religions"). To emphasize these divisions, the signatures following the body of the petition were often likewise divided according to the government's view of the natural cleavages within Syrian society. The Arab government frequently reproduced these divisions physically in the arrangement of the line of march of the demonstration.[14]

Typical of the petition demonstrations staged by the Arab government was the demonstration held in Damascus on 20 February 1919, following the most intensive petition campaign theretofore undertaken by the government and its allies. Two months before, the French foreign minister, Stephen Pichon, had delivered a speech before the French Chamber of Deputies reaffirming France's historic interests in Syria. The ostensible purpose of the February demonstration was to present to entente representatives posted to Damascus petitions that protested Pichon's remarks, ratified the appointment of Faysal as Syrian representative to the Paris negotiations, and affirmed the commitment of the signatories to a united and independent Syria.

Although, as will be seen below, the demonstration did not actually take place as planned, the Arab government and Arab Club—cosponsors of the event—did distribute a program that attests to the designs and motivations of its planners. According to the program, the participation of the crowd in the demonstration was to be brief (less than an hour), and its role marginal: under the direction of local government functionaries, demonstrators, arranged within designated categories and in accordance with a predetermined line of march, were to parade from their separate quarters to the city hall. There, while the crowd listened to speeches delivered not only in Arabic but also in French and English—languages incomprehensible to most demonstrators—delegations of *mutanawwirun*, hand-picked members of the Arab Club, would present the petitions to foreign legates. Thus, according to the plan, the central drama of the demonstration was to take place off stage and behind closed doors.[15]

Over the course of the next year—that is, until the Arab government lost control of the streets to the popular committees—the government and its supporters organized a series of demonstrations that shared characteristics with the demonstration of 20 February.[16] The fundamental building blocks of these demonstrations were government-supported primary and secondary schools, any one of a number of political or charitable associations allied with or sponsored by the government, guilds that had been established or newly reconstituted by the Arab government, and the Arab army and functionaries of the Arab government. The enlistment of these groups in demonstrations served two purposes for the Arab government. First, it enabled the government to effect a controlled mobilization of the Syrian population while simultaneously bypassing—and therefore potentially enervating—its rivals, such as oppositional members of the indigenous Damascene notability and, later, the popular committees. In addition, the process of assembling each demonstration—the selection and physical organization of the participants, their arrangement in the line of march, their participation or nonparticipation in various sequences of the ceremony—permitted the government to define, reinforce, legitimate, and expand the institutional networks under its control.

Furthermore, because all government-sponsored demonstrations shared a common outward-directed purpose—to show the entente powers that the Syrian population was prepared for independence and stood united behind the Arab government and Amir Faysal—they scripted similar roles for the schoolchildren, guild members, political activists, soldiers, and functionaries they incorporated. Unlike many of the demonstrations later organized by the popular committees—demonstrations that would, in effect, celebrate the crowd itself—the participants in government-sponsored demonstrations were rarely the focus of the ceremony or even the principal actors in the drama. Often the government or its allies assembled demonstrators to act as a backdrop for the true focus of attention, such as the aforementioned presentation of petitions. At other times they cast demonstrators as bit players in a drama that primarily concerned Amir Faysal, the *mutanawwirun*, and the entente powers. Because government-sponsored demonstrations thus conveyed their meaning and fulfilled their function without the active participation of the crowd in their central drama, and because the government feared lest the unruliness of the crowd discredit it in the eyes of foreign powers by casting doubts on the preparedness of Syrians for independence, the crowd's presence at government-sponsored demonstrations was uniformly fleeting and its participation restricted.

The demonstration held in Damascus in the spring of 1919 to greet Amir Faysal upon his first return from the Paris peace conference was typical of the celebratory demonstrations organized by the Arab government and its allies. Faysal, who had been away from Syria for over five months, returned to Damascus to direct the preparations for the upcoming visit of the King-Crane Commission. As soon as the word of the amir's departure from Europe reached Damascus, the Arab government began preparing ceremonies of greeting. "It is unnecessary to tell you that all activity here is directed to assure him a grand reception," the French liaison officer resident in Damascus reported, "[T]he police have personally invited all the inhabitants to fly the Arab colors; the schools have been mobilized; victory arches have begun to be raised practically all over, and there promises to be innumerable speeches. The arrival of the amir will certainly be a capital event in Syrian affairs."[17]

For days before his arrival in the capital, local newspapers carried news of the amir's journey from Rome to Beirut, reported on celebrations held in his honor in Beirut, then followed his progress from Beirut to Damascus.[18] To ensure a fitting reception in the Syrian capital, *al-ʿAsima* printed a front page editorial on 2 May entitled "His Exalted Highness Amir Faysal," which praised Faysal's efforts in Europe and recounted his qualities as an Arab hero "who was and still is working tirelessly to guarantee the future of the nation" and who "rescued the nation from slavery and the misfortunes of slavery."[19]

The demonstration organized in Damascus to greet the amir, like the above-cited demonstration that provided the background for the delivery of petitions to entente representatives, was coordinated by the municipal government of Damascus. It was staged as a triumphal celebration of the amir, whose entrance into the city was described by a Syrian observer as follows: "When His Highness Amir Faysal arrived at Damascus, he rode in a carriage drawn by eight horses. On the carriage were trimmings of gold and silver. Victory arches had been set up for him and were decorated with jewels donated by the women of Damascus. Spread before him in his path were twenty-five thousand carpets."[20]

According to *al-ʿAsima*, crowds of Syrians had turned out to greet Faysal; nevertheless, the public ceremony was mere window dressing planned for the benefit of the entente powers. After briefly acknowledging the crowd, Faysal adjourned to a nearby park to speak with a small group that had been invited to attend this invitation-only event.[21] In the park, orators delivered speeches of greeting and recited paeans to the amir, the entente powers, and the Arab government. The amir responded by thanking the entente representatives in attendance for the support of their governments, which had "saved the nation from the enemy" and had "offered [the Arabs] independence." In addition, he thanked the population of Syria "for remaining calm during the past five months, enabling him to push on for complete independence." Following the ceremony in the park, the military governor hosted a banquet in Faysal's honor to which "members of the [Arab] government, groups of ulama, [progovernment] notables, spiritual leaders from the minority communities, and delegations from the surrounding areas" also had been invited. The public and private aspects of the ceremony greeting Faysal thus replicated the binary division of Syrian society described above: while the members of the Arab government, *mutanawwirun*, etc., decided affairs of state, ritual planners, having cast the populace in a passive role, removed them from center stage. Ironically, then, this demonstration, like others organized by the Arab government, affirmed the fact that real political decisions were to be made neither democratically nor in the streets.

Government demonstrations did not convey meaning just through their form, however. The Arab government and allied organizations carefully vetted the slogans shouted by demonstrators and the messages inscribed on their banners. The government also took advantage of the theatricality of demonstrations and the inactivity of the populace to impart information and to inculcate specific values they deemed appropriate. This was perhaps most evident in the parade that preceded the demonstration held in Damascus on 16 November 1919. According to official accounts, the purpose of the parade was to confirm unity, the desire for complete independence, and the rejection "of any patriotism or nationalism in any part [of Syria] but Arab nationalism." Embedded within the ranks of the marchers were floats constructed to symbolize this message. Some demonstrators, for example, carried a table decorated in the black, white, and green of the Arab flag. On the table, parade organizers had placed copies of the Old Testament, the New Testament, and the Qur'an, an obvious reference to the unity of the separate Jewish, Christian, and Muslim communities within the framework of the new "civic religion" endorsed by the state. Also included in the parade was a cart on which a man stood wearing a costume representing a map of Syria divided into sections labeled "eastern zone," "southern zone," and "coastal zone," corresponding to the entente's planned division of the Arab provinces of the Ottoman Empire. As reported in the official government journal, "this man, representing the nation, asked the people if they would be satisfied with his division or colonization, and they answered in unison expressing principles upon which the nation had decided unanimously." To ensure that the message was not lost on the population, another float, containing newspapermen working a printing press, printed nationalist slogans and distributed them to the crowd.[22]

Ultimately, the demonstrations organized by the short-lived Arab government accomplished neither their outward—nor their inward-directed goals. As can be ascertained from the dispatches sent home by the foreign legates based in Syria, the entente representatives did not regard the demonstrations as genuine expressions of popular will, nor is it likely that it would have much mattered if they had.[23] Furthermore, while the Arab government was unable to instill its brand of nationalist ideology among the Syrian population for a variety of reasons unconnected to the manner in which it arranged demonstrations, the demonstrations it did sanction did little to bolster its support among the populace. There were several reasons for the inefficacy of these demonstrations: government-sponsored demonstrations relied on didactic signs, which were relatively weak in comparison with the widely recognized multivocal symbols of which the popular committees took advantage; the message of the demonstrations was diluted because there was no inherent link between their central drama—the presentation of petitions, for example—and the physical organization of the participants; the Arab government lost control of the streets after the autumn of 1919 to the popular committees and therefore spent as much effort on repressing demonstrations as it did on promoting them; and finally (and perhaps most important) the nationalism that the Arab government attempted to promote through the demonstrations—a nationalism that the government encouraged as much for its efficacy in promoting foreign policy goals as it did because of a commitment to its predicates—just did not inspire the population.

The circumscribed capacity of government-sponsored demonstrations to instill among the population a world view and ideology that, in all probability, most Syrians deemed alien becomes apparent when the plans for the demonstrations are compared with accounts describing their actual realization. For example, the above-cited demonstration of 20 February 1919 was, in reality, neither as popular nor as disciplined as planners had anticipated: as estimated by an obviously pleased French observer, only three or four hundred participants—including a number of curious onlookers—attended the ceremonies, a far cry from the thousands expected by the Arab government. Moreover, the display of decorative flags and bunting, which lent the demonstration a festive quality, and the performance of music belied the seriousness of the occasion.[24] It was, perhaps, a result of the carnivallike atmosphere that only two speakers actually harangued the crowd instead of the larger number listed in the official program. In addition, through their activities, the demonstrators seemed to flaunt both their detachment from and inattention to the principal themes of the ceremony. To cite one example, although the government staged the demonstration in large measure to display to foreign legates a Syria that was prepared to join the "civilized" nations of the world, according to an eyewitness account, the impatient crowd chanted a slogan—"The religion of Muhammad is the religion of the sword"—that was fundamentally at odds with this purpose.[25]

Nevertheless, the crowd did not remain entirely detached from the central drama of the demonstration. To the contrary, the focus of the demonstration shifted from the delegated and almost secretive presentation of petitions to foreign representatives to a collective presentation of copies of the petitions to the military governor who assumed responsibility for passing them on.[26] Thus, whether as a result of active or passive resistance on the part of the participants, last-minute adaptation on the part of organizers who anticipated popular indifference or antipathy, or a combination of both, those whom the Arab government had mobilized to bear witness to the central drama of the demonstration instead both recast the ceremony and assumed the role of active participants in it. As will be seen in the next section, the alteration in the central dramatic sequence of the demonstration, which, in effect, transformed an event designed to confirm a specific structuring of society and political program into an event that challenged that structuring and program, attests to the underlying tension, present in all ceremonies that are staged primarily for didactic purposes, between the designs of the mobilizers and the aspirations of the mobilized.

## The Demonstrations of the Popular Committees

In early September 1919, the Arab Club of Damascus, with the apparent sanction of the Arab government, organized a demonstration "to glorify the Arab army . . . by insisting on the right to unity and independence."[27] This demonstration merits special scrutiny for two reasons. First, even though the demonstration took place two months before the founding of the popular committees, evidence indicates that the Arab government and the Arab Club agreed to its staging in response to the same popular pressure as that which would soon inspire the formation of the committees. Furthermore, the popular impetus behind this demonstration influenced its distinctive morphology, the content of the accompanying speeches, and the symbolism embedded within its ritual sequences. These alterations in form and oratorical pronouncements set this demonstration apart from those previously mounted by the Arab government and establish it as a precursor to—if not the source for—demonstrations sponsored by the popular committees.

According to official reports,[28] the demonstration began when representatives of political parties, guilds, and "youths of nationalist organizations . . . of every quarter" mobilized by the Arab Club converged on the club's headquarters to display their support for compulsory military service. After arriving at the clubhouse, they were joined by another procession, which, as the ensuing speeches pointed out, was the true focal point of the demonstration. Led by a cavalry unit drawn from the regular Arab army, this group of marchers included "young men and the sons of notables" from various quarters of the city who had already registered in a battalion sponsored by the Arab Club and who now marched behind the club's banner. Immediately behind them, a phalanx of newly enlisted youths from the Qanawat quarter of the city followed a litter-bearing camel "which served as a symbol for the glory of the nation which the sons of the nation would have to protect to their last soul." From the Arab Club, the entire assemblage marched a short distance to a location where Amir Faysal, his brother, and their retainers awaited them. After an exchange of speeches involving orators chosen by the Arab Club, on the one hand, and Amir Faysal, on the other, the crowd adjourned to Martyrs' Square for another ceremony, this time without the amir. An orator once again addressed the crowd, but now from the same municipal building balcony that Faysal and other government officials customarily used for their addresses to the nation. After the speech, the crowd returned to the Arab Club building to disband.

At first glance, this demonstration appears similar to other ceremonies and demonstrations planned by the Arab government or its allies before and subsequently: a parade before the amir, the exchange of speeches, the invocation of national heroes, didactic exhibits, and speakers representing exemplary social categories ("an *'alim*," "a priest," and "an educated youth," in the words of the official government newspaper). Even Faysal's speech to the demonstrators differed little from others he had delivered and would continue to deliver on countless other occasions: having introduced himself as "the person whom you entrusted with your interests and to whom you handed over your political leadership," he defended the integrity of the entente powers, assured his audience that the powers would not violate their wartime promises, and vindicated the diplomatic strategy and negotiating tactics of his government.

In spite of these similarities, however, this demonstration differed from previously described demonstrations in significant ways. During other ceremonial occasions, for example, it had become common practice for a crowd to pay symbolic obeisance to Faysal by gathering below the balcony of the royal residence or a government building while the amir addressed them from on high; on this occasion, not only did Faysal ride out to await the crowd at a location midway between his residence and the Arab Club building, but after the encounter, the crowd withdrew from the amir to hold its own ceremony. Significantly, although the amir did not attend this ceremony, it took place below the very balcony associated with official pronouncements. Moreover, as indicated by the speeches delivered by the crowd's representatives, the encounter with the amir was not petitionary; rather than representing the fulcrum of power as he had done in previous ceremonies, on this occasion, it was the amir rather than the crowd who assumed a passive role, bearing witness to the activities of the nation. Calling attention to Faysal's transformed ceremonial function, one of the designated orators asserted, "We have come to this place in order to renew in front of you and under this Arab banner a covenant made between us [the volunteers] and the nation." According to the newspaper transcription of the speech, the speaker repeated the formula, "a covenant made between us and the nation," twice in his speech.

This demonstration might also be distinguished from those described earlier by the role assigned to its participants. Unlike other demonstrations and ceremonies with which the Arab government and its allies were associated—demonstrations in which the crowd, barred from direct participation in the focal ritual sequence, assumed the role of backdrop or, at best, audience—the participants in this demonstration assumed a central, performative role. But not only were the participants the principal celebrants, they were the objects of the celebration as well. "We have become at this hour soldiers," proclaimed another of the speakers, "the youth of this nation meet now because they feel that our freedom and independence will necessarily continue because we are soldiers."

Two aspects of this demonstration directly foreshadowed the demonstrations sponsored by the popular committees. First, as the text of the initial speech quoted above, the encounter between the demonstrators and Faysal, and the subsequent ceremony held in Martyrs' Square all make clear, the demonstration symbolically separated the "nation" from the ruling institution and privileged the former over the latter. Because the popular committees claimed to embody the nation and represent its will, and because the demonstrations they sponsored thus exemplified the nation assembled, this separation and privileging became a consistent theme in their demonstrations as well. Second, not only did the demonstration present the crowd as instrumental; it confirmed both its instrumentality and autonomy by engaging it in activity that was entirely self-referential. The use of the participants as the motive force to advance the central drama of the demonstration would come to characterize all demonstrations sponsored by the popular committees. As the authority of the Arab government weakened further during the spring and summer of 1920, the committees attenuated or even eliminated from the demonstrations they sponsored ritual sequences that dramatized dissent from the policies of the Arab government and/or the entente powers. By deleting all referents extraneous to the demonstrators themselves, the popular committees were, in effect, sponsoring demonstrations that had no purpose other than to represent in microcosm a nation that was self-contained and self-directed. In these demonstrations, the celebration of the nation and its autonomy did not merely accompany other symbolic messages; it superseded them.

The first and most common large-scale demonstrations organized by the popular committees were petition demonstrations. In most cases, these petition demonstrations might be distinguished from analogous demonstrations staged by the Arab government by their central dramatic sequence: during the demonstrations mounted by the popular committees, the crowd submitted petitions to representatives of the Arab government either to be acted on by the government itself or to be passed on to the entente powers. This shift in the identity of the petition recipient had important symbolic connotations: by means of the presentation of a list of demands to the Arab government in the name of the nation, demonstrators, under the leadership of the popular committees, not only reenacted the confrontation between the nation and the government but symbolically reestablished the proper equilibrium between the two distinct entities. As a result, even those demonstrations that submitted petitions beginning with professions of devotion to the amir—like the demonstration of January 17, 1920, described below—were in fact confrontational rather than supplicatory.

By the spring of 1920, the popular committees mounted a series of petition demonstrations throughout the unoccupied eastern zone of Syria that underscored the autonomy and primacy of the nation even more bluntly. Instead of petitioning the government to intercede with the entente powers on behalf of the nation, these protests ignored the Arab government entirely and directly petitioned the entente powers. The Higher National Committee in Damascus, along with local affiliates in Aleppo, Homs, and Hama, organized several demonstrations of this type throughout the spring and early summer of 1920 to protest issues that were of particular concern to their constituents, such as Zionist immigration to Palestine, French actions in Lebanon (including the issuance of a franc-backed Syrian currency and the censorship of sermons delivered in mosques), and the San Remo Agreement dividing Syria into separate mandated territories.[29]

While the popular committees continued to organize demonstrations that, like the above, alluded to the autonomy and primacy of the nation while protesting entente actions or Arab government irresolution, they also organized demonstrations solely to celebrate that autonomy and primacy. Like the demonstration of September 1919, these demonstrations were a radical departure from petition demonstrations because, by eliminating ritual sequences that adverted to external events or authorities, they were comprehensive in themselves. Many of these demonstrations were festive, small-scale, ostensibly leaderless, and/or haphazardly organized. On some occasions, armed demonstrators chanting slogans or singing songs marched through residential quarters. On others, the demonstrations culminated with speeches lauding the Syrian nation or with the administering of an actual or symbolic oath of allegiance that pledged the participants to defend the fatherland or reformulated the social contract that united Syrians with each other or linked the nation with the state.[30]

The internal structure of both the celebratory and petition demonstrations organized by the popular committees further reinforced their thematic content. The fundamental building block of these demonstrations was the local popular committee, and most individuals who participated in them did so under the auspices of the local committees with which they were affiliated. Because, as discussed above, these local committees had assumed responsibility for a variety of day-to-day functions, and because the committees fulfilled their functions on both local and national levels, these demonstrations in effect recreated the nation in microcosm. In more elaborately structured demonstrations, the popular committees allowed other groups to maintain their individual or corporate identities in the line of march. However, because these groups paraded behind a vanguard representing the popular committees, and because their arrangement in the demonstration was seemingly arbitrary and nonhierarchical, individuals and groups not affiliated with the committees were symbolically subsumed to them and therefore to the Syrian nation.[31]

The accuracy with which the demonstrations staged by the popular committees displayed in symbolic form the ideology of the committees was hardly fortuitous. The ritual planners associated with the popular committees, like those associated with the Arab government, well understood the meanings that participants and spectators might derive from their efforts, as the juxtaposition of two articles printed in sequence in the journal *al-Kawkab* demonstrates. *Al-Kawkab*, a newspaper affiliated with the Arab Club, was financed by the British and Arab governments in order "to support the Arab movement and further good relations between England and the Arabs." Thus, in his report on the demonstration held to celebrate the return of Amir Faysal to Damascus from his second trip to Europe on 17 January 1920, an unidentified staff writer contributed an account of the event correspondent to the views held by the government, emphasizing, for example, the central role played by the amir in the drama:

> While His Highness Amir Faysal was in the palace today, he met well-wishers who had organized a great demonstration in which 120,000

participated, demanding unity and complete independence. His highness announced that he was firmly committed to unity and that he
would accept nothing but complete independence. . . . The entire city
was locked up tight so that all might participate in the demonstration,
and enthusiasm was great.

The article that followed, however, was submitted by Kamil al-
Qassab, president of the Higher National Committee. It reported on the
same demonstration from the standpoint of the popular committees, this
time underscoring the authority and activity of the crowd/nation while
downplaying the significance of the amir and the government:

A great, patriotic demonstration took place today, bringing together
more than 100,000 people from all estates. . . . The demonstration presented a declaration of the nation calling for complete independence,
the unity of Syria, and the amir's support for military service which the
nation planned to use as a shield. The people assembled before the government building, orators spoke, and the amir came down and spoke
with them, saying that he did not strive and would not strive for anything other than complete independence, and that there was nothing
separating him from the nation—that there was, fundamentally, agreement for an independent, indivisible Syria. He praised the nation for
demanding conscription.[32]

Demonstrations of the type sponsored by the popular committees
generated enthusiasm during those periods when participation in government-sponsored demonstrations waned. On 9 November 1919, for
example, a demonstration that ended by the crowd marching to Faysal's
residence while shouting, "To war, to war," attracted a crowd estimated
at between fifteen and twenty thousand. The next day, only a fraction
of that number participated in a demonstration that culminated in the
presentation of a petition by the president of the municipality of Damascus to foreign consuls. French observers noted a similar phenomenon
when demonstrations organized by the Arab government and the popular committees competed on 16 and 17 January 1920.[33] Such occur-
rences cannot simply be attributed to the ability of the popular committees to mobilize resources more effectively than the Arab government or
to their ability to exert social pressure on residents of those quarters in
which they were active; these capabilities were, after all, derived from
the prestige already accorded the popular committees. Furthermore,
while the Arab government's capacity for coercion and suasion did
decline as a result of ongoing financial difficulties, it never entirely dis-
appeared.

Overall, then, demonstrations organized by the popular committees
were successful because they reenacted in ceremony and symbolized in

form a national narrative and a societal structure that more accurately reflected the aspirations of a majority of Syrians than did demonstrations mounted by the Arab government. In so doing, they manifest the multiform character of nationalisms that emerged in the post-Ottoman Arab Middle East and confute the mythopoetic constructions proffered sometimes ingenuously, sometimes cynically, by apologists for the contemporary nation-building project.

## SELECT BIBLIOGRAPHY

*al-ᶜAsima*, 2 May 1919; 7 May 1919; 11 September 1919; 16 October 1919; 15 November 1919; 17 November 1919. Syria: Dimashq.

al-Husri, Satiᶜ. 1947. *Yawm Maysalun*. Beirut: Dar al-Ittihad.

alᶜIyashi. 1955. *al-Idahat al-siyasiyya wa asrar al-intidab al-faransi ᶜala Suriyya*. Beirut: al-Matbaʿah al-kathulikiyah.

*al-Kawkab*, 8 October 1918; 27 May 1919; 3 June 1919; 2 December 1919; 27 January 1920. al-Rahirah: Ikhwan.

Bek, Khalil Mardam. 1978. *Dimashq wal-Quds fi al-ᶜishrinat*. Beirut: Mu'assesat al-Risalah.

Chatterjee, Partha. 1993. *Nationalist Thought and the Colonial World: A Derivative Discourse?* Minneapolis: University of Minnesota Press.

Daghir, As ad. 1956. *Mudhakkarati ᶜala hamish al- qadiyya al-ᶜarabiyya*. Cairo: Markaz.

Gelvin, James L. 1996. "The Ironic Legacy of the King-Crane Commission." In *The Middle East and the United States: A Historical and Political Reassessment*, David W. Lesch, ed. Boulder: Westview Press.

## NOTES

1. This is the third account of Syrian demonstrations mounted in the aftermath of the First World War I have published. An earlier version of this chapter, entitled "Demonstrating Communities in Post-Ottoman Syria," appeared in *The Journal of Interdisciplinary History* 25:1 (Summer 1994): 23–44. A more expanded version can be found in my *Divided Loyalties: Nationalism and Mass Politics in Syria at the Close of Empire* (Berkeley: University of California Press, 1998).

2. *al-Kawkab*, 8 October 1918, 4–5.

3. See statements of Amir Faysal in Aleppo, 11 November 1918, transcribed in al-Husri 1947, p. 213.

4. *al-ᶜAsima*, 7 May 1919, 5–6.

5. *al-ᶜAsima*, 16 October 1919, 1–2. Also see *al-ᶜAsima*, 15 November 1919, 4; 11 September 1919, 6; *al-Kawkab*, 27 May 1919, 9; 3 June 1919, 8–9; Laforcade to Pichon, 19 August 1919, Ministère de la défense, Vincennes, France (hereafter MD), 7N4182/dossier 4.

6. ʿAli Rida al-Rikabi, as quoted in Bek 1978, p. 43.

7. Chatterjee 1993, pp. 29–30, 43–49.

8. Foreign Office, London (hereafter FO) 371/5188/E7808/42. "Arabic Press Abstracts for Week Ending 14 June 1920."

9. For use of *mankubun*, see leaflets contained in Ministère des affaires étrangères, Paris (hereafter MAE) L:SL/vol. 43/62, 64. n.d.; MD 7N4182/4/340. Picot to MAE, 21 July 1920.

10. See also leaflets and transcriptions contained in the following: MAE L:SL/Vol. 43/62–171. Original copies of "nombreux tracts, affiches, et mani-festes . . . répandus à profusion à travers la ville (Damas) avant et pendant le séjour des délégués (Americains)," n.d.; Archives diplomatiques, Nantes (here-after AD) 2345. 5 March 1920; AD 2372/dossier propagande antifrançaise. 8–9 March 1920; *al-Kinana*, 15 July 1920, 2, 3.

11. *al-ʿAsima*, 17 November 1919, 1–2.

12. Salafiyya Library, Cairo, Lajna Wataniyya File, "Nizam al-lajna al-wataniyya al-ʿulya fi al-ʿasima al-suriyya," 17 November 1919.

13. *al-ʿAsima*, 7 May 1919, 1–2. For more on the King-Crane Commission and its impact on the evolution of nationalism in Syria, see my "Ironic Legacy of the King-Crane Commission" 1996, pp. 11–27.

14. Originals and translations of petitions have been preserved in various archives in Britain, France, and the United States. In addition, many petitions were printed in contemporaneous Syrian newspapers such as *al-ʿAsima* and *al-Kawkab*.

15. AD 2430/no no. Cousse to Haut commissionaire (hereafter HC), 21 February 1919; AD 2430/dossier confidentiel—départ/65. Cousse to HC, 21 February 1919.

16. For descriptions of these demonstrations, see AD 2429/42. Mercier to Pichon, 11 November 1918; AD 2430. Cousse to Dame, 20 March 1919; MAE L:AH/vol. 4/237–38; Picot to Pichon, 22 May 1919; AD 2430/240. 11 August 1919.

17. AD 2430; Cousse to Dame, 20 April 1919.

18. See, for example, *al-ʿAsima*, 2 May 1919, 2.

19. Ibid., 1.

20. al-ʿIyashi 1955, p. 32.

21. *al-ʿAsima*, 7 May 1919, 5–6.

22. *al-ʿAsima*, 17 November 1919, 3–4; AD 2344/c1/149–51.

23. MAE L:AH/vol. 4/237–38; Picot to Pichon, 22 May 1919.

24. AD 2430/no no. Cousse to HC, 21 February 1919; AD 2430/dossier confidentiel—départ/65. Cousse to HC, 21 February 1919.

25. AD 2367/10/1/146. Cousse to HC, 14 February 1919; AD 2430/no no. Cousse to HC, 21 February 1919; AD 2430/65. Cousse to HC, 21 February 1919; Daghir 1956, p. 105.

26. AD 2430/no no. Cousse to HC, 21 February 1919; AD 2430/65. Cousse to HC, 21 February 1919.

27. *al-ʿAsima*, 11 September 1919, 4–6.

28. The following description of the demonstration, along with transcrip-tions of speeches, can be found in *al-ʿAsima*, 11 September 1919, 4–6.

29. See, for example, India Office, London, L/PS/10/802/P4953. "Renseignements: semaine du 18 au 24 mai 1920"; AD 2346. "Extraits des renseignements du 19 mai 1920."

30. See, for example, AD 2344/327; Cousse to Picot, 10 November 1919; MAE L:SL/vol. 121/1–2. "Rapport de renseignements hebdomadaire," 10–17 November 1919; FO 371/4185/152060/I.707S. GHQ (Egypt) to DMI, 11 November 1919; FO 371/4238/160100/8–11. "Situation in Egypt, Syria, and Arabia," 14 November 1919; AD 2344/c1/149–51. 17 November 1919; FO 371/4185/158008/408–9. "Summaries of Telegrams," 29 November 1919; United States National Archives, Washington, D.C., 59/867.00/1035/1682. US Consul (Aleppo) to Sec. of State, 1 December 1919; al-Kawkab, 2 December 1919, 6–7; FO 371/4186/165787/I.1224. GHQ (Egypt) to DMI, 23 December 1919; FO 371/4186/174490/FO 10 (CPO331/6). Meinertzhagen to GHQ, 13 January 1920; MD 4H114/5/700. Cousse to Gouraud, 16 July 1920; MD 4H60/1. "Bulletin quotidien #1264," 20 July 1920; MD 4H60/1. "Bulletin quotidien #1266," 21 July 1920.

31. See, for example, the order of march for the demonstration organized in Damascus by the committees of national defense on 17 January 1920, which can be found in a leaflet contained in AD 2372/dossier: propagande antifrançaise, 17 January 1920. See also al-Kawkab, 27 January 1920, 5.

32. al-Kawkab, 27 January 1920, 5. For information about al-Kawkab see Arbur to Sirdar (Khartoum), 13 November 1916, Sudan Archives, University of Durham, Wingate Files 143, 2, 167 (AB202).

33. AD 2344/296. Cousse to HC, 28 October 1919; AD 2430/dossier confidentiel—départ/325–26. Cousse to HC, 10 November 1919; FO 371/4185/152060/I.707S. GHQ (Egypt) to DMI, 11 November 1919; FO 371/4238/160100. Admiralty Report, "Situation in Egypt, Syria, and Arabia," 14 November 1919; MD 4H114/2/37. Cousse to Gouraud, 17 January 1920.

# PART II

## *Gender*

# CHAPTER 5

# Humanist Nationalism

# Miriam Cooke

In this chapter, I examine three Lebanese women's texts in order to study the concept of humanist nationalism. In most formulations of nationalism, the state is a central component, it being understood that for a nation to exist it should have, or aspire to have, a political dimension, which would be the state. Such nationalisms, whether they are termed "popular," "official," "liberal," "romantic," "racist," "cultural," "authoritarian," "ethnic," "long-distance," or "religious," I subsume under the umbrella term of *statist*, because of their insistence on the overlaps among an imagined community, the nation, and a public entity called "the state." There are some few nationalists, however, who imagine nations as able to function as human units without formal political institutions. These are the humanist nationalists.

Statist nationalisms may be imposed from above as a form of official propaganda, or they may proliferate at the grassroots level, often coming into conflict with each other. Syria and Lebanon provide interesting contrasts within an area that was originally united. In both cases, the production of culture has played a key role in the definition and projection of a national identity and imaginary.

The Syrian regime, which is founded on a form of pan-Arab secular nationalism, today propagates a form of top-down statist nationalism that accords with Benedict Anderson's notion of "official." It is an "anticipatory strategy adopted by dominant groups which are threatened with marginalization or exclusion from an emerging nationally imagined community . . . (its policy levers are:) compulsory state-controlled primary education, state-organized propaganda, official rewriting of history, militarism . . . and endless affirmations of the identity of dynasty and nation" (Anderson 1991, pp. 101, 110).

The national slogan reads: "*Umma 'arabiya wahida dhat risala khalida.*" This translates that socialist, secular Syria is: "A single Arab *umma* with an eternal message." In other words, it is both *Arab* and—despite its secular pretensions—*Islamic.* Why Islamic? Because the word *umma* means "community" and it refers to the original seventh-century Islamic community of which the Prophet Muhammad was the leader. This is not a pluralist society, but a *single* community, and as such it has an eternal message. Since it stretches forward beyond time into eternity, it must also extend back.

The Syrian government has used cultural production to create, enhance, and project a sense of national cohesion that submerges any threat of cultural pluralism. The Ministry of Culture puts out 130 to 150 books a year that range from children's books to prison narratives, all of which are chosen because of the way in which they serve the national story. Additionally, it sponsors some fairly subversive novels, films, and plays that give the impression that they are written in a context that encourages the free flow of ideas, all in the interests of promoting a stronger, healthier national climate. For example, despite the need for cultural homogeneity, the regime allows for the representation of regional cultural differences, but in such a way that these differences are acknowledged without being taken seriously. How does that work? Plays or films that include multiple regional dialects make the audience laugh. Those who do not speak Damascenc Arabic are peasants, stock characters in Arab cinema and theater, whose role is to amuse. Their difference we are led to believe is not one of essence but of class, it will be neutralized with education. However, these plays and films have short, if any, public lives lest the joke reveal its message: regional differences not only exist, but they are so marked that they sometimes erect barriers to understanding; speakers of different dialects may be as mutually incomprehensible as speakers of different languages who usually inhabit different nation-states. Such speakers of different dialects should not be led to believe that they can put forward claims to separateness. These spectacles are allowed to proceed only as long as the audience laughs. However, a film like Muhammad Mallas' *Al-Layl* (The night, 1991), although sponsored by the Ministry of Culture, cannot be shown. This is probably the case because this film questions what actually happened at the capital of the Golan—Qunaytra—in 1967, when it was lost to the Israelis, and then in 1973, when it was recovered, without buying into the Israelis-sacked-the-city story. Such questioning disrupts the national narrative about defeat and victory on the Golan. The Qunaytra story is one of the key strands in the fabric of the state's self-narration and -legitimation: Qunaytra is another good reason that the Syrians are united. One wonders why *Al-Layl* was allowed to go through to production since the censors had had their eye on every stage of its production. The answer would seem to be that the production of such films serves the national self-image, their circulation does not.

The Ministry of Information has also enlisted intellectuals in its effort to support the national program. It oversees the publication in the three government newspapers of weekly columns by marginal intellectuals. Most of these columnists, were originally verging on the dissident, deluding themselves perhaps that they might create the possibilities for civil society. The Ministry of Information gives them the opportunity and officially sanctioned space to express their views, even to become spokespersons, albeit within certain constraints, and thus coopts their opposition. In such a context, their criticism of the Syrian regime is read as a wish to help it, to improve the national image. Thus has a highly pluralist society been pulled together and contained under the canopy of a single identity and loyalty.

The regime counters theories that Syria has never had a coherent political and cultural identity with ubiquitous images of the nation as family with President Hafiz al-Asad as its father. Wherever one travels in the country, one sees statues, banners, posters, and messages engraved into the side of hills proclaiming the paternity of the president. This campaign—that is said to be spontaneous and not orchestrated by the government—was helped by the untimely death of the heir apparent, Basil al-Asad, in January 1994. The Syrian Constitution does not have any provision for dynastic succession, yet Basil was clearly being groomed to take over from his father. His death and subsequent hero-cum-saint cult has legitimized the Asad family's right to rule. Hafiz al-Asad became Abu Basil. The father of the one who was to have been the beloved ruler becomes himself beloved. It became urgent to find a substitute, so another son, Bashar, is entering public iconography along with the father and dead brother. Statist nationalism in Syria revolves around the authoritarian but benign rule of the male members of the family of the president. Citizens—including the Lebanese—are united as brothers in the family of the masculinized nation.

Many inside praise President Hafiz al-Asad for bringing security to a state that had been plagued by political instability after the departure of the French in 1946. They point to neighboring Lebanon as an example of what happens when there is no strong government to control individual ambitions, cause civil strife. Syrian hegemony over the whole region is proposed as a solution to regional strife. The Lebanese in turn point back, warning of the loss of freedom threatened by a government that would flatten political, social, regional, and religious differences. They are particularly worried by Syrian claims that Lebanon is not a separate country but rather a Syrian province and that the Lebanese are brothers to the Syrians.

Wariness of Syrian nationalist ambitions is a goad to the construction of yet another Lebanese nationalist ideology. Throughout its fifty-year history, Lebanon has enjoyed very weak central government that has been unable to control the proliferation of countless grass-roots statist nationalisms in competition with each other. During the civil war of 1975 and until 1992, many groups invoked nationalism as their raison d'etre. The labels attached to these groups might be political (e.g., Marxist, Nasserist) or religious (e.g., Maronite, Shiite) or feudal (e.g., Zghorti, Jumblati). Yet, however particular these identifications might be, they were always assigned nationalist meaning. Only members of the Kataib, an extreme right-wing Maronite militia; or of Saiqa, a left-wing Palestinian group; or of the Ahrar, another right-wing Maronite militia; or of Amal, a moderate left-wing Shiite militia; or of Hizbollah, a pro-Iranian Shiite fundamentalist organization, really understood and therefore were qualified to respond to Lebanon's needs and to represent its aspirations.

In its extreme form and without regard for whether it is top-down or bottom-up, statist nationalism may become manically xenophobic. Foreigners, regardless of whether they are in power or not, become fair game. But who are these foreigners? Fragmentation of centers in the postcolonial era, provides groups who had not previously thought of themselves collectively with the possibility of projecting autonomous ethnic purity. Differences are highlighted, some might say invented, that open up divides in what had seemed to be a homogeneous community. New myths of origin allow groups to remember or discover or create a uniqueness that "spontaneously" produces a shared identity—a national essence—and promises the fruits of a common destiny. They then segregate and exclude those who do not fit, those who threaten their freshly constructed and thus fragile group ethos, This process is inherently violent because it involves imposing ideology on geography. Statist nationalists place the state first and the nation second but always as though the nation were at once primordial and immortal.

Statist nationalists claim to represent all the people comprising their imagined community. In general, however, they have been indigenous male elites, who invoke without listening to others' voices. I am not trying to judge statist nationalism as evil nor am I labeling it inherently masculine. Globally, women are as much at the forefront of violent statist nationalist movements as they are advocates of nonviolence. To cite only a couple of examples of what Jean Bethke Elshtain calls the "Ferocious Few," we have women of the Shining Path fighting peasants in Peru, Serb women blocking aid convoys to Bosnian Muslim civilians, and Israeli feminists establishing Zionist settlements on Palestinian land. Yet they have rarely, if ever, been the leaders of these movements. Highlighting the gender of statist nationalist groups and their leaderships reveals the stake of the one group in advocating a particular identity. Once such a stake is made transparent, individuals are seen to be talking not so much about and for others but about and for themselves, those who dominate the group that aspires to dominate. Such decentering of a particular statist nationalist discourse assigns it a place *alongside* others.

Equal consideration of competing nationalist ideologies of multiple centers within the confines of a single state suggests that before becoming a collective ideology, nationalism is an individual state of mind, an emotional experience that engenders a sense of belonging to an entity that is thus created as that to which people may choose to belong. This complex of emotions is what I call "humanist nationalism." Whereas statist nationalism is absolute and constructed within a binary framework of differentiation and recognition, positing the nation out there waiting from time immemorial to be discovered by those who "naturally" belong to it, humanist nationalism construes the nation as dialectic, as both producing and produced.

Humanist nationalism is a program of action that may be pursued without reference to a state. It unites individuals without prejudice of gender or race or class. It accounts for the subjectivities of those who are not considered nationalists because they do not belong to a group that designates itself as first and foremost nationalist, and, those who, like women's groups, call themselves nationalists but whose individual needs have been marginalized. How can one recognize a nationalism that does not necessarily name itself as such? How do individuals first begin to understand themselves as belonging to a unit larger than the family or the neighborhood? When does love of a neighbor or of a friend radiate out to encompass others who are then joined by the fact of that love? Are we in the realms of religion and mysticism, or of politics, or is there another arena in which humanist nationalism manifests itself? It is in literature that we can read most clearly those earlier stages of nationalist feeling that need not necessarily develop into a political program. How do the outlines of the nation first become visible?

In what follows, I shall use the term *nation* to denote a psychic space in which individuals feel rooted and to which they belong. This space can be but need not be coterminous with a political entity, a piece of land, a human collectivity organized around a culture, a religion, or a language. Nationalism is action derived from that feeling of connectedness. In general, its goal is the fostering of a conceptual community that shares an understanding of what the nation is. Thus construed, nationalism may be primordial. It may indeed go back to the earliest records of human history that describe men fighting together as members of a chosen people to assert their right to and control over a piece of land promised to them because they speak the language of their god. However, as all the chapters in this volume assert, what is different about today, the expanded today of the post-Enlightenment, is that nations are imagined and nationalisms are played out within the context of nation-state ideology. In other words, each nation once imagined is almost expected to agitate for a state that will give it political autonomy. This context must shape our considerations of nation and nationalism.


Lebanon has long been the site for contestation over the meanings attached to nation and nationalisms. Lebanese have announced their loyalties both from within and outside the country. Even when they have opted to make their physical homes elsewhere, they have attempted to carry their cultural homes with them. These expatriates Benedict Anderson would call "long-distance Lebanese nationalists." Current estimates put the number of Lebanese living outside the country at five to six times the number remaining on the soil of Lebanon. At the annual convention of the Middle East Studies Association in the Research Triangle Park, November 13, 1993, the poet Henri Zghaib articulated succinctly the expatriate understanding of the Lebanese nation when he said that Lebanon was not only its *soil*, it was, most important, its *soul*. However, from the soil of Lebanon, and especially after the ravages of the seventeen-year war, the nation was less mystical. As the writings analyzed below will show, the soul was inextricably intertwined with the soil.

Women's literary constructions of the nation in 1980s Lebanon emerged in response to a sense that not only had statist nationalist projects failed but that they bad been responsible for the damage of the civil war. This poetry and fiction allow us to connect the first stirrings of nationalist sentiment in the individual psyche with its mobilization and organization into a collective movement when the nation that was imagined by the individual requires that the collectivity invent it. Lebanese women's writings redefine and extend nationalism to reveal its humanist dimensions. The women write of the individual's construction of links with a piece of land, the geopolitical dimensions of which are rarely defined, that is then instrumental in an individual's self-definition.

This focus on individual agency in constructing political selfhood creates the possibility of seeing nationalism as a meaningful and dynamic way of belonging and caring rather than of dominating. Such a redefinition of nationalism from the perspective of the individual subject position would seem to vindicate Fredric Jameson's contested claim that throughout the twentieth century Third World writers have produced national allegories (Jameson 1986). For him, citizens of this so-called Third World cannot write of themselves except as metonyms of their nations. Critics suggested that Jameson's theory depended on the omission of all literature written by any but the indigenous male elites. However, if we accept the promise of humanist nationalism, then it may well be that twentieth-century postcolonial male and female writers of all classes and all nations—not only those of the Third World—may be engaged in a nationalist enterprise. Their project begins in the individual imagination and may in some cases ally itself with others to escalate to some form of statist nationalism. They are inscribing a sense of belonging in a global economy that is less and less hospitable to the individual and in a world which is increasingly fragmenting just as it seems to be unifying; their goal is to accommodate, reintegrate, and empower its alienated citizens.

Lebanese war literature by women provides readers with several humanist nationalist allegories. What is key is the definition of nationalist sentiment. From the beginning of the war, Emily Nasrallah was creating maternal prototypes of the ideal Lebanese citizen. It was not that this citizen was necessarily and essentially a woman but that she was capable of what Sam Ruddick has called "preservative maternal thinking" (Ruddick 1989). Whoever had stayed during the war could redefine nationalism so that it should become a positive force. Nasrallah imagines writing itself to be that space in which the nation can be constructed. "The word has become a refuge and a life boat—the poem or story a substitute nation" (Nasrallah 1985, p. 12).

In "All of Them Are His Mother" (1985), Nasrallah focuses on nationalist sentiment or *hiss watani*. She suggests that it may be experienced as empathetic grieving, an ineffable feeling that is paradoxically, yet inevitably, packaged in words. The narrator finds herself the tone audience for a drama acted out by masked, screaming players. Although they "seem oblivious" to her, she cannot leave the theater because it has no exits. Then one of the players raises his mask. How long has she been there? "Since the curtain went up." Briefly, the boundary between stage and audience, between fiction and fact is sketched. So she is in a real theater. He asks her what she has seen and understood. She is relieved. Maybe the anonymous masked players were just screaming, and there was nothing more to understand? However, her relief is short lived: since she had understood nothing, why had she stayed? There were no exits. He pulls down his mask, plunging her back into her confusion and frustration. Her illusions of communicating and understanding—that the screams were screams—are shattered.

Next a woman separates herself from the mass of actors. How, she wonders, does she know that this is a woman? "From the voice. Yes. It was a wounding voice erupting out of the depths of creation and fluttering off into space, spreading fear and pain. 'She's weeping for her son.' A voice from nowhere reaches me" (pp. 197–98). The woman's voice is distinctive. Even if it does not utter words, it imparts meaning by creating spontaneous empathy. The father joins the mother, and they scream together. At this point, when the parents melt into a single scream, the narrator begins to weep, to share the feelings of those people with whom she could not otherwise communicate. She has touched on the core of the others' intensity, of their terrible grief for their son. Comparison with contemporary women's writings on the civil war suggests that this intense grief is for the nation. To grieve during this war is to feel with, to belong, and only then somehow to communicate nationalist sentiment.

However, at that very moment of identification with the grief, the same disembodied voice tells her that unlike the rest of the actors, she is not "his mother" because her tears are outside the theater. Next, she sees "the mother's shape separate for the second, third and fourth time. Then, that recurrent mother began to form a wide circle and the others became a dot to that circle. All of them are his mother" (pp. 199–200). The symbiosis of dot and circles, of mother and mothers, is assured through the maintenance of the scream. The story ends when one of the mothers approaches the narrator with arms stretched out like "ropes of unearthly light," beckoning her onto the stage. The narrator is about to react when the mother turns into a huge tree. The voice explains that the mother has "taken root in the soil" (p. 204). The materiality of the soil is vivid.

It is as mother that she unites with the soil. When the voice leaves, the narrator realizes that the theater has become a forest. All of the actors have become mothers, have become trees, and their roots reach down to the "living principle." This ending, the transformation of a mother into a tree, echoes other writings about women's growing strength during the Lebanese civil war. All who wish to consider themselves Lebanese must stay in the country and become organically part of its regenerative soil. It is not enough to participate in its soul. But who can plant such roots? People who feel together and intensely for something that is at once their child and, paradoxically, their parent, the source of their communal identity. These are the humanist nationalists.

Nur Salman's 220-page poem *To a Man Who Did Not Come* (1986) extends this definition of humanist nationalism from a complex of emotions to a self-awareness that allows her to distinguish the Lebanese citizen from the one who has forfeited the right to such a designation. The title immediately signals the tone and message: a love poem filled with blame and pain. The dedication indicates the audience: "To my mother Zahiyya and to my sisters Najla and Widad and Saqala." On behalf of the women of her family, she is writing to the men who did not come to Lebanon. She is not explicit about who and when. Yet, put into the context of women's literature on the Lebanese civil war, it is probable that she is referring to expatriates who continue to think of themselves as Lebanese, much like the Iranian exiles in the United States whom Mandana Limbert describes in this volume. The accusation directed at absent Lebanese recalls criticisms by Aijaz Ahmad and Benedict Anderson of emigrants who claim exile status. Both insist on the importance of clarifying these nomenclatures, which Anderson calls "long-distance politics without accountability" by "emigres who have no serious intention of going back to a home, which, as time passes, more and more serves as a phantom bedrock for an embattled metropolitan ethnic identity" (1992, p. 20). These emigres who are far from the nation that continues to shape their identity push against international frontiers in the hopes that they will blur into national boundaries.

Throughout *To a Man Who Did Not Come*, the poet summons and then immediately repels "My Distant One." She grieves for his distance. Again and again, she calls to him, even begging him to "Be a man for my nation!" (p. 17). Yet almost in the same breath, she warns him not to come. She fears for him

> the narrowness of the pavements . . .
> I fear for you our wailing, our lamentations
> Our screaming in small valleys.
> I fear for you our confusion. Our wretched delusion.
> (Pp. 124, 190)

As the poem progresses, her warnings, always sad and never angry, escalate. He, like the others who left (p. 88), is not safe in this land of martyrs, prophets, and poets who have lived the terrors and who have learnt to break down the barriers between death and life and between life in death and life in life. There is in them a life that death cannot touch. The martyrs are

> the creators of the single echo
> They are the ones who remain . . .
> All that remains of the body of the nation are its martyrs.
> (Pp. 100, 104)

These martyrs, this human vestige of the nation, are the prophets whose lives were cut short, so that "we might live" (p. 89); yet these are martyrs who do not die. They are the bedrock of the new nation. How can others become like them? Stay, but also write, because the poets

> plant the nation in the earth
> Master creators. They fecundate our history with fire . . .
> The earth holds its head high because of them and is called nation.
> (P. 103)

The poets will return "my nation to its land" (p. 104). These people who have stayed, these martyr-prophet-poet-survivors are dangerous for those who have not shared their experiences. The poet is threatening her lover, while claiming as a mother to be protecting him against the harm that will spontaneously befall him, even from herself.

> I fear for you the voracity of my fading
> I fear for you the voracity of my loneliness.
> (Pp. 169, 172)

Finally, Cassandralike she intones the prohibition:

> Beware of coming!
> Do not come to our grief (nation), my Distant One . . .
> I longed for you. Do not come tonight!
> (Pp. 189–90)

The only relief is in this final protem prohibition, namely "tonight." Is she offering hope for ultimate forgiveness? There is the possibility that he can find a niche in this dangerous place if, once he has returned, he can learn to love the land.

Yet, despite her longing, the poet fears his return lest

> my body end in a blocked pulse . . .
> We are doomed to miscarry we
> who are caught between our own wombs, the wombs of
>     time and place
> A dead fatherhood and a crippled motherhood.
> (P. 221)

She is trying to survive in a death world that has destroyed the possibility of parenting. The dream of her Distant One enables her to hold on to her own individual power of reproduction, in fact to be at once both mother and father. His presence might render her body sterile. She has managed to retain her fertility because of her dream of him, the dream that made her mother to a child/nation that is at once feminine and masculine.

The absent presence of the Distant One remains the muse of her poem and also of her love that is creating the nation. Her love for him feeds and is, in turn, fed by her love for her nation, and each of these loves is made possible by the greatest love of all, that of the nation for its people:

Your love brought me love of nation
My love for you would be worth nothing if my nation
    did not love me
My love for you would be worth nothing without a nation
    for me to love . . .
Our love is not enough for my nation
It loved me more, more, more
I dissolve into the earth.
(P. 15)

What is the nation? For Salman as for Emily Nasrallah, the nation is the grief of the people who have stayed and survived and whose staying has allowed them to push down roots into the soil, the earth of the nation. This grief of the survivors is an empathy that links and creates a community out of those who have experienced it. Women have the greatest share of grief, of the nation: "I am a woman whose only right is to grieve" (p. 134). The earlier association of grief with nation allows us to read the woman whose only right is to grieve as the humanist nationalist writ large. This nationalist, this grieving woman is powerfully creative, because grief, when it is found in the body of a woman, is "fertile with the mercy of childbirth" (pp. 120, 205). Indeed, the grief/nation—like the anguished dream of the beloved—makes a woman's body fertile. Salman anchors her hope in the notion of intellectual fertility. As long as the earth/woman's body is fertile, the nation will survive.

Who is this fertile woman? She is both mother and writer: the mother who nurtures and the woman writer who sows fear. The poet's father, "the man who was jealous of the thin pen" (p. 41), had warned her mother when she was small that her pen would "turn into nails in the coffin of her happiness" (p. 38). How is the reader to understand this mother-writer who represents both the ethic of care and a symbol of terror? Through the transformation of the meaning of the nation, which becomes the product of the citizen's love as well as its source. The mother-writer is the source of the new nation; she is the one who has "no choice but to love because (she) constantly give(s) birth" (p. 43). Her work, and by extension she also, produces while being the product or the nation. Each needs the other to exist and to survive.

A recurrent image in this poem is of the womb. This quintessentially female organ becomes in Salman's hands the symbol of renewal. As such, it is no longer attached to a particular body but is generalized to all regardless of sex. How does it work? Twice, Salman repeats verbatim that, like Saraswati, the Hindu goddess with her many hands, the woman writer has many wombs:

> A woman's body has more than one womb
> My hands are a womb
> My heart is a womb
> My eyes are a womb
> My lips are a womb.
> (Pp. 153, 159)

In a move that I read as strategically essentialist, she extols woman's body as powerful in its pride, its seclusion, its pain, its creativity, its freedom, its chasteness (156, 157). This woman's body recreates "a nation that has left her" (p. 11). It defies the blades of men's logic to release "the glorious laborpains which weave the body to the soul for constant childbirth" (p. 159). Nations regenerate themselves through the mother-poet's many wombs. The woman poet-prophet-martyr must write the abandoned nation back into existence by giving birth to sons who will replace the absent sons.

Is Nur Salman excluding men from citizenship in a nation for whose production everyone should be responsible? What does she mean when she insists on the woman's body and the sons of the nation which women must produce? Does the womblessness of men's bodies disqualify them from producing new sons and creating the nation? Surely not, and I believe that her focus on the woman's reproducing body is key. For just as she seems to be connecting the production of a nation to the physicality of women's bodies, she undermines the gender specificity of the connection. She displaces the womb from its natural place so as to allow it to proliferate throughout the body and into parts and organs that are not gender specific, such as the hands, the heart, the eyes, and the lips. This dislocation and multiplication of a woman's reproductive organs extends an invitation to men to join in this process of self- and nation regeneration. Humanist nationalists who have earned the right to call themselves Lebanese can and should join together to preserve the nation.

In *The Laughing Stone* (1990), Huda Barakat examines the ways in which a humanist nationalist is drawn to statist nationalism. During this process, he rejects his blood kin so as to create a new family out of a military matrix. Khalil is a homosexual who floats through the novel in a limbo that is that space that divides humanist from statist nationalism. He loves several men in a manner he describes as nationalist, but it is in defiance of the norms of statist nationalism he has been taught, for example, censure of laughter. Only extreme seriousness and a consorting with death are truly indicative of nationalist feeling: "History is constructed by death alone, full of hatred and contempt for laughter. Khalil had known two history teachers. He remembered them well. Neither had laughed. Both were infatuated with nationalist sentiment and with death" (p. 131).

Laughter is a sure sign of deficient nationalism if not betrayal. The list of those who laugh is telling. Those involved with militias laugh alot; they tell terrible jokes at parties and burst their sides laughing. Laughter rings loud when the bombing starts because this is the signal that a holiday has started. Women laugh because they can meet each other to chat. The shopkeeper and the baker laugh because everyone is panic buying. The restaurateur also laughs because people care less about their safety, and they risk dining out. The gas station owner laughs because suddenly he is powerful and may even become a political leader. The money changers laugh because remittances start to pour in. Poets laugh because their moral authority is renewed by elegizing the newly dead. Foreign correspondents laugh because they are sure of a good story. Everyone in real estate laughs because bombs are good for business. Worst of all, "all the people laugh, even the mothers of the dead will laugh because new delegations will join their sons and thus lessen the loneliness of the mothers." But the ones who laugh the most are the armed elements, "blue-blooded laughter turns black from laughing . . . dies from laughing. You, Khalil, who drink your tea coldly, why do you not laugh?" (pp. 145–50). Khalil, it seems, is the only one in this carnival of laughter, of antinationalism, who retains dignity and composure and nationalist sentiment.

Khalil controls his laughter, but he has no stomach for that aspect of nationalist sentiment that is obsessed with death. When he sees the fountain of blood at the Ministry of Tourism exhibition, he faints and hallucinates his dead lover, and then he vomits blood because his ulcer has been irritated. Khalil is mortified that he cannot be a better nationalist. He loves his nation and understands its prohibition on laughter. However, love interfered with his expression of appropriate "nationalist feeling." When his lover Yusuf returned home from some mission alive, Khalil laughed and named what he did and felt "nationalist" (135). Although both laughter and affirmation of life are antinationalist, Khalil's love defiantly redefines them. Has his love for Yusuf turned the negative mandate of statist nationalist feeling into something positive? Or is his desire a threat to his nationalism?

This love had held the potential for a reprieve, but it is never realized. I suspect that this is the case because the attraction of statist nationalism became overwhelming. Khalil describes his first brief membership in a nationalist group in glowing terms. He recalls the joy he had experienced to be part of "a group, even if only on its margins." He recalls how comrades dropped by whenever they needed anything and confided their fears and their dreams: "In front of you they strip off their family to choose you. . . . When you leave the group you become a real orphan because you have lost your chosen family to whom you gave birth because you had become a man. Your friend becomes your ultimate father and you forget the first one. You have relegated him to the edges of childhood memories so as to be able to create new loved ones" (pp. 122–23). The need to belong to a statist nationalist group drives Khalil to create surrogate fathers who include, beyond such companions, Dr. Waddah. This doctor had successfully operated on Khalil for his ulcer. When Khalil comes out of his coma, he turns his savior into both father *and* mother. In the recovery room, he felt the touch of his hand whose "warmth gave me more than had the umbilical cord connecting me to my mother. . . . While I slept, he looked at me more than had my mother when I was a child. . . . Like my father when I recovered he was happy with me." Later, Khalil leans his head against Dr. Waddah's chest and finds himself nestling into two large breasts, and he realizes that this man is "more than my mother and his eyes are more than her milk" (pp. 204–5).

These created parents are more real and loving than are the natural ones. Khalil is particularly repelled by his beautiful mother. Toward the end of the novel, when he has come to terms with his homosexuality, he thinks about his mother, who, unlike "the women of Carthage who cut their hair and melted their precious metal for the national fleet . . . laughs alot . . . Khalil began to hate his mother a little, and her laughter a lot, and he came out top of his history class" (p. 133). It is almost as though to despise his mother and her laughter garnered him academic rewards.

Through Khalil, Barakat demonstrates how the statist nationalist group displaces the individual member's family through a reconceptualization of birth, men's birth at both the passive and the active levels. To give birth to the new family, the boy must become a man. So how did the boy become a man? Barakat glosses over the transformation writh a simple causative conjunction: "*because* he had become a man." Looking elsewhere for elucidation of masculine birth in a nationalist context, we find Klaus Theweleit's analysis of German Freikorps writings of the inter-World Wars era. Theweleit claims that all military formations provide the womb for the gestation and birth of the properly masculinized man, the only person qualified to be a citizen. The military corps renders irrelevant and redundant the mother's body. The mother cannot give real birth to real men, real citizens. This real birth must be out of the all-male fighting killing corps whether it be an official military unit or a militia (Theweleit 1987). The mother must be eliminated. However, Barakat takes the transferral of birthing beyond Theweleit. She proposes that the real birth, acquiring a militarized masculinity and right to citizenship, relegates not only the mother but *also the father* to the margin of memory so as to allow for the imagining of new bonds that are based not on kinship but on ideology. Theweleit writes that the Freikorps writers *"desire* a father—a man less weak than their own fathers were in reality. . . . While real fathers are silenced by the soldier males, their texts express unmistakable desires for better ones" (Theweleit 1989, p. 369). Statist nationalism remasculinizes by giving birth to new beings.

After recovering from the ulcer operation, Khalil suddenly sees the world differently. He gives up thoughts of death and turns to self-indulgence. He gives in to his old friend Nayif who for weeks had been trying to convince him to start working for his militia's newspaper. He goes to a party thrown by the militia and discovers that the editor is interested in him sexually. Although Khalil does not reciprocate the interest, he becomes involved knowing that such an affair will improve his life. It does. Now he can convince himself that morality and nationalist sentiment are meaningless in this city and that what really matters is to love oneself even if that love means hating others. By the end, he takes this new philosophy so far that he rapes the woman upstairs. He has succumbed to the temptations of the drugs and arms trade and to the lure of the group—the real family—that makes him one of the boys. He laughs with the others when racist jokes are told (p. 219). He has entered a nationalist unit, but in defiance of what he had considered to be the necessary conditions for nationalist sentiment. In Khalil's journey from humanist to statist nationalist, the reader witnesses the steps taken from the lonely struggle to love one's nation to compromise for the sake of power and domination, but in the name of this same nation.

My reading of these three texts indicates that these women's conceptions of Lebanese nationalism do not engage with notions of national essence. They propound a humanist nationalism rooted in an individual, nurturing relationship with Lebanon. It is a dynamic, reciprocal relationship in which they belong to the Lebanese nation, sometimes defined as the extended village or even family, because they have adopted a quasimaternal responsibility for the people and above all for the land denoted by the name *Lebanon.*

Humanist nationalists in Lebanon were also concerned with inclusion and exclusion. Like the statist nationalists, they designated those who were qualified to assume Lebanese citizenship and those who were not. Unlike the statist nationalists, these qualifications did not pertain to membership in political, religious, or feudal groups, but rather to individual evidence of loyalty to the nation. How could this loyalty be recognized? It manifested itself in the impossible decision to stay in Lebanon and to write of the staying as transformative; those who left forfeited citizenship. Writing the decision to stay became part of the new social and civic contract between the Lebanese and their nation as defined by these same texts.

Emily Nasrallah, Nur Salman, and Huda Barakat write the nation not as an ideological construct despite its discursive nature, but rather as an individual sense of belonging and then of responsibility, which radiates out from multiple centers. It is first of all personal, and it *may* become collective. This nation is the context within which each individual constructs a center for her/himself, the new citizen. Citizenship is neither a birthright nor an earned reward for military service; it is an affective identity that becomes a building block in the construction of the nation, the center of another humanist nationalist. The process is circular and keeps renewing itself in terms of itself. For those who are humanist nationalists, there is no single polity but multiple, fragmentary projects, constantly disassembling but also reassembling and self-regenerating because they foster, above all, survival.

## BIBLIOGRAPHY

Anderson, Benedict. 1992. "Long-Distance Nationalism: World Capitalism and the Rise of Identity Politics." Paper delivered at University of Michigan, September.

___1991 (1983). *Imagined Communities*. New York: Verso.

Barakat, Huda. 1990. *The Laughing Stone* (Hajar al-dahak). Beirut.

Elshtain, Jean Bethke. 1987. *Women and War*. New York: Basic.

Jameson, Fredric. 1986. "Third World Literature in the Era of Multinational Capitalism." *Social Text* 15 (Fall).

Nasrallah, Emily. 1985. "All of Them Are His Mother" (Kulluhunna ummuhu). In *The Lost Mill* (Al-tahuna al-da'i'a). Beirut: Nawfal.

Ruddick, Sara. 1989. *Maternal Thinking*. Boston: Beacon.

Salman, Nur. 1986. *To a Man Who Did Not Come* (Ila rajul lam ya'ti). Beirut.

Shehadeh, Lamia Rustum. 1993. "Sexual Conflict in Lebanon." Paper given at Conflict Resolution in the Middle East Conference, Larnaka, Cyprus, July.

Theweleit, Klaus. 1987. *Male Fantasies*. Minnesota University Press.

# CHAPTER 6

# Nationalism and Sexuality in Palestine

## Julie Peteet

On a hot and muggy summer day in Saida, Um Salih and her son were chatting about her neighbors upstairs with whom she was having an argument. While giving a negative characterization of everyone in the household, she zeroed in on their recently divorced daughter. She kept repeating, "Where is her certificate? Where is her certificate? If she really fell from a tree and lost her virginity she should have a certificate!" In castigating the daughter for her recent divorce, she launched into a story of how on her wedding night no blood appeared to assure the groom of her sexual innocence. The young woman claimed to have fallen from a tree as a youth and thus lost her virginity. Her parents verified the story. But Um Salih didn't buy it. For her a certificate from a medical doctor was necessary. She couldn't understand why the girl's parents had been so lax as to neglect to have her examined by a doctor and issued a certificate explaining the conditions under which she had lost her virginity.

Sexuality, as this anecdote underscores, is hardly a private affair. It has a public, exhibitive aspect where knowledge of it is circulated and its legitimacy or illegitimacy is verified. Thus the knowledge of a person generated by sexual practices and history is often the affair of the public. This management of sexuality, and its public nature, raises one more problematic in the by now highly dubious distinction between private and public. Ethnographic accounts of the first sexual encounter point to its enactment in a public domain—that is, with meaning and performative value beyond the persons of the bride and groom. Abu-Lughod describes the Egyptian Bedouin defloweration as one where the bride waits with a few female relatives in the bridal chamber for the groom to take her virginity with a cloth-covered finger. "All eyes were on it (the door). The women and children sang wildly . . . it seemed like forever (though later they said two minutes, stopwatch timed). . . . I jumped as the guns went off and the men rushed away. . . . The cloth with its faint red spot of blood, a faint mark, was waved above our heads."[1] In her richly detailed description of a Moroccan defloration, Combs-Shilling suggests that it is a rite of passage into publicly sanctioned gendered adulthood. The bride's bloodied trousers were given to the "women who are waiting outside the door of the nuptial chamber. The women ululate with joy upon seeing the blood and either parade the bride's trousers through the crowds or hand them over to the men."[2] While one cannot generalize from Egyptian Bedouin and Morocco to the rest of the Middle East, in the past there has been a discernable pattern of virginity being required and some proof of its existence as knowledge for the consumption of others. What is possible to state with some certainty is that virginity is often a requirement. While ceremonies for its public display are on the wane, knowledge of its absence still circulates and can bring on disgrace.

Among Palestinians, stories are still told of rural, peasant wedding night ceremonies where the bloodied sheet or gown was handed out to the crowd gathered to celebrate a marriage. Reema, a young upper-middle-class bride from Nablus, told me about her wedding night. Fearful of her involvement in nationalist activities, her parents forced her into marriage with a man she hardly knew. The marriage took place in Jordan under the supervision of her aunt and uncle. Her aunt entered the bridal chamber the next morning and politely asked her to give her a bloodied sheet or nightdress. Reema handed it over, and her aunt promptly and neatly wrapped it up and tucked it away to be presented to the bride's parents when they next came to visit.

In the Middle East, as elsewhere, sexuality is not necessarily a private matter of relations between two people. Rather, as Geertz noted, sexuality "is not felt to be matter for inner control, but rather for exterior regulation, mainly on the part of the social community, but with the aid of the sanction of fear of the judgment of Allah."[3] Because sexuality is considered normal and natural, and both men and women are accorded active sexual natures, the control of sexuality is vested in society, particularly the family. Farah, writing on Islam and sexuality, notes that "the sexual drive is a natural instinct that God has ordained. Islam has placed sanctions on this drive in order to avert transgressions, especially that of fornication. Both the penal code and the ethical view regulate the manner in which the instinct is satisfied."[4] Structural features such as segregation and modest clothing are also means of regulating sexuality by defining the kinds of contact permissible between the sexes and the notion of what is visually permissible. In part, this external control stems from the notion of unregulated sexuality leading to social chaos (*fitna*).

One might ask what all this has to do with nationalism. I suggest that the Palestinian resistance movement (PRM) has, in explicit and implicit ways, taken up the public management of sexuality, female sexuality in particular, and that the construction, deployment, and meaning of sexuality is not independent of nationalism. The larger issue at stake is how these categories—sexuality and nationalism—are constitutive of one another.

## LOCATING THE SCHOLARLY PRODUCT

I will argue that the Palestinian resistance movement has in explicit and implicit ways taken up the public management of sexuality, claiming it under its purview. The fragmentary quality of scholarship on Palestinian women does not emerge solely from the fact of exile and geographical dispersal. Scholarship on Palestinian women has tended to focus on singular locales and times: the era of autonomy in Lebanon, 1968 through 1982, and the intifada in the West Bank and Gaza Strip, 1987 to the present. In other words, the problem is one of focus on the immediate to the neglect of past histories on which the present is built.[5] Part of the problem is political and part a matter of funding. The era of the Palestinian resistance movement in Jordan (1967–71) fostered a questioning of gender boundaries and meaning in a national context. Women guerillas made their appearance, and women began to organize on a mass base for the first time. Yet very little has been written about this period because of the political limitations imposed on research in Jordan.

Scholarship on the Palestinians in Lebanon, where the women's movement was highly active and where there was an informal, although discernible, experimentation with sexual and gender ideologies and practices, was limited by the high level of violence during the civil war (1975–90) and the security considerations of the resistance movement, which limited access to all but a few scholars. Since the beginning of the intifada in 1987, the West Bank has been the primary focus of scholarship on Palestinians. Funding has been more readily available for research on the intifada than it has been for research on Palestinians in Lebanon or elsewhere in the diaspora. The academic atmosphere in which research takes place has tended to give priority to those areas of Palestine occupied in 1967, while the experiences generated by the resistance era in Lebanon, among refugees from 1948, have been relegated to the background.

If we look at Palestinian history without privileging one time or place, we arrive at a much more nuanced and complex view of the intersection of gender, sexuality, and nationalism. An examination of two different times, places, and kinds of power relations enables us to arrive at an idea of the ambiguity, contradictoriness, and tensions in this intersection.

Texts can hardly be critiqued without reference to the conditions in which their research was undertaken. In this vein, I would like to insert a brief comment on my research among the Palestinian communities in Lebanon and the West Bank. When I first did field work on Palestinian women and the resistance movement in the late 1970s and early 1980s, posing questions about sexuality was difficult for a number of reasons. Political ideology cast issues of sexuality as frivolous and superfluous in a period of war. Assigned to an interior domain, sexuality was thought to hold little meaning vis-à-vis what were categorized as serious political issues.

I feared questions about sexuality would cast doubts on my seriousness as a researcher. In the cultural politics of ethnographic research in Arab communities, the marital status of the researcher can be an issue. In Muslim Arab societies, unmarried women are considered innocent of direct, firsthand sexual knowledge, and thus conversations about sex are unsuitable arenas for them. As an unmarried woman, posing sexual questions would have put my own standing and reputation at stake in this community. While I still find it difficult to ask direct questions about sexuality in a community where it is spoken of euphemistically, I am now, over a decade later, more at ease. Married and a mother of two children, I now have access to those conversations previously somewhat off limits. And the political situation is now more conducive to discourses that are less bound by official rhetoric and restrictions. In addition, a long-term relationship with a research community, as Narayan[6] points out, carries certain benefits, not just of enhanced knowledge of the community but also of the ability to observe change over time.

## NATIONALIST FRAMES, GENDER, AND SEXUALITY

For much of the past century, nationalism has been a privileged frame for discussing and theorizing Palestinian political and social life. Gender and sexuality have not been exceptions in the nationalist order of things, being consigned to the interior as Chatterjee[7] pointed out.

Standard texts on nationalism[8] as well as literature on Palestinian nationalism[9] have not identified sexuality or the gendering of nationalist practice or ideology as analytical issues. In part, this is related to the fostering of an epistemological distinction between public and private domains whereby the kinds of knowledges and experiences arising from experiences and affinity with an assumed private social zone were not constitutive of profound, agential, nationalist thought or action. Yet in everyday social life, the cultural field of sexuality was endowed with a nationalist meaning and subjected to nationalist regulation, and gender identity and discourse were subsumed under and subordinated to the national. Concomitantly, feminist political practice was constrained by a nationalist framework and organization of power.

Recently the gendering of nationalism has been taken up by scholars of feminism and nationalism.[10] A common denominator in this literature is an unwillingness to accept the notion that social or political life is organized in bounded public/private spheres as well as a refusal to traffic in the troublesome notion of the national subject as a preconstituted, singular category of analysis and action. The assumption of national homogeneity or a common experience of national identity is not sustainable in the face of multiple subject positions and sources of identity.

Mosse approached the issue of nationalism and sexuality from another angle, one that may have resonance in the context of Palestinian nationalism and Islamism. In detailing the intimate relationship between European nationalisms and respectability, he states, "Nationalism helped control sexuality yet also provided the means through which changing sexual attitudes could be absorbed and tamed into respectability."[11] It is precisely this dual project of control and taming of change that makes Mosse's work relevant to a discussion of Palestinian nationalism and sexuality.

If identity has multiple nodes embedded in a plurality of contexts, nationalist discourse is problematic, as it is fixed upon, indeed often insists upon, the primacy of national identity, ranking other aspects of identity as secondary. Contemporary feminist discourse and practice has confronted this problematic. Palestinian activists recognize multiple points of identity such as gender, class, and nationality, yet organizational linkages to the larger national movement have often muted the tensions that might possibly be raised by a forefronting of this multiplicity.

Let us examine the issues of how sexuality was scripted and managed during the Resistance era in Lebanon and second, how sexuality was positioned in the intifada. How are these positionings of sexuality constitutive of gender and nationalism? The following discussion of nationalism, gender, and sexuality will draw upon ethnographic research in Palestinian communities in Lebanon (1979–82 and 1993, 1994, and 1995) and the West Bank (1990).

Palestinian women activists are acutely aware of the space opened up for transformations in gender relations by over seventy years of conflict, social upheaval, and nationalist organizing. Within this new space, nationalism, sexuality, and gender intersected in a particular field of power. I suggest that while official nationalist discourse and practice have promoted a nationalism that is a bounded, essential phenomenon assuming ethnic and cultural homogeneity, there are forms of consciousness and subjectivity that openly claim other forms of identity as points of political organizing, a point iterated in Göçek's introduction. Palestinian nationalism recognizes other subject positions such as "woman" but has denied them the status of independent agency and articulation on a equal footing with national struggle. It has accomplished this disarticulation and process of exclusion through a ranking of forms of subjectivity, subordination, and struggle.

Is Palestinian nationalism male and heterosexual? Is the nation a fraternity? These are the sorts of questions that contemporary reflections on nationalism, sexuality, and gender raise. This chapter proposes that the Palestinian nationalist struggle has opened spaces in which gender and sexuality could become, in a very subtle way, open to experimentation.

Elsewhere I have argued that Palestinian nationalism contains a contradictory potential at once creative and enabling yet also constraining.[12] It constituted a legitimate spatial arena in which a women's movement could thrive, and yet it strove to contain that movement and has had the means—coercive, financial, and ideological—to do so. It had the potential in some instances to rescript gender in progressive fashion, but equally, it contained the potential to rescript it in traditional ways.

## LEBANON 1968–82: MOBILIZATION, EXPERIMENTATION, AND CONTAINMENT

The Palestinian resistance movement had an openly armed presence in Lebanon from 1969 to 1982. A self-styled political as well as social movement, its goal was to struggle for Palestinian rights to a homeland and in the process mobilize the mass of people to participate. The project of mobilization and participation of all sectors of society inevitably brought to the fore the issue of reformulating notions and practices of gender, generation, and class. The younger generation leading the movement in Lebanon engaged in a critique of traditional culture, which was seen as partly responsible for the defeat in 1948. The notion of honor residing in women was one such critique, and it was often casually brought up in the informal self-critique—"We left to save women's honor."

The Palestinian refugees residing in Lebanon since 1948 are by and large from the Galilee and coastal cities of Haifa and Akka. When they spoke of the differences between themselves and other Palestinians, they often drew attention to the conservative social practices and attitudes of Palestinians from the West Bank. They did not openly define themselves as more socially liberal, for to do so would situate them on a moral lower ground. Rather, their statements about the conservativeness of Palestinians from the interior were euphemistic forms of expression, or codes, pointing to the moral nature of their social order as less restrictive for women. What they meant in terms of actual social practice was that women have greater mobility, are subject to less restrictive dress codes, and interact with men with fewer constraints on their behavior and demeanor. The issue was not whether these features were true or not but that they were an integral part of constructing a sense of self and a national culture inclusive of some level of diversity. These self-characterizations were formulated vis-à-vis a geosocial interior that was spatially and culturally perceived as closed and less exposed, such as the West Bank and the cities of Nablus, Hebron, and Jerusalem, which were construed as more socially conservative. Difference was also constructed between Lebanese and Palestinian through deployment of a sexual idiom. Girls were warned not to marry Lebanese who are "poor husbands" and "likely to be unfaithful." Lebanese girls were considered loose and not as committed to their families as were Palestinian women. In asserting difference with the Lebanese in terms of sexual practice and morality, Palestinians were defining themselves as occupying the moral high ground.

Under the resistance in Lebanon, there was no call for a return to "authentic" gender relations or sexualities. The mobilization and the interpretation of culture were highly selective. Indeed, what one noticed were the forms of experimentation in both sexual practice and in the gendering of activism. Yet this process of experimentation operated within a national framework that both legitimized and yet constrained its potential for radical social transformation. It did so in two ways: first, by assuming control over and defining legitimate sexualities, and second, by hierarchizing forms of identity and political struggle.

One of the most succinct and telling examples of the confluence of gender, sexuality, class, and nationalism concerns Palestinian domestic servants. Until the early 1970s, it was not uncommon for women from the refugee camps to work as domestic servants in Lebanese (or Palestinian) households. In the Arab world, domestic work has an extremely low status and is associated with poverty, subordination, and sexual vulnerability.[13] Soon after the resistance came to power in 1968 in Lebanon, they called for Palestinian women to discontinue domestic service. The economic reverberations of the oil boom contributed to an enhanced standard of living of many Palestinian households and a near end to domestic service. In addition, the resistance offered employment as well as welfare services, easing the margins of poverty.

For Palestinians in the camps, the maids stood as an immediate and daily signifier of an intertwined national and familial humiliation. Maids not only cleaned after others but were thought to be sexually vulnerable to male members of an employer's family.[14] From the concurring perspectives of their employers and of the resistance, their appropriated bodies signified subordination and concomitant exploitation, on the one hand, and humiliation and sexual transgression, on the other. In calling for an end to Palestinian domestic service, the resistance was proclaiming the inclusion of Palestinian female sexuality in its domain of moral authority and influence and signaling the end of refugee subordination to Lebanese and upper-class Palestinians. With the end of Palestinian autonomy in Lebanon in the early 1980s and after years of siege and official discrimination and extreme poverty in the 1990s, some Palestinian women have again taken up domestic service in order to feed their families, a clear sign of the demise of the resistance movement in daily life and extreme economic marginalization.

The question of militarization poses a problem for the construction and reproduction of gender identities and their deployment during sustained conflict. Feminist literature on militarization points to the construction of militarized masculinity vis-à-vis a feminized and subordinate other.[15] Developed in the context of militaristic movements operating in support of what could commonly be called "narrowly" nationalist, sectarian, and expansionist movements such as the Serbs or Zionism, or in terms of U.S. militarism in the Gulf and the Vietnam Wars. What about nationalist movements that are neither expansionist nor narrowly defined in terms of ethnic or sectarian composition? In such instances a rethinking of the relationship between gender and militarism developed in the context of the West may be in order.

Palestinian militarization in exile was not accompanied by an organized, vocal, gendered opposition movement. Unlike women's peace movements in Europe and the United States, women did not demand an end to militarization in Lebanon or the uprising in the West Bank and Gaza Strip, both of which situations claimed the lives of significant numbers of young people. Cooke's article (this volume) reminds that women can be as much "at the forefront of violent statist resistance as they are advocates of nonviolence." In the aftermath of defeat and resubordination in Lebanon, while there has been a critique of the leadership,[16] it has not encompassed the notion of armed militancy itself and the era of its heyday.[17]

Participation in militancy was voluntary in Lebanon; there was neither a draft nor forced recruitment. In the West Bank and the Gaza Strip, the mass nature of the uprising precluded coerced involvement. Anderson notes that it is "astonishing how insignificant the element of hatred" is in national sentiment among the colonized.[18] Thus the demonization of an other is absent to some extent.

While militarism and sexism can be closely linked, the relationship, I would argue, is culturally and politically specific. One cannot argue, with any consistency, that notions of Palestinian masculinity have, at all times, been constructed against a female other. The consequences of women in the military for male gender identity have not been uniform. In examining responses to women in the military, one finds few people publicly opposed it, many welcomed it, and most did not react either way. Women were involved in armed struggle, but certainly not in numbers comparable to men. It posed less of a threat to male identity and hegemony than it did to concerns about women's possible sexual transgressions in a space of mixed sexes, distant from family surveillance and control. The threat was to patriarchal control of women and male identity vested in the family control over women, not a male identity caught up with militancy. The implications for sexuality of women in the military was highly ambiguous. In some bases, sexual activity was forbidden. In others, it was allowed as long as it took place away from the base. Military activities offered a space and a veil of legitimacy to these kinds of experiments. Militancy was a critical component of Palestinian culture, but men were not its sole exemplars, and thus it is difficult to claim it as a male preserve. This is particularly so as all aspects of political work were increasingly couched in a militaristic idiom.

Reference to the pervasive experience of conflict and crisis stands out in a discussion of why there was no mobilized women's opposition to militarization. The dailiness and routinization of military assault and the accompanying chronic fear fostered an atmosphere where one's daily life experiences and fears were referenced to being a Palestinian above all else. The ability to individuate and elevate a selected aspect of identity, in this case the national, over others was compatible with exile, assault, and the routinization of fear. Palestinians as a national category were targeted, and this diluted the potency of militancy to define masculinity against a female other.[19] An interesting contrast can be noted in Cooke's article where during the same crisis, Lebanese women writers formulated a critique of the war that embodied a humanist nationalism that was highly gendered.

Palestinian militancy mobilized certain defining qualities of masculinity—mainly being defenders of the community. There was little of the conquer and cleanse impulse. The willingness to die was perhaps more crucial than the willingness to kill in the juxtapositioning of masculinity and femininity in war. I would refer to femininity as "ambiguous" under conditions of militancy. The woman activist in nontraditional activities could be highly gender ambiguous. Whether carrying the gun or engaged in mass work, the female activist expanded the parameters of the feminine and thus unsettled the gendered order of society. Women were expected to be militants in a number of capacities, ranging from carrying arms to mass work to remaining steadfast. Women's status was most ambiguous when they carried arms. Then it could encode a range of positions from a beloved member of the community to a woman of dubious moral reputation. Women with exemplary reputations could became honorary men and thus be cast as sexual neuters. Therefore caution should pervade attempts to argue that militarization necessarily constructs a masculinity formed against a female other.

An incident that occurred in 1976 during the height of the civil war in Lebanon gives a sense of the ways in which the categories of gender, national identity, and agency can be collapsed and sexualized. A young Palestinian Christian woman was captured by the resistance movement and accused of having supplied information to the Phalangists (Lebanese Christian rightists) about resistance activities. When she was brought to a military base for questioning, some of the young guerrillas were visibly agitated and angry. Referring to her as a "whore," they started saying they wanted to kill her and bandying about suggestions as to what they would like to do to her—all very sexual. Their commander was a young woman who had attained her rank through well-known acts of bravery such that she commanded the respect of her male subordinates. She listened without a word while the comments flew. Finally she stood up and very calmly announced that it was time for a political discussion. She sat with these young men and explained to them very firmly but without a hint of reprobation that this was a movement that did not rape or sexually abuse women. She said that this young woman was a traitor to the Palestinian cause and would be punished as such. For the young men, national betrayal by a woman was sexually framed. This young woman was castigated as a whore, and the punishment hinted at was gendered and sexualized, while the female commander saw transgression only in the national sense.

Given the experimentation with and the ambiguity of gender in the national movement, what kinds of gendered iconography circulated and what was their nationalist ranking and cultural acceptability? The images and practices of the mother of the martyr in Lebanon or, during the intifada, the mother saving boys involved very little gender ambiguity. They mobilized traditional feminine qualities of sacrificial mothering for the sake of the national cause. These images and actions had impeccable national credentials precisely because they were of women adhering to tradition in the service of the national struggle. Political credentials were derived not just from service to the nation but from the way that politics had violently dissolved the home/front distinction while upholding the dominant nationalist narrative of women as mothers and keepers of the home front. The "mother" was an activist and was ranked and celebrated as such; mothering itself was constitutive of political agency but in a way that did not seriously contest the gender boundaries of the nationalist narrative.

What is perhaps most suggestive of the relationship between nationalism and sexuality was the resistance movement as an arena of control over women's sexuality, marriage, and reproductive potential. In Lebanon, the resistance movement encouraged, and indeed members took upon themselves, the task of trying to arrange marriages between fellow members. The resistance identified itself as an endogamous space and defined its outer borders in terms of membership or affiliation somewhat similar to Cooke's (this volume) evocation of author Barakat's antihero Khalil's sense of kinship derived from membership in a political group. Yet the direction of endogamy was gender specific. Women members who married exogamously had doubts cast on their political standing and trust, while men's out-marriage, which tended to be more frequent, occasioned little comment and hardly affected their political standing and credibility.

Women's belonging to the nation and their political reputations were heavily referenced to their moral and sexual reputations. Specific devices such as gossip about sexual activities, which was usually expressed euphemistically as "looseness," were deployed as exclusionary devices. Evaluations of a young woman's moral comportment was often part of an assessment of whether she was material for political mobilization or advancement in rank.

While the resistance movement exercised these kinds of controls over women's sexuality and defined it as licit or illicit—sort of an extension of family control and management into the national sector and a nationalization of its meaning—it also offered a spatial arena in which women and men explored alternative sexual mores and practices. The resistance movement offered an arena not only spatially and ideologically removed from the family for testing and negotiating the boundaries of sexuality, but it offered protection and empowerment as well. While not flaunted, sexual relations between members were certainly not uncommon. Women who faced parental opposition to marriages of their own choosing were supported by the resistance movement morally, emotionally, and often financially as well. Parents might have a visit from several high-ranking members to try to persuade them of the soundness of their daughters' choices and their right to make them. In cases of total breakdown in family relationships, young women could seek a sort of sanctuary with the resistance.

## THE INTIFADA: STOICISM AND AUSTERITY

The intifada, the uprising in the occupied territories against Israeli occupation, generated a body of literature in both English and Arabic too numerous to list. One of the more curious aspects of this literature was that the intifada was going to liberate women.[20] The fact that this idea initially circulated so easily and with so little critique is an indication, on the one hand, of the extent to which scholarly knowledge of Palestinian women is embryonic, and on the other, of the euphoric atmosphere of the early intifada and the hopes it embodied for social transformation.

The initial activism of women could be attributed to the mass nature of the uprising, which mobilized broad sectors of society and temporarily and contingently diluted gendered domains, activity, and norms. The neighborhood committees that emerged in the first year absorbed much of women's energies and activism. In the midst of social chaos, women organized neighborhood-based committees to provide medical care, education, food preparation, and distribution and other local services. The committees served to negotiate a boundary, giving a new definition to the permissible limits of women's activism. While the committees were a space of activism, they were also an extension of traditional domesticity. By the summer of 1988, the committees had lost much of their momentum. Banned by the occupation authorities, their demise, along with the lessening of the spontaneity and mass nature of the uprising and ideological shifts, signaled the beginning of women's demobilization.

The uprising was accompanied by a gendered national political culture where personal qualities of stoicism, austerity, and moral rectitude were called for and highly valued. Women were central to its embodiment and public performance. Specific to the national culture of stoicism was an absence of frivolity, bodily adornment in the form of cosmetics and fashionable dress, merriment, celebration, and expressive forms such as song and dance. Weddings were a primary target of an enforced austerity. The culture of stoicism was gendered because it is women who are typically visible as sites for the display of conspicuous consumption and the enactment of frivolity, and it is their bodies that are adorned and decorated in public displays of the cultural aesthetic. Thus the culture of denial and defriviliousness took aim at women; to enact the culture of stoicism, women were asked to engage in restraint in public dress and the organization of celebrations. To do so signified a kind of inclusion, although limited, in the national body.

The Israeli ban on popular neighborhood committees effectively closed off one potential avenue of women's culturally legitimate participation. The banning coincided with a development in the Palestinian political and social arena that signaled a serious challenge to secular, nationalist frames of liberation.

The most serious challenge to the leadership of the PLO and Fatah has come from Hamas (*Harakat al-Muqawama al-Islamiya*). With few exceptions, women are not an overriding topic of concern in Hamas texts or in the literature on Hamas, yet they initially played an important role as the grounds on which a Fatah-Hamas tension was encoded and played out.[21] In 1988, Hamas heightened its campaign in Gaza to impose the veil on all women. Coercion, violence, and intimidation accompanied this campaign to impose a new visually acute boundary around women. It also pointed to this community's vision of the nation as one that excludes women from the polity as well as sight. A reading of the Hamas charter suggests that it was part of the organization's perception and strategy of struggle well before that. Prior to the liberation of Palestine, society has to be reformed along Islamic lines. Thus with few resistance activities as political credentials, Hamas engaged in the coercive construction of a moral society through a campaign of forced veiling. Veiled women were assigned the task of being highly visible embodiments of a nationalism that forefronted Islamic morality. The Islamic veil was re-interpreted to signify nationalism, and enforcement of veiling by young men was considered a national act.[22]

As Göçek reminds us in the introduction, the "discourse is thus about women but not often by them." While women actively and intrepidly resisted this assignment, they received little support from the secular national movement whom they accused of offering the morality/woman issue as appeasement to the Islamists. In this atmosphere of serious setbacks and cultural retrenchment, women produced a critique of the national movement and its inability to deal with the question of gender and the emergent Islamist movement.[23] And the critique deployed notions such as "un programme feministe clair."[24] Women activists were vividly aware of the extent to which enforced veiling served as a barometer of Hamas' social acceptance. With veiling equated with nationalism and morality, women who resisted were equated with collaboration and treachery.[25] In short, nationalism, morality, and religiosity were inscribed on women, whose comportment and dress were now subject to an intense surveillance.[26]

The question remains whether women will be sacrificed to the

Islamists in a bid to forge national unity. Will they be the grounds of a battle waged between secularist and religious nationalism? Hamas has set forth an agenda of social transformation that locates women and the family—assigned to an interior space—as central to their project of constructing an Islamic society.

## CITIZENSHIP

The following is a story related to me by a Palestinian friend and activist in the United States. When I told her I was writing a chapter that included the issue of citizenship, she said:

> I'll tell you about an interesting incident. I hadn't really thought of it in terms of citizenship and gender, but now that you bring up this issue the story makes more sense. We have a Palestinian Women's Association here in the U.S. We drew up our by-laws, and in them we said any woman can be a member whose father or mother [is] Palestinian. We have another category called "friends" or "affiliates" for non-Palestinian women who wish to work with us. In any case, a woman came from the leadership of the GUPW in Tunis, and she read over our by-laws to make sure they are in tune with larger PLO and GUPW policy. When she came to this section on being eligible for membership if one has a Palestinian parent, this women was astonished. She told us in no uncertain terms that "you can't be a Palestinian if only your mother is Palestinian!" We tried to explain to her that we have women here who are of mixed parentage—sometimes only the mother is Palestinian— but that these young people feel they are Palestinian and are committed to the struggle. She wasn't convinced. I never really thought about these issues until she had this reaction, and now you are thinking about it as well.

Curthoys[27] calls attention to the "recent reorientation within feminist debates from theorizing the state to theorizing citizenship." Because there is as yet no Palestinian state, one can only speculate about some of the issues involved in theorizing the gendering of Palestinian citizenship. The positioning of women within the national movement, their spheres of activity, and nationalist thought on identity are points of departure for thinking about possible relations to a future state. The question becomes whether and how relations to a state are gendered, and, in the Palestinian instance, the question has to be expanded to encompass how one relates to a fragmented national community and political entity and the possibilities these relations entail in the event of a state.

There is as yet no such thing as Palestinian citizenship. Palestinians hold a variety of documents; for example, those in Jordan have Jordanian citizenship, which is only transmitted through males; those in

Lebanon and Syria hold refugee identity cards, which are only transmitted through males.

For Palestinian women, and other women in most Middle East states, relation to the state cannot easily be conceptualized in terms of the Enlightenment-based notion of the universal citizen. Nor is the matter as simple as stating that women's relationship to the state is dependent on her relationship with a male. It is to the realm of kinship that we must turn and to the progression through the life cycle. As minors, a category of age in the life cycle, the citizenship of both males and females is derived from their kinship with a father, a relationship based on the concept of blood. Men's citizenship has a continuity in that it can be transmitted to their children. A woman's citizenship is terminal; it ends with her. She can transmit it neither to her children nor to a nonnational husband. Naturally if she marries a Palestinian, the issue of citizenship both for herself and for her children does not arise. What seems like continuity, however, is contingent upon marriage. If a woman married a non-Palestinian, her children are not considered to be Palestinians either in terms of belonging to the imagined community or to a possible political entity.

In short, access to citizenship is contingent upon a relationship to a male whether by descent or marriage. As McClintock has argued for postenlightenment Europe, "A woman's political relation to the nation was submerged as a social relation to a man through marriage."[28] I would argue that analysis of women's political relation to the nation through males should include her position as a daughter—that for Palestinians (for the purpose of citizenship), the relationship to a male be expanded to include the relationship to a man through descent. Descent and marriage are the contingent categories in the assigning of citizenship. A Palestinian woman can keep her refugee identity card (or Jordanian citizenship if that is the case) even if she marries a non-Palestinian. But her daughter or son cannot claim the same sort of belonging. The patrilineal categories of blood and descent are conceptualized as natural and thus immutable categories of affiliation and belonging.

A more immediate way of elucidating some of these issues in the absence of a state and citizenship is to examine how women officially belonged to the resistance movement. The resistance movement can be cast as a family writ large. Terms of reference and address are indicative of a kin ethos. Leaders are commonly referred to as "father(s)" and addressed as "father of (the name of his first born son, fictitious or real)." Young unmarried women were "sisters." Married women were referred as Um so-and-so "mother of (either their own sons' first name or the female form of their husband's nom de guerre)" or as the mother of a martyr. Mobilization was often conducted through kin structures, locales, and relations.[29] We have seen how the resistance movement could be an endogamous unit where women who married out were politically suspect. Framing resistance in a family trope endowed the movement and affiliation with it a sense of the "natural" and called forth kinlike obligations and sentiments of loyalty.

The Palestinian nation may be represented symbolically as female (the land and its products, Palestine as the lover), but so far its privileges of full and complete belonging and its transmittal are male preserves. In terms of citizenship, I would argue not only that it is potentially highly gendered but that it has been somatized, that bodily processes of reproduction and substances of blood and milk figure centrally in its imagining.[30] Palestinian women in Lebanon critique the resistance movement's 1982 departure from Lebanon, which exposed them to over a decade of assault and massacre, "after taking our milk and blood!" The latter is a reference to the children lost to war and in a sense implies that an unspoken agreement has been breached.

The Palestinian National Covenant (1964, and the 1968 amended version) states that identity and belonging are based on patrilineal descent. Article 5 of the 1964 document states that the Palestinian identity is "transferred from fathers to sons." Palestinians are defined in article 6 as those Arab citizens living in Palestine up to 1947 and "every child who was born to a Palestinian father after this date." Will this change? Official discourse has tended to posit women as transmitters of Palestinian sentiment and cultural identity but not national belonging or citizenship. Women are expected to reproduce the nation through their reproductive potential and ideologically through the maternal task of socializing youth as nationalists and in cultural heritage. Yet in the realm of law and citizenship, women's role is neither recognized nor validated. They have been consigned to a bounded interior; only males are able to transmit formal national identity and belonging to the nation. The issue is blood, bodily substances, their gendering, and the construction of national belonging. Women's blood and milk infuse raw human material into the national body, and their nurturing transmits the emotional sentiments of national belonging. But it is men's blood that gives formal belonging. Men's blood not only defines belonging through descent but also its shedding for the sake of the national struggle through martyrdom. Thus there is a distinct gendered binary in terms of ways of relating to the national body.

During the intifada, those accused of collaborating with the occupying Israeli authorities were often attacked or killed. Occasionally women were accused of collaboration and killed. What is noteworthy is how these killings were framed and knowledge of them circulated.

Since 1967, Israel had recruited Palestinians as collaborators often from the prison population, which included drug dealers and prostitutes. There were rumors and many people were firmly convinced that recruiters attempted to photograph young women in morally or sexually compromising situations to compel them to collaborate. The killing of women collaborators was presented in a somatized discourse that conflated treason, gender, and morality. Prostitutes had betrayed the nation and the community. What was deemed morally illicit female behavior, which could range from prostitution to simple sexual relations, was recoded as national betrayal. National betrayal by women was configured as moral deviance. What was hard to discern in this conflation of morality with treason was what had actually occurred. Were prostitutes being killed who were not collaborators because of moral house cleaning undertaken in the name of nationalism? What is significant for my purposes is the public presentation of these killings. Women killed as collaborators were usually deemed to have been prostitutes or as morally suspect.

While Hamas has not approached the issue of citizenship, it is not difficult to envision their concurrence with the nationalist policy of citizenship for women being contingent upon the relation to a male. Kinship terms run through the Hamas Charter, in particular male kinship terms. Hamas spokespersons refer to members as "Sons of the movement";[31] Hamas critiques of Fatah contain an element of kinship as well. In an interview, Jamil Hamameh, the Hamas leader, said, "Fatah, because of its hegemony and because of its belief that it was the mother of Palestinian people, adopted a cortical stand as it did not accept any other claims of parentage."[32] The Hamas Charter outlines in gender-specific terms the relationship between Hamas and the secular, nationalist organizations, as "of a son toward his father and the brother toward his brother" (article 27).

In a telling conversation on how difference is constructed, one member of a group of several hundred Hamas activists deported to Lebanon by the Israeli authorities in the early 1990s explained to an interviewer that the attitude of the Lebanese toward the Palestinians began to change with the presence of the deportees. The deportees' behavior was in marked contrast to the more secular Palestinians of Lebanon—the "fedayeen" (guerillas) who used to run around villages without supervision and chase after women.[33] Setting up a moral opposite to the fedayeen, Hamas again uses women and moral behavior to try to establish itself as the leader of the struggle.

An article in the Hamas Charter concerning the state of jihad[34] explains that the "woman is allowed to go fight without permission of her husband and the slave without the permission of his master" (article

12). Thus the state of jihad suspends the usual relations of subordination and, like the slave, allows women to be active subjects, but only in the fight against the enemies of Islam.

The Charter contains an article entitled "The Role of the Muslim Woman" in which it is stated that woman play a role equal to men in the battle for liberation. Yet that role is different; it is one that revolves around her reproductive capabilities—"for she is the factory of men." It also takes up the issue of women as having been coopted without knowing it by enemies of Islam. It is the role of Hamas to regain women from these enemy organizations. In this article, women have little subjectivity or agency. Indeed they are in need of rescue. They are one of the grounds upon which enemies destroy Islamic communities; to regain those communities, women must be regained.

The Palestinian Declaration of Independence (1988) includes an article specifying equal rights for women.[35] The document may well become the site for a contentious debate over the meaning of national belonging, citizenship, and gender. Reports have circulated that a subgroup working on a constitution removed this article in order to appease the Islamists.

In the construction and maintenance of national belonging, men and women have been assigned different and somatized tasks. Men transmit formal, blood-based belonging, which confers citizenship, while women reproduce the community physically. And most significant, women's sexual comportment now has national implications, not just familial ones.

## AUTONOMY

The new, although highly circumscribed, spaces of political autonomy in parts of the West Bank and the Gaza Strip may facilitate the proliferation of organizing poles around a plurality of subject positions that a nationalist frame has muted and subsumed. While some Palestinians see the contemporary era as the first step toward statehood, others see it as the consolidation of occupation and the working out of a relation of subordination and dominance. In either case, for women, one key issue is the legal structure of autonomy. What kind of a legal system will prevail in the autonomous areas of Palestine?

A discussion of current shifts in Palestinian women's strategies requires cognizance of the transitional nature of the present. What do new spatial arenas offer women, and how are they responding to them? The ranking of struggles as primary and secondary has lost steam and certainly credibility and has been by-passed by the discourse of democracy and human rights. A second and related key issue of course is the religious/secularist confrontation.

The relationship between feminism and nationalism has changed from the early nationalist era when feminism was rejected. A discourse of hierarchy of struggle located a feminist consciousness and struggle as threatening to national identity and unity and as a secondary struggle in both time and space.[36] Palestinian nationalism supposed a predetermined national identity that stood above and subsumed other forms of identity such as gender and class. Gender was to be addressed after national liberation and within the structures of a state. The problem was not that nationalism didn't recognize other subject positions—it did—but that it ranked them and privileged nationalism. Mouffe argues that only by de-essentializing the homogenous and coherent subject can we be "in the position to theorize the multiplicity of relations of subordination."[37] Palestinian women have long recognized the "social agent as constituted by an ensemble of subject positions," but the nature of the linkage to the national movement effectively precluded serious theorization of multiple relations of subordination and ways of politically organizing around them.

*Feminism* is now a term of some currency, whereas when I initially did fieldwork in Lebanon, it had little legitimacy. During the course of the intifada, women moved beyond the national frame of ranking subject positions. If nationalism and feminism are juxtaposed as competing spheres of interest, identity, and locality, one runs the risks of a binary construction that is not borne out in everyday experience. An insistence on one or the other forces a split between dimensions of women's identity forcing multiple, dynamic phenomena into unidimensional categories. The perception of a split has both an interior and an exterior manifestation. A decidedly vocal Palestinian feminist discourse is emerging from a critique of nationalism as an ideology and mobilizational frame that subsumed, either implicitly or explicitly, alternative or dissonant interpretations of the social order and the formation of the Palestinian subject.[38] With some form of autonomy on the horizon, however limited, Palestinian feminist discourse is enmeshing itself in the discourse of democracy.[39] For example, activists and intellectual women's critiques of the Islamists' imposition of veiling is framed within a democracy discourse rather than solely one of women's rights. Kuttab writes that involuntary veiling contradicts the political pluralism and democratic spirit which characterizes women's militancy.[40] Feminist agendas and discourse may be in a tense relationship with the national movement, but the women's movement seems to be committed to a both/and relationship.

What women activists seem to be advocating is a form of citizenship in which sexual difference is irrelevant, where women relate to the state as rights-bearing individuals and not through kin-based relationships with males. With the advent of a limited form of autonomy in the occupied territories, women have formed "lobbies" to work on issues such as the Constitution and women's participation in elections.[41] In the pre-autonomy stage, women were hesitant to separate their movement too dramatically from the larger national movement. The tensions involved in doing so have often been expressed in the common refrain of "How can we take our rights from men who have none?" This refrain is less pronounced now as women are carving out some critical distance between their issues and those of the larger national movement. Framing demands for equality in a democratic vision does not preclude organizing around the category of women. In the General Union of Palestinian Women's (GUPW) Declaration of Principles, they engage in a critique of the Palestinian nationalist movement's past, where "national concerns were prioritized over social issues. Bitter experiences, however, have made Palestinian women conscious of the specificity of women's issues which are linked to the struggle for justice, democracy, equality, and development."[42] The Declaration also demands "equality in civil rights, including the right to obtain, maintain, or abdicate citizenship and in a woman's right to grant it to her spouse and children."

To conclude, one pattern stands out clearly: the transformation in Palestinian women's activist discourse from a narrowly national focus to a nationalist-feminist one embedded in multiple subjectivities and grounded in the discourse of equal rights and democracy. The women's movement and the national movement have been rather quiet but certainly not inactive on the issue of sexuality. It is still categorized as in the private realm and referred to euphemistically by Hamas, in commands to veil and be moral and in the nationalist conflation of sexual activity and national betrayal. The GUPW's Declaration refers to women's mobility and autonomy but does not mention sexuality. We need to be looking at the ways in which women claim management and control of sexuality from both Islamic and nationalist appropriations. With their demands for equality in personal status laws and intervention in violent practices, they are clearly signaling that women can no longer be easily and uncontestedly assigned to a culturally representative interior, bounded off from the public, and that intervention, from a national, democratic authority in which women are full participants, is in order.

## ACKNOWLEDGEMENTS

An earlier version of this chapter entitled "Nationalism and Sexuality in the Palestinian National Movement" was presented at Harvard University, February 8, 1995. A shorter version of this chapter appears as "Gender and Sexuality: Belonging to the National and Moral Order" in *Gendering Public Space: Mediation of the Feminine in Muslim Societies*, ed. Asma Asfaruddin (Harvard University Press: Cambridge, 2000). Research was made possible by funding from a Fulbright Research Grant and an Advanced Research Award from the Social Science Research Council.

## BIBLIOGRAPHY

Abu-Lughod, Lila. 1993. *Writing Women's Worlds: Bedouin Stories.* Berkeley: University of California Press.

Ahmad, Hisham. 1994. *Hamas: From Religious Salvation to Political Transformation: The Rise of Hamas in Palestinian Society.* Jerusalem: Palestinian Academic Society for the Study of International Affairs.

Anderson, Benedict. 1991. *Imagined Communities.* Revised edition. London and New York: Verso.

Chatterjee, Partha. 1993. *The Nation and Its Fragments: Colonial and Postcolonial Histories.* Princeton: Princeton University Press.

Cobban, Helena. 1984. *The Palestinian Liberation Organization: People, Power, and Politics.* Cambridge: Cambridge University Press.

Combs-Shilling, Elaine. 1989. *Sacred Performances: Islam, Sexuality, and Sacrifice.* New York: Columbia University Press.

Curthoys, Ann. 1993. "Feminism, Citizenship and National Identity" *Feminist Review*, no. 44:19–37.

"Declaration of Independence." 1988. Palestinian National Council. 19th Session. Nov. 12–16, Algiers.

Enloe, Cynthia. *1993. The Morning After: Sexual Politics at the End of the Cold War.* Berkeley: University of California Press.

———. 1990. *Bananas, Beaches & Bases: Making Feminist Sense of International Politics.* Berkeley: University of California Press.

Farah, Madelain. 1984. *Marriage and Sexuality in Islam: A Translation of al-Ghazali's Book on the Etiquette of Marriage from the Ihya.* Salt Lake City: University of Utah Press.

Fleischmann, Ellen. 1996. "Crossing the Boundaries of History: Exploring Oral History in Researching Palestinian Women in the Mandate Period." *Women's History Review* 5, no. 3:351–71.

Geertz, Hildred. 1979. "The Meaning of Family Ties." In H. Geertz, C. Geertz, and L. Rosen, *Meaning and Order in Moroccan Society.* Cambridge: Cambridge University Press.

General Union of Palestinian Women. 1994. "Declaration of Principles on Palestinian Women's Rights." *Journal of Palestine Studies* 24, no. 1:137–38.

Giacaman, Rita, and Penny Johnson. 1989. "Palestinian Women: Building Barricades and Breaking Barriers." In *Intifada: The Palestinian Uprising against Israeli Occupation*, Zachary Lockman and Joel Beinin, eds. Boston: South End Press.

Hammami, Rema. 1994. "L'Intifada a-t-elle emancipe les femmes?" *Revue D'Etudes Palestiniennes* 51: 59–65.

――. 1990. "Women, the Hijab and the Intifada." *Middle East Report* 164–65: 24–28, 71.

Heng, Geraldine, and Janadas Devan. 1992. "State Fatherhood: The Politics of Nationalism, Sexuality and Race in Singapore." In *Nationalisms and Sexualities*, A. Parker, M. Russo, D. Sommer and P. Yaeger, eds. New York and London: Routledge.

Hobsbawm, Eric. 1990. *Nations and Nationalism since 1780*. Cambridge: Cambridge University Press.

Kuttab, Elaine. 1994. "Liberation des femmes, liberation nationale." *Revue D'Etudes Palestiniennes* 51: 67–72.

McClintock, Anne. 1993. "Family Feuds: Gender, Nationalism and the Family." *Feminist Review* 44: 61–80.

Menchu, Rigoberto. 1991. *I, Rigoberta Menchu. An Indian Woman in Guatemala*. Edited and introduced by Elisabeth Burgos-Debray. London and New York: Verso Press.

Mosse, George. 1985. *Nationalism and Sexuality: Middle-Class Morality and Sexual Norms in Modern Europe*. Madison: University of Wisconsin Press.

Mouffe, Chantal. 1992. "Feminism, Citizenship, and Radical Democratic Politics." In *Feminists Theorize the Political*, Judith Butler and Joan Scott, eds. New York and London: Routledge.

Muslih, Muhammad. 1988. *The Origins of Palestinian Nationalism*. New York: Columbia University Press.

Narayan, Kirin. 1993. "How Native Is a 'Native' Anthropologist." *American Anthropologist 95*, no. 3:671–86.

Norton, Anne. 1991. "Gender, Sexuality and the Iraq of Our Imagination." *Middle East Report* 173: 26–28.

Parker, Andrew et al. 1992. Nationalisms and Sexualities. New York and London: Routledge.

Peteet, Julie. 1995. "'They Took Our Milk and Blood': Palestinian Women and War." *Cultural Survival* 19, no. 1:50–53.

――. 1991. *Gender in Crisis: Women and the Palestinian Resistance Movement*. Columbia University Press: New York.

Quandt, William B., Fuad Jabber, and Ann Mosley Lesch. 1973. *The Politics of Palestinian Nationalism*. Berkeley: University of California Press.

Said, Edward. 1989. "Intifada and Independence." In *Intifada: The Palestinian Uprising against Israeli Occupation*, Zachary Lockman and Joel Beinin, eds. Boston: South End Press.

Sharoni, Simon. 1993. "Gender and Middle East Politics: The Fletcher Forum." *World Affairs* 17, no. 2:59–73.

Taraki, Lisa. 1989. "The Islamic Resistance Movement in the Palestinian Uprising." *Middle East Report* 156: 30–32.

Thapar, Suruchi. 1993. "Women as Activists; Women as Symbols: A Study of the Indian National Movement." *Feminist Review* 44: 81–96.

Tucker, Judith. 1994. "Muftis and Matrimony: Islamic Law and Gender in Ottoman Syria and Palestine." *Islamic Law and Society* 1, no. 3:265–300.

—————. 1992. "Ties That Bound: Women and Family in 18th and 19th Century Nablus." In *Women in Middle Eastern History*, Nikki Keddie and Beth Baron, eds. New Haven: Yale University Press.

## NOTES

1. See Abu-Lughod 1993, pp. 190–91.
2. Combs-Shilling 1989, p. 207.
3. Geertz 1979, p. 332.
4. Farah 1984, p. 33.
5. This is being remedied by the recent work of Fleischmann 1996 and Tucker 1992, 1994.
6. See Narayan 1993.
7. See Chatterjee 1993.
8. See Anderson 1991 and Hobsbawm 1990.
9. See Cobban 1984; Mushin 1988; and Quandt and Lesch 1973.
10. See Enloe 1990 and 1993; Mosse 1985; Parker et al., 1992; and Thapar 1993.
11. See Mosse 1985, p. 10.
12. See Peteet 1991.
13. Foreign domestics have all but replaced local domestic workers in the Arab world. Foreign servants (from Sri Lanka, the Philippines, Thailand, and India) are preferred over Arab women because they accept lower wages and cannot easily leave if dissatisfied.
14. The positioning of domestics as sexually vulnerable knows few cultural borders. Guatemalan activist and Nobel Peace Prize winner Rigoberto Menchu 1991 offers a poignant and harrowing account of a period in her life as a domestic servant in urban Guatemala; sexual services were often expected of young servant girls.
15. See Enloe 1993 and Norton 1991.
16. See Peteet 1995.
17. The critique is aimed at a leadership that they feel used them during the resistance movement era (1968–82) in Lebanon and then abandoned them. The heavy losses of life are considered wasted since they were intended to bring a modicum of political gain, and yet the Palestinian refugee community in Lebanon ended up political and militarily defeated and socially marginalized in the post-1982 period.
18. See Anderson 1991, p. 142.
19. A similar situation prevailed among the indigenous population resisting the Guatemalan military. Under attack as a group and responding as communities, masculinity was not forefronted in defining militancy or activism.
20. See Said 1989 and Giacaman and Johnson 1989.
21. See Hammami 1990 and Taraki 1989.
22. See Hammami 1990.
23. See Kuttab 1994 and Hammami 1994.
24. See Kuttab 1994, p. 70.

25. See Hammami 1990 and 1994 for the first and most solid analysis of the veiling campaign.

26. See Hammami 1994, p. 62.

27. See Curthroys 1993, p. 34.

28. See McClintock 1993, p. 65.

29. See Peteet 1991.

30. In the context of Singapore and its exhortations to educated upper-class Chinese women to produce more children, Heng and Devan suggest that nationalism was so gendered that "a sexualized, separate species of nationalism . . . was being advocated for women." They argue that women's relation to the nation was "uterine nationalism" (as opposed to a male phallic nationalism). See Heng and Devan 1992, pp. 348–49.

31. See Ahmad 1994, p. 39.

32. Ibid., p. 61

33. See Ibid., pp. 94–95.

34. *Jihad*, which translates as "holy war," refers to the righteous struggle against the enemies of Islam, which includes injustice and corruption. It also refers to the inner, more spiritual and practical striving to realize God's will on earth and the inner struggle against human impulses that contravene Islamic laws.

35. The document states on page 6, "Governance will be based on principals of social justice, equality and non-discrimination in public rights of men or women, on grounds of race, religion, color or sex under the aegis of a constitution which ensures the rule of law and an independent judiciary." Included in the text on page 8 was a "special tribute to that brave Palestinian woman, guardian of sustenance and life, keeper of our people's perennial flame."

36. For discussions of how the politics of national liberation and national security have deployed the notion of priorities of struggle and development to deflate women's demands for equality, see Peteet 1991 and Sharoni 1993, pp. 65–66.

37. See Mouffe 1992, p. 372.

38. Palestinian national identity has a fundamental point of difference not always highly relevant in other nationalisms. Scattered in exile in various countries for nearly fifty years, Palestinians have developed exilic, nationalist identities highly bound with particular places. For example, the Palestinians of Lebanon see themselves as different in some ways from the Palestinians of Syria or Jordan. Their experiences of exile form another layer of identity upon an imagined common Palestinian cultural identity. In addition, Palestinians live under differing legal systems, which has implications for their legal status, identity, and rights. With the recent peace accords, there is now a further category of Palestinians legally and in terms of relationship to the homeland—the Palestinians of Jericho and the Gaza Strip.

39. On the feminist/democracy discourse, see Kuttab 1994. Palestinian women are not alone in this avenue. Tujan Faisal, woman member of Jordan's Parliament, concerns herself with questions of human rights and democracy. She argues that women's rights are within the domain of human rights. She has submitted amendments to the Passport and Nationality Law to permit women to

obtain a passport without the consent of a male relative and to be able to transmit citizenship to their children. Faisal sees this as a human rights issue.

40. See Kuttab 1994, p. 72.

41. See comments by Rada Zeraid, director of the Palestinian Link Center, reported by Oded Lipshitz in *Al-Hamishmar* January 21, 1994, and reprinted in *Review D'Etudes Palestiniennes* 51, 1994, pp. 229–35.

42. See Peteet 1994, p. 137.

# CHAPTER 7

# Civil Society, the Public/Private, and Gender in Lebanon

## Suad Joseph

"Lebanon is not a civil society,"[1] Edward Shils asserted shortly after the 1958 civil war and only twenty years after Lebanon's independence from France (which had established a mandate over Lebanon during the dismantling of the Ottoman Empire after World War I). Such pronouncements echo thirty years later in the corridors of Western political discourses about the Middle East. Indeed, the question of civil society in Lebanon and in other Middle Eastern countries has reemerged as a critical issue in the past decade. As scholars and activists struggle for and about the possibilities of democratic nationhood in the Middle East, questions about the meaning and centrality of civil society for democracy and nation building have become center staged.

Despite the longevity and increasing intensity of the civil society debate and its centrality to discourses of democratic nationhood, relatively few political theorists have considered the relevance of these debates for women in the Middle East.[2] For their part, Middle Eastern feminists have only begun to critically challenge civil society theorists' neglect of gender issues.[3] To the degree that civil society notions are pivotal to nations, nationalism, and democracy, then civil society debates must be informed by research on gender. The assumptions of the civil society model must be tested against local cultural dynamics, including local gender systems, as crucial threads in the cloths of cultures.

Civil society generally has come to mean the existence of nongovernmental institutions and agencies that carry out significant social activity and restrain the state from arbitrary exercises of power.[4] The presence of autonomous social agencies operating as limits to state power has been taken as the litmus test of national democratic potential.[5] The engagement of a citizenry in civil society has come to be seen as a measure of their active construction of their communities and nationhood.[6] While communities and nations may be imagined,[7] their social construction requires the active participation of their members in sites that are socially and politically recognized.[8] Democratic construction of communities and nations is usually analyzed by political theorists in terms of a citizenry's participation in the nongovernmental arena of civil society. The nature and dynamics of civil society, therefore, have been regarded as a central site for the assessment of nature and dynamics of democratic nationhood.[9]

These assumptions of the civil society model are Western-centric. Cultural bias, however, is not, by itself, my concern, nor, by itself, the crucial test of the efficacy of theory. Culture, like theory, travels.[10] As culture crosses borders, components are selectively borrowed, reconfigured, and adapted to create new cultures and theories. The origins of an idea only partially inform us of its local meanings and uses.[11]

More disconcerting to me, in the uncritical application of civil society theory to Lebanon or other Middle Eastern countries, has been the transportation of gendered Western political notions and the consequent neglect or glossing of local dynamics impacted by local gender systems.[12] Gender is woven into the fabric not only of the Middle Eastern political systems about which the civil society model is contested, however, but also into that of the Western societies, which produced the civil society model of democratic governance.[13] The outcome has been a double gender blindness—to Western and local gender issues.

While a few Middle Eastern feminists theorists have analyzed civil society, they, like their Western counterparts, have suggested that neither the state nor the nation is gender neutral. Mervat Hatem has argued that there has been an enduring alliance between nationalism and patriarchy in Egypt, which has been most explicitly manifested in the enduring sexism of Muslim personal status laws.[14] Boutheina Cheriet similarly argued that in the aftermath of the nationalist struggles in Algeria, the state elite sold out women in their efforts to appease and compromise with Islamicists.[15] The use of women to symbolically represent the advances nationalist struggles promise but rarely deliver has also been documented in Turkey,[16] Palestine[17] and many other Third World nations such as Iran, China, and Vietnam.[18] Nationalist struggles and nation-making movements must always address the question of the participation of the citizenry in the making of the nation and state. Western political theory has taken civil society as the central site of that activity. Yet, civil society theory has been largely uninformed by debates and controversies in Western feminist research and has been critiqued by Western feminist theorists for its masculinist assumptions.[19] Western masculinist assumptions have driven much of civil society theorizing in the Middle East as well, glossing local gender systems, which are quite different from Western gender systems. To unravel the assumptions in the civil society model of nationhood and democracy from the positionalities of women requires double excavation—for gendered assumptions vis-à-vis Western societies and vis-à-vis Third World societies.

Central to the problems of civil society theory, in its application to both Western and Third World societies, has been its assumption that a democratic nation is, and needs to be, divided into relatively autonomous public and private spheres; that the democratic nation is founded on boundary making.[20] As Göçek argues, gender is one of the significant sites at which the boundaries of nationalism are negotiated.[21] It is, as Göçek asserts, a process of inclusion and exclusion. I, like many feminists theorists, am particularly concerned about the exclusion of women from civil society—an exclusion achieved by the systematic weaving of patriarchy throughout society, rendering the classical understandings of the boundaries between civil society/state, public/private relatively meaningless. Civil society theorists have blamed the weakness of the public/private division, and particularly the minimal autonomy of the private sphere, for the absence or weakness of nationhood and democracy in Third World societies. The assumption of a public/private binary in civil society theory has its parallels in feminist theorizing.[22]

Paradoxically, early structuralist feminist theory, in the 1970s and 1980s, argued that it was just the (purported) universal division of social orders into public and private domains and women's association with the devalued private domain that led to women's (purported) universal subordination to men.[23] The engendering of the public/private paradigm, long standing in Western discourse, by feminist theorists set into motion much theorizing about differing modes of operation of males and females, especially the notion that differing modes of operation characterize behavior in masculinized public and feminized private spheres. The public sphere was argued to be a sphere of rational discourse, abstract principles, the rule of contract law, and objective and impersonal judgments and relationships. The private sphere was argued to be the sphere of emotionalities, subjectivities, specificities, and the rule of natural law.[24]

Later feminist theorists—Marxists, poststructuralists, critical theorists, and others—challenged the universalism of the public/private binary and its usefulness in understanding gendered domination, even in the West.[25] Scholars argued the historical recency and cultural specificity of public and private sphere binaries.[26] Some argued for relationalities between the spheres, the porousness of the boundaries, or the impact of boundedness on the visibility of women's activities.[27]

Despite the controversies in feminist theory concerning the meaning and uses of the public and private paradigm, there has been widespread agreement among feminists that Western public and private spheres have been gendered. Discourses predicated on this binary, such as civil society theory, presume the gendering of social/political spaces. Western civil society discourse, a number of feminist theorists have argued, is therefore gendered.[28] In this chapter, I analyze the appropriateness of the assumptions of the civil society model for the historically and culturally specific case of Lebanon.

For purposes of this chapter, I outline five key assumptions of civil society theory that must be challenged in terms of Lebanon.[29] Civil society theorists have presumed, first, that civil society, and therefore nationhood and democracy, requires a division of social life into dichotomous spheres, public (governmental) and private (nongovernmental) spheres.[30] Second, these theorists have argued that democratic nationhood requires the autonomy of these spheres based on an assumption that the state is inclined toward autocracy.[31] They assume that democratic impulses of a nation are generated in the nongovernmental sphere or in the tension between public and private spheres. Third, civil society theorists have assumed democratic nationhood requires a differentiation of structures, modes of operations, and idioms of discourse in public and private spheres. Fourth, civil society theorists have presumed a tension between the binary poles: the private restrains the public; the public attempts to control the private. It is in this oppositionality that democratic opportunities for a nation are created according to civil society theory. Finally, civil society theorists have assumed the gender neutrality of civil society (and the nation and state). Counter to these presumptions of civil society theory, I argue that the binary between public and private assumed in the civil society model conflates multiple domains of social activity in such a way as to gloss gender issues, particularly by glossing the impact of patriarchy across social fields. Minimally, the binary becomes a triad when gender is taken into account: the public (governmental), the private (nongovernmental), and the domestic (kinship). Second, I argue that autonomy of spheres is a meaningless goal if uninformed by analysis of gendered domination. Antidemocratic forces have multiple sites of construction.[32] Patriarchy is an antidemocratic force. The patriarchal impetus to gendered and aged domination, found in the domestic sphere, is also found in public and private spheres.[33] Third, the differentiation among the public, private, and domestic has not been a social presumption in Lebanon. I argue that continuities of structure, modes of operation, and idioms of discourse in multiple spheres have been linked to systemic patriarchy in

Lebanon. Fourth, I suggest that in Lebanon, the oppositionality between public and private presumed by the civil society model has been mitigated by the continuities in patriarchal structures, modes of operation, and idioms in public, private, and domestic arenas.[34] For women, this has limited the productivity of the civil sphere as a constraint to the arbitrary exercise of patriarchal power in the state or domestic arenas. Fifth, I contend that civil society in Lebanon, as in the West, has been gendered.[35] Finally, I argue that the dynamics described and analyzed in this chapter have not been fixed, stable features of Lebanese society but the outcomes of specific historical processes—and therefore, comparative analyses to processes of nation-building and state-building with other Middle Eastern societies and other historical periods in Lebanon becomes crucial.

## LEBANESE CIVIL SOCIETY

Western scholars, according to Yahya Sadowski, have tended to regard Middle Eastern societies as incapable of producing civil societies.[37] Classical Orientalist scholars viewed Middle Eastern states as being too strong. They portrayed Middle Eastern states as autocratic, despotic, in control of social resources and social activities. Classical Orientalists viewed Middle Eastern societies as too weak. They saw nongovernmental groups as too personalistic and inefficient. More recently, particularly in the wake of the Islamic revolution in Iran, Neo-Orientalist scholars, according to Sadowski, have viewed Middle Eastern states as too weak and societies as too strong. In particular Neo-Orientalists have stressed strong religious communalism as a deterrent to the development of civil society. Whether society or state has been too strong or too weak, civil society has not grown (and apparently cannot) on Middle Eastern social soils, according to classical and Neo-Orientalist scholars. The hopes for democracy in this region, from the classical and Neo-Orientalist reading of Middle Eastern history and culture, are nil.[38]

Few scholars have faulted the Lebanese state for being too strong. For Shils, the central reason that Lebanon was not a civil society was that primordial attachments, particularly to religious communities and kinship, superseded attachments to the nation and state.[39] Citizens prioritized their obligations to these subnational communities over and above those to the nation. Primordial communalism resulted in weak state institutions and obstructed the growth of civil society in the 1960s, according to Shils. In my earlier work, I argued that the description of Lebanon as sectarian communalist was an essentialized view of

Lebanese nationhood.[40] I argued that, in their local communities, persons in Lebanon created and used relationships across religious and ethnic boundaries for affective and instrumental purposes.[41] When dealing with formal public and private institutions, people used social ties across all sorts of social boundaries as they needed them.[42] Formal institutions, however, were often organized along sectarian lines and pressured persons to use their religious identity and their social relationships as political tools to gain access to resources and services. As Peteet describes for the Palestinian case, formal governmental and nongovernmental agencies exert critical power in authorizing and institutionalizing certain forms of domination.[43] In the Lebanese case, I argued that the viability of sectarian communities could not be explained only as a result of primordial attachments. Rather, sectarianism was structurally, institutionally, and politically constituted and reconstituted daily as Lebanese encountered the necessity and efficacy of deploying sectarian identities socially, politically, and economically in a state that inscribed sectarianism into its foundational social charter. This social charter was itself the legacy of five hundred years of an Ottoman and then French rule, which had institutionalized sectarianism as the channel to membership in the political community.

I based my analysis on research in Lebanon starting in the late 1960s. The core research, begun in 1971, was in the urban working-class neighborhood of Camp Trad, in the Greater Beirut municipality of Burj Hammud. Burj Hammud in the early 1970s was primarily an urban working-class municipality in the Greater Beirut area. About 40 percent of the population were Armenian (mostly Orthodox, but also Catholic and Protestant). About another 40 percent were Lebanese Shi'a. The remaining 20 percent were Maronite, Roman Catholic, Greek Orthodox, Greek Catholic, Arab Protestant, Syrian Orthodox, Syrian Catholic, Sunni, Druze, 'Alawite. The population was also mixed in terms of nationalities: Lebanese, Syrian, Palestinian, Greek, Jordanian, Egyptian.

My observations in Burj Hammud were corroborated by observations of other social classes and regions of Lebanon. That Burj Hammud, in the 1970s, housed, in addition to Lebanese, relatively recently immigrated Palestinians, Syrians, Iraqis, Jordanians, Egyptians, and Armenians of all religious sects suggests that some of these patterns were not foreign to surrounding Arab countries. I would not, however, generalize an "Arab" pattern from this data. This earlier work, challenging the sectarian communalist view of Lebanese society, led me, early on, to argue that the public/private dichotomy did not accurately capture the organization of social life in Lebanon when gender was taken into account.[44]

## MULTIPLE SPHERES, NOT BINARY

To the degree civil society theorists have based democracy on having a private sphere systematically differentiated from the state, democracy has been based on the necessity of a social binary—the public and private. This binary has been misleading, particularly in relation to gender issues. The shifting uses of *private* (or domestic) by scholars to mean nongovernmental agencies and also kinship, family, and marriage has had the effect of glossing the dynamics of patriarchy. *Public* has been used to mean governmental, as well as any nondomestic activity. Compounding the confusion, according to Carole Pateman, has been the ambiguous uses of *civil society* to mean both the whole of those societies with constitutional governments and one component of those social orders, the private, nongovernmental, sphere of "civil society."[45]

The origins of the public/private binary is historically linked to the emergence of the state and the attempts of state institutions to delineate domains of authority for themselves. The assumed necessity of differentiation between public and private has perhaps been spurred by the expansion of the state and an overprivileging of the agency of the state. What counts as public and as private historically has and continues to shift, however. Overprivileging of state agency and the almost exclusive focus on the public/private dichotomy by political theorists has led to a glossing of structures of domination in other spheres. Not apprehending the multiple sites in which antidemocratic forces are produced, statist theorists have been particularly blind to gender domination.

For purposes of this discussion, I stabilize (temporarily) the terms *public* to mean governmental institutions, *private* to mean nongovernmental agencies, and *domestic* to mean kinship, in order to argue the specificity of their relationship in Lebanon.[46] The binary between public and private transforms, minimally, into a triad: public (state), private (nongovernmental activity) and domestic (kinship). I propose this triadic distinction strategically to foreground gender-related issues. I do not intend to suggest, however, that this captures the organization of social life in Lebanon, nor do I propose a fixed description of Lebanese social order. Indeed, social life, I suggest, is not only organized by multiple spheres, but the spheres continually shift and transform.

Earlier I argued against Shils' sectarian communalist model of Lebanon. I now add a concern over his essentializing and overprivileging primordial attachments. His model presumes a single-site construction of "primordial" attachments, the domestic sphere that extends into religious communities. I argue that social life in Lebanon (perhaps in most societies) is organized by multiple, shifting social spheres. Primordial attachments are constructed at multiple sites and take multiple forms. In particular, I argue for the multiple-site construction of patriarchy and its concomitant de-privileging of women and juniors.

## RELATIONAL SPHERES AND GENDERED DOMINATION

Civil society theorists have assumed democratic impulses are generated in the private sphere or in the tension between the private and public spheres. The overprivileging of the private sphere as a source of democracy and the exclusive focus on the public/private binary has been made possible by the glossing of gendered antidemocratic forces and the multiple sites in which they are constructed.[47] Patriarchy, in particular, has been a primary antidemocratic force neglected by most civil society theorists.

I define *patriarchy* as the privileging of male and elder rights and the use of kinship structures, morality, and idioms to legitimate male and elder privilege. This definition of patriarchy and its uses in Lebanon differ from Carole Pateman's definition and uses of patriarchy in her critique of liberal theories of civil society. For Pateman, patriarchy is fraternal. She argues, "Modern civil society is not structured by kinship and the power of fathers; in the modern world, women are subordinated to men *as men*, or to men as a fraternity."[48] The distinction between Pateman's fraternal patriarchy and my kin-based patriarchy is crucial for understanding patriarchy in Lebanon. I stress the structural, moral, and idiomatic location of patriarchy in kinship in order to clarify its operation in the Lebanese context. That is, in Lebanon, patriarchy is forceful, in part, because of its rooting in the family system. Patriarchy in Lebanon, however, is constructed not only in family dynamics, but also in political, economic, and social dynamics in private and public spheres. To appreciate these dynamics it is productive to focus on relative relationality, rather than on relative autonomy, of spheres.

The model of civil society has assumed the relative autonomy of public and private as arenas that rely on but have relatively independent means of restraining each other. The assumption of autonomy between civil society and state, as Pateman argues, assumes the irrelevance of kinship, family, and marriage to politics and civil life. The assumption of their irrelevance made possible the "perception of civil society as a post-patriarchal social order."[49] In Lebanon, the structures, modes of operation, and idioms of kin-based patriarchy are pervasive. In the Lebanese cultural ideal, patriarchy has been accompanied and supported by cultural values of patrilineality and patrilocality. The family has been a set of values, expectations, cultural rules, and psychodynamics, central to which has been the view that kin relationships are key to all social, political, and economic life. Family has been considered the basic unit of society. A person's fundamental sense of self, political identity, security, and access to social resources and services has been generated from family relations. Reverence of family has brought with it expectations of deference to family elders, particularly male elders.[50]

The patriarchal organization of domestic relations has given males and elders (including female elders) considerable domestic power over female and junior (including male junior) family members. Though there is empirical variability, male household heads, generally, have been socially expected to be in charge of household affairs and the behavior and well-being of their household members. Arranged marriages have not been not uncommon in the urban and rural working classes. In middle and elite social classes, persons have had more say (often complete control) in their spousal choice, but usually parental approval has been sought and expected. Single people, even if educated and employed, usually have lived with their parents. Men as well as women prioritized kin relations and received their primary identity, resources, and social agency from family membership. Recognizing men and elders' embedding in familial relationships further challenges the falsifying gendered paradigm of public/private spheres. Women and juniors have been expected to continue respecting and deferring to family elders, even after marriage. The degree of women and juniors' subordination often has been affected by material considerations. Given economic constraints and gender-linked earning power, women have been more financially dependent than men. Women, like men, usually have retained primary identification with their families of origin who continued to be responsible for them, life-long, regardless of their marriages. Since brothers have been likely to live longer than fathers, uncles, or grandfathers, they (especially elder brothers) have often exercised considerable authority over sisters (and younger brothers).[51] Women have been encouraged to identify with brothers and fathers as primary sources of security. As Andre´ Chedid so simply stated, "[E]ven when you're grown up, you're still accountable to your family, to your father and brother."[52] Security has been purchased through subordination, however. To insure the protection of kin males, women have had to defer to them.

To argue the power of patriarchy as an antidemocratic force that has multiple sites of construction and to argue the rooting of patriarchy in kinship is not to stabilize either patriarchy or kinship as essentialized entities. Part of my rejection of Shils' sectarian communalist view of Lebanon was his essentialization of religious communities. A similar essentializing of patriarchy and kinship as stable givens determining social arrangements in the Arab world advances us no further.[53]

Patriarchy in Lebanon has not been a stable construct nor a stable set of relationships. The fluidity of patriarchy and kinship in Lebanon has been a part of the power of patriarchal institutions. Brothers, fathers, and extended male patrilineal kin often have not protected sisters and juniors. Younger brothers at times have come to have more familial authority than older brothers, particularly if they have gained more wealth or political influence. Maternal kin, if wealthy or powerful, can have more domestic authority than paternal kin. Elder male kin might defer to younger kin. Economic, social, and political circumstances have shaped the specificities of domestic power dynamics. Yet, despite the variability, the idioms and moralities of patriarchal kinship continually have been invoked to legitimate shifting social arrangements. And despite the variability, gendered and aged domestic domination were culturally and socially normative.

In addition, family and kinship have also been fluid constructs. Contrary to the presumptions of functionalist accounts of kinship, the family in Lebanon has not been a fixed bounded entity.[54] Given the ethnic, religious, and national diversity of Lebanon and the disruptions of wars, migrations, and political persecutions, normative family forms were contested, and empirical household forms were complex.[55] Definitions of family boundaries shifted depending on perceived needs, shifting structural situations, memberships, and alliances. While boundary shifts did not always follow normative codes, the language used to justify new boundaries often did. That is, people justified the new family boundaries and relationships in culturally normative terms. "This is my real family." "This is my real brother." The domestic sphere in Lebanon has been, therefore, a fluid, shifting space characterized by gendered and agist domination. It was one of the multiple sites for construction of patriarchy. For women and juniors, domestic relations relied on the conflation of love, affection, security, identity, and sense of selfhood with relationships of subordination and domination.[56] Patriarchal moralities have not been simply produced in the family and reactively reproduced in public and private arenas, however. Patriarchal structures, modes of operation, and idioms have been as actively produced and reproduced in public and private as well as in domestic spheres. To the degree that civil society theorists claim that the creation of autonomous spheres of social activity is necessary for a democracy, they must address the role of patriarchy in undermining such autonomy. In Lebanon, the arbitrary exercises of patriarchal domestic power, which were enacted systematically also in private and public spheres, were immediate and distinctive sources of domination for women.

## CONTINUITIES OF STRUCTURES,
## MODES OF OPERATION, AND IDIOMS OF DISCOURSE

The civil society model has assumed differentiation of structures, modes of operation, and idioms of discourse in public and private spheres. The civil society theorists assume it is this differentiation that has fostered democratic possibilities. Gendered domination is assumed to be irrelevant to civil society, because, as Pateman argued, civil society was assumed to be postpatriarchal. The assumptions of difference of structure, modes of operation, and idioms of discourse glosses similarities of structures, operations, and idioms which are crucial to women. I contend that patriarchy in Lebanon has multiple sites of construction. The continuities of patriarchal structures, modes of operation, and idioms of discourse in the different social spheres are expressions of the power of patriarchy in not only the domestic but also the public and private spheres.

In civil society theory, the private (nongovernmental, nonkin) has been assumed to be voluntary, competitive, recruiting membership by diverse criteria, generally acting for the benefit of limited constituencies, and lacking legitimate coercion to mandate compliance. The public (governmental) has been assumed to be compulsory, monolithic, universally recruiting membership undifferentiated by primordial criteria, acting on behalf of the political whole community, and monopolizing legitimate coercion to mandate compliance. Distinctions among public, private, and domestic are made in Lebanon. Social life is not seamless. The distinctions, however, are not premised on the notion that the spheres of social life are bounded, autonomous, utterly differentiated entities. The boundaries between and among spheres of social activity in Lebanon have been porous, elastic, and shifting.[57]

First, the state has reinforced the control of sectarian institutions over citizens, making membership in a religious sect a legal requirement for citizenship. Since representation is formally on the basis of religious sects, each citizen has borne his religious membership on his national identification card. Additionally, the Lebanese state has delegated control over matters of personal status to the seventeen formally recognized religious sects. Sponsoring religious institutions' control over matters of marriage, divorce, child custody, and inheritance and providing few civil alternatives, the states has pressured persons to submit to the control of religious authorities on these matters. Given the male dominance of religious institutions and the tendency of religious institutions to support patriarchal family structures, this has disadvantaged women. This has created a series of intermediaries between the state and citizens—state-sanctioned sectarian intermediaries to control citizens.[58] Membership in a religious sect is therefore not voluntary as the civil society model presumes, but a practical requirement of citizenship in Lebanon. The state used its coercive forces to mandate compliance with the rules of sectarian (patriarchal) authority.

Second, rather than building effective public institutions, the Lebanese state has invested public monies in private institutions that, in the civil society model, would have been independent of the state. Schools, social services; social welfare organizations; cultural, recreational, and social groups relied in part on public funds for their functioning. This has made many of those groups dependent on the state for their existence, undermining their autonomy.

Third, and most crucial, has been the systematic deployment of structures, modes of operation, and idioms of patriarchal kinship in public and private spheres of social activity. There have been multiple mediations between patriarchal kinship and public/private spheres. Kinship has been central in all spheres of social activity in Lebanon. Given the weakness of the state, the perceived externalness of state institutions, and the state's deference to centers of power outside the state, persons experienced their security as resting on kin relations. The strength of kinship has been evidenced by the use of kinship idioms to create short- and long-term relationships. Persons in Lebanon, in all social classes and religious/ethnic communities, regularly sanctioned relationships by referring to them in kin terms. Persons called each other "brothers," "sisters," "uncle/aunt/niece/nephew," "cousins." In referring to each other by kin terms of address, they evoked the expectations and obligations of kinship for instrumental and affective purposes. Using idiomatic kinship, they incorporated extended kin, in-laws, and nonkin into familial boundaries, speaking of them as family.

Such incorporations were not perceived as disruptions to family boundaries and life, but continuous with them. They were also perceived to be and were enacted as continuous with kinship morality. Not only has it been a linguistic elision that has made patriarchy relevant to public and private spheres. Rather, it has been the transportation of specific domestic patriarchal relationalities from domestic to public and private spheres that made the idiomatic usages so powerful. Political leaders pulled their actual relatives into public offices. Lay people expected their relatives in public offices to act as kin to them, rather than as public officials. The fluidity of kinship provided a lubricant for social relationships outside domestic spheres. Transported with the idiomatic uses of kinship, then, were the structures, modes of operation, and idioms of patriarchy.

The public and private not only were recipients of domestic patriarchy but were sites for the production of patriarchal structures, modes of operation, and idioms. Patriarchal modes of operation were produced in the public and private spheres. The distribution of resources on the basis of highly personalistic, face-to-face relationships grounded in kinship reinforced patriarchy in public and private spheres. They encouraged the expectation that citizen and civic rights would be conditional on the particular set of relationships one could muster.[59] The privileging of males and elders was a foundational principle of both public and private spheres. Political leaders privileged the rights of males and elders over familial females and juniors in distribution of resources or in the adjudication of legal matters. They often deferred to family heads in matters related to members of their families. They were often more willing to give services to women and juniors if they were represented by their men and elders.

Thus public, private, and domestic spheres in Lebanon have been all marked by patriarchy. That is, specific patriarchal relationships, morality, modes of operation, and idioms have been socially acceptable, expected, and ascendant in each arena. Given the centrality of kinship and kinship idioms and the multiple sites in which patriarchal kinship has been constructed and operated, patriarchy has contributed to forms of domination in public and private, as well as domestic spheres. These continuities among public, private, and domestic structures, modes of operation, and idioms have been, I argue, constitutive of patriarchy and politics in Lebanon.

## DEMOCRACY OUT OF OPPOSITIONALITY?

Given the fluidity among public, private, and domestic arenas, the structures, modes of operation, and idioms upholding patriarchy in Lebanon have flowed relatively freely across the boundaries of state, civil society, and kinship. From a woman's point of view, the public and private reinforced domestic domination. The state and civil society not only did not restrain the arbitrary exercises of patriarchal power but were themselves sites for the construction of patriarchy. Women in Lebanon often have not experienced civil society as a democratic recourse but as another site in which to struggle against gendered and aged domination. That is, the oppositionality of public, private, domestic spheres presumed in the civil society model has been ameliorated in relationship to women because of systemic patriarchy.

The lack of oppositionality and the fluidity of boundaries among public, private, and domestic spheres, however, has not been, I believe, the central problem for women. It is that all arenas have been marked by patriarchy.[60] That is, it is not the absence of autonomy of spheres, but the presence of patriarchy in all spheres.

While I would not argue that state and civil spheres in Lebanon have been domesticated, there were significant continuities in structure, modes of operation, and idioms among public, private, and domestic spheres. From the perspective being developed here, this is not surprising, because, as I have argued, systemic patriarchy linked spheres of social activity. Since patriarchal relationality flowed mutually among family, civil society, religious institutions, economy, and the state, the priviledging of males and elders was mutually reinforced in multiple arenas.

## GENDERED STATE AND CIVIL SOCIETY

Neither state nor civil society has been gender neutral in Lebanon or in any other society, I would argue. Patriarchal structures, modes of operation, and idioms flowed among public, private, and domestic spheres in culturally acceptable ways. Patriarchal family relations flowed into the state, and political relationships became familial, patriarchal. Political relationships were justified in the idiom of kinship. The *zaim* (political leader, political patron) was seen as a family member, an honorary family patriarch. Political leaders often presented themselves as the senior patriarchs of extended political families, and the loyalty, deference, and service due them was that of the head of the family. Patron-client relationships worked precisely because of the expectation that the morality and commitments of kinship upheld in public and private spheres.

Officials in nongovernmental public agencies or in the economy similarly preferred working through males and elders, often requiring women and juniors to seek the mediation of men, particularly senior men of their families. *Wasta* (mediation, networks) contact was required for almost all social processes. The intervention of males and elders was usually more effective than that of women or juniors. From the highest level of state to the neighborhood level, Lebanese expected and were expected to privilege patriarchal kin-based (and patriarchal idiomatic kin) relationships.

State officials were expected to act upon personal/familial obligations in their official roles. Political leaders have priviledged their own kin relationships in the state. They have privilege kinship as a principle of organizing their followings and distributing resources to their followings. Political leaders have favored direct contact with male family heads, allocation of services and resources to and through heads of families, and mobilizing clients through family heads. State officials often set up idiomatic patriarchal relations with those seeking their services.

Citizens expected the demands of personal relationships to take precedence over civil procedure. Persons needing services, protections, or resources from political leaders have found themselves best served when they have used family connections to reach political leaders. They have known they were best served vis-à-vis political leaders when they could present themselves as a unified family block, offering the leader a strong following. While often such family unity has been not possible, the recognition of these dynamics among those in Lebanon has served to reinforce family structures, moralities, and idioms. The conflation of the rules of public, civil, and domestic operations nurtured the production of patriarchy in multiple sites.

## HISTORICAL, NOT ESSENTIAL, FEATURES

The fluidity among social spheres; the continuity of structures, modes of operation, and idioms among social spheres; and the reproduction of patriarchy in multiple sites have been characteristic of the politics and patriarchy in Lebanon in the contemporary period. Lebanon's is a historically and culturally specific form of patriarchy. The patriarchy I found in Lebanon, unlike Pateman's fraternal patriarchy, has been based in gendered and agist domination justified by the structures, modes of operation, and idioms of kinship.

Patriarchy, like civil society, class, and state, is a historically specific construct. Patriarchy not only has multiple sites of construction in any particular society but is organized in around different social structures, modes of operations, and idioms from society to society. Patriarchy is useful to describe such different systems of gendered inequality but must be historically situated.

The specific patriarchal dynamics I have described are not essentialized, fixed features of Lebanese culture, Arab culture, Islam, or the minds or world views of the people involved. Historically and culturally specific conditions have given rise to the circumstances that have empowered and institutionalized these patriarchal patterns in Lebanon and the sites on which they are constructed. The Ottoman state used indigenous patriarchal institutions to undermine local state building by bolstering the powers of religious institutions over their members.[62] French, British, American, and Russian powers in the nineteenth and twentieth centuries played religious communities off against each other. The French mandate, after the fall of the Ottoman Empire following World War I, formalized patriarchal sectarianism in the Lebanese Constitution.[63]

The Lebanese elite both inherited this legacy and participated in its creation. The elite supported the institutionalization of religious sectarianism in the system of governance providing a further ground for patriarchal controls. They used state resources to build their personal power outside the state, further decentering the state and reinforcing citizens' experiences of the state as distant and alien. Patronage, *wasta* (brokerage), personal networks, and relationships of mutual obligation became and remained pivotal in the allocation of state resources from the top down and in gaining access to state resources from the bottom up. These relationships, regardless of location and religious sect, often directly or idiomatically built on kinship.

The frequent use of actual or idiomatic kinship relations and morality reinscribed patriarchal patterns in the Lebanese social life in public, private, and domestic arenas. Weak from inception and by design, the state elite made implementation of patriarchal modes of operation, structures, and idioms necessary to political survival in Lebanon. These dynamics among public, civil, and domestic spheres in Lebanon, like Western political and social dynamics, are the products of specific historical processes.

## CONCLUSIONS

I have argued that the civil society model has deployed Western constructs with a double gender bias. The problems with the gendering of civil society model are not Lebanon's alone. As Carole Pateman observed, the original social contract created a patriarchal civil society with the separation of public and private as constitutive of patriarchal liberalism.[64] Western civil society was patriarchal from conception. While Western feminists have critiqued the masculinist assumptions of the civil society model, these assumptions have continued to be applied to Third World countries. The model does not account for the power of patriarchy as an antidemocratic force in Western or in Third World nations.

I caution, however, against overprivileging or essentializing patriarchy as a source of domination. As everywhere, there are multiple systems of domination in the Middle East (gender, class, race, tribe, ethnicity). I have focused on in this paper patriarchy because an analysis of gender and civil society must take account of patriarchy, because of the centrality of patriarchy in Lebanon, and because patriarchy has been overlooked in most analyses of civil society.

There is nothing inherent or unchanging in Lebanese culture that disallows the development of democratic nationhood, whether democratic nationhood is achieved through the construction of civil society or alternative social arrangements. As such, public, private, and domestic arenas continue to be sites of struggle, contestation, and transformation. Lebanon, like most Third World nations and states, is relatively young. It had not had time to grow its institutions when Shils proclaimed its dysfunctionality. Shortly thereafter it became the prime site for Arab-Israeli battles and ultimately succumbed to a war that has been both regional and civil.

That democratic nationhood should be participatory I do not doubt. What constitutes participation in the making (imagined and concrete) of a nation, however, can take many forms. The Lebanese, I would argue, are highly involved in the making of their nation through numerous venues. Contestation over Lebanese nationalism and the evocation of the nation as an actively pursued vision were paramount in the Civil War through literary[65] and material means.[66] Given the small size of Lebanon and the highly personalized character of political leadership, lay people, even the relatively disempowered, have not been many steps removed from social networks leading them to sites of power.[67] That family dynamics have woven together "public," "private," and "domestic" spheres has enhanced the access of the ordinary citizen to national and state leaders.

Whether citizens are involved in the project of making the nation is not the issue here, however. The issue is the gendered nature of the involvement and the gendered bias in the theoretical constructs that have been used to analyze their involvement. In Lebanon, patriarchy has woven through the various sites in which nationhood has been constructed systematically biasing the state, the nation, civil society, and the very dynamics of citizenship in favor of males and elders.[68] That the debates on civil society have reflected so little on this structurally enduring form of domination is a result of the double gender bias in theory.

This account of Lebanon does not lead me to argue for the separation of the public, private, and domestic. The connection of social spheres is not only inevitable but also socially necessary.[69] What I argue for[70] is a notion of democracy based on the elimination of gendered (as well as other forms of) domination. I have argued that civil society remains a site of domination of women and therefore a site for the construction of antidemocratic structures, modes of operation, and idioms. Without recognition of the dynamics of gendered domination, scholars and activists concerned with democratic nationhood will devise a liberty blind to gendered injustice.

## BIBLIOGRAPHY

Anderson, Benedict. 1983. *Imagined Communities: Reflections on the Origin and Spread of Nationalism*. London: Verso.

Arat, Yeşim. 1996. "On Gender and Citizenship in Turkey." *Middle East Reports*, no.198, vol. 26, no. 1: 28–31.

Barakat, Halim. 1985. "The Arab Family and the Challenge of Social Transformation." In *Women and the Family in the Middle East: New Voices of Change*, Elizabeth W. Fernea, ed. Austin: University of Texas Press.

Benn, Stanley I. 1983. "Private and Public Morality: Clean-Living and Dirty Hands." In *Public and Private in Social Life*, ed. S. I. Benn and G. F. Gaus, eds. London: Croom Helm.

Benn, Stanley I., and Gerald F. Gaus. 1983a. "The Public and the Private: Concepts and Action." In *Public and Private in Social Life*, S. I. Benn and G. F. Gaus, eds. London: Croom Helm.

———. 1983b. "The Liberal Conception of the Public and the Private." In *Public and Private in Social Life*. S. I. Benn and G. F. Gaus, eds. London: Croom Helm.

———. 1983c. "Private and Public Morality: Clean-Living and Dirty Hands." In *Public and Private Social Life*, S. I. Benn and G. F. Gaus, eds. London: Croom Helm.

Chedid, Andre. 1989. *The Return to Beirut*. London: Serpent's Tail.

Cheriat, Boutheina. 1996. "Gender, Civil Society and Citizenship in Algeria." *Middle East Reports*, 198, vol. 26, no. 1: 22–26.

Chodorow, Nancy. 1974. "Family Structure and Feminine Personality." In *Women, Culture, and Society*, Michelle Zimbalist Rosaldo and L. Lamphere, eds. Stanford: Stanford University Press.

Dwyer, Kevin. 1991. *Arab Voices: The Human Rights Debate in the Middle East*. Berkeley: University of California Press.

Eisenstein, Hester. 1983. *Contemporary Feminist Thought*. Boston: G. K. Hall.

Elshtain, Jean Bethke. 1981. *Public Man, Private Woman: Women in Social and Political Thought*. Princeton: Princeton University Press.

Fuller, Ann. 1966. *Buarij: Portrait of a Lebanese Muslim Village*. Cambridge: Harvard University Press.

Giacamen, Rita, I. Jad, and P. Johnson. 1996. "For the Public Good? Gender and Social Citizenship in Palestine." *Middle East Reports*, no. 198, vol. 26, no. 1: 11–17.

Giddens, Anthony. 1987. *The Nation-State and Violence*. Berkeley: University of California Press.

Harik, Iliya F. 1968. *Politics and Change in a Traditional Society: Lebanon, 1711–1845*. Princeton: Princeton University Press.

Hartsock, Nancy C. M. 1983. *Money, Sex, and Power: Towards a Feminist Historical Materialism*. New York: Longman.

Hatem, Mervat. 1986. "The Enduring Alliance of Nationalism and Patriarchy in Muslim Personal Status Laws: The Case of Modern Egypt." *Feminist Issues* 6, no. 1: 19–43.

Hernes, Helga Maria. 1987. *Welfare State and Woman Power. Essays in State Feminism*. Oslo: Norwegian University Press.

Hijab, Nadia. 1988. *Womanpower: The Arab Debate on Women at Work*. Cambridge: Cambridge University Press.

Hudson, Michael. 1968. *The Precarious Republic: Political Modernization in Lebanon.* New York: Random House.
Jagger, Alison. 1983. *Feminist Politics and Human Nature.* Totowa, NJ: Rowman & Allanheld.
Jayawardena, Kumari. 1988. *Feminism and Nationalism in the Third World.* London: Zed.
Jones, Kathleen B. 1993. *Compassionate Authority: Democracy and the Representation of Women.* New York: Routledge.
Joseph, Suad. 1997. "The Public/Private—The Imagined Boundary in the Imagined Nation/State/Community: The Lebanese Case." *Feminist Review*, no. 57 (Autumn): 73–92.
———. 1996. "Gender and Citizenship in Middle Eastern States." *Middle East Reports*, no. 198, vol. 26, no. 1: 4–10.
———. 1994a. "Brother/Sister Relationships: Connectivity, Love and Power in the Reproduction of Arab Patriarchy." *American Ethnologist* 21, no. 1: 50–73.
———. 1994b. "Problematizing Gender and Relational Rights: Experiences from Lebanon." *Social Politics* 1, no. 3 (Fall): 271–85.
———. 1993a. "Gender and Civil Society: An Interview with Suad Joseph." By Joe Stork. *Middle East Reports*, no. 183, vol. 23, no. 4 (July-August): 22–26.
———. 1993b. "Connectivity and Patriarchy among Urban Working Class Arab Families in Lebanon." *Ethos* 21, no. 4 (December): 452–84.
———. 1990. "Working the Law: A Lebanese Working Class Case." In *The Politics of Law in the Middle East*, Daisy Dwyer, ed. South Hadley, MA: J. F. Bergin.
———. 1983. "Working Class Women's Networks in a Sectarian State: A Political Paradox." *American Ethnologist* 10, no. 1: 1–22.
———. 1978. "Muslim-Christian Conflicts in Lebanon. A Perspective on the Evolution of Sectarianism." In *Muslim-Christian Conflicts: Economic, Political and Social Origins*, Suad Joseph and B. L. K. Pillsbury, eds. Boulder: Westview Press.
———. 1975. "Urban Poor Women in Lebanon: Does Poverty Have Public and Private Domains?" Paper presented at Association of Arab-American UniversityGraduates Annual Meeting. Chicago.
———. Forthcoming. "Women between Nation and State in Lebanon." In *Between Women and Nation: Feminism and Global Issues*, Norma Alarcon, C. Kaplan, and M. Moallem, eds. Durham: Duke University Press.
Kandiyoti, Deniz. 1993. "Strategies for Feminist Scholarship in the Middle East." Paper presented at the Middle East Studies Association Annual Meeting, Research Triangle Park, NC.
———. 1991. "The End of Empire: Islam, Nationalism and Women in Turkey." In *Women, Islam and the State*, Deniz Kandiyoti, ed. London: MacMillan.
Keane, John. 1988. a*Democracy and Civil Society.* London: Verso.
———. 1988b. "Despotism and Democracy: The Origins and Development of the Distinction Between Civil Society and the State." In *Civil Society and the State*, John Keane, ed. London: Verso.

Kohli, Atul. 1988. *India's Democracy: An Analysis of Changing State-Society Relations*. Princeton: Princeton University Press.

Kondo, Dorinne. 1990. *Crafting Selves: Power, Gender and Discourses of Identity in a Japanese Workplace*. Chicago: University of Chicago Press.

Mayer, Ann Elizabeth. 1991. *Islam and Human Rights: Tradition and Politics*. Boulder: Westview Press.

Meo, Leila M. T. 1965. *Lebanon: Improbable Nation: A Study in Political Development*. Bloomington: Indiana University Press.

Nedelsky, Jennifer. 1993. "Reconceiving Rights as Relationship." *Review of Constitutional Studies* 1, no. 1: 1–26.

———. 1990. "Law, Boundaries, and the Bounded Self." *Representations* 30: 162–89.

———. 1989. "Reconceiving Autonomy: Sources, Thoughts and Possibilities." *Yale Journal of Law and Feminism* 1, no. 7: 7–36.

Ortner, Sherry B. 1974. "Is Female to Male as Nature Is to Culture?" In *Woman, Culture and Society*, M. Zimbalist Rosaldo and L. Lamphere, eds. Stanford: Stanford University Press.

Pateman, Carole. 1988. *The Sexual Contract*. Stanford: Stanford University Press.

———. 1983. "Feminist Critiques of the Public/Private Dichotomy." In *Public and Private in Social Life*, S. I. Benn and G. F. Gaus, eds. London: Croom Helm.

Phillips, Ann. 1991. *Engendering Democracy*. Cambridge: Polity Press.

Prothro, Edwin Terry. 1961. *Child Rearing in Lebanon*. Cambridge: Harvard University Press.

Rosaldo, M. Zimbalist, and L. Lamphere, eds. 1974. *Woman, Culture, and Society*. Stanford: Stanford University Press.

Sadowski, Yahya. 1993. "The New Orientalism and the Democracy Debate." *Middle East Reports* 183, vol. 23,.no. 4: 14–21, 40.

Said, Edward. 1983. *The Word, the Text, and the Critic*. Cambridge: Harvard University Press.

Seligman, Adam B. 1992. *The Idea of Civil Society*. New York: Free Press.

Sharabi, Hisham. 1988. *Neopatriarchy: A Theory of Distorted Change in Arab Society*. New York: Oxford University Press.

Shils, Edward. 1966. "Lebanon: The Development of a Political Society." In *Politics in Lebanon*, edited by Leonard Binder, ed. New York: John Wiley & Sons.

Spelman, Elizabeth. 1988. *Inessential Woman: Problems of Exclusion in Feminist Thought*. Boston: Beacon Press.

Springborg, Patricia. 1992. *Western Republicanism and the Oriental Prince*. Austin: University of Texas Press.

Suleiman, Michael. 1967. *Political Parties in Lebanon: The Challenge of a Fragmented Political Culture*. Ithaca: Cornell University Press.

Trinh, Minh-ha. 1989. *Woman, Native, Other*. Bloomington: Indiana University Press.

Walton, Anthony S. 1983. "Public and Private Interests: Hegel on Civil Society and the State." In *Public and Private in Social Life*, S. I. Benn and G. F. Gaus, eds. London: Croom Helm.

Williams, Judith R. 1966. *The Youth of Haouch El Harimi: A Lebanese Village.* Cambridge: Harvard University Press.

Young, Iris Marion. 1987. "Impartiality and the Civic Public. Some Implications of Feminist Critiques of Moral and Political Theory." In *Feminism as Critique*, Seyla Benhabib and D. Cornell, eds. Minneapolis: University of Minnesota Press.

———. 1983. "Is Male Gender Identity the Cause of Male Domination?" In *Mothering: Essays in Feminist Theory*, Joyce Trebilcot, ed. Totowa, NJ: Rowman & Allanheld.

Yuval-Davis, Nira and F. Anthias, eds. 1989. *Woman-Nation-State.* London: MacMillan.

Zubaida, Sami. 1989. *Islam, the People and the State: Essays on Political Ideas and Movements in the Middle East.* London: Routledge.

## NOTES

1. Shils, 1966, p. 2.
2. Sharabi 1988; Dwyer 1991.
3. Hijab 1988; Mayer 1991; Joseph 1993b; 1996; Kandiyoti 1993.
4. Sadowski, 1993, p. 15.
5. Keane 1988a; Seligman 1992.
6. Kohli 1988.
7. Anderson 1983; Göçek, this volume.
8. Gelvin, this volume; Hanioğlu, this volume.
9. Sadowski 1993; Seligman 1992.
10. Said 1983, p. 226.
11. See Cooke's use of humanist nationalism, this volume.
12. See Peteet, this volume.
13. Pateman 1988; Phillips 1991; Young 1987.
14. Hatem 1986.
15. Cheriet 1996.
16. Arat 1996; Kandiyoti 1991.
17. Giacamen, Jad, and Johnson 1996.
18. Jayawardena 1988; Yuval-Davis and Anthias 1989; Joseph 1996.
19. Elshtain 1981; Hernes 1987; Young 1987; Pateman 1988; Phillips 1991; Jones 1993.
20. Young 1987; Pateman 1988; Nedelsky 1989.
21. Göçek, this volume.
22. Joseph 1997.
23. Ortner 1974, pp. 67–87; 1974; Rosaldo and Lamphere 1974.
24. Jagger 1983; Hartsock 1983.
25. Eisenstein 1983; Young 1987; Spelman 1988; Pateman 1988.
26. Nedelsky 1989; Trinh 1989.
27. Kondo 1990; Nedelsky 1990; Young 1993.
28. Pateman 1988; Nedelsky 1989; Young 1987.
29. Benn 1983c, 155–81; Benn and Gaus 1983a; 1983b; Giddens 1987; Keane 1988a; 1988b; Seligman 1992.

30. Göçek, this volume.

31. Peteet, this volume.

32. See Armbrust (this volume), Limbert (this volume), and Balaghi (this volume) for a similar argument. A fuller account of antidemocratic forces in Lebanon (and elsewhere) would have to take into account dynamics of domination based on ethnic, racial, religious, regional, and national groupings as well. For purposes of this chapter, I limit my discussion to gender.

33. Sharabi 1988.

34. See Peteet, this volume, for Palestinian parallels.

35. Pateman 1988.

36. Göçek, this volume.

37. Sadowski 1993.

38. Springborg 1992; Sadowski 1993.

39. Shils 1966.

40. Joseph 1978, pp. 63–98.

41. Joseph 1983.

42. Joseph 1990, pp. 143–60.

43. Peteet, this volume.

44. Joseph 1975.

45. Pateman 1988.

46. I use *public* to refer not to the nation/state but to governmentalities—the institutions of public decision making, appropriation and allocation of resources, and management and control of the behavior of those within the political boundaries of the state. I am indebted to Smadar Lavie for suggesting that I clarify this distinction.

47. One could also add the glossing of antidemocratic forces based on race, class, ethnicity, nationality, and sexual orientation as well here.

48. Pateman 1988, 3.

49. Ibid., 10.

50. Joseph 1993b.

51. Joseph 1994b, pp. 271–85.

52. Chedid 1989, p. 73.

53. Sharabi 1988; Barakat 1985, 27–48.

54. Prothro 1961; Fuller 1966; Williams 1966.

55. There were many household forms: nuclear, joint, extended, duo-focal, single-headed.

56. Joseph 1994a.

57. The boundaries between public, private, and domestic in Western nation states, I would argue, are also more fluid in practice than public political discourse would suggest.

58. Joseph, forthcoming.

59. Joseph 1990 and 1993a.

60. Sharabi 1988.

61. Harik 1968.

62. Meo 1965.

63. Suleiman 1967; Hudson 1968.

64. Pateman 1988, p. 12.

65. Cooke, this volume; Chedid 1989.
66. Joseph 1978.
67. Joseph 1990.
68. Joseph 1993a and forthcoming.
69. Walton 1983, pp. 249–66; Young 1987; Nedelsky 1993.
70. Like Cooke, this volume.

# PART III

# *Cultural Representation*

# CHAPTER 8

# The Iranian as
# Spectator and Spectacle:
# Theater and Nationalism in the
# Nineteenth Century

## Shiva Balaghi

### THE HOUSE OF SPECTACLE: THEATER AND
### REPRESENTATION IN NINETEENTH-CENTURY IRAN

After eating dinner, the sun was still up, and we went to the theater
(*tamashah-khanah*) [literally, the "house of spectacle"]. There were
many people in the streets. When we arrived at the theater, we
ascended many steps, passed through the lobby, and sat in the box in
front of the space where they perform plays. It is a large theater, one
of the structures of the Emperor Nicholas. It has six levels, and in each
level there were many women and men. There was a large chandelier
hanging from the middle of the theater. . . . The curtain went up and a
strange world appeared.[1]

This description by Nasir al-Din Shah-i Qajar (r. 1848–96) recounts his
evening at the theater in Moscow in 1290/1873, at the outset of a journey that would take him through Russia, Prussia, Germany, Belgium,
and England. The shah's journal documents the details of most of his
outings, but the theater was clearly of special interest to him, and discussions of it take up much space in his journal. When he was not en
route by boat or train, he seems to have visited the theater, the ballet, or
the opera nightly. Little evaded his keen eye. He carefully noted the
lighting of the stage, the orchestra that played throughout the performance from a section beneath the stage, and the actors who were
dressed in fantastic or realistic costumes. His travel journal, which was

printed and read in Iran, allowed him to share the spectacle of nineteenth-century Europe with his Iranian countrymen.[2]

The theater also offered the nineteenth-century European observer a vantage point from which to view Iran. In the late nineteenth century, European scholars of Iran discovered Persian theater. In his preface to *Théater Persan*, the first anthology of Persian drama to appear in a European language, A. Chodzko noted, "The Persians have dramas, spectacles, and a complete dramatic literature, that can astonish the Orientalists. We are astonished, that among all of us, among the great many scholars and tourists who study and observe the Orient, we know of no one who before us has reported on this literature that is so remarkable."[3] Chodzko introduced the European reader to the *taziyeh*, a form of popular religious theater likened by some to the passion plays of the European Middle Ages.[4] Through the nineteenth century, the *taziyeh* continued to be performed, yet Iranian theater was to undergo a major transformation with the creation of a new form of theater that was secular and nationalist by Mirza Fath 'Ali Akhundzadeh and Mirza Aqa Tabrizi. Their plays offer an example of the innovative use of culture by some of Iran's intellectuals seeking to define and thereby remedy Iran's internal woes in order to strengthen her in the face of European colonial incursions. The theater was a "spectacle house" in which the Iranians created representations of Iran and of "Farangistan" (Europe) as nations with distinct cultural boundaries. In return, these plays offered a new venue to the Orientalists who studied Iran.

The study of theater can elucidate aspects of the interrelationships of culture, colonialism, and nationalism. And for the historian seeking to integrate cultural and social history, the theater is particularly inviting, for as Raymond Williams noted, "dramatic forms have a real social history."[5] Though Williams admitted that drama has very different expressions within different historical and cultural contexts, the theater nevertheless retains an implicitly social quality as it entails not only the creation but also the transmission and reception of representations.[6]

## THE TRADITION OF POPULAR THEATER IN IRAN

One of the main attractions of studying the emergence of secular nationalist theater in Iran is that one can trace the creation, documentation, and reception of a new cultural form. Clearly one cannot fully understand a "new" cultural form without studying the "old" forms that preceded it. And before the rise of a secular, nationalist theater in the nineteenth century, Iran had an array of theatrical arts such as the *ruhowzi*, *arrusak-bazi*, *naqali*, *siyah-bazi*, and *taziyeh* that could best be described as popular theater.[7] Perhaps the best known of these forms of popular theater in Iran prior to the nineteenth century was the *taziyeh*, which were representations of religious scenes, primarily those revolving around the martyrdom of Hussein and Hasan, two Shi'ite imams.[8] The *taziyeh* flourished in the nineteenth century, both in its street festival form and in its magnificent stage representations that took place on especially constructed stages (*takiyahs*). A German diplomat/Orientalist included a photograph of a *taziyeh* production in his book, that captures the mystical aura of the plays that reenacted the martyrdom of Hussein and Hasan, Shi'ite imams. From a distant vantage point, we see the production taking place in a large circular room. The actors and the audience are indistinguishable from one another; only a thin stream of light from a hole in the ceiling illuminates the scene.[9]

On his trip to Iran, the indefatigable Lord Curzon experienced the *taziyeh* firsthand. In his *Persia and the Persian Question*, he described the occasion in his characteristically colorful prose:

> At the time of my visit Meshed was in one of its chronic spasms of religious excitement. The anniversaries of the martyrdom both of Hasan and the holy Imam were being commemorated. *Taziehs*, or religious plays, were being acted; the holy places were crowded to suffocation; and beaten tomtoms and clamored convocations made the night hideous. Judging from the noise that he made, there must have been some particularly holy personage living near my quarters in the British consulate; and freely did I anathematise this insufferable saint, as I lay awake at night listening to his long-drawn lamentations and plaintive howls.[10]

Indeed travelers to Iran had noted the *taziyeh*, but it was not until the late nineteenth century that the Europeans attempted a systematic study of these plays. In the preface to his *Théatre Persan*, Chodzko noted the absence of critical study of the *taziyeh* by Europeans. "This can be easily explained, " he wrote. A European has certain fixed ideas about the theater and matters relating to it. For example, it takes place in specially constructed buildings. One expects a certain "personnel du théâtre" such as the promoters and the actors. None of these can be found in Iran. Furthermore, the Persians lack a dramatic language. What drama the Persians had, Chodzko wrote, was completely different than that of the Europeans. And finally, he observed that the character of Persian drama was exclusively religious.[11]

Chodzko saw the lack of a theatrical tradition resembling the European style to be of major consequence. It was nothing less than evidence of the lack of civilization. He was heartened, he wrote, though amazed at the site of the Turkish Sultan walking down the Champs-Elysées and partaking in the fruits of French civilization. He viewed the travels of

Nasir al-Din Shah to Europe as a hopeful sign and remarked that his own copy of the Shah's *Ruznameh* was within sight as he wrote this preface. Though the Iranian writers had nothing by way of a substitute for the *taziyeh* as yet, he hoped that their increasing travels to Europe would remedy this situation.[12] Though Chodzko claimed to be introducing the *taziyeh* to the European readers for the first time, he was clearly not a fan of the art. In fact, he commented on the brief translation of a *taziyeh* that Gobineau included in his book, "In my view, the charm of the French style of the scholar/traveler sheds a light that brings life to the work, which when read in the original language" offers nothing to the European scholar that cannot be found in the mysteries of the Middle Ages.[13] What is of interest in the *taziyeh* for the history of art, he claimed, was the absolute religious conviction of the men involved in the productions. Men of riches were known to channel these energies in order to increase their religious and political influence by sponsoring *taziyeh* productions.[14]

Indeed *taziyeh* productions were often sponsored by the Qajar kings. I'timad al-Saltanah, the minister of publication and the head of the Translation Bureau (Dar al-Tarjumah) wrote an article on the building of a new state *takiyah*. An entire issue of a state-sponsored gazette, *Sharaf*, was devoted to the article and drawings of the structure.[15] I'timad al-Saltanah emphasized the largeness of the structure, enumerated on the specific building materials used in its construction, and estimated the total cost of the *takiyah* approached three hundred thousand tumans, though the great roof had yet to be built. When visiting the Gulistan Palace and its surrounding grounds, Curzon saw the *takiyah* in its finished form. he wrote of the infamous *takiyah*'s roof:

> At the further extremity of the Gulistan rises the extraordinary circular structure, the arched ribs and girders of whose open roof I had seen from a distance as I approached Tehran, rising above the low level of the housetops. . . . From the upper rim of the building rise the great arched and iron-bound traverses of the roof. It was originally intended to cover the whole with a dome, the Shah, it is said, having been so impressed with the Royal Albert Hall in London, as to long for the reproduction in Teheran; but the substructure was found to be inadequate to the burden. Accordingly, these spans were thrown across and awnings are stretched over them when the play is acted in the heat of day; the precise counterpart of the *velarium* of the Roman amphitheater.[16]

In the *Sharaf* article, I'timad al-Saltanah had expressed his hopes that future generations would view the building of the *takiyah* as a sign of the generosity and piety of Nasir al-Din Shah. Indeed, it appears that the rental of boxes in the *takiyah* was a source of revenue for the state.

Curzon noted that in 1888–89, the state derived 16,250 krans from these rentals, which was about 485.07 pounds sterling according to the exchange rates of that year.[17]

The year after the publication of Chodzko's anthology, Colonial Sir Lewis Pelly's English anthology of *taziyah*s was printed in London by William H. Allen, publishers to the India Office.[18] Pelly had served as secretary of legation and political resident in the Persian Gulf from 1862 until 1871 prior to his transfer to Rajputana. Pelly noted the impact of the *taziyah* on Iranians of all rank, "I was . . . struck by the effect produced upon all classes of society at the capital as they listened, day after day, to this unprecedently long tragedy. From the palace to the bazaar there was wailing and beating of breasts, and bursts of impassioned grief from scores of houses wheresoever a noble, or the merchants, or others were giving a tazia."[19] Pelly determined to inscribe this tradition and render it into English. "It so happened that I was acquainted with a Persian who had long been engaged as a teacher and prompter of actors. I arranged with this man that, assisted by some of his dramatic friends, he should gradually collect and dictate all the scenes of the Hasan and Husein tragedy."[20] Here we get a different sense of the *taziyah* from Chodzko's description. There does appear to be a "personnel du théâtre" attached to the *taziyah*, one whose cooperation Pelly enlisted in order to produce his book. After leaving Iran, Pelly turned over the project to A. N. Wollaston, a translator for the Indian Service with whom he corresponded regularly about the completion of the manuscript, primarily discussing matters of cost and speed of printing the book.[21]

A striking feature of Pelly's explanation of the *taziyah* is that it is *one* play. The European reader who was for the first time being introduced to the *taziyah* by Pelly would inevitably have the false impression that all across Iran, all *taziyah*s were one and the same and that Pelly had inscribed that "oral tradition" into a fixed text. He wrote:

> [T]his drama is singular. It is so in many respects. It is singular in its intolerable length, in the fact of the representation of it over many days, in its marvelous effects on the Mussulman audience, both male and female; in its curious mixture of hyperbole and archaic simplicity of language; and in the circumstance that the so-called unities of time and space are not only ignored, but abolished. . . . Mohammed appears on the scene at will . . . it seems to be a universal Here and a universal Now."[22]

Indeed, such consistency in the genre of *taziyah* hardly exists, either in contemporary productions or in historical ones. There was no unity of plot. Rather, various representations of events and characters from the Quran and the Bible were enacted in the *taziyah*. Furthermore, *taziyah* productions were very much contingent on place and context. Which is to say that local and contemperaneous politics were likely to enter into the scenario.

Chodzko and Pelly inscribed and translated the *taziyah* and offered it to the European consumers of Oriental cultural material. This cast of characters is, in itself, of import. Chodzko was on the faculty of the Collège de France when he wrote his anthology, but his interest in Iran began when he was the Russian consul in Rasht. Pelly was an officer of the Indian government who undertook literary studies in his spare time in the field. Their anthologies of the *taziyah* were more than simple literary studies. They were investigations of language, form, ritual, and religion. They were elements in the study of civilization, or the lack thereof, in the colonial world. As theater critiques, they noted the formatic difference of Iranian drama as digressions from the civilized norms, as further examples of the difference of the Iranian. Iranians may be more civilized than other Orientals because of their dramatic arts, but the seeming inability of the Iranian dramatists to adhere to the rules of drama (i.e., European dramatic mores) offered further proof of the inherent cultural superiority of the European. The process of translation was important, for by translating the plays into a European tongue, the Orientalist would inevitably improve upon the original, as had Gobineau. By rendering a text from an oral tradition, by making the mysterious *taziyah* productions readable and understandable to European audiences, these Orientalists were defining, coding, and ordering Persian culture.

There was an attempt at fixity in the Orientalist reification of the *taziyah* that is not present in the Persian form of these plays. Indeed, the very act of transcribing, editing, and translating these plays in a sense disembodied them. They were not meant to be scripted dramas. They were not meant to be literary masterpieces. The essence of the *taziyah* went beyond simple plots. There was little to no distinction between the audience and the actor. The producer/director, known as the *mu'in al-buka* (the one who brings tears), stood in the midst of the actors on stage, preparing props, giving stage directions, and distributing scripts to the appropriate actors as the plays progressed.[23] These productions that blurred the line between ritual and theatrical representation. Indeed, this very malleability of the *taziyah* allowed it to simultaneously traverse both the secular and profane cares of Iranians. In translation, this feature is lost and "Persian culture" as constructed in this genre by European Orientalists fails to encompass the intertextuality of the everyday with the divine, which is characteristic of the *taziyah*. For the average participant, the *taziyah* may have offered a release from the daily tensions of life, an opportunity to shed tears for the martyrs of this life and the past.[24] For the Occidental scholar/traveler, the *taziyah* was a spectacle of Shi'ite sentiment, a venue into the sacred, and further proof of European cultural superiority.

## MIRZA FATH 'ALI AKHUNDZADEH AND MIRZA AQA TABRIZI: THE BEGINNINGS OF NATIONALIST THEATER IN IRAN

In 1859, Mirza Fath 'Ali Akhundzadeh published a series of *tamsilat* or comedies formed on the models of Molière and Shakespeare. Written in Azeri Turkish and published in Tiflis, these plays have come to be known as the first secular plays written in the Islamic world and the first nationalist plays written by an Iranian. Influenced by Akhundzadeh, Mirza Aqa Tabrizi wrote the first modern secular Persian plays in the 1870s. Together, these men have been credited with creating a new theatrical form in Iran, one that marks a clear departure from the traditional theatrical representations discussed in the preceding sections. Their plays were written with a clear text, were intended to be read and seen by an audience that was clearly set apart from the action in the plays but who could relate to the forms that were theatrically represented. In *Selection from Cultural Writings* Gramsci observed that theater was a controlled cultural form; and the theater of Akhundzadeh and Tabrizi stood in juxtaposition to previous kinds of theatrical art forms in Iran in this important aspect.[25] In their plays, extemporaneous theatrical representation gave way to controlled plots and dialogue; theater as religious expression gave way to theater as education; the sacred ritual gave way to profane performance. No longer was Shi'ism the assumed link of the audience. For the first time, the audience was assumed to be a *millat* or a nation. The *taziyahs*' fluidity contained both religious and secular qualities. In this new theatrical form, a specific sphere of the secular is being constructed—one that has significance for the articulation of nationalism in the Qajar era.

Why did these men feel compelled to create a new literary form? Both Akhundzadeh and Tabrizi left behind explanations of their motivations for writing these plays. Akhundzadeh's appear in his autobiographical essay, in the preface to his plays, and in his correspondences. In a letter to Mirza Aqa Tabrizi, he wrote, "[T]he purpose of the art of drama is the refinement of the character of the people and the edification of the readers and listeners. . . . The era of 'Gulistan' and 'Zinat al-Majlis' is past. Today, these kinds of writings are not useful for the nation (*millat*). Today, the writings that are useful for the nation and agreeable to the taste of the readers are the art of drama and the novel."

Encouraging Tabrizi's own interest in writing plays, Akhundzadeh wrote, "I hope you will devote much time to this noble art . . . and that you will make great progress and will become a guide to your compatriots, those of the same language as you and your co-religionists (*hamvatanan, ham-zabanan*, va *ham-kishan*) in this art."[26]

Tabrizi wrote a dialogue on the usefulness and purpose of drama in which he asserted that "studying these plays and becoming informed of the stories, the narrations, thoughts and counsel that is in them will lead to [a] vision and the increase in education . . . of the nation and the cause of progress and the prosperity of the country and these two will contribute to the ordering and strength of the government."[27] Above all, it is this focus of using the theater as a vehicle to communicate with the nation that sets these plays apart, for in the process, Akhundzadeh and Tabrizi were constructing the nation with whom they were communicating. If the theater is to serve as a means of edifying the nation, then the audience must clearly *be* a nation.

Both Akhundzadeh and Tabrizi used theater as a way to discuss certain social and political issues that they perceived to be problematic. Their plays were written in simple colloquial Persian and did not retain the complex and intricate symbolism of classical Persian literature. Their *tashbih* or representation was simple to decode. Their candid discussion of everyday life, thinly cloaked in satire, offers the historian a glimpse into segments of Iranian society who rarely appeared as actors in classical literature. Again and again they refer to theater as a venue for the edification and the education of the nation. In fact, the subtitle of Akhundzadeh's plays as they appeared in the Persian was *The Book of the Edification of Behavior*. In its preface, Akhundzadeh noted that human beings were capable of happiness and sorrow, that they were confronted in life with good and bad. However, he had observed a strong resistance to constructing representations of "the bad" in literature. In Europe (*Farangistan*), he noted, this had been done to great advantage. By viewing representations of social maladies, he contended, one could better understand them and therefore remedy them.[28] If these playwrights sought to remedy social ills, what did they consider these maladies to be?

Tabrizi's plays are generally set in urban settings and deal primarily with the corruption of the government at various levels and its implications for Iranians of all classes, genders, and ethnicities.[29] In his *Tariqqih-yi Hukumat-i Zaman Khan*, which takes place in Burujird in 1266/1849, he confronts the issue of the corruption of provincial governors and their rank and file quite openly. The play begins with the governor telling his main *farrash* (attendant), "This year in this state, I want to govern and behave in such a manner that the residents will forget all of the previous governors and bureaucrats (*mubashirrin-i divan-i*) and as long as they have life, they will praise my governance."[30] He complains that something must be done about all the wine-making and prostitution in his province. His main *farrash* understands that his governor seeks to make greater profits from *pishkish* (favors). He first approaches Vartanus, the Armenian, with false claims that his neighbors have been complaining about his wine-making. Vartanus is stunned, as he has an established arrangement with the local officials, providing them with some of his product as well as regular cash payments in order to carry out his business. Vartanus becomes quite distraught and pleads with the *farrash* saying, "In the Church, I will say a big prayer for you." Whereupon the *farrash* motions towards some money saying, "You know, this all will not be fixed with money." A relieved Vartanus whispers to the *farrash* that he finally understands the purpose of the visit and agrees to make a payment. Take it, he says, "and still say that Armenians are stingy."[31]

The *farrash* then searches for a prostitute in town. To his great disappointment, they all seem to be out of work, having passed away, become married, or retired. He calls on one who has retired and convinces her to contact a former client, a wealthy merchant in town. Together, they plot to entrap the merchant in order to bribe him. He is lured to the prostitute's house and is caught with his pants down (literally) by the local officials who receive healthy bonuses for their silence.

Another play, *Sarguzasht-i Ashraf Khan, Hakim-i Arabistan* further demonstrates the directness and harshness of his criticisms of the corruption in the government and acquiescence by the people. Akhundzadeh and Tabrizi were well aware of the dangers of writing plays that too closely resembled the state of affairs in Qajar Iran. Indeed, Akhundzadeh warned Tabrizi that this particular play may cause him problems with the government, "Writing and publishing these sorts of things . . . [given the realities of our time] is a dangerous thing. And especially in a kingdom (*mamlikat*) like Iran where freedom has not yet been extended to printing, writing and thinking, what is one to do? [Yet] the issue is very worthy."[32] The setting of this particular play is the capital Tehran in 1815. A local official of the province of Arabistan has come to the city to clear up his accounts for the taxes of his province for the past three years, to pay the percentage owed the central government, and to receive the *khil'at* (customary robe) of governance for his province. He hopes that his meetings with the chief *mustawfi* (tax collector) will be quick and that his stay in Tehran will be short. Realizing that he must pay some favors in order to get through the bureaucratic machine, he has made arrangements to bring several bags of gold with him. Unbeknownst to him, the prime minister and the chief tax collector have conspired to overestimate the tax intake for his province, in order to get a larger commission from him. In addition, they have agreed to stall Ashraf Khan in the capital as long as possible in order to receive as many favors as possible for making arrangements for his stay.

Ashraf Khan's original bags of gold that were meant to last for the duration of his trip begin to dwindle with great speed as everyone from the *farrash*es to the prime minister ask for more bribes than he had anticipated. Every time he takes a meal or smokes a *nargil* (water pipe), it appears that he must pay a dozen people. After a few days, Ashraf Khan becomes distraught. Speaking to himself, he says, "God, what a mistake I have made! What governance! What account!" That night, poor Ashraf Khan sleeps in great discomfort and dreams that he is in a courtyard surrounded by seven or eight great snakes that are attacking him. He awakes screaming. In the morning, he enters the courtyard, calling for Karim Aqa to come and interpret his dream for him, when suddenly five men dressed in red appear before him. Ashraf Khan recalls his frightening dream and becomes frozen in fear; his stomach becomes tied up in knots and makes loud noises till finally he defecates on himself. He runs to the outhouse and proceeds to carry on a dialogue with the *farrash*, requesting a clean pair of pants to replace his soiled ones. Stepping into the courtyard once again, Ashraf Khan is still riddled with fear and faints. As he is resuscitated, he moans, "O dreams of snakes, O snakes of dreams!" The play's twisted plot continues with incident upon incident requiring Ashraf Khan to pay more favors, until he finally sneaks out of town quietly, with great doubts about the value of the governance of his province.

Akhundzadeh took great offense at certain aspects of the play, especially the use of the words *outhouse*, *defecation*, and *filth*. He cautioned Tabrizi to remove these words from his script.[33] Some contemporary theater critics also deride the plays of Aqa Tabrizi as they defy the rules of the theater. This play, in particular, is sometimes cited as evidence of his lack of familiarity with the basic rules of drama.[34] Others, however, see his plays as innovative and in mood with the theatrical breakthroughs that were made on the stages of late-nineteenth-century Europe:

> Mirza Aqa shocked the conformists and the believers in classical conventions in theater . . . who criticized his free language and disregard for the three unities. Precisely these 'mistakes' gave his work an unintended boldness and modernity. A. Bricteux believes that the comical situations and funny everyday dialogues make these masterpieces of humour comparable to Gogol's 'Revisor' and Jules Romain's 'Knock'. These plays denounce, in an uninhibited way, moral simperings, corruption of absolute rulers, and the sheepishness of the people.[35]

Akhundzadeh's plays are set in rural Azerbaijan and deal with lives of peasants. Like Tabrizi, Akhundzadeh portrays the consequences of various social problems and the passive acceptance of them by the peasantry. He questions the value of arranged marriages, suggesting that women should have a greater say in the choice of their spouses. He exposes the corruption of alchemists and sorcerers. He draws attention to the corruption of local Islamic courts, which could be manipulated by local officials and corrupt mullahs, meting out injustice in the name of Islamic law. And he includes several characters who are foreigners appearing in rural Azerbaijan.

Akhundzadeh was born in the Persian Empire. By the time he was an adult, his hometown was part of the Russian Empire. As a translator for the Russian viceroy in Tiflis, he was in a position to meet various foreign intellectuals and diplomats. As Adamiyat noted, Georgia at the turn of the century was a crossroads of Persian, Armenian, Russian, Turkish, and European cultural influences. It was at this crossroads that Akhundzadeh derived his inspiration for cultural innovation.[36] H. Algar portrayed Akhundzadeh as a reformer who along with Mirza Malkum Khan stood in awe of the West and sought to remake Iran in its shape. He cites the play *M. Jordan and Musta' 'Ali Shah* as evidence that Akhundzadeh favored Western-style sciences over traditional forms such as sorcery that still retained an influence among the Iranian people.[37] I suggest that the play can be read quite differently leading to a very different understanding of Akhundzadeh's position on Western science and his general attitude toward reforms of Iranian society.

M. Jordan, a European botanist, visits a village in Azerbaijan in order to collect some specimens that he will take back to "farangistan" where there is a giant chart. If M. Jordan manages to add enough new specimens to this chart, he will become famous and probably rich as well. The local villagers watch with amazement as he plucks away at the weeds, wildflowers, and leaves that grow around their village, preserving them carefully as though they were rare and valuable possessions. His amazed unfamiliarity with the things that seem so ordinary to the peasants may be seen as Akhundzadeh's critique of the nineteenth-century Orientalists, with whom he undoubtedly had contact in his official duties.

During his stay in the village, M. Jordan befriends a young man who is slated to be married to a local girl. But M. Jordan fills his head with ideas of going to Paris to learn French so he can get a bureaucratic job in the city. The women of the village suspect that the boy's real motivations for making the trip to Paris are to see the women who reportedly walk around nearly naked and dance with men who are not even their husbands. The village women enlist the help of the local sorcerer, who convinces them that this grave situation will require gross measures. Requesting a huge fee (which is payed with the money that had been set aside for the impending nuptials), he promises to cast a spell on Paris itself so that it will be destroyed once and for all. The spell is cast, and when M. Jordan hears of it, he pretends to be in great anguish. The village people regret their actions, feeling pity for the people of Paris, including M. Jordan's friends and family, who have now met with their demise. M. Jordan takes advantage of the ensuing chaos to sneak the young man out of the village and takes him to Paris after all.

The play ends with a peasant asking why it is so easy to fool people who clearly have the capacity for wisdom. In my view, in this duel between the botanist and the sorcerer, there is no clear winner. It does not appear that Akhundzadeh meant to endorse Western sciences over the more traditional local forms. Rather, he reveals flaws in both and calls on the people to employ their own wisdom and to not be so easily dooped by practitioners of either sort.

In the preface to his Persian translations of Akhundzadeh's *tamsilat,* Mirza Ja'afar Qarajedaghi wrote that the readers of these plays should employ patience and wisdom in reading them. They will then be justly rewarded by the book, which had been produced under great difficulty for the purpose of "opening the eyes and ears" of the people.[38] Both Tabrizi and Akhundzadeh remarked repeatedly on the power of drama to edify and educate people through the production of representations of the social ills that dogged Iran in the Qajar period. They very consciously chose to write in a theatrical form that was "new" to Iranian literature. The form that they constructed, a highly satirized drama set in naturalistic settings dealing with everyday problems for the purpose of critiquing the society in which they lived, was an attempt at cultural innovation to meet the challenges faced by Iran. The particular cultural sphere that they they helped to construct through their playwriting helped to produce certain shifts in the culture of Iran at the time. In these plays, the domain of culture is being constructed as part of emergent social classes to which both Akhundzadeh and Tabrizi belonged—a class loosely consisting of midlevel bureacrats, traders, and merchants. Furthermore, they introduced an inherently multiethnic quality to the dramatic form they created. In their correspondences and the prefaces of their plays, they referred again and again to the nation, the *millat,* as their chosen audience. In some respects, then, Akhundzadeh and Tabrizi constructed a sense of *milliyat* in this particular sphere that was class based, secular, and multiethnic. Having focused thus far on the production of a "new" cultural form, it is important to attempt to establish the history of the transmission and reception of these plays.

## TRANSMISSION AND RECEPTION:
## RECONSTRUCTING THE AUDIENCE OF IRANIAN
## NATIONALIST THEATER IN THE NINETEENTH CENTURY

Studies of the cultural production by scholars such as Raymond Williams, Roger Chartier, and Robert Darnton have shown that an assessment of the role of cultural production in nationalism is incomplete without an evaluation of cultural consumption. That is to say, who saw or read the plays of Akhundzadeh and Tabrizi? How were they received and perceived by the audience? Akhundzadeh promoted his plays vigorously, sending copies to his network of intellectual friends in Iran and taking copies with him on his trip to Istanbul in 1873 with which he gifted the sultan. He set about the task of getting his plays translated into Persian to make them more accessible to an Iranian audience. In a letter to Mirza Ja'afar Qarajedaghi, he wrote that the Persian translations had not only captured the essence of his plays but had possibly improved on them. He urged Mirza Ja'afar to see to the quick printing and distribution of the book. The lithographed Persian edition that appeared in 1874 certainly did not go unnoticed.

Akhundzadeh claimed that his plays were performed in the Caucuses in Russian translation and were favorably reviewed in literary magazines in Berlin and St. Petersburg.[39] H. W. Brands confirms that they were published in Russian in the journal *Kavkas* and were performed in Russian at Tiflis and St. Petersburg. Apparently the only time they were performed in the original Azeri Turkish was by school children at state schools in Azerbaijan at the end of the 1870s.[40] We have no evidence that they were ever performed in Iran until the late Pahlavi era (1960s and 1970s),[41] but we do know that they were read by Iranians at gatherings in the nineteenth century. This is not unusual as Akhundzadeh meant for his plays to be read and seen, often referring to theatrical audiences as "listeners" (*mustama'in*). Mirza Tabrizi, Mirza Ja'afar, and Akhundzadeh all gave specific directions on how their plays should be read, noting the importance of using a different voice for each character, of maintaining appropriate voice inflection, and of avoiding reading stage directions. The speech of older men, foreigners, and Armenians should be read with appropriate intonations and accents.[42]

In fact, Mirza Aqa Tabrizi wrote that he first heard Akhundzadeh's plays at a gathering (*majlis*) where talk had turned to the art of rhetoric. The host of the gathering then brought out a copy of Akhundzadeh's plays, which were read aloud. "Its simple and sweet words and meaningful and pleasant expressions hung like . . . gems . . . from the ears of the listeners. . . . Retelling these sorts of stories and articulating these sorts of plays will lead to the progress and education of the nation (*mil-*

*lat*)."[43] And so Mirza Aqa Tabrizi took it upon himself to translate the plays. Failing at that task, he decided to write some plays in Persian using Akhundzadeh as his model. He sent a copy of his plays to Akhundzadeh, asking that he remain anonymous. Given the fact that his plays were highly critical of the government and that Tabrizi worked as a bureaucrat, this is not surprising. Clearly this anonymity led to the confusion that caused his plays to be for years ascribed to Mirza Malkum Khan. Only in 1956 did two Soviet Azeri scholars discover original drafts of the plays, which Tabrizi had sent to Akhundzadeh and of which Tabrizi was rightfully credited with the authorship.[44]

This "new" dramatic Iranian form also had an audience in Europe and British India, among Orientalists, diplomats, and students alike. It was in their Persian translation that Akhundzadeh's plays first came to the attention of W. H. D. Haggard and G. Le Strange. Haggard had served as the second secretary to Her Majesty's legation in Tehran and G. Le Strange was an Orientalist who had already translated major Persian works. In 1882, they published an English translation of the *Vazir of Lankuran* as "a text-book of modern colloquial Persian for the use of European travelers, residents in Persia, and students in India." Their edition included a transcription of the play in Persian, an English translation, an introduction that paraphrased the preface to the Persian translation, a grammatical introduction, several pages of notes, and a vocabulary that also indicated the pronunciation of the words. Here was an opportunity for Europeans wanting to learn Persian to have a colloquial text. "[I]t may safely be said that there is hardly a sentence in the whole Play that he might not find daily occasion to use in the Bazars."[45] Subsequent translations were rendered in French and English throughout the 1880s and 1890s by Barbier de Maynard, S. Guyard, A. Cillière, and G. Le Strange. A German translation was rendered by Adolf Wahrmund, an Austrian Orientalist, in 1889. A few of these were published in *Le Journal Asiatique* and the *Journal of the Royal Asiatic Society*. More commonly, they were collated, glossed, and published as textbooks of colloquial Persian.

The potential use of the plays for the study of colloquial Persian was not lost on residents of British India. Several editions of the plays and their English translations were printed and lithographed in India. One edition of particular interest was produced in 1905 by Muhammad Kazim Shirazi, the Persian instructor to the Board of Examiners and one of the editors of the influential Persian newspaper *Habl al-Matin*. Shirazi made interesting selections to include in his textbook for the lower standard examination in Persian. In his *Ganjina-i Muhawarat*, he published a literal translation of the Vazir of Lankuran by Akhundzadeh alongside an excerpt from Nasir al-Din Shah's travel journal.[46] In fact, the segment of the Shah's journal recounts his travels through Rasht and Lankaran, the same cities in which Akhundzadeh's play is set. Perhaps this is coincidence. However, the readers may have found the juxtaposition of a play that ridiculed the corruption of local officials and the description of the shah's travels through the same region along with his large entourage noteworthy. Perhaps this was an attempt to draw attention to Akhundzadeh's critique of the power plays that infested much of provincial Qajar politics. Nevertheless, the use of Akhundzadeh's play in a textbook for the examination of Persian ensured it a wide readership in British India in 1905, just as the Iranian Constitutionalist Revolution was underway. It is interesting that the man who produced such a text, Shirazi, was a known critic of the Qajar regime who had come under fire more than once from Tehran for his publication of oppositionary articles in *Habl al-Matin*. It was his presses that often printed and lithographed books that were censored in Iran.

The publication of some of Akhundzadeh's plays in translation in the *Journal of Royal Asiatic Societies* was noted in several letters to the editor. In one such letter published in 1890, F. J. Goldsmid reacted quite strongly to the appearance of these plays, claiming that they addressed "no less important a question that the regeneration of Persia. . . . If Mirza Fath'Ali's plays do not attempt at high teaching, they are at least suggestive of a healthy innovation, which the Persians now living are capable of turning to good account, both for themselves and their countrymen."[47]

Goldsmid further commented that these plays had not been performed in Persia, a fact that Haggard and Le Strange had also noted. Pondering the reasons for this, Goldsmid wrote:

> May it be that they touch too keenly the sore points of the Persian character, and interpret too plainly the national vanity which kills every germ of enlightenment obtained from outside influences? They lay bare for the first time in Oriental literature a painful Truth, acquaintance with which is the first step to reformation. My humble opinion is that a drastic treatment such as this would open the minds of the more simple-minded native to the wretched shams which he has been taught to acknowledge as Justice and equitable government, and to the real character of those whose decisions he has been trained to respect and obey—consequently, to the consciousness of power to rise from his self-imposed abasement and become a free and thinking creature.[48]

That Goldsmid had very strong opinions about the need for reform in Iran and the potential power of these new plays is undeniable. But who was he? F. J. Goldsmid could best be described as colonial grout. From the time he began his military service for the Indian government in Madras in 1839, he appeared in various capacities at a host of colonial sites. He began a journal in 1841 while in Hong Kong by writing out a list of places, including Russia, Turkey, America, Persia, Aleppo, Damascus, Florence, and Jerusalem. Beneath them he wrote, "How many, if any, shall I be permitted to see?"[49] Indeed his career offered him the chance to see many countries and to learn several languages, including Hindi, Persian, Arabic, Sindi, and Turkish.

In 1841, Goldsmid won a Chinese war medal for his service in the capture of the Forts of the Bocca Tigris. In 1855, he served in the Crimean War, after which he returned to his post in Sind as the assistant commissioner for a special inquiry into alienated lands in Sind. After the Indian mutiny, his services were used to translate "addresses to the native troops and the promulgation of sentences to the Mutineers."[50] He later worked with the Indo-European Telegraph and served as its director-general at one point. In this capacity, he traveled to Iran to negotiate a telegraph treaty and wrote a pamphlet, "Telegraph and Travel" about this journey.

In 1870, he was the official arbitrator of the Perso-Afghan frontier, after which he served in various diplomatic capacities in India and Egypt. As his official biography explains:

> He was in Egypt during the outbreak in September, 1881, to June, 1882, when he proceeded to London, and thence, by special order from Lord Granville, to Constantinople. Reaching Alexandria again on July 8th, he remained, under instructions, on board the P. and O. Tanjore pending the bombardment. Under the authority of Sir Beauchamp at Alexandria he organized an Intelligence Department at Alexandria, and remained its chief until it was broken up at the end of the war. In this capacity he made constant reports of the enemy's movements, examined suspected persons, controlled the despatch of telegrams, and was Censor of the local press.[51]

In 1883, Goldsmid undertook his final colonial mission in the Belgian Congo, where he was sent "to carry out special measures for the organization of the new State."[52] Upon retiring from the colonial service, Goldsmid continued to be active, principally through his work for the Royal Geographical Society and his writing. His personal papers show that his dual and sometimes intertwined interests in the theater and the East continued.

The plays also came to the attention of another colonial official. While writing his tract *Persia and the Persian Question*, Lord Curzon contacted countless experts on Persia. One British diplomat in Iran, Mr. Churchill, from whom Curzon solicited information, wrote disparagingly of corruption of the provincial governors:

> In the towns the Gov[ernor] has many sources of income. But his most successful one is the administration of Justice. . . . In the judicious

administration of what is called "moeurs" by the French the Gov[ernor] has a goose and a golden egg. If there are no prostitutes in his district it is to the Gov[ernor]'s interest to introduce some. By means of them as a decoy the Gov[ernor] can do a great deal. He can surprise wealthy merchants entertaining them and . . . [engaging in] heavy blackmail as a bribe to prevent any scandal.[53]

If this story sounds suspiciously like one of Tabrizi's plays discussed above, that is not surprising, for Churchill continues: "I have some comedies written by a very smart pen which w[oul]d—in translation—give you more insight into the Persian character and its government than you would get in ten years of sojourn among them."

Indeed, the plot of Tabrizi's play, which was read by Churchill and relayed to Curzon in personal correspondence, was relayed in Curzon's *Persia and the Persian Question* in a chapter on Persia's taxation system:

[E]very wheel of the judicial machine will require constant greasing. Another device is the introduction of prostitutes into a district where they were previously absent. Using them as a decoy, the Governor suddenly pounces upon some wealthy merchant, giving a convivial entertainment on the sly, and extorts a heavy blackmail as the price of silence. These and many other expedients are devised by the Governors, in order to meet the troublesome inquisition of the Ministry of Arrear, which has a beautiful way of producing all sorts of arrears, and defecits, and objections to provincial budgets. No final acquaintances can be obtained without considerable "palm-oil."[54]

The line between theatrical representation and reality was crossed. The playwright's attempt at social criticism in order to remedy Iran's internal social ills was used by the colonial officials to assert the weakness of Oriental morals, the corruption of the Persian system. These were necessary justifications for colonial interjection into the internal administration of Iran.

## CONCLUSION

The above discussion of Iranian theater in the late nineteenth century has been illustrative. It has helped to show the specific and concrete use of culture by both colonial and nationalist thinkers and writers. The "discovery" of Persian theater by Europeans in the nineteenth century was not accidental. Scholars of Orientalism have shown that an important feature of colonialism was the study and packaging of Oriental cultures into consumable units for the colonizers. Demonstrating the weakness of the culture of the Orient strengthened the moral imperative of the colonial powers by adding a civilizing mission to the colonial enterprise. Culture was the key feature in constructing the colonial other. In fact, many of the Europeans who translated, edited, anthologized, and critiqued Iranian theater in the nineteenth century were colonial officials who had entered the ranks of Orientalists. These included A. Chodzko, who had been the Russian consul at Rasht; Sir Pelly, who had been the British Consul at Bushire; Sir Goldsmid, who had been the boundary commissioner for the Seistan and Baluch borders; and George Curzon who was a Conservative MP about to become the viceroy of India. Discussions of the colonial efforts have shown a linkage between the colonization of the Middle East and India. This chapter has shown that often the same men were a part of the British colonial hierarchy, traveling between posts in India, Iran, and Egypt. Goldsmid, for example, was present in India during the time of the Indian mutiny, in Iran during the drawing of her Western boundaries, and in Egypt during the British bombardment of Alexandria. The link between parts of the empire are clear, on the level of both ideology and personnel. The link between culture and the use of colonial power is also significant.

The discussion of the rise of a new cultural form in Iran, the secular, satirical theater shows that culture was also used by the indigenous intellectuals to articulate and propagate nationalism. Although Akhundzadeh borrowed his models of play writing from European dramatists, he created a uniquely Iranian cultural form that allowed him to write the language of the peasants, to recreate the rural setting he witnessed around him in Azerbaijan, and to address the weaknesses in the Iranian character that he deemed most problematic. Among them are the corruption of local officials, the lack of basic rights by women in terms of inheriting their due property and choosing their spouses, the usurping tendencies of practitioners of traditional sciences such as sorcery and alchemy. But Akhundzadeh, who worked in the employ of the Russians in Azerbaijan, was no blind admirer of the West. Western characters in his plays receive the typical satirical treatment and look to be self-serving, naive, and markedly out of place in his rural Azeri settings.

Following the model of Akhundzadeh, Tabrizi wrote plays dealing with the problems that beset urban Iran in the nineteenth century. Showing the problems of corruption at the local and central levels of government, Tabrizi used the theater to communicate scenes he must have witnessed as a member of the bureaucratic system. His liberties with the theatrical art were criticized by Akhundzadeh and subsequent theater critiques. However, he was writing plays at the same time that modernist theater was being written and produced in Berlin and Munich.[55]

The connection between form and content must not be overlooked here. It is significant that Akhundzadeh and Tabrizi consciously created a unique Iranian cultural form. Recognizing that they were operating in a changing political climate, that they were addressing new problems in a new context, Akhundzadeh and Tabrizi eschewed other Iranian cultural forms and instead chose to construct their own cultural genre; as such, they were sending an important signal that cultural production could not continue as before. They created a form that was more useful for their attempt to use culture to help create a sense of national identity and commitment from the Iranians whom they hoped would be the audience of their plays. They had a new objective; they claimed to be using their plays as vehicles for social criticism in hopes of remedying the social ills that beset Iran. Indeed, the concept of self-strengthening was a key feature of all forms of nationalism in nineteenth-century Iran. This positionality allowed them to be authors, social critics, and political players all at once. They were creating new openings into the political life of Iran. They were also able to define what they perceived to be the "social woes" that beset Iranians at the time—thus creating a potentially powerful process of subjectivity in which they could play a pivotal role as the artist/social critic. They perceived the importance of the power of interpretation in helping to affect political changes. The value of constructing symbolic images of the Iranian national scene was not lost on these men.

The plays of Akhundzadeh and Tabrizi had a significance beyond Iran itself. In translation, their plays were made available to readers in British India, Russia, and Europe. Their reception in translation shows the irony of cultural production in a colonial context. While their stated intention may have been to edify and educate the Iranian nation, their plays in translation were used to great advantage by the colonizer. Indeed, they helped untold numbers of British and French colonial officials in Europe and India learn to speak the idioms of colloquial Persian. Whereas the publication of the *taziyah* offered Europeans entry into the realm of the sacred Shi'ite ritual, the plays of Akhundzadeh offered them a chance to study the spoken Persian that the common man used. Again and again, Orientalists had noted their frustration at being limited to the classical Persian texts. The theater offered them a different venue through which to study Iranian culture. Akhundzadeh and Tabrizi's representations of a weak and corrupt Iranian society were manipulated by the Orientalists who used them to draw attention to the weakness of Oriental society. For some colonial officials, the line between reality and artistic representation seems to have been blurred. Clearly, the theater played a significant role in mediating the changing relationship between the realms of politics and the arts in ways that reveal aspects of the construction of Iranian nationalism in the late Qajar era.

# BIBLIOGRAPHY

Adamiyat, F. 1970. *Andishahayi Mirza Fath 'Ali Akhundzadeh*. Tehran: Kharazmi.

Akhundzadeh, Mirza Fath 'Ali. 1291/1874. *Tamsilat*. Mirza Ja'afar Qarajedaghi, trans. Tehran: Karkhanah-i Ustad Muhammad Hussein.

Algar, H. 1973. *Mirza Malkum Khan*. Berkeley: University of California Press.

al-Saltanah, I'timad. 1304. "Takiyah-i Mubarak-i Humayuni." *Sharaf*, no. 53.

'Ata'i, A. Jannati. 1333/1955. *Bunyad-i Namayish-i dar Iran*. Tehran: Chap-i Mihan.

Bahadur, Khan, and Douglas Craven. 1911. *English Translation of the* Vazir of Lankuran: *A Play in Four Acts*. Calcutta: Baptists Mission.

Brands, H. W. 1960. "Akhund-zada." In *The Encyclopedia of Islam*, 2d edition, vol. 1. Leiden: E. J. Brill.

Chelkowski, Peter J. 1979. *Ta'ziyeh: Ritual and Drama in Iran*. New York: New York University Press and Soroush.

Chodzko, A. 1878. *Théatre Persan: Choix de téazies ou drames, traduit pour la premier fois du persan*. Paris: Ernest Leroux.

Curzon, George. 1892. *Persia and the Persian Question*. vol. 1. London: Longmans and Green.

Curzon, Marquess, of Kedelston. Personal Papers, the Oriental and India Office Collection, EUR. MSS. F. 112, Volume 614, part 2.

Durand Personal Paper Collection, the Oriental and India Office Collection, EUR. MSS. D727, Volume 5. Lithographed under the supervision of Mirza Muhammad 'Ali Shirazi.

Gaffary, F. 1984. "Evolutions of Ritual and Theater in Iran." *Iranian Studies*, pp. 361–89.

Ghanoonparvar, M. 1989. Introduction to *Iranian Drama: An Anthology*, M. Ghanoonparvar and J. Greene, eds. Costa Mesa: Mazda.

Gobineau, A. 1866. *Les Religions et Les Philosophies dans l'Asie Centrale*. Paris.

Goldsmid, F. J. 1890. "Le Theatre Persan." *JRAS*, pp. 663–64.

Goldsmid, Sir F. Private Papers, the Oriental and India Office Collection, EUR. MSS. F. 134, Box 4.

Haggard, W. H. D., and G. Le Strange, eds. 1882. *The Vazir of Lankuran: A Persian Play*. London.

Isherwood, R. 1986. *Farce and Fantasy: Popular Entertainment in Eighteenth-Century Paris*. New York: Oxford University Press.

Jelavich, P. 1985. *Munich and Theatrical Modernism: Politics, Playwriting, and Performance, 1810–1914*. Cambridge: Cambridge University Press.

Malikpur, J. 1963. *Adabiyat-i Namayish dar Iran*. 2 vols. Tehran: Intisharat-i Tus.

McCormick, J. 1992. *Popular Theaters in Nineteenth-Century France*. London: Routledge.

Pelly, Colonel Sir Lewis. 1879. *The Miracle Play of Hasan and Husain*. London: W. H. Allen.

Pelly Private Collection, Oriental and India Office Collection, MSS. EUR. F 126/11.

Qajar, Nasir al-Din Shah-i. 1293/1876. *Ruznamah-i Safar-i Farangistan* (Journal of a trip to Europe). Bombay.

Qarajedaghi, J. 1291/1874. Preface to *Tamsilat*, Mirza Ja'afar Qarajedaghi, trans. Tehran: Karkhanah-i Ustad Muhammad Hussein.

Rizavi, Muhammad Baqir, ed. 1933. *Tiyatr-i Mirza Malkum Khan.* Mirat: Matba'a-i Ahsan al-Mutba.

Rosen, F. 1926. *Persien, in Wort und Bild.* Berlin: Franz Schneider Verlag.

Sadiq, H., ed. 1975/76. *Namayishhayi Mirza Aqa Tabrizi.* Tehran: Kitabkhanah-i Tahouri.

Shirazi, Muhammad Kazim. 1905. *Ganjina-i Muhawarat.* Calcutta: H. D. Chatterjee.

Williams, Raymond. 1992. *The Long Revolution.* Rpt. 1962. London: Hogarth.

## NOTES

1. Qajar 1293/1876, p. 25. All translations from Persian and French that appear in this chapter are by myself. Citations refer the reader to the original work. At times, nineteenth-century translations are quoted, and this has been noted.

2. Nasir al-Din Shah traveled to Europe three times during his reign. British consular reports indicate that the shah dictated his journals to his secretary on a daily basis. The published journals were widely read in Iran and British India and influenced Persian prose writing with their simple style. Sections were included in the Persian examinations of Indian universities. The shah's journals were recommended reading for students of Persian, as the British minister noted to the Marquis of Dufferin, "For the modern Persian idiom the best book is said to be the present Shah's diary. In case you have not got it, I shall send you a copy." (Durand to the Marquis of Dufferin, Gulahek, June 18, 1895, in the Durand Personal Paper Collection.) An English translation was reportedly a popular read in Victorian England.

3. Chodzko 1878. He notes that while he was preparing this preface, A. Gobineau published his book, which includes a discussion and a transcription of some Persian theater. See Gobineau 1866, pp. 359–79.

4. Whether he actually was the first Orientalist to introduce the subject of *taziyah* to European readers or not, Chodzko makes the claim in his book. Of course, some chronologizing of texts can have important historical implications. As M. Tavakoli-Targhi, Abbas Amanat, and other historians currently engaged in writing the cultural and intellectual history of Qajar Iran have been showing, the discussions of "modernity" in Iran need to be pushed further back in time than has been the case in much of the literature on modern Iranian history.

5. Williams 1992, p. 273.

6. Ibid., p. 243.

7. See Gaffary 1984, 361–89, and Ghanoonparvar 1989, for brief discussions of these forms in English. Persian readers can consult 'Ata'i 1333/1955 and Malikpur 1963.

8. For discussions of popular theater in Europe at this time, see Isherwood 1986 and McCormick 1992.

9. Rosen 1926.

10. Curzon 1892, p. 164.

11. Chodzko 1878, pp. vi–vii.

12. Ibid, pp. viii–ix.

13. Ibid, p. ix.

14. Ibid, pp. ix, xx.

15. al-Saltanah 1304.

16. Given the prevalence of domed structures in Islamic architecture, it seems odd that the desire to dome the building was assumed to be the shah's desire to replicate the Albert Hall. Curzon 1892, pp. 327–28.

17. Ibid., p. 481.

18. *The Miracle Play of Hasan and Husain*, which was collected from oral tradition by Colonel Sir Lewis Pelly.

19. Ibid, p. iii.

20. Ibid, p. iv.

21. Pelly Private Collection.

22. Ibid, p. v.

23. Gaffary 1984, pp. 361–89.

24. B. Beeman in Chelkowski 1979.

25. Gramsci, *Selections from Cultural Writings*.

26. See a copy of the letter in Persian in Sadiq 1975/76, pp. 149–63.

27. Ibid.

28. Akhundzadeh, in the preface of the Persian translation of his plays, *Tamsilat* 1291/1874, p. 17.

29. When Mirza Aqa Tabrizi's plays were first published, in serial form in the newspaper *Ittihad*, they appeared under the name of Mirza Malkum Khan. Subsequent reprints of his work into compilations were all printed under the name of Malkum Khan, including those published by the Kaveh Press in Berlin (1921), in Russian translation in Tashkent (1927), and in Persian in *Mirat* (1933).

30. Rizavi 1933, p. 29. See also Sadiq 1975/76.

31. Rizavi edition, p. 32–33.

32. Ibid., p. 153.

33. Ibid., p. 150.

34. A discussion of this subject apprears in Ghanoonparvar 1989, introduction.

35. See Gaffary 1984, p. 375. For a discussion of concurrent trends in German modernist theater, see Jelavich 1985.

36. Adamiyat 1970.

37. Algar 1973.

38. Qarajedaghi 1291/1874, p. 6.

39. Malikpur 1963.

40. Brands 1960, pp. 331–32.

41. Ghanoonparvar 1989.

42. For such remarks by Mirza Ja'afar and Akhundzadeh, see the preface to the Persian translation (1874), pp. 12–15. For Mirza Tabrizi's instructions to the reader, see his preface in *Namayishahyi Mirza Aqa Tabrizi*, ed. H. Sadiq.

43. See Persian translation again.

44. See appendix in Algar 1967, for a discussion of this matter.

45. Haggard and Le Strange 1882, p. xii.

46. A copy of this textbook is available in the Oriental and India Office Collections. Shirazi 1905. Again in 1911, the vazir of Lankuran was used in a textbook for the Persian examination in an edition by Lieutenant-Colonel Phillott and Khan Bahadur. This edition included an Urdu translation as well. An introductory note claims that the original translators, Haggard and Le Strange, "have laid a whole generation of students under a deep debt of gratitude." Bahadur and Phillott 1911.

47. F. J. Goldsmid, "Le Théatre Persan," *JRAS* (1890): 663–64.

48. Ibid.

49. Private Papers of Sir F. Goldsmid. Though Sir Goldsmid's papers have not been properly indexed as of yet, the India Office staff generously allowed me to view the collection.

50. Private Papers of Sir F. Goldsmid. Notes on his life are taken from his official biography contained in the collection.

51. Private Papers of Sir F. Goldsmid.

52. Ibid.

53. Churchill to Curzon, Tehran, October 6, 1891, Personal Papers of the Marquess Curzon of Kedleston.

54. Curzon 1892, p. 474.

55. See Jelavich 1985.

# CHAPTER 9

# The Rise and Fall of Nationalism in the Egyptian Cinema

## Walter Armbrust

By the late 1930s Egypt possessed a substantial infrastructure for producing and exhibiting films. The cinema built upon habits of consumption already familiar through other media, which were then amplified in film narratives. Few phenomena are more suggestive than the cinema of the modern practice of consuming objects and images that individuals themselves do not produce "in the first instance."[1] It is therefore surprising how rarely the cinema enters into analyses of modernity in Egypt or the rest of the Arabic-speaking world. However, past sins of omission are not a good reason for continuing to ignore the Egyptian cinema.

This chapter examines Egyptian national identity through films. The cinema was an important component in the construction of modernity, and by association, nationalism. At a certain juncture, films were also instrumental in expressing the decline of modernity as expressed in popular culture. Two films form the basis of the analysis. One is *The White Rose*,[2] a classic, which I use to illustrate a modernist metagenre prevalent in the cinema for several decades. The other is *Ragab on a Hot Tin Roof*,[3] a film that illustrates the eventual crystallization of a counternarrative to that of earlier media.

The films are indicative of the development of both modernity and nationalism in Egypt. One way of looking at modernity is to emphasize

---

*Note on Transliterations*: Transliterations from Arabic follow a simplified version of the *International Journal of Middle East Studies* format. The "ayn" is indicated by a " ' "; the "hamza" by a " ` ". Long vowels and emphatic consonants are not marked. Where appropriate, transliterations follow colloquial Egyptian rather than standard written Arabic.

its association with nationalism. The process of decisively associating a group of people to a particular territory, and more important, of enabling such a group to imagine itself as a community[4] is a quintessentially modern practice, and one that paradoxically requires a conceptualization of the national community as ancient. The central concern here is vernacular imagery as elaborated in films. A vernacular is most often associated with spoken language, in opposition to standardized written varieties. In the context of nationalism, the standardization of national vernaculars is a common goal, if not necessarily a universal one.[5] Films, of course, utilize language both in the conventional verbal sense and visually through the manipulation of images, motion, and sounds. Egyptian cinema is an institution potentially involved in standardizing a national vernacular, and vernacular identity—the "local" so often counterpoised to global processes—is a vital aspect of modernity.

It is unsurprising that one of the symbols of the continuity so important to Egyptian modernity is the Arabic language. But which Arabic? Nationalist ideology in an Arabic-speaking context formally recognizes only written Arabic, which must be conceptually (if not practically) linked with classical Arab heritage. Actual similarities between modern and medieval written Arabic are another matter. Linguists and lay persons alike recognize that modern written Arabic is not identical to the medieval Arabic sometimes described as "classical," or "eloquent" (*fusha*). But at the same time, the scope of change permitted modern written Arabic has been sufficiently limited that the gap between it and the vernacular is described as "diglossic." Ferguson's "Diglossia" article,[6] originally published in 1959, was an influential milestone in discussions of the issue. The article stipulated that some languages (including Arabic) are characterized by functional division into "high" and "low" variants; the high variant is written Arabic, used also in formal situations, and the low is the vernacular. In modern times Arabic never actually worked this way. Since Ferguson's article, many linguists have identified intermediate varieties of Arabic between the conceptual ideals of the classical Arabic of antiquity—which is of course still taught in religious institutions, and to some extent in secular institutions—and the spoken Arabic of uneducated individuals.[7] Some have called into question the degree to which modern written Arabic, the conceptual descendant of the classical variety, is standardized,[8] while others[9] contend that the sense of linguistic bifurcation between written and spoken Arabic is primarily a product of Western analyses. Much Egyptian popular culture does operate through a contrastive imagery of just the sort of oppositions suggested by linguistic bifurcation. However, the point of popular culture was often not to maintain absolute separation between realms of culture; rather it was to synthesize them. In many contexts the vernacular in linguistic terms was associated with "backwardness," and the modern—or modernizable—was the classical heritage, which could be linked with European technological progress by virtue of its status as a vehicle of sophistication. As in many other places, the vernacular was nonetheless a potentially valuable medium for constructing a sense of national community. Consequently synthesis of written and vernacular expression—with fewer concessions made in favor of the vernacular—is a goal of modern Egyptian culture and one realized most potently in Arabic used in the media, particularly (as one might expect given Anderson's arguments) newspapers.[10] But the idea of a persistent wide gulf between spoken and written styles of Arabic occurs often in both official and folk sociolinguistics, and it is often described as a "problem" that must be solved by bringing spoken language closer to the written.[11]

In nationalist discourse a link is often made between territory and language, but the territory associated with Arabic potentially encompasses all presumed speakers of *classical* Arabic (or its modern standard counterpart)—everyone and no one at the same time. No person speaks classical Arabic or its modern standard descendant in daily life, and yet everywhere in the Arabic-speaking world states have created an institutional apparatus to defend linguistic purity. Descriptions of Arab nationalism have always heavily emphasized the ideological attraction of the classical language, which usually alludes to a modernized, and presumably standardized, variant of the written Arabic used in antiquity. This emphasis excludes from consideration much cultural production in primarily oral (and vernacular) media. Written Arabic, however, differs markedly from the sort of vernacular expression emphasized by recent theorists of nationalism as a general phenomenon.[12] Classical languages, according to Anderson, belong to a nonnationalist world of religious community in which religious texts unite believers through a kind of scriptural iconography: "[T]he deader the written language—the farther it was from speech—the better: in principle everyone has access to a pure world of signs."[13] Arabic in its modern written form, although conceptually and ideologically linked to heritage, could never be classed among the "dead" languages. Literate Arabs, including thoroughly secularized writers, consider it the only natural means of written expression. Any attempt to replace it with writing in the vernacular would be resisted fiercely—more fiercely than was the abortive attempt to make Ebonics a language of instruction in California schools. But the teaching of written Arabic nonetheless bears some resemblance to the teaching of a second language. The grammar, syntax, and vocabulary of written Arabic differ considerably from those of any of the various spoken varieties of the language.

The scope of change permitted to modern written Arabic is in principle (but not always in practice) relatively limited compared to the vernaculars adopted in European writing during the late medieval period and later standardized under the pressure of modernity. One reason for this is that Arabic "is a sacred language linked to a super terrestrial order of power."[14] The importance of Arabic as the perfect vessel of ontological reality is not just that modern Arab nations want to maintain a palpable link to their common classical heritage; the Arab heritage is not inherently more important as the foundation of modern Arab nations than the Latin heritage was to modern European nations. The linguistic basis of Arab heritage lies more in the notion that the heritage is an extension of the sacred text. The modern Arab state can no more discard the heritage than it can discard the core text from which it derives—the Qur'an—because the former is an extension of the latter. There is a kind of symbiosis between the two, and by definition this must extend through history as what Anderson calls "simultaneity-along-time" rather than "transverse, cross-time, marked not by prefiguring and fulfillment, but by temporal coincidence."[15] In other words the emphasis by Egypt and all other Arab states on modernized classical Arabic as the vehicle of national authenticity assures a continuing emphasis on the "vertical" dimension of time (linking the present with the past and future) in addition to the "horizontal" dimension (linking all individuals in a specified territory as a "sociological organism" moving through empty time.)[16]

The relationship between nationalism and vernacular language in Egypt and other Arabic-speaking societies is therefore different than that typically found in Europe. The "official language," as Bourdieu calls it, "is the one which, within the territorial limits of that unit, imposes itself on the whole population as the only legitimate language, especially in situations that are characterized as more *officielle* (a very exact translation of the world 'formal' used by English-speaking linguists)."[17] Through a combination of official regulation and "normalization," the standard language is eventually "capable of functioning outside the constraints and without the assistance of the situation, and is suitable for transmitting and decoding by any sender and receiver, who may know nothing of one another."[18]

In Arabic-speaking societies the official language was not abstracted from the vernacular of an elite but from a language that was not used in everyday life. Arabic-speaking societies saw a devaluation of nonstandard language similar to that of Europe,[19] and this devaluation was no doubt reinforced by the development of modern cultural hierarchies along the same lines as those in Europe and America.[20] In relation to official language, the vernacular had to be kept at arm's length, and was, by definition, not the proper medium for art or print media. But cinema and other nontraditional oral media (the gramophone, theater, and radio) were another matter. In these media the vernacular was never completely banished in constructions of Egyptian nationalism. To the extent that the nation was "imagined"[21] or "narrated,"[22] the medium of expression was *both* the official language and the vernacular. Nationalist discourse on the one hand functioned within the terms of a conceptual linguistic bifurcation and on the other hand sought to effect a merger between them.

## THE CINEMA: FORTY YEARS
## OF MODERNISM VICTORIOUS

Although the importance of nontraditional media in constructing Egyptian and Arab nationalism is generally underemphasized,[23] it is commonly said that the cinema could be a powerful tool for educating the masses, although it usually falls short in this regard. This is as likely to be said by people within the entertainment industry as by lay persons. Specifically it was the illiterate masses who, theoretically, could most profitably be targeted for education by popular culture. Educating the masses meant popularizing education and promoting the style of the bourgeoisie. This was the dominant theme of the Egyptian cinema from its beginning in the 1930s until the 1970s.

At a glance "bourgeois style" meant "Western style." Early Egyptian films were often set in mansions lavishly appointed with French furniture, statuary, and paintings. Characters dressed in the traditional *galabiya* were less often given extensive treatment in films.[24] A Western suit, perhaps topped off by the red tarbush emblematic of the middle-class effendi (bureaucrat), was the standard dress of early Egyptian films. Much of this material is now derided as divorced from Egyptian reality. As critic Samir Farid put it,

> In Egypt, over the course of the more than two thousand films produced in half a century, and then shown again on television and destined to continue being aired on the video, the image of the Egyptian prevalent in Egyptian films is Egyptian in his clothes, his accent and manner of speaking, his movements. But he is not Egyptian in his traditions and customs, behavior, thoughts, actions and reactions. The reason for this is the prevalence of the Western model in Egyptian film making. The film makers are Egyptian, and the films are made in Egypt, but their content is Western.[25]

Few films are excepted from this general accusation, and most of the exceptions tend to come after the early years. Nonspecialists do not necessarily agree with such assessments. Many Egyptians regard "old films" with a substantial degree of nostalgia. For nonspecialists, "old" often mean black-and-white films, which may be as recent as the late 1960s. But for some, the reason that people like old films is that they have been corrupted by them. Farid again expresses this sentiment:

> Filmmakers realized that most of their audience was illiterate—because most of the Arab people were illiterate—and they directed [their work] to them. They made their films an extension of folklore such that it gratified both the merchant and the state at the same time. . . . It is as if the cinema is running parallel to society. We say parallel because this cinema, despite the fact that its films are not art in the true sense of the word, perfectly expresses a view on how to explain life and the world. But it is a backward point of view divorced from reality.[26]

In other words the masses were attracted to films with "Western content" because they were unable to see past their superficial aspects— "clothes . . . accent . . . manner of speaking . . . movements."

Considering the scorn heaped on most of the Egyptian cinema, and the oft-expressed nostalgia for films of the old days on the part of the audience, the favorable treatment of films made by the singer Muhammad 'Abd al-Wahhab seems odd. 'Abd al-Wahhab is a national icon— a cultural figure generally above criticism in the popular press (though musicians are more divided on his legacy). But when he died in the spring of 1991, the reaction to his films was not what one might have expected: complete indifference on the part of the audience (which often professes a liking for "old" films) and an outpouring of admiration on the part of the establishment (that tends to be sparing in its praise of old films).[27]

One reason for this disparity is that almost everyone, including Farid,[28] allows that the production of early films was a national triumph over colonialist occupiers, who had every intention of keeping Egypt in a position of dependency. But beyond the general patriotic significance of Egyptian film production in the abstract, the content of 'Abd al-Wahhab's films—especially his first film, The White Rose[29]—was nationalistic. In fact, contrary to Farid's blanket condemnation of commercial Egyptian cinema, 'Abd al-Wahhab's first film was both thoroughly commercial and vigorously modernist.

The White Rose was released in 1933, and immediately became a huge hit.[30] The film was primarily a vehicle for 'Abd al-Wahhab, who was already famous by the time it was produced. At the time of its release The White Rose was hailed by critics as a new standard of filmmaking technique in the Egyptian cinema; it fits in a "star is born" genre that dates at least to the Victorian era and has been made and remade all over the world. The dark side of the genre tells cautionary tales about the evils of show business that leave the protagonist addicted to drugs and alcohol, or dead. Another variant of the genre chronicles a rise to greatness. Such films can be based on real people. *The Glen Miller Story* [31] and *The Benny Goodman Story* [32] are examples from the American cinema. In Egypt most of these biographical star narratives tend to be about dancers: *Shafiqa the Copt*;[33] *Bamba Kashr*;[34] *Badi'a Masabni* [35] One exception is *Sayyid Darwish*,[36] which tells the story of a major Egyptian singer of the early twentieth century and one who is strongly associated with nationalist iconography.

But not all star narratives are biographical. Many are fictionalized stories creating a persona for an already well known figure. In the American cinema a good example would be Elvis Presley's *Jailhouse Rock*.[37] In Egypt 'Abd al-Wahhab's *White Rose* and Umm Kulthum's *Anthem of Hope*[38] are outstanding examples. Neither of these two films is biographical; both are more in the *Jailhouse Rock* mode in that they create a fictional narrative for a star already famous through other media.

'Abd al-Wahhab's *White Rose* was not the first Egyptian musical,[39] but it was undoubtedly the first Egyptian star narrative. In terms of its style, *The White Rose* appears at first glance to be as relentlessly Westernized as Farid said it should be. The story was set in a gaudy mansion decorated in French fashions (the interior scenes were shot in France); it depicted a style of living that bore no relation whatsoever to the homes of most Egyptians. Some of the women were aggressively décolletées, and a few of the men casually imbibed liquor. For some characters the plot gave off a whiff of self-indulgent party going. Viewing *The White Rose* today, one might find little difficulty in dismissing it as a forthright attempt to sell the bourgeoisie to a gullible public.

The film revolves around an ill-starred love affair between Galal effendi ('Abd al-Wahhab), a talented young singer who has been recently orphaned, and Raga`, the daughter of Isma'il Bey, a rich man who has no intention of marrying his daughter to a mere singer. In the end Galal effendi makes a success of himself as a musician but loses the girl, who is forced to marry Shafiq, a libertine relative from her mother's family. What makes the story an exercise in Egyptian-style modernism is that the love story is not so much the "content" of the film as the circumstances within which it takes place; the social matrix of *The White Rose* is both conservative and radical at the same time. Like modernized classical Arabic, it modernizes through extending the old rather than by creating ruptures with the past. In Benedict Anderson's terms, the film emphasizes the horizontal relations common in novels but also a vertical temporal dimension allegedly associated with "sacred languages."

One aspect of the film's modernity derives from the idea of Galal striving to become a respectable musician. At the time this was unusual, if not outright bold. The public did not automatically differentiate between musicians and other sorts of entertainers, such as dancers, and the attitude toward the moral attributes of them all was not favorable.[40] Later biographers of ʿAbd al-Wahhab made much of his presumed role in elevating the public's taste in music from a kind of premodern musical *jahiliya* (pre-Islamic "time of ignorance"),[41] and the film indeed highlights this aspect of ʿAbd al-Wahhab's public image. In one scene the singer woos Ragaʾ, who has just learned of his predilection for music, by telling her morosely, "My lady, music is a beautiful art, the art of goodness and love. But what a shame. It isn't well appreciated." Indeed it is not, as the chagrined Galal learns when Ismaʿil Bey, angry at his discovery that his daughter is involved with a musician, and worse, a musician who had been his clerk (Galal's position at the start of the film), categorically forbids him from seeing his daughter.

But the point of the film is not just to lament that art is not properly appreciated but also to point out by *whom* it is unappreciated. The sort of art appreciation championed in *The White Rose* was an innovation. *The White Rose* was not just inculcating a Western attitude of "art for art's sake" in a gullible Egyptian public; the film always carefully distinguishes between those who imitate the West and those who adapt it to Egyptian culture. The unfavorable attitude of Ismaʿil Bey contrasts strongly with a later scene in which we see crowds of Western-suited, tarbush-wearing *efendiya* (bureaucrats) flocking to see Galal perform in the same opera house built by Khedive Ismaʿil to commemorate the opening of the Suez Canal. In *The White Rose* Egyptians take over the cultural infrastructure built by openly Westernized rulers and then used by the British rather than slavishly imitate it.[42]

The difference between inauthentic imitation of the West and adaptation on Egyptian terms comes through in parallelisms between Ragaʾ and her mother and between Galal and Shafiq, the suitor from Ragaʾ's mother's family. The contrast between Ragaʾ and her mother is expressed through clothes: the mother is décolleté (we see her pointedly modeling a low-cut backless dress to her husband, who appears a bit embarrassed), while the daughter remains unveiled, but relatively unexposed. Ragaʾ only begins to dress as immodestly as her mother at the end of the film, when her mother finally gets her way and forces Ragaʾ to marry Shafiq, whom she loathes.

As for the men, the contrast is expressed through education, occupation, and their emotional predispositions. Both men have attained at least a secondary-school diploma, which, in the 1930s, was sufficient to land the recipient a respectable bureaucratic job. Galal cannot continue his education because his parents have died, forcing him to find whatever work he can. We see him in the opening scene of the film asking Isma'il Bey for a lowly clerk's position, which Bey grants. Shafiq, on the other hand, has obviously obtained a position in the civil service through family connections; we see him seeking Isma'il Bey's intercession with his superiors so that he can obtain a promotion at the far more prestigious *diwan* (government office).

The work habits of the two men also make a strong contrast. We see Galal hard at work collecting rent from a surly foreigner living in one of Isma'il Bey's properties. Shafiq, however, takes time away from work "in order to entertain some foreign friends." We get a hint of the nature of Shafiq's "entertainment" in a scene showing Shafiq waking up at three o'clock in the afternoon. He pulls back the covers to reveal that he is still dressed from the party the night before and promptly begins preparing to go to another party.

And of course the two men are completely at odds in their attitudes toward Raga`. Shafiq is interested only in her money. We know this from his conversations with Raga`'s mother, who is constantly trying to push him into the marriage and who finally pays for the *shabka* (a gift of jewelry from the groom to the bride) herself, presumably with her husband's money. Shafiq's essential disinterest in Raga`, as opposed to her father's money, is also clear from a scene in which Raga`'s mother enters Shafiq's room and surprises him making suggestive gestures to a shameless neighbor girl who stands on a balcony across the street from his apartment. He denies any interest in the girl when Raga`'s mother brings up the subject of his engagement to Isma'il Bey's daughter. Galal's love for Raga`, by contrast, is pure—symbolized by a white rose given to him by Raga` early in the film. He pines for her when she is away. There is no question of interest in any other woman.

But all this is not enough to establish a sense of authenticity in *The White Rose*. The carefully drawn contrasts between imitative Westernized Egyptians and an alternative model of a bourgeois, but authentic, lifestyle serve to draw a line between what is Egyptian and what is not. On the other hand, the contrastive aspect of the film only gives a negative definition of the "new man" represented by Galal. Something more positive was required to associate Galal with an image of tradition. This is because while Galal and Raga` may be more modest than their opposite numbers (Raga`'s mother and Shafiq), their brand of independent romantic love (even to the point of kissing on the screen) was nonetheless beyond the pale for most Egyptians in the 1990s, let alone the 1930s, when the film was released. Making Galal a faithful lover in contrast to Shafiq was not enough when the very idea of a girl having a lover was shocking.

The scene that follows is important in authenticating the character played by 'Abd al-Wahhab in the film. Without it 'Abd al-Wahhab makes a convincing radical (or a Westernized pseudo Egyptian in the view of the cinema's harshest critics) but does not convincingly evoke the conservatism befitting a nationalist. One authenticating twist in *The White Rose* was provided by the songs 'Abd al-Wahhab performs at regular intervals throughout the film. 'Abd al-Wahhab's admirers have always insisted that his music was terribly innovative, but in *The White Rose* innovation was not necessarily always in the foreground. One of his innovations was to add Western instruments to the traditional Arabic ensemble. By doing so 'Abd al-Wahhab—along with other composers—created something resembling an orchestra. This helped put Arabic music into new public contexts and created new sounds for composers to work with, but by itself did not necessarily change other key characteristics of Arabic music.[43] But the ensemble with which he appears in *The White Rose* is not particularly large or impressive. In addition to some of the conventional instruments,[44] the ensemble includes a pair of cello players and two violinists rather than one. Despite his reputation as an avant garde musician, 'Abd al-Wahhab's ensemble in *The White Rose* is puny compared to the orchestras featured in *Anthem of Hope*, the star narrative of his rival, Umm Kulthum, made in 1937. If one were to have seen the two films in 1938, the impression would have been of Umm Kulthum the modernist and 'Abd al-Wahhab the traditionalist, or at least the less avant garde.[45] But this was not to be the overriding public image of the two singers; ultimately it was Umm Kulthum who was seen as more of a traditionalist and 'Abd al-Wahhab as the innovator.[46]

'Abd al-Wahhab was also known for having adapted Western rhythms, especially Latin rhythms, to Arabic music—an innovation conspicuously employed in one of the *White Rose* songs.[47] But in other ways 'Abd al-Wahhab always remained grounded in musical convention. Particularly in the early years of his fame, his vocal technique was strongly rooted in traditional Arabic music, which was also studied by reciters of the Quran. A well-trained traditional singer had tremendous facility, and this was important for 'Abd al-Wahhab because he never strayed far from the traditional Arabic quarter tone modalities of Arabic music. A third traditional element of 'Abd al-Wahhab's style his reluctance to venture into harmony.[48] All these attributes of 'Abd al-Wahhab's music kept him rooted in Arabic tradition, while the love story and his fruitfully bureaucratic lifestyle put him out in the social vanguard.

But even the songs 'Abd al-Wahhab performs in the course of *The White Rose* are not the most explicit ties to a musical *isnad* leading back to authentic Egyptian tradition. The most important scene for linking 'Abd al-Wahhab to tradition (and perhaps the most important scene in the entire film) is both visual and musical. The scene comes late in the film, when 'Abd al-Wahhab's love affair with his boss's daughter has been discovered.

When Galal's love affair with Raga` is revealed to her father, he immediately fires the young musician, forcing him, finally, to make a living by his art rather than through his education. We see Galal come home to his apartment after having been fired from his job and told he can no longer see the woman of his dreams. He walks through the street, stopping in front of a poster for a performer. As he stares at it, the performer's name fades into his own—Muhammad Galal. He is obviously imagining the greatness that could be his if he only devoted himself to art. He signals his intention to become a star. 'Abd al-Wahhab enters his apartment and does an interesting thing: he looks at three portraits. The first is a painting of Abduh al-Hamuli, who was the major musical figure of the late nineteenth century. An al-Hamuli tune plays in the background as 'Abd al-Wahhab looks at the painting. 'Abd al-Wahhab then looks at the second portrait: Salama al-Higazi, a prominent performer of 'Abd al-Wahhab's youth, who was credited with having founded the musical theater in Egypt. An al-Higazi tune plays in the background as 'Abd al-Wahhab looks at the picture. Then on to the third portrait: Sayyid Darwish, again with one of his songs playing in the background. Darwish was a nationalist hero who was publicly associated with Egypt's 1919 revolution against the British. 'Abd al-Wahhab actually worked with Darwish. The scene ends with the camera swinging onto a closeup of Ab al-Wahhab's face. The effect is unmistakable: he receives the authentic tradition from his predecessors. It is a kind of modernity without rupture, which makes it the perfect modernity for a nationalist.

*The White Rose* was a prototypical film. Most important, it built a vernacular imagery that was locally rooted and temporally continuous. This was not a vernacular imagery that corresponded to stereotypical notions about "low" vernacular language counterpoised to a sharply differentiated "high" language—the vernacular of "diglossia." Other films worked through more explicit juxtapositions of social types than *The White Rose*, but these too revolved around a synthesis of narrative elements into a specifically Egyptian modern identity. What made *The White Rose* a paradigmatic film was that it created 'Abd al-Wahhab as a figure who combined local identity with both heritage and worldly sophistication—worldly sophistication, and even technological and managerial expertise to which the character's education and rent-collecting scenes allude (he pointedly makes a foreigner pay his due), but explicitly *not* Westernization. Shafiq, the corrupt suitor, was an obvious manifestation of that, just as the scheming mother signaled the dead hand of tradition.

*The White Rose* was a template for Egyptian films through the 1960s. It was not the only one (although it is the oldest Egyptian film available on commercial video tape), and not necessarily the one that comes to mind most readily when one thinks of the standard-setting Egyptian films. But it was certainly an early and outstanding example of how Egyptian cinema created a sense of national community. And the pattern continued for several decades. In 1969 'Abd al-Wahhab himself financed the production of an updated variation of the same tale of radical conservatism. This was *Papa's Up a Tree*,[49] starring 'Abd al-Wahhab's protégé 'Abd al-Halim Hafiz. The story is about a singing college student (although not, as in *The White Rose*, a professional musician) who chafes under traditional practices barring him from seeing the girl he loves without a chaperone. By the end of the story, the boy learns the value of tradition, and everybody lives happily ever after. From *The White Rose* until the end of the Nasserist period, this was the dominant metagenre.

But by the late 1980s such films were sometimes ridiculed, or even more often remembered with a degree of nostalgia, as something from a bygone age. *The White Rose* often fit in the former category. Many Egyptians of the younger generation sneered at the idea of watching 'Abd al-Wahhab films, even if they liked 'Abd al-Wahhab's music in principle. Although the older type of metagenre continues to be produced (especially on television, which is controlled by the government), at a certain point it began to compete with a new style of entertainment, which, at least for a time, overtook the old modernism in popularity. This brings us to 'Adil Imam.

## EGYPTIAN "POSTMODERNISM": FROM AUTHENTICITY TO HUMILIATION

'Adil Imam might seem an odd character to associate with a discussion of Egyptian nationalism. To many Egyptians of the older generation, the very idea of counterpoising Muhammad 'Abd al-Wahhab with 'Adil Imam inspires revulsion. But the point here, of course, is *not* that the two are similar but that they provide a clear contrast between two different metagenres. Both are metagenres developed through mass culture; it is the promulgation of the two men's contrasting imagery that draws them together and that facilitates a comparison between different historical periods.

'Adil Imam is a comedian—a very popular one, but until recently, a phenomenon taken lightly by those who create nationalist iconography. The 'Adil Imam film discussed here is *Ragab on a Hot Tin Roof*.[50] This film is not about the social construction of Egyptian modernity, but rather about a moment of radical doubt about the effectiveness of such a construction. The construction of an image of modernity lies at the heart of Egyptian nationalism; thus the decline of modernism is closely linked to a crisis in the Egyptian national self-image. As Sivan[51] suggests, the period in which the film was produced was one in which the attractiveness of the state was severely tarnished. However, the film's scathingly critical tone suggests that a certain amount of protest from within the establishment was tolerated. In this case criticism of the modernist edifice built up by the state is by no means couched in terms of "Islamic resurgence."[52]

Although 'Adil Imam is mentioned in the media relatively infrequently—far less often than 'Abd al-Wahhab in any period since the singer first rose to prominence in the 1920s—his current popularity far outstrips that of 'Abd al-Wahhab. In fact, 'Adil Imam's popularity outstrips that of any actor in Egypt. Many now complain that Imam has been spoiled by success and that his audience is dwindling. Nonetheless, the only film I ever attended in Egypt at which tickets were being scalped was Imam's *Playing with the Bigshots*.[53]

Until the early 1990s, when Imam achieved a degree of critical success to go with his commercial appeal, one could not have guessed the actor's popularity from what was said about him in the press. There were, if anything, rather fewer articles written about him than about many entertainment figures who are far less active ('Abd al-Wahhab for instance). His breakthrough performance was in the play *School of Troublemakers*,[54] which ran from 1971 to 1974. Although he had the leading role, and the play was remembered primarily for the students' performances, reviews barely mentioned him. One review published during the play's first flush of success devoted only a single line to Imam in a one-page article.[55]

As a text, *School or Troublemakers* revolved around a female teacher's efforts to tame a number of wild undisciplined students. But primarily she must come to terms with the students' ringleader, the wildest troublemaker of all, who was played by 'Adil Imam. The students' resistance is chronicled in a number of colorful antics, but in the end, she convinces them of the value of education, thereby transforming them into useful citizens—a cheerily affirmative view of modern society. However, as a performance, *School of Troublemakers* was very different. The actors literally hijacked the script, turning a ninety-page text into a four-hour play through shameless ad-libbing, much of which was of a political nature. They downplayed the ending in which all problems were neatly resolved and the value of education affirmed. Not only did they treat education—a key modernizing institution—with a degree of disrespect bordering on contempt, but they also made jokes about the recently deceased Gamal 'Abd al-Nasser, and even laced the performance with mockery of the 1970s free-market economic policies of Sadat. Audiences liked Imam's subversion of the text; critics did not. Reviews of the play ignored Imam's character and wrote mainly in praise of the school administrators, who, in the performance, were nothing more than straight men for Imam and his gang of troublemakers to send up. Establishment intellectuals grumbled about cheap sensationalism in the commercial theater, which they often compared unfavorably with the golden era or state-subsidized theater in the 1960s. And by most formal criteria the critics were right: *School of Troublemakers* was a terrible play, but it was nonetheless a turning point in the career of 'Adil Imam and indeed of post-1960s Egyptian culture. The floodgates were open, and for a time, a surly spirit of cynicism and divisiveness reigned. The primary targets were modern institutions and the new economy. By the standards of the earlier metagenre of Egyptian popular culture typified by 'Abd al-Wahhab's *White Rose, School of Troublemakers* was downright antimodernist.

A few years after *School* finished its then-unprecedented four-year run, Imam began to appear in a number of films that carried the antimodernist theme of his breakthrough performance a step further. Among these post-*School of Troublemakers* productions was *Ragab on a Hot Tin Roof*,[56] which was Imam's breakthrough performance in the cinema—the performance that transformed him in that medium from star to superstar. The film is part of a trilogy that includes *Sha'ban below Zero*[57] and *Ramadan on the Volcano*.[58] Although the films are not formally a trilogy, one reviewer noted that when the first film, *Ragab*, came to the theaters, there were plans for "two or three Ragab films."[59] There were, in fact, no more Ragab films, but there were two more films in which the main character was named after an Islamic month and in which this character was described as "over" or "under" something. Also, the three characters were all very similar—naively believing in the system at first, corrupted and in prison by the end.

The three films illustrate a break with the sort of metanarrative developed in *The White Rose* and then reworked in many later films. Whereas *The White Rose* depicts the popularization of high art, in *Ragab* the starting point is vernacular identity—a localized ideal that corresponds roughly with the associations of vernacular language. A common gloss for such a figure is *ibn al-balad* (son of the country). The "son of the country" is a stereotypical figure with either social (class) referents or nationalistic referents, depending on whether the man who uses the phrase wants to emphasize his class position within Egyptian society or his authenticity vis-à-vis non-Egyptians. Just as vernacular language must be "elevated" through association with the eloquence of classicism, so must the authenticity of vernacular identity be improved through the benevolent action of the state. As one writer put it in an article on the depiction of "sons of the country" by a well known colloquial poet:

> The "son of the country" . . . is a man who, despite his poverty, is intelligent, aware, of ready insight, light-hearted, cheerful by nature, a joker, brave and gallant in his boldness. But social circumstances impose upon him ignorance and poverty, so he flees from reality in drugs and participates—unknowingly—in cultural backwardness through which his country drags him. If someone would stand ready to work for his treatment, and for his revival, his awakening would be magnificent.[60]

By itself the *ibn al-balad* persona is insufficient; it needs the salutary influence of higher ideals. This is not unlike the discourse on language, which stipulates a role in modern society for the vernacular only insofar as it can be made "eloquent" through association with classical ideals. Passages such as the one quoted above are either a call for greater attention to the needs of the poor, or, at their worst, a justification for intervention in the lives of the poor. This is quite common in nationalist ideology. Elites both need the authenticating aura of the "lower classes" (often composed of newly urbanized rural folk) and the radically transforming uniformities of industrial society. Fishman describes these dual requirements of nationalism as a "built-in dialectic."[61]

In contemporary Egypt one often encounters both a widespread realization of the constructed nature of such ideal types as *ibn al-balad* and a feeling that such constructions no longer move audiences the way they once might have. *Ragab on a Hot Tin Roof* typifies a mass-media treatment of the "son of the country" that differs sharply from the officially sanctioned stereotype. The 'Adil Imam trilogy as a whole parodies a movement from the presumed authenticity of the lower classes toward synthesis with the sort of higher ideals implied by both classical values and the modern educational system. The first film, *Ragab*, is about a peasant, and with each successive film, the protagonist becomes more "enlightened": in *Sha'ban* Imam plays a bureaucrat with a high school education who lives in the countryside; in *Ramadan* he plays a college dropout who works in a government ministry in Cairo. In the first film Imam starts out as a beleaguered "son of the country," crude but honest—"a man who, despite his poverty, is intelligent, aware, of ready insight, light-hearted, cheerful by nature, a joker, brave and gallant in his boldness." But though Imam moves progressively closer in each film to the urban center of enlightenment, he never prospers materially or morally other than by foul means. Some of the characters 'Adil Imam meets along his three-film journey into hell possess all the material marks of success that had been mainly the preserve of the "enlightened" class in Egyptian cinema since *The White Rose* in 1934. But such characters in post-1960s cinema typified by *Ragab* are more "Westernized," than "enlightened." Egyptian films have always featured such corrupted characters, but prior to the 1970s their nonauthenticity was frequently contrasted to other characters who more wholesomely embodied progress without abandoning heritage. In *Ragab* and the other films of Imam's trilogy, the handful of decent characters are mostly figures who have either rejected modern life or simply have not yet been affected by it.

The journey of mock-modernist transformation begins in the first film, *Ragab on a Hot Tin Roof*, which is adapted from the American film *Midnight Cowboy*.[62] *Midnight Cowboy* might seem to be an unlikely candidate for adaptation to the Egyptian screen. Not only is the original nihilistic, but Joe Buck, the film's protagonist, is a homosexual. *Ragab* retained the nihilism but carefully excised the homosexuality by substituting women for some of the characters and in some of the events that centered around men in the American film.

Ragab, the hero of the film, is a peasant played by 'Adil Imam. We first see him laboring in the fields, hacking at the hard earth with a *fas* (a heavy hoelike implement). He and a fellow peasant decide that if they are to prosper, the village must buy a tractor to do such onerous labor. The village elders agree, and after the Friday prayer[63] they announce that they will collect money from each family to buy the tractor and then set about choosing someone to go to the big city to buy it. Initially they want the *'umda* (headman) to go, but he is afraid of not being able to cope with the crowds and confusion of the city. Instead Ragab is selected as the most trustworthy man in the village and sent off ill-prepared for the big city.

Although this opening sequence occupies no more than five minutes of the film, it is one of the most important devices for making *Ragab* an Egyptianized adaptation of *Midnight Cowboy* rather than a purely imitative film. In *Midnight Cowboy* Joe Buck starts out in amoral squalor and goes nowhere. He goes to the city planning to make a living as a male prostitute, not realizing that most of the clientele for male prostitutes are men. There is no question of "spoiling" Joe Buck: he is already ruined. In fact, there is not a single character in *Midnight Cowboy* who is not similarly ruined. Ragab, however, starts off as naive as Joe Buck, but not particularly corrupt. In fact his fellow peasants choose him to make the journey to the city because he is considered morally outstanding. The journey itself is not for the purpose of sexual adventure and immoral profit, but to buy a tractor and bring prosperity to the entire village. *Midnight Cowboy* is about the state of alienation; *Ragab on a Hot Tin Roof* is about a transformation to alienation. This is one of the main devices for stamping the film as Egyptian rather than a copy of a foreign film. *Ragab* starts off from the same modernist premise as countless other films but then goes in a different direction. This is not to say that many other films do not feature peasants. Particularly in the partially nationalized cinema of the 1960s, peasants were in vogue. But such films tend to depict a very urban view of peasant life and to be concerned with bringing "progress" to the countryside or are a commentary on an assumed lack of same.[64] *Ragab* is unusual in that it portrays the countryside as a site of morality and progress, albeit a fragile morality rooted more in the absence of temptation than in true conviction, and a pale, somewhat rudimentary progress. But compared to what Ragab encounters in the city, the countryside appears relatively enlightened.

Ragab arrives in the city on the train clad in *galabiya* (robe) and a brown felt peasant's *taqiya* (a simple cap), hanging out of the window, eyes popping out of his head from the sight of so many people. The train pulls into the station to the sound of American bluegrass "hillbilly" music—banjos and fiddles. When I watched the film with some Egyptian students, they told me that the scene was funny because of Ragab's obvious naiveté—because he was a "hick," but that bluegrass music by itself would not necessarily evoke such an image. Nonetheless, virtually all of the music in *Ragab* was Western, the only exceptions being a singer at a nightclub in which Ragab gets swindled and a belly-dance song.

Ragab is taken by the swindler (the Egyptian equivalent of *Midnight Cowboy's* Ratso Rizzo) to a restaurant, where the peasant wolfs down roasted meat as a bemused con-man looks on—all this to a recording of a 1960s American novelty song called "Manamana." Later the swindler robs Ragab and leaves him with a bill for whiskey at a nightclub. The owner calls in three bouncers to shake down the frightened peasant. As Ragab eyes the huge men, the theme from "The Sorcerer's Apprentice" starts up. "The Sorcerer's Apprentice" theme returns when Ragab is discovered wandering the darkened Cairene streets by a policeman. Ragab runs, so the policeman pursues as the music becomes wilder. In another scene Ragab is about to have sex with a hideous old woman who has bought him a meal in a restaurant: we hear the high-pitched pulses played in the background of the murder scenes of *Psycho*; the woman's face appears distorted and threatening, and Ragab flees. When Ragab is searching for the Ratso character—we see Ragab lurking by a sleazy hotel where he hopes to find his tormentor—the James Bond theme plays. When "Ratso" dies at the end of the film, it is to a tune from *Ben Hur*. Audiences understand the irony in the use of these songs,[65] the

point comes across that this city moves to alien rhythms, never to familiar Arabic sounds.

The "Ratso" of *Ragab on a Hot Tin Roof* is named Bulbul—
"Nightingale." Bulbul, an unsuccessful gambler and hustler like his
American predecessor, spots Ragab lost in the crowd at the train station,
looking around himself and muttering "minayn yiwaddi 'ala fayn?"
(From where heads to where?). Bulbul hooks his bewildered prey by pre-
tending to recognize Ragab and telling the peasant that he comes from
the same village. He then keeps the gullible Ragab from spending his
money on the tractor by asking a tractor salesman if the tractor comes
with a *siks(i)bis* (six piece). Both Ragab and the salesman are embarrassed to admit that they don't know what a *siks(i)bis* is, and the negotiations quickly break down. A few scenes later Bulbul has Ragab guz-
zling whiskey and ogling the women at a nightclub thick with Bulbul's
fellow con men and women. "Di labsa min ghayr hudum" (She's dressed
without any clothes), says the astonished Ragab when he sees the belly
dancer.

One of Bulbul's accomplices working this nightclub is Bulbul's mis-
tress, Iglal, a buxom redhead wearing a skintight, strapless top, who
leads Ragab into thinking that he will sleep with her when the night is
through. Ragab gives his money to Bulbul "for safekeeping." Bulbul
quietly makes his exit while Ragab is drinking toast after toast to the
smiling Iglal; the money is quickly lost by the hapless Bulbul in a card
game. Ragab is freed from having to pay his bill at the nightclub by
another of Bulbul's accomplices, a fat man dressed as a peasant, who
claims that he was rescued in similar circumstances when he first came
to the city. When Ragab is sent on his way, the man promptly goes to
Bulbul's card game and collects his cut of the booty.

The remainder of the plot is similar enough to that of *Midnight
Cowboy* that no summary is necessary. Ragab searches for Bulbul, finds
him, and befriends him after a fashion. Along the way he endures
numerous indignities. Ragab tries to repent, but repentance is expensive:
how will he live? In the end only Bulbul can help him, but he does so by
turning Ragab into himself. Finally, Bulbul is killed by a sore loser in a
card game Ragab has won through beginner's luck. The man tries to
stab Ragab, but Bulbul throws himself in the way of the knife—the only
decent thing he has done in his entire life.

There are some other significant differences between *Ragab* and
*Midnight Cowboy*. Both the homosexuality and the psychological flashbacks of *Cowboy* are addressed differently in *Ragab*. There are two
sides to *Cowboy*'s homosexuality. One aspect of the matter is that it is
degrading: Joe Buck must endure sex in a movie theater with a frightened boy. The other aspect is Joe Buck's relationship with Ratso. Ratso

is virtually the only kind face Joe Buck sees in the entire film. Ratso and Joe Buck may not be lovers in a physical sense, but this is because Joe Buck cannot face that part of his nature.

Degradation is not communicated in *Ragab* through homosexual encounters (which are, in any case, not less degrading than Joe Buck's heterosexual encounters in *Cowboy*). Instead degradation is communicated by putting Ragab into a world that is completely emasculated. Scantily dressed women live alone in splendid villas while men scavenge in the ruins, which we see near the end of the film when Bulbul takes Ragab to his lair. The most humiliating scene in *Ragab*—very much the opposite number of the movie theater scene in *Midnight Cowboy*—is of Ragab washing a prositute's feet. Ragab protests weakly that "this is women's work," but he washes the prostitute's feet anyway because his only alternative is starving in the streets.

The friendly side of Joe Buck's relationship with Ratso is adapted to *Ragab* through a female character, Inshirah, whom Ragab stumbles upon when fleeing from the police. Inshirah is another red-haired woman—a poor, modest girl who looks like Iglal, but who functions in the film as Iglal's alter ego. Inshirah lives with her ailing father in a desperately poor area and works preparing *ful* (fava beans, a staple of poor Egyptians' diet) in large clay pots, which are distributed all over the city after a night of slow cooking; Iglal haunts penthouse nightclubs. When we first see Inshirah, she is ascending from a sooty pit where the pots are fired. Ragab thinks she is an *'afrita* (demon). Periodically Ragab returns to Inshirah and her kindly old father. They try to help him, but the non-corrupted characters in the world Ragab now inhabits are marginalized and helpless. Ragab eventually leaves Inshirah and sleeps with Iglal, only to discover that she was in league with Bulbul all along. Scenes featuring the two women are often paralleled—the good Inshirah coming directly after the corrupt Iglal so that the contrast between the two women is obvious. The scene in which Ragab washes the prostitute's feet is also immediately juxtaposed to a brief scene of Inshirah massaging her poor father's tired feet. The two women in *Ragab* take on the human characteristics, both good and bad, of *Midnight Cowboy*'s Ratso, but avoid the homosexuality of the original.

The flashbacks to Joe Buck's past in *Midnight Cowboy* are transferred in *Ragab* to occasional scenes of Ragab's village. The villagers wonder what has happened to Ragab, but there is surprisingly little sentiment to condemn him. Instead the villagers gather more money and send someone else to buy the tractor. By the end of the film the villagers have their tractor and are still wondering what happened to poor Ragab. As noted above, this is one of the chief differences between the Egyptian and American versions of the story. The village is a symbol of decency that is lacking in *Midnight Cowboy*. There may be no way Ragab can return to it, but at least the village flashbacks remind the viewer that somewhere there is a place where small bits of modern life can be absorbed without corrupting the salutary aspects of tradition, whereas the flashbacks in *Cowboy* serve only to affirm Joe Buck's brutalization. But as the tenuous position of Inshirah and her father shows, there is little hope of integrating village life with the city. Local identity—the vernacular in linguistic terms—does not benefit from the elevating influence of higher values in this film. Rather they are opposed to simple corruption.

The final difference between *Ragab* and *Midnight Cowboy* is that in the former Ragab complains openly to Inshirah that evil people seem to be gaining the upper hand in the world. Two other rather clumsy and didactic scenes involve the police. At least one critic attributed these scenes, especially those with the police, to pressure from the censors.[66] If this is true, Imam or his director, Ahmad Fu'ad, dealt with censorship pressure by trying to turn necessity into a virtue. In the first police scene Ragab is running witless on the corniche of a wealthy neighborhood, where he has just suffered yet another bewildering mishap in the big city. He happens upon a police officer, grabs at his arm breathlessly, and says, "Are you ready?" "For what?" says the officer. "For thieves and swindlers and smugglers. I tell you, the people are multiplying, and when they multiply, the bad people multiply with them. Are you ready?" "For what?" "To catch the bad people who are multiplying." The officer shoos him away. The scene is so obvious that it makes the police look ridiculous and draws more attention to the likelihood of censorship than to the supposedly honorable role of the police in catching criminals. The second time the police appear in *Ragab* is in the final instant of the film. Ragab has taken Bulbul's place hustling newcomers at the train station. Just as he latches onto a new mark, a policeman grabs Ragab's other arm and starts to hustle him off to prison. The picture freezes on this scene, and the film ends. Ragab, the peasant "son of the country," has been transformed, but transformed by the corrupting influence of the city rather than by the salutary intervention of modern life. This is not the transformation that modernists had envisioned.

## MODERNISM PAST AND FUTURE

There was a simple dichotomy between the reception of *Ragab* by the audience and that by the critics. Critics despised the film. As Rafiq al-Saban said,

> [*Ragab on a Hot Tin Roof* is] the story of a simple peasant in a small village, most of which is inhabited by naive villagers living as their

grandfathers had lived a hundred years ago, knowing nothing of progress and civilization except rumors. We find ourselves confronted not just by a character representing ignorance, but by a real contempt for the intelligence of the viewer. [The director] treats the audience as intellectually backward. The ultimate moral conclusions of the film completely ruin it—make it a despicable work. One cannot tell if it is criticism or an admonition, a lesson in morals, or a view of society. . . . How I wished that Ragab would actually jump from that hot tin roof and stop the affected convulsions that we saw through three-quarters of the film . . . and tell us what ignorance and backwardness do to a good man who comes from a green branch of a tree rooted in the generous soil of Egypt.[67]

In al-Saban's view it was entirely Ragab's backwardness that was at fault, not the social milieu into which he was thrust. The problem was that Ragab was living as his "grandfathers had lived a hundred years ago." Modernity had passed him by, and it was the duty of the film-makers to show how Ragab could be enlightened, not how he could be morally perverted.[68] For Saban, to leave the enlightenment of modernity entirely out of the film makes the story unrealistic or even nonsensical. Saban's criticism implies that the institutions of modernism are imbued with values—the values inherent in classicism—and that these values will raise the naive man from the "generous soil of Egypt." He echoes a discourse of reform evident in such fields as language, where high values are contained in the vessel of high language and modernizable classicism redeems the localism inherent in "low" language. The *ibn al-balad* (son of the country) ideal that *Ragab* parodies fits within the same discourse. Some parts of the passage on *ibn al-balad* quoted earlier could have been written by Saban: "Social circumstances impose upon [the *ibn al-balad*] ignorance and poverty, so he flees from reality in drugs and partici-pates—unknowingly—in cultural backwardness through which his country drags him. If someone would stand ready to work for his treat-ment, and for his revival, his awakening would be magnificent."[69] It is precisely the "revival and awakening" of an ideal created through ear-lier media of which *Ragab* makes fun.

It is unlikely that the audiences of *Ragab* felt those responsible for making the film, or 'Adil Imam, were contemptuous of them, as al-Saban claims. *Ragab*'s fans kept the film in the theaters for thirty-three straight weeks—a long run for the Egyptian cinema. Ten years later it was not the "unenlightened" who found *Ragab* appealing, but college students—the very audience that was supposed to be most conversant with the "progress and civilization" that Rafiq al-Saban saw as the nat-ural antidote to *Ragab*'s assumed vulgarity. *Ragab* was one of the films recommended to me by college students when I asked for opinions on

good popular films. After I had obtained a video copy of *Ragab*, I found
no difficulty in convincing students who had seen the film before to view
it with me again.

Conversely, I found scant interest among college students in seeing
the more critically acceptable 'Abd al-Wahhab films. After 'Abd al-
Wahhab died, two of these films were shown on the big screen, followed
by a panel discussion of his musical legacy. None of my friends attended
either the films or the discussion. Indeed, none of these events drew a
larger audience than twenty, half of whom were American students
studying Arabic.[70] "Overexposure" was the explanation given by the
organizers of the event for the poor attendance; there had been too
many showings of 'Abd al-Wahhab films at other locations and on television. But none of the students I spoke to had gone to any of these other
showings, and all had equal opportunity to see 'Adil Imam (whose films
they were not averse to seeing again) on video.

This is not to say that old films in general are shunned in all cases.
Indeed, one commonly hears the sentiment that "old films are better
than the ones being made today." And the old films are readily available
because the rise in the 1970s and 1980s of the new metagenre typified
by *Ragab* corresponds to the saturation of the Egyptian television market. By some time in the early 1970s essentially everyone in urban Egypt
who wanted to watch television was able to do so on some basis,
whether at home, in friends' homes, or in public places such as cafes. As
television became prevalent in Egypt, the "old" films migrated to the
new medium. But television films are chosen by employees of the state-
run television station, not marketed. It was in the movie theaters, where
culture had to be marketed, and where the audience had to choose how
to allocate its money, that the new style arose. The old popular culture
metagenre of progress built on a foundation of local and classicist ideals was forged very much under commercial conditions, but by the
1970s, it no longer maintained the ability to get audiences to spend
money on it.

The music market in some ways parallels and in other ways contrasts with the cinema. The music industry long remained relatively centralized by the expense of records and particularly by the impossibility
of cheaply copying records. This process of centralization was intensified in the 1950s when a newly independent Egyptian state increased the
broadcasting power of the national radio station and eliminated any
competition from nonnationalized stations broadcasting from Egyptian
soil. But in the 1970s the relationship between the musical product and
its potential media was redefined. The cassette recorder became easily
affordable to consumers, and suddenly music became both highly
portable and easily reproducible. A suddenly decentralized music indus-

try gave rise to a new breed of performer much less beholden to the tastes of state-appointed gatekeepers. The new singers who arose in this technological/consumer milieu are like 'Adil Imam's films in relation to those of Muhammad 'Abd al-Wahhab. Since the 1970s a common complaint is that "there are no more great voices." The new singers are almost always found wanting in comparison to those of a golden age of the past.[71] Of course 'Abd al-Wahhab himself is one of the great old voices against which the newcomers pale in comparison. He makes an apt figure of comparison in the fields of both music and cinema.

The significance of the changes in media technology, marketing strategy, and consumption habits since the 1970s is not that the old metagenre of popular culture has ceased to be heard or seen. State-controlled radio and television broadcasts assure that it lives on. But in popular culture, the modernist synthesis of vernacular and classicist cultural ideals typified by *The White Rose* is now the object of nostalgia, nostalgia for something no longer there. The agglutinative process of extending modernity along an unbroken line—Abduh al-Hamuli to Salama al-Higazi to Sayyid Darwish to 'Abd al-Wahhab for example—has been problematized since the 1970s. Nostalgia also can function as a commentary on the present. Thus the often-voiced opinion that the old films and songs were better, cleaner, and more artistic is not necessarily incompatible with the rise of the more bitter kind of criticism conveyed by films such as *Ragab on a Hot Tin Roof*.

A comparison of these two films, *The White Rose* in 1933 and *Ragab on a Hot Tin Roof* in 1979, indicates a shift in the metagenres most often employed in Egyptian mass culture. From the 1930s until the late 1960s, mass culture tended to parallel a certain type of modernist ideology prevalent in schools, universities, official institutions, and much writing. Films, songs, and the theater were an integral part of the vernacular culture of Egyptian nationalism. The narratives developed in such mass culture, and the discourse elaborating them in the popular press, aimed at a synthesis of local, Arab classicist, and foreign (usually technological) elements into a coherent national identity. Print capitalism, the engine of Benedict Anderson's well-known "imagined" national communities, was fully able to articulate the intellectual goals of such a synthesis. But other forms of capitalism were instrumental in vernacularizing the means of nationalist expression. "Screen capitalism," "song capitalism," and "theater capitalism" are important components of the nationalist project in Egypt, components that constructed vernacular identity in media less problematized by the social and religious conventions of writing.

*Ragab on a Hot Tin Roof* suggests a change in the metagenre of mass culture. Like *The White Rose*, it is a sample of a large body of works that express a similar construct of Egyptian identity. But the neat synthesis—"newspaper Arabic" in linguistic discourse; bourgeois society in many a film—does not occur in such works as *Ragab*. The old metagenre, like the discourse of simplified but still recognizably classical newspaper Arabic, was a centripetal construct, forcing the social extremes to the center. *Ragab* is centrifugal; it suggests fragmentation of the social body.

There is, of course, no clean dividing line between the old metagenre of national identity and the new one. Indeed, the ideal of social synthesis lives on in the state-controlled media and could conceivably continue to thrive if the television and radio were privatized. But in the most commercialized media, where individuals make conscious choices on what they consume, for a time the old metagenre of nationalist synthesis substantially gave way to a new and more fragmented metagenre often denounced as vulgar. This began to happen in the late 1960s and gained commercial force by the mid 1970s. There are obvious proximate causes for such a shift. The two enormously disruptive wars fought by Egypt in 1967 and 1973 caused many to question old cultural formulas. New technology made centralized control of any medium much more difficult. The "open door" economic policies of the 1970s brought a flood of controversial economic and political changes to Egypt.

The timing of the shift suggests even wider forces at work. The 1970s are often seen as a period of transition from a predominantly modernist cultural paradigm to one of postmodernity.[72] Such a shift assumes a transition from a centralized "Fordist" regime of capitalist economics to one of "flexible accumulation," from a preoccupation with internal structures of relatively coherent social entities to an emphasis on surfaces juxtaposed to one another in ways previously considered strange or untenable. Most important in this context, postmodernity problematizes boundaries, and most conspicuously, boundaries of the nation-state. Currently discussions of the relation between modernity and national identity[73] tends to emphasize the spread of modernity rather than the emergence of postmodernity. But in terms of the way nationalism is understood, the result is the same: national boundaries are no longer considered the primary frame of analytical reference. This chapter focused on a shift from a type of nationalism understood to be organically connected to modernity. Alternatively, the spread of modernity has been connected to the occurrence of globalization, which implies the erosion or even irrelevance of national borders in favor of transnational constructions of identity.

Egypt is certainly engaged in the flows of people, products, and cultural practices across borders that globalization discourse emphasizes. But this does not mean that national borders or national identity are irrelevant to Egyptians. By many standards nationalism is still a very potent ideal in Egypt as it is elsewhere. However, globalization discourse tends to see nationalism as a negative and archaic force: "Maimed bodies and barbed wire in Eastern Europe, xenophobic violence in France, flag waving in the political rituals of the election year here in the United States—all seem to suggest that the willingness to die for one's country is still a global fashion."[74] Such depictions of nationalism deny the intellectual validity of the view that a nationalist framework might, in some circumstances, be the best way to pursue a modern future.

The rise of an antimodernist expressive culture such as *Ragab on a Hot Tin Roof* does not necessarily imply an embrace of globalist antinationalism. By the early 1990s some Egyptian films began to revisit the sort of modernist narrative common before the 1970s. 'Adil Imam was a conspicuous part of this movement. The low opinion of Imam common in official cultural circles changed—perhaps temporarily—in the early 1990s when Imam began working with director Sharif Arafa and writer Wahid Hamid, with whom Imam made five well-received films and a play. Perhaps the best known of these was *Terrorism and Kabab*,[75] a comedy in which Imam's character, a well-meaning and highly ethical bureaucrat, gets mistaken for a terrorist, holds the government security forces to a standstill for a night, and finally escapes from his predicament through the sympathy of his fellow citizenry. The film depicts a society in which the sort of middle-class bourgeois values featured in pre-1970s films are endangered but very much worth fighting for. *Terrorism and Kabab* builds an optimistic image of potential social harmony within a national framework that was missing in many of Imam's previous blockbusters.[76] The relation of this film to Imam's previous work, and to the wider cultural milieu of contemporary Egypt, suggests an indeterminate status for nationalism. The nationalist ideal and its close ties to "enlightenment" and modernity, are often proclaimed with greater fervor than ever before. But some of the most popular depictions of contemporary society revolve around the struggle to maintain a coherent social body rather than its ultimate triumph depicted in the popular culture of an earlier age.

## REFERENCES

'Abd al-Rahman, Mustafa. 1989. *The Poetry in the Music of 'Abd al-Wahhab.* Cairo: Akhbar al-Yaum (Arabic).

"'Abd al-Wahhab al-Mumaththil" (n.a.). 1991. *Sabah al-khayr* 1844 (May 9): 63.

Abu-Absi, Samir. 1991. "The 'Simplified Arabic' of *Iftah Yaa Simsim*: Pedagogical and Sociolinguistic Implications." *Al-'Arabiyya.* 24: 111–21.

Abuhamida, Zakaria. 1988. "Speech Diversity and Language Unity: Arabic as an Integrating Factor." In *The Politics of Arab Integration*, Ciacomo Luciani and Ghassan Salamé, eds. Vol. IV. London: Croom Helm.

Anderson, Benedict. 1991. *Imagined Communities: Reflections on the Origin and Spread of Nationalism*. New York: Verso.

Appadurai, Arjun. 1996. *Modernity at Large: Cultural Dimensions of Globalization*. Minneapolis: University of Minnesota Press.

Armbrust, Walter. Forthcoming. "Egyptian Cinema and the Polemic on Islamism," International Institute of Asian Studies (Leiden), Working Papers of the IIAS.

———. 1998. "Terrorism and Kabab: A Capraesque View of Modern Egypt." In *Images of Enchantment: Performance, Art, and Image of the Middle East*, Sherifa Zuhur, ed. Cairo: American University in Cairo Press.

———. 1996. *Mass Culture and Modernism in Egypt*. Cambridge: Cambridge University Press.

'Asfur, Jabir.. 1993. *Difa'an 'an al-Tanwir*. Cairo: al-Hay'ah al-'Ammah li-Qusur al-Thaqafa.

'Ashari, Galal al-. 1971. "The Troublemakers Pass, but the Egyptian Theater Fails." *Ruz al-Yusuf* 2257 (September 13): 44–45 (Arabic).

Awad, Mahmud. 1991 (1971). *The Muhammad 'Abd al-Wahhab that Nobody Knew*. Cairo: Dar al-Ma'arif (Arabic).

'Azab, Yusri al-. 1986. "Ibn al-Balad as Bayram Saw Him." *Sabah al-khayr* 1580 (April 17): 36–37.

Badawi, E. M.. 1973. *Mustawayyat al-'Arabiyya al-Mu'asira*. Cairo: Dar al-Ma'arif.

Bhabha, Homi, ed. 1990. *Nation and Narration*. New York: Routledge.

Blanc, Haim. 1960. "Style Variations in Spoken Arabic: A Sample of Inter-dialectical Educated Conversation." In *Contributions to Arabic Linguistics*, Charles A. Ferguson, ed., Harvard Middle Eastern Monographs. Cambridge: Harvard University Press.

Bourdieu, Pierre. 1991. *Language and Social Power*. Cambridge: Harvard University Press.

Brown, Nathan. 1990. *Peasant Politics in Egypt*. New Haven: Yale University Press.

Catholic Egyptian Office for the Egyptian Cinema. n.d.. File on the film *Ragab on a Hot Tin Roof*.

Danielson, Virginia. 1997. *Shaping Tradition Arabic Song: The Career and Repertory of Umm Kulthum*. Chicago: University of Chicago Press.

———. 1996. "New Nightingales of the Nile: Popular Music in Egypt since the 1970s." *Popular Music* 15, no. 3 (October).

Farid, Samir. 1988. *The Identity of Arab Cinema*. Cairo: Dar al-Farabi (Arabic).

———. 1986. "The Image of the Egyptian on the Screen between Commercial Films and Art Films." In *The Egyptian Man on the Screen*, Hashim al-Nahhas, ed. Cairo: General Egyptian Book Organization (Arabic).

Ferguson, Charles. 1971 [1959]. "Diglossia." In *Language Structure and Language Use: Essays by Charles Ferguson*. Selected and introduced by Anwar S. Dil. Stanford: Stanford University Press.

Fishman, Joshua. 1972. *Language and Nationalism: Two Integrative Essays.* Rowley, MA: Newbury House.

Ghanim, Fathi. 1991. "The Struggle of Art, Politics and Culture from the 1919 Revolution to the 1952 Revolution." *Ruz al-yusuf* 3283 (May 13): 8–9 (Arabic).

Harvey, David. 1990. *The Condition of Postmodernity.* Oxford: Basil Blackwell.

Hasanayn, 'Adil. 1991. *Muhammad 'Abd al-Wahhab.* Cairo: Traykrumi (Arabic).

Hassan, S. A. El-. 1979. "Educated Spoken Arabic in Egypt and the Levant: A Critical Review of Diglossia and Related Concepts." *Archivum Linguisticum* 10:112–25.

Hifni, Ratiba al-. 1991. *Muhammad 'Abd al-Wahhab.* Cairo: Dar al-Shuruq (Arabic).

Hobsbawm, Eric. 1992. *Nations and Nationalism since 1780: Programme, Myth, Reality.* New York: Cambridge University Press.

'Imara, Muhammad. 1994. "Al-Tajdid al-Islami Yu'id al-Tawazun ila Masadir al-Ma'rifa." *al-Sha'b* (April 8, 1994): 9.

Kamal, 'Abd Allah. 1991. "*Singer for the Ages.*" *Ruz al-Yusuf* 3283 (13 May): 74–75 (Arabic).

Karim, Muhammad. 1972. *Memoirs of Muhammad Karim* (two volumes). Cairo: al-Idhaca wa al-Tilifizyon (Arabic).

Landau, Jacob. 1958. *Studies in the Arab Theatre and Cinema.* Philadelphia: University of Pennsylvania Press.

Levine, Lawrence. 1988. *Highbrow/Lowbrow: The Emergence of Cultural Hierarchy in America.* Cambridge: Harvard University Press.

Mahmud, Yousseff. 1986. "Arabic after Diglossia." In *The Fergusonian Impact.* J. A. Fishman et al., eds. Vol. 1. New York: Mouton de Gruyter.

Malkmus, Lizbeth, and R. Armes. 1991. *Arab and African Film Making.* London: Zed.

Miller, Daniel. 1995. "Anthropology, Modernity and Consumption." In *Worlds Apart: Modernity through the Prism of the Local,* ed. Daniel Miller. New York: Routledge.

Mitchell, T. F. 1986. "What Is Spoken Educated Arabic?" *International Journal of the Sociology of Language* 61.

Najmi, Kamal al-. 1992. *Muhammad 'Abd al-Wahhab: Singer of the Century.* Muhandisin, Egypt: Awraq lil-Nashr wa al-I'lam (Arabic).

Nassar, Fayiz. 1975. *Memoirs of 'Abd al-Wahhab.* Beirut: Dar al-Nahda al-Haditha (Arabic).

Parkinson, Dilworth. 1991. "Searching for Modern Fusha: Real-life Formal Arabic." *Al-Arabiyya* 24: 31–64.

Radwan, Lutfi. 1991. *Muhammad 'Abd al-Wahhab: A Biography.* Cairo: Dar al-Hilal (Arabic).

Ramadan, 'Abd al-'Azim. 1991. "'Abd al-Wahhab and the Middle Class." *Uktubir* 759 (May 12, 1991): 16–17 (Arabic).

Saban, Rafiq al-. n.d. "Ragab on a Hot Tin Roof." File in the Catholic Egyptian Office for the Cinema (Arabic).

Sahhab, Salim. 1991. "What 'Abd al-Wahhab added to the legacy of Sayyid Darwish." *Al-Musawwar* 3474 (May 10): 26–27 (Arabic).

Shusha, Muhammad al-. 1975. "Introduction" to Kamal Salim, *The Complete Text and Scenario of the Film Resolution.* Cairo: General Egyptian Book Organization (Arabic).

Sivan, Emanuel. 1990. "The Islamic Resurgence: Civil Society Strikes Back." *Journal of Contemporary History* 25: 353–64.

Tabarak, Muhammad. 1991. *The Riddle of 'Abd al-Wahhab.* Cairo: Akhbar al-Yaum (Arabic).

Taufiq, S'ad al-Din. 1969. *The Story of Cinema in Egypt.* Cairo: Dar al-Hilal (Arabic).

Tayyar, Rida` al-. 1981. *The City in the Arab Cinema.* Beirut: al-Mu'assasa al-'Arabiya lil-Dirasat wa al-Nashr (Arabic).

———. 1980. *The Peasant in the Arab Cinema.* Beirut: al-Mu'assasa al-'Arabiya lil-Dirasat wa al-Nashr (Arabic).

Twitchell, James. 1992. *Carnival Culture: The Trashing of Taste in America.* New York: Columbia University Press.

van Nieuwkerk, Karin. 1993. *A Trade Like Any Other: Female Singers and Dancers in Egypt.* Austin: University of Texas Press.

## FILMOGRAPHY

'Arafa, Sharif. 1992. *Terrorism and Kabab* (Al-Irhab wa al-kabab). Cairo: Wahid Hamid Films.

———. 1991. *Playing with the Bigshots* (Al-Li'b ma' al-kubar). Cairo: Wahid Hamid Films.

Badr Khan, Ahmad. 1966. *Sayyid Darwish.* Cairo: General Cinema Organization.

———. 1937. *Anthem of Hope* (Nashid al-amal). Cairo: Studio Misr.

Barakat, Henri. 1980. *Sha'ban below Zero* (Sha'ban taht al-sifr). Cairo: Aflam al-Karawan.

Davies, Valentine. 1955. *The Benny Goodman Story.* Hollywood: Universal Studios (Aaron Rosenberg).

Fu'ad, Ahmad. 1979. *Ragab on a Hot Tin Roof* (Ragab foq safih sakhin). Cairo: Husayn Yaqut.

Galal, Nadir. 1994. *The Terrorist* (Al-Irhabi). Cairo: Mustafa Mitwalli.

Imam, Hasan al-. 1975. *Badi'a Masabni.* Cairo: Ahmad al-Haruni.

———. 1974. *Bamba Kashr.* Cairo: Ahmad al-Haruni.

———. 1963. *Shafiqa the Copt* (Shafiqa al-qibtiyya). Cairo: Hilmi Rafla.

Kamal, Husayn. 1984. *The Boy Sayyid, the Servant* (Il-Wad sayyid il-shaghghal). Cairo: Samir Khafagi (videotaped play).

———. 1969. *Papa's up a Tree* (Abi fauq al-shagara). Cairo: Saut al-Fann.

Karim, Muhammad. 1933. *The White Rose* (Al-Warda al-bayda'). Cairo: Muhammad 'Abd al-Wahhab.

Kramp, Fritz. 1938. *Lashin.* Cairo: Studio Misr.

Mann, Anthony. 1954. *The Glen Miller Story.* Hollywood: Universal Studios (Aaron Rosenberg).

Sab'awi, Ahmad al-. 1985. *Ramadan on the Volcano* (Ramadan fauqa al-burkan). Cairo: Aflam al-Karawan.

Salim, Kamal. 1939. *Resolution* (Al-'Azima). Cairo: Studio Misr.

Schlesinger, John. 1969. *Midnight Cowboy*. Hollywood: United Artists (Jerome Hellman).

Sharqawi, Galal al-. 1972. *School of Troublemakers* (Madrasat al-mushaghibin). Cairo: al-Fannaniyin al-Muttahidin (videotaped play).

Thorpe, Richard. 1957. *Jailhouse Rock*. Hollywood: MGM.

Volpi, Mario. 1932. *Anthem of the Heart* (Unshudat al-fu'ad). Cairo: Nahhas Sphinx Films.

## NOTES

1. Miller 1995, p. 1.
2. See Karim 1933.
3. See Fu'ad 1979.
4. Anderson 1991.
5. See Fishman 1972, pp. 54–55; Anderson 1991, pp. 41–49; Bourdieu 1991, pp. 45–48; Hobsbawm 1992, pp. 102–20.
6. See Ferguson 1971.
7. See, for instance, Badawi 1973.
8. See Parkinson 1991.
9. See Abuhamida 1988.
10. See Parkinson 1991.
11. For views on the need to bring written Arabic closer to spoken expression (or conversely, the observed convergence of the two in some circumstances), see Abu-Absi 1991, Hassan 1979, Blanc 1960, Mitchell 1986, and Mahmud 1986.
12. See, for instance, Anderson 1991, pp. 41–49.
13. See ibid., p. 20.
14. See ibid.
15. See ibid., p. 30.
16. See ibid., p. 31.
17. See Bourdieu 1991, p. 45.
18. See ibid., p. 48.
19. See ibid., p. 47.
20. See Levine 1988 and Twitchell 1992.
21. See Anderson 1991.
22. See Bhabha 1990.
23. However, as the globalization of media exposes Egypt to a much greater variety of media sources—both regional (primarily the Gulf) and beyond (Europe and the United States)—the state has responded by investing very heavily in media technology over which it can exercise a measure of control.
24. The most common traditionally dressed characters appeared in comedies, especially those of Nagib al-Rihani and 'Ali al-Kassar, both of whom had popularized "traditional" characters in the theater; see Landau 1958. Another 1939

film, *Resolution* by Salim 1939, is often cited as the forerunner of a more sympathetic style of treating traditional characters; for more on *Resolution*, see Armbrust 1996; Malkmus 1991, p. 30; al-Shusha 1975; and Taufiq 1969, pp. 65–80.

25. See Farid 1986, p. 209.

26. See Farid 1988, pp. 8–9.

27. Throughout his life the press faithfully reported 'Abd al-Wahhab's activities, long after the peak of his singing, and perhaps even composing, prowess. When he died on May 3, 1991, his funeral caused barely a ripple in the streets, although every major newspaper and magazine devoted a great deal of attention to him, eulogizing the deceased singer as "the last of the giants." All of the daily and weekly press ran special issues on 'Abd al-Wahhab and continued to do so for several weeks after his death. Also a number of books on 'Abd al-Wahhab were either published or reissued; see Awad 1991 [1971]; Radwan 1991; Tabarak 1991. This is far from a complete list of the books written about 'Abd al-Wahhab, but only those readily available on downtown Cairo street corners at the time. Some other biographies of 'Abd al-Wahhab (again, there is no pretense to comprehensiveness in this list) include Nassar 1975; 'Abd al-Rahman 1989; Hasanayn 1991; al-Hifni 1991; al-Najmi 1992. Virtually all of these books and special issues gave 'Abd al-Wahhab's films prominent mention.

28. See Farid 1986, p. 208.

29. See Karim 1933.

30. See Karim 1972, pp. 194–201.

31. See Mann 1954.

32. See Davies 1955.

33. See Imam 1963.

34. See Imam 1974.

35. See Imam 1975. This is a selection of the dancer biographies made in the Egyptian cinema. They were largely the labor of one man, director Hasan al-Imam, who reveled in a reputation for making melodramatic and sexy films.

36. See Badr Khan 1966.

37. See Thorpe 1957.

38. See Badr Khan 1937.

39. That distinction goes to *Anthem of the Heart*; see Volpi 1932. Egyptian film Historians tend to ignore *Heart* because it was directed by an Italian, Mario Volpi, and because the director made no effort to use music as part of the story. See "'Abd al-Wahhab al-Mumaththil" 1991.

40. For more on the status of entertainers see Danielson 1997 on musicians and Van Nieuwkerk 1993 on dancers. Both are more concerned with female rather than male performers, but both extensively describe general social attitudes toward performers.

41. See, for instance, Awad 1991, pp. 41–43, and Kamal 1991.

42. Indeed, the history of *The White Rose* mirrors the events of the film to some degree. When the film opened in December of 1933, it became something of a national cause. Egyptian students opposed to British rule had been trying to organize a boycott of foreign-owned theaters. They enforced the boycott by leaving chlorine "stinkbombs" in the aisles. Unfortunately, *The White Rose* was to open in the Royal Theatre, which was foreign owned. But the students agreed

to relax the boycott for the opening week, and a sign was affixed to the theater, saying, "You are Egyptian, and it was Egyptians who made what you are seeing here. Be proud of your *Egyptianness* and see the film *The White Rose* in the Royal Theater beginning on December 4, 1933"; see Karim 1972, pp. 198–99. Politicians had the film moved during the second week to the Metropole, which was also owned by foreigners. The idea was to spread the "protection" around. Then the film was moved to the Fu'ad Theater, which had been founded by a group of business school students who made up the Cinematograph Company. The group included 'Abd Allah Fikri Abaza (who first introduced Karim to 'Abd al-Wahhab—see Karim 1972, p. 162). The Fu'ad Theater had been the Gozi Palace, but it was soon abandoned by the group in favor of the Cosmo, which was also temporarily renamed the Fu'ad. *The White Rose* moved to the new theater on January 10, 1934, but then closed in May of the same year with a loss of LE 12,000; see Karim 1972, p. 199.

43. According to Danielson 1997 a genre called the *"ughniya"* (song) developed during the interwar period. The *ughniya* differed structurally from previous genres. Danielson does not, however, ascribe its development to any single composer.

44. A traditional *takht* could also include a *riqq* (tambourine), and a *qanun* (zither), as well as an *'ud* (lute) and violin.

45. Ultimately both singers used a mixture of modernist and traditionalist imagery; see Danielson 1997. Umm Kulthum's public reputation eventually tilted a bit toward evoking conservatism and 'Abd al-Wahhab's toward the modernist.

46. Others consider aspects of his life that were not strictly musical to have contributed to his innovativeness. His association with Shauqi, for example, is often mentioned as having been important in raising music from a state of "vulgarity" to a true artistic level; see Ghanim 1991. Such arguments, however, neither account for the pervasiveness of "vulgar" music nor attempt to give a wider view of singers in 'Abd al-Wahhab's generation (other than Umm Kulthum) who may have also have consciously tried to portray themselves as "art" singers. One author cautions that Western categories of art music and popular music do not necessarily transfer to an Egyptian or Arab context; see Danielson 1996. This is undoubtedly true in terms of how the formal characteristics of musical categories map onto a given singer or song's popularity in simple quantitative terms. But it has never stopped Egyptian or Arab intellectuals from trying to define high/low cannons of musical taste. Possibly modernists everywhere have an urge to create such categories; see Levine 1988 for a comparative case.

47. In the end, the most unambiguous musical innovations attributed to 'Abd al-Wahhab are expanding the *takht* (traditional ensemble) and introducing Latin rhythms. Even in these cases the literature on 'Abd al-Wahhab doesn't give a very clear or extensive picture of what other musicians of the period were doing. In the press a great deal of emphasis is placed on 'Abd al-Wahhab's innovativeness. For example, see al-Najmi 1992 and Sahhab 1991.

48. There is no consensus on the compatibility of harmony with Arabic music. But by the 1930s other composers were experimenting with it. For example, the background music to the films *Lashin* and *Resolution* was harmonic and

was composed by Egyptian 'Abd al-Hamid 'Abd al-Rahman; see Kramp 1938. Also, a composer named Muhammad Hasan al-Shaja'i was praised in a popular magazine as early as 1934 for arranging Sayyid Darwish music from the plays *Shahrazad*, *Al-Hilal*, and *Rahit 'Alayk* with harmony; see *Al-Ithnayn*, no. 2, p. 46 [June 25, 1934]. Several of the songs composed by Muhammad al-Qasabgi in Umm Kulthum's second film, *Anthem of Hope*, were harmonized; see Badr Khan 1937, and Danielson 1997. It is possible that most of the "firsts" attributed to 'Abd al-Wahhab were in fact developed by many people over time. This does not, of course, imply that 'Abd al-Wahhab was not an outstanding musician and the most popular singer of his day, but his main virtue may have been that he integrated new elements into Arabic music better than his contemporaries, not that he invented such elements.

49. See Kamal 1969.

50. See Fua'd 1979.

51. See Sivan 1990, pp. 356–58.

52. It should be pointed out, however, that *Ragab* and other films like it criticize without offering any specific alternative to the bankrupt image of modernity it presents. Islamists, of course, do offer at least the hope of an alternative. By the 1990s, filmmakers began to distance themselves from the deconstructivist criticism some of them had been emphasizing. This was reflected in Imam's career, particularly in *The Terrorist*; see Galal 1994. For more on *The Terrorist*, see Armbrust (forthcoming).

53. Another measure of Imam's popularity is that his play *The Boy Sayyid, the Servant* played continuously for eight years, from 1984 to 1992; see Kamal 1984. It is often said that what kept the play going was tourists from the Gulf. However, *Sayyid* came after a five-year run for *Shahid Mashafsh-(i) Haga* (The witness who witnessed nothing, starting in the mid 1970s), and *School of Troublemakers* ran for eight years. Parts of both of the earlier plays are regularly aired on television, and they also spanned a period when Gulf tourism was much less significant than today. Imam's play *Al-Za'im* (The leader, directed by Sharif Arafa) started in 1993 ran until 1998. The play has received far more critical acclaim than Imam's earlier stage work. The director of the play stated that he hoped *The Leader* would last even longer than *The Boy Sayyid*; interview between Sharif Arafa and author, August 28, 1994.

54. See al-Sharqawi 1972.

55. See al-'Ashari 1971.

56. See Fu'ad 1979.

57. See Barakat 1980.

58. See al-Sab'awi 1985.

59. The information is from the Catholic Egyptian Office for the Egyptian Cinema n.d.

60. See al-'Azab 1986, p. 36.

61. See Fishman 1972.

62. See Schlesinger 1969. The general resemblance of the two films is obvious, although there are also some fairly significant differences. At least one critic also noted in an article that *Ragab* was based on *Midnight Cowboy*; see Catholic Egyptian Office for the Cinema n.d.

63. The way the Friday prayer is incorporated into the story is typical of how the film took a pastiche of elements from the American original and adapted them to the local setting. *Midnight Cowboy* also featured a "prayer," which was intended to consecrate a task that is about to be undertaken. The "task" in *Cowboy* is for Joe Buck to begin working as a male prostitute, and the "prayer" is initiated by a dangerously addled old pimp (who appears to be planning on being Joe Buck's first customer). Aside from the general outline of the two stories, many of the elements of *Cowboy* appear scrambled throughout *Ragab*, some changed greatly, and some changed very little. Some of these elements are as follows: arriving in the big city (on a bus in *Cowboy*, and on a train in *Ragab*); being awakened by a policeman after being swindled (on the street in *Ragab*, in a movie theater in *Cowboy*); a hopeless search for the swindler in a vast and confusing city; eventually finding the swindler; eventually teaming up with the swindler; fleeing in revulsion from a corrupt old man (*Cowboy*)/old woman (*Ragab*); imagining that he could be hired by the opposite sex as a prostitute; being taken in by a woman with a dog (the woman wants sex in *Cowboy*, wants a dog trainer in *Ragab*, although *he* thinks she wants sex); a hopeless longing to "go straight" long after there is any possibility of doing so (on the bus to Florida in *Cowboy*, with an honest girl who will sell her father's mule so that he can travel abroad in *Ragab*). Not all the elements match perfectly, and there are some differences (although not in the alienated tone of the films), but there are enough similarities that *Ragab*'s pedigree is not in doubt.

64. For more on the image of the peasant in Egyptian cinema, see al-Tayyar 1980 and 1981, pp. 45–46. For more on urban attitudes toward the Egyptian peasantry, see Brown 1990, pp. 59–82.

65. Very likely some of these musical references were understood by the audience. For example, sections of *Fantasia*, the Disney cartoon featuring "The Sorcerer's Apprentice," are played often on the television (although nobody I knew remembered if it was played when *Ragab* was first run). The *Psycho* tune was very likely also familiar to many viewers; I found that Hitchcock was well known and liked by many of my friends and acquaintances. The same was true of James Bond.

66. The information is from the Catholic Egyptian Office of the Cinema n.d.

67. See Saban n.d.

68. The enlightenment so heavily emphasized by al-Saban is currently a bone of contention between the cultural establishment and its Islamist critics. For example, 'Asfur 1993 is a prominent figure in the state-sponsored campaign to defend *tanwir* (enlightenment). 'Imara 1994 typifies the Islamist line on *tanwir*, which in this case consists of an attempt to undermine the establishment chain of authority tracing the descent of modernist thought in Egypt from the midnineteenth century to the present.

69. See al-'Azab 1986, p. 36.

70. The event was held at the American University in Cairo July 8, 9, and 10, 1991. Film festivals featuring Salah Abu Sayf and Yusuf Shahin had been held the previous two summers at the same location and with the same level of publicity. Both the Abu Sayf and the Shahin festivals had nearly filled the one thousand-seat capacity of the American University's Ewart Hall.

71. Danielson describes the development of Egyptian music since the 1970s; see Danielson 1996 and Armbrust 1996.

72. See, for instance, Harvey 1990.

73. See Appadurai 1996.

74. See ibid., pp. 159–60.

75. See Arafa 1992.

76. Both *Terrorism and Kabab* of ʻArafa 1992, and *Ramadan on the Volcano* of al-Sabʻawi 1985, the final film of Imam's "over and under" trilogy, are set in a well-known government building on Cairo's main square. For a comparison of the two films, see Armbrust 1998.

# CHAPTER 10

# *Visions of Iran: Persian-Language Television in the United States*

## Mandana Limbert

In the fall of 1992, the talking head on a Persian-language television program broadcast in Washington, D.C. said, "[Even] if they were in a foreign country for ten years, twenty years, thirty years, they still wouldn't be from here. That is why we will never abandon our identity, our national identity."[1] I was struck by the implications of this statement: no matter when an Iranian left Iran, what she remembers, or even if she never goes back, her *national* identity should always be Iranian. What was also implied by this avowedly proroyalist program was that she was supposed to be an Iranian *despite* the present regime of the Islamic Republic. The television program called upon the nation without the present state. Her connection to Iran was supposed to be to the land, to particular versions of history, and to a culture and society unchanged by the current regime. The Iran that this television program in Washington, D.C., envisioned, one that was both thousands of miles away and overturned by a revolution, alerted me to a novel dimension of Middle Eastern nationalism, one constructed in the United States. In this chapter, I examine three Persian-language television programs aired in the United States and analyze their constructions of Iranian national identity almost twenty years after the 1978–79 Islamic revolution. As each program negotiates who and where Iranians are, there is a tension between appealing to an all-encompassing Iranianness and defining that national identity.

Nationalist images are not confined to the physical boundaries of nations themselves. As people cross borders, sometimes even acquiring new passports, their places of emotional and nostalgic reference may remain the homeland.[2] In a world where having a nationality is generally taken for granted, migrating can mean taking that nationality to the next nation and adopting a hyphenated identity. As scholars[3] have illustrated in different ways, images and descriptions of nations serve as proof that peoples' lives continue simultaneously in different sites, as nostalgic reminders of the recent or ancient past and as continuing enactments of the reproducing present. Since these images and descriptions are not restricted to the borders of nation-states, diaspora communities easily see, hear, and read about how their homelands continue to exist without them. Picking up the telephone, writing and receiving letters, watching films and television, reading the newspaper, faxing, using the internet, and flying back and forth all enforce the continuing presence of the distant land. Diaspora television works toward evoking Iranian national identity by reminding its viewers of their shared origins and by enacting a supposedly shared culture.

## MASS MEDIA AND THE MIDDLE EASTERN CONTEXT

Recent studies on mass media in the Middle East have examined the place of nation-ness in television and film productions. Abu-Lughod[4] focuses on the condescending and misguided attempts of urban middle-class television and film producers to educate and modernize the Egyptian nation as well as on the absence of religion, even as an alternative morality, in soap operas. Armbrust[5] analyzes how the style and content of Egyptian films have changed toward a pessimism about the modernist nationalist projects of the earlier part of this century. Whereas these studies focus on a community of producers who have similar aspirations and analyze viewers' differing interpretations, this chapter compares several visions of a distant nation. This emphasis highlights the complex and sometimes contending ways television programs play with national identity.

Naficy[6] has carefully documented the history and transformations of Iranian television in Los Angeles. He emphasizes the centrality of nationalism in exile television, distancing himself from Bozorgmehr, Sabagh, and Der-Martirosian, who have argued that the varying assimilation speeds and social networks of Iranian subgroups in Los Angeles prevent an all-encompassing national identity. Naficy focuses on the liminality of Iranians in Los Angeles and suggests that this position, as evident in the television programs, produces "the consolidation of nationality."[7] While Naficy does not deny the internal differences between the programs, he stresses how this diversity is muted. My interest is to describe the variations in the television programs showing the ways each portrays an all-encompassing Iranianness; confronts questions of ethnic, political, religious and social affiliations; and negotiates the problem of place. The contending images establish the boundaries within which differences are played out: a Foucauldian field formed by the very enactments and declarations of difference.[8] The dispersed and opposing signs of national identity form the limits and possibilities of Iranianness.

## IRANIANS AND PERSIAN-LANGUAGE TELEVISION IN THE UNITED STATES

The majority of the recent Iranian immigrants to the United States left Iran due to opposition to and fear of the present regime or because of the eight-year war with Iraq (1980–88). Nevertheless, the postrevolution population in the United States is heterogeneous and includes a number of religious groups such as Assyrian and Gregorian Christians, Baha'is, Jews, Shi'ite and Sunni Muslims, and Zoroastrians, as well as ethnic groups such as Arabs, Armenians, Baluchis, Kurds, Persians, and Turks.[9] While there are large populations of Iranians in New York and Washington, D.C., most settled in Southern California. The number of Iranians in Southern California is highly contested and varies between eight hundred thousand, according to the *Los Angeles Times* in 1992, and fifty-three thousand to seventy-four thousand, according to a UCLA-based study six years earlier in 1986.[10] Despite the drastic differences between these figures, even over six years, Los Angeles is the city with the largest population of Iranians outside Iran[11] and is frequently called "Tehrangeles" or "Irangeles"; it has become a center of Iranian diasporic literature, art, politics, and music. There, Iranians quickly established a variety of services, including restaurants, markets, publishing houses, nightclubs, Persian-language classes, travel agencies, and television programs, that foster connections, material and otherwise, with a land thousands of miles away.

Despite political restrictions and concerns, many of the hundreds of thousands of Iranians who immigrated to the United States after the 1978–79 Islamic revolution maintain connections with Iran through personal contact, international monetary transactions, and the media. Although these recent immigrants do not tend to return to Iran to live, many have returned for short trips to visit family. By the same token, family members who live in Iran and who do not want to or cannot immigrate also occasionally come to the United States. Iranians living in the United States also sent and continue to send capital to Iran either in times of crisis, such as during the earthquake in 1990, or regularly to support family or business interests. And Iranians in the United States continue to be connected to Iran either through news from Iran or about Iran by means of telephone conversations, movies, Persian-language radio, the internet, newspapers, and television programs.

The first Persian-language television program in the United States was aired in Los Angeles in 1978, the year riots and strikes began to threaten seriously the stability of the Pahlavi regime. Only one episode of the thirty-minute program was aired in 1978, and it was not until March 1981 that a thirty-minute weekly program, "Iranian" (Iranians), began to be aired regularly.[12] By March 1981, the regime of the Islamic Republic was continuing to consolidate its power, fighting both the Mojahedin, an Islamic Marxist guerrilla opposition group, and the Iraqis in a war that would last eight years and claim more than 1 million lives. By then, the American hostages had been released, and the first wave of Iranians had already moved to Los Angeles. This first regularly scheduled program was soon followed by other Persian-language programs, some of which have lasted more than ten years, although most have not. Between 1981 and 1993 thirty-seven producers created sixty-two regularly scheduled programs. In 1993 there were twenty-six programs produced in Los Angeles and two produced in Iran.[13] These programs are transmitted via satellite or tape to a variety of cities throughout the United States. Each of the programs usually includes time for news, advertisements, music videos, skits, and advice.

The short life span of most Persian-language programs is usually due to lack of funding, which comes from advertising or sometimes directly from exiled political groups. This direct political funding, needless to say, affects the content of the programs and their representations of Iran and Iranians. The television programs broadcast throughout the United States are divided among a number of political, ethnic, and religious factions. In many ways the programs reflect the population politically: while most of the Iranian television programs aired in the United States oppose the Islamic Republic, there are differences, differences that index the major political divisions of the last forty to fifty years in Iran.

Although the political affiliations of the programs are not highly emphasized, they are significant. While the majority of the programs are proroyalist and secular, some programs actively support the return of the Pahlavi regime to Iran, and others who had supported the Pahlavis in the early years after the revolution, do not today. In addition, there are programs that are sympathetic to the National Front, a political party that supported Prime Minister Mohammad Mossadegh and his nationalization policies in 1953. The National Front was also active in the 1978–79 revolution but could not compete with the organization and popularity of the religious movement. It is noteworthy that the Communist Party, known as Tudeh, which also played a role in the 1978–79 revolution, does not have a television program. From time to time there have been programs produced by the Mojahedin. According to Naficy, one such program ran in Los Angeles in 1986 but was briefly forced off the air by the U.S. government until it was aired on another television station.[14] Another such program ran in Washington, D.C., in 1992 to celebrate the birthday of Mariam Rajavi, one of the leaders of the Mojahedin. The year 1992 also marked the first program sponsored by the Islamic Republic, "Aftab" (Sunshine), to be aired in the United States. Although many Iranians severely criticized this program, and some royalist groups unsuccessfully called for boycotting it, it has gained large audiences mainly because the program maintains a serious format; has few, if any, advertisements; and does not emphasize its affiliations with the Islamic Republic. Together, these programs illustrate a variety and at times contending images of Iran and Iranians. The boundaries of what should constitute the nation are continually negotiated in these programs: although they may not seem to be in direct dialogue, their emphases and absences become evident in relation to each other.

In Los Angeles, Persian-language television is broadcast at different times on a number of cable and broadcast television stations, including KRCA and KSCI. In Washington, D.C., the television programs run every Sunday on WNVC in Fairfax, Virginia. In both cities, the different Persian-language programs, which run from thirty minutes to one hour each, are allotted times next to each other, creating blocks of several hours of successive Persian-language broadcasting. Often, families leave televisions on during these times, allowing the programs to play one after the other. For the most part, people pay little attention to the programs, which basically form a background sound of Persian-language ambiance.

Here I focus specifically on three programs that aired in Washington, D.C., on November 15, 1992. The first program, "Pars," opposes the Islamic Republic. The second program, "Melli," openly supports the return of the Pahlavis to Iran. The third program, "Peyk," is religious and supportive of the Islamic Republic. Using one day as the basic unit of analysis enables me to demonstrate how together these programs illustrate different visions of Iran. I describe each program in its entirety from beginning to end to illustrate its sequences, contents, and contexts. It is in the complete description of each program, one next to the other, that the reader gets a sense of the debates and common ground around Iranian national identity in the United States.

## SITES OF LONG-DISTANCE NATIONALISM:
## IRAN IN WASHINGTON, D.C.

In Washington, D.C., each program is framed by the voice of a non-Persian–speaking announcer stating that the program is supplied by a particular producer and that the "news segments within this program may have been produced by a television station in a foreign country." The announcer continues: "The views expressed in this program do not reflect the opinions or views of the management or staff of this public television station. This is WNVC, channel 56 in Fairfax, Virginia— bringing the world to Northern Virginia." This announcer, who pronounces the names of the programs with an "American" accent, introduces the programs and marks each of them as distinct. The announcer reinforces the foreignness of the programs both by stating that the program may have been produced in a foreign country and by his accent. The irony is that most of the programs are produced in Los Angeles, and thus, the world that is brought to Northern Virginia is most likely none other than that of Los Angeles. Different sites on a circuit of migration—namely, Los Angeles, Iran, and Washington, D.C.—are here visible from the opening statements of the programming.

### "PARS"

The first program begins with an image from Persepolis and the name of the program, "Pars," immediately connecting the show with a pre-Islamic past. Persepolis was the ceremonial capital of the Achaemenid empire (550—330 BCE) and was one of the central symbols of the Pahlavi regime. The Pahlavi regime continually emphasized Iran's pre-Islamic past with images of Persepolis, and it was there, in 1971, where a celebration was held to mark the (supposed) twenty-five hundred years of continuous monarchy. For this program to begin with such images not only immediately connects it not only with a pre-Islamic heritage but also with the Pahlavi regime, which propagated such imagery. Thus, here the nation and its people are shown to have a heritage long before Islam, attesting to the continuing tradition of a people. The continuity of Iran as a glorious and great "empire" is inextricably tied to images of Persepolis.

Moreover, the very name of the program, "Pars," is not a neutral choice. It is the name of the southwestern region of the Iranian plateau that was taken up by Western Orientalists and travelers: Persia became the established name for the entire plateau. The name *Pars* also emphasizes the unity of the country in terms of language and ethnicity since it portrays Persian-language speakers as the citizens, ignoring all other people and languages of Iran. The name of the program and the image of Persepolis together represent Iran as seemingly both unified and ancient, as linguistically homogeneous and primordial. Now, after the revolution, many in the United States insist on calling themselves Persians rather than Iranians because, faced with prejudice, many feel that being called Iranian would associate them with the Islamic Republic and stereotyped fanaticism. Many Iranians in the United States prefer to associate themselves with an exoticized land of carpets, poetry, and gardens than one supposedly full of religious revolutionaries and militants.

The background music of the opening of the program is an anthemish song beginning with "Iran, Iran . . ." As the music continues, views of different buildings and monuments in Iran come to the screen; we are confronted with more images of Persepolis. The music and the images fade away, and a woman appears to introduce and host the show. She is wearing makeup and is without a hair cover. The use of makeup and absence of the hair cover is especially important: the hair cover is not only iconic of a certain religiosity but also, for some, indexical of a connection with either the Islamic government or the Mojahedin. The presence or absence of the hair cover can be, therefore, a strong indication of political, as well as religious, association in these programs. After a brief welcome, a music video begins. The music video is about travel, return, tears, and longing. The scene is the Amtrak station in Glendale, California, where a man is leaving on a train and singing to his female lover or wife that he will come back soon. The man is wearing a sport jacket, and the woman, a short black dress with high heels and no hair cover. The camera focuses on her long brown curly hair defying the laws of the Islamic Republic. The video ends, and several advertisements begin: one for an Iranian grocery store, one for a restaurant, and one for a music concert.

Next is the news. A map of Iran covers an image of the globe. The woman who introduced the program reappears and begins the news, and after several lines, the camera shifts to a male newscaster. The man is wearing a tie, which is also indexical of a polemic in Iran: ties were so marked with the image of the Pahlavi era and its Western orientation that during and after the revolution, most men in Iran stopped wearing them in conformity with a new "dress code."[15] In Iran, dress codes for men and women have been the subject of a number of laws, which have attempted to regulate characteristics of national identity. For example, in 1929 Reza Shah Pahlavi ordered that all men wear "modern, western" dress to illustrate that Iran was an advanced nation.[16] The man and woman alternate reading the news, which mainly revolves around relations between Iran and the United States. The spectrum of news demonstrates a certain image of Iran: the two newscasters inform the viewers that the State Department announced that its allies should stop selling technology, which could be used for military purposes, to Iran, that Iran is still on the list of "terrorist" countries, that the "regime" would not allow foreign diplomats to visit an imprisoned American, that the *fatwa* (legal opinion) issued against Salman Rushdie cannot be revoked, and that a bomb exploded in Tehran. This news on *Pars* presents Iran as unstable and unpredictable, juxtaposing it to the majestic and solemn scenes of the monuments of Iran's past.

After the news and a number of advertisements, a music video begins. This time the video is of a woman singing about her husband and how happy she is to be with him. The camera follows the man through one of his usual days at work. His name, Javoonmard (gentleman), appears on the checks he signs, his business cards, his reserved parking spot, and his office building. He is shown driving a Rolls Royce and a Mercedes, talking on his car telephone, driving to his airplane, buying flowers that his driver takes to his wife, exiting Gucci's, helping an African American man cross the street and then giving him money, and returning home to his mansion, his singing wife, and playful daughter. This fantasy of money and power, aired after the news, highlights the distinctions between life in the United States and life in Iran: the video places images of wealthy Iranians in the present United States, while the news refers to instability in Iran. More important, however, this video illustrates the successful reproduction of the Iranian nation outside the boundaries of the physical nation as well as beyond the control of the present state. After the video, there are several advertisements, an announcement for a lecture entitled "What Is History?" and a request by an Iranian diagnosed with leukemia at Johns Hopkins hospital for help with a bone marrow transplant. He ends by saying that his ultimate wish is to return to Iran to see his family. Next is another music video showing a train moving slowly through tunnels and around mountains in Iran, an advertisement for a doctor, and one for an Iranian grocery store, which is superimposed on a scene from a market street in Iran.[17] The market street in Iran authenticates the grocery store: it has the same food one would find in that market thousands of miles away. The market street is also an image that could evoke nostalgia. Unlike the music video for Javoonmard, this advertisement blurs the lines between here and there, making little distinction between the United States and Iran. Moreover, rather than highlighting the successful reproduction of the nation, this advertisement emphasizes the authenticity of Iran in Iran. After the advertisements, there is advice from a lawyer who explains the drinking and driving laws of Virginia quickly resituating the viewer back in the United States where it is both legal and even possibly acceptable to drink alcohol. The television program ends with a final advertisement for cheap tickets to Iran, reinforcing the connections between the United States and Iran, and a farewell from the host. The voice of the non-Persian–speaking announcer returns and announces the beginning of the next program.

## "MELLI"

*Melli* means "national." As the name of a television program, it signifies the Pahlavi regime's policies of propagating the image of Iran as a single, unified nation and also suggests that the nation continues despite the present government in Iran.[18] The nation and its people belong to a land on which Persepolis, also presented during the opening seconds of the program, stands. This program is openly royalist, and in the beginning scenes, after advertisements for a lawyer, a concert, a car dealer, electrolysis, and a travel agent, the image of the Iranian flag with the Pahlavi regime's insignia of the lion appears. There is a quick image of the Shah's son, the present "Shah in exile," and the news segment begins. The Pahlavi flag and the image of the "Shah in exile" evoke more than nostalgia—they are political statements based on the continuance of the monarchy. Unlike "Pars," as a project for the future, "Melli" overtly emphasizes the rightful rule of the Pahlavis. A man, wearing a jacket and tie, appears and speaks of the 1992 U.S. presidential election. Then a woman, wearing makeup and no hair cover, appears and reads more news about the U.S. elections, situating the program in the United States. While this emphasis on the elections alludes to the rights of the new citizens to vote, the focus is on the possibly detrimental implications of Clinton's victory for U.S.-Iranian relations.

After the brief news update, there is a music video, explicitly about Iran rather than about life in exile as those shown on "Pars." There are images of nature, mosques, monuments, and finally of a street with a BMW and a cart. The BMW could be seen to refer to the wealth of some of the proroyalist community, placing them within the authentic home, Iran with the cart. That home is not only poor, but also and perhaps more important in this video, authentic and natural. As the music video ends, a quasipedagogic editorial begins about the differences between Republicans and Democrats in the United States, noting that it is always when Democrats are in power that Americans become involved in world problems; the connection between Carter and the Iranian Revolution is given as an excellent example. After the editorial, another series of advertisements, and immigration advice, a skit begins.

A male television producer in the United States sits at a typewriter, singing to himself. He is a bit disheveled, wearing a sport jacket and an open shirt with no tie. The telephone rings, and the television producer answers the telephone with the name of the company. The image switches back and forth between the producer and the caller, a man who is wearing a collarless shirt. When the caller makes an unusual statement about the time of night, the man at the typewriter becomes confused and, in English, asks "Can I help you?" The caller then complains: "[S]o, since when have you become so American? At least speak correctly."[19] Slightly offended, the man in the United States returns to Persian and asks who is calling. The caller says he would rather not answer the question since it may not be safe where he is. The man in the United States becomes intrigued and asks from where the other man is calling. When the man who called says, "Iran," the television producer becomes excited that he has received a call from Iran and says: "*my* Iran." At this point, the man in Iran corrects him and says, "No, I am calling from *my* Iran." Here the television producer replies that yes, that is what he meant, *that same* Iran.

When the television producer asks how the man in Iran knew the telephone number, he replies from the programs which are all available in Iran. They have a conversation about work: taking turns, they explain that life is not easy and that they have to work hard. They then begin a conversation about what each has in the different countries. The man in Iran points out that what there is in America, they do not have in Iran, while what is available in Iran, they have in America. He finally adds, however, that there is one thing that they have that is not in the United States: *pasdaran* and *hezbollahi*.[20] At this, the man in the United States laughs and says, that in fact they have them too, however, instead of beards, in the United States they wear ties. The producer then asks if their telephone conversation is dangerous for the man in Iran. After responding that everything should be fine, the man in Iran asks the same question of the television producer, who declares that America is a free country and that he can say whatever he wants. This declaration is exaggerated, as if to mimic and perhaps even mock American rhetoric. Suddenly, in the corner of the screen showing America, a third man appears and stands over the television producer, who becomes very nervous and puts down the telephone. The man who just entered, an Iranian with a beard and no tie, sits down at the desk. If the tielessness is not enough to indicate the man's affiliations, the beard unmistakably indicates to the viewer that the man is a supporter of the Islamic Republic. Then, "To Be Continued" flashes on the screen.

Each of the two men represents working men in different societies, each exploring stereotypes of the other. For the man in the United States, Iran is a place where old customs and hopes still exist even though a constant fear of the state pervades all conversations and aspects of life. For the man in Iran, the United States is where those who gave up Iran now live. The problem of losing the use of Persian and, thus, "becoming American" is noted here. This show, which is written from the view of the royalists, highlights a tension mentioned at the beginning of this chapter. Here, though, the royalist program places the words of pointing out the tension in the mouth of the Iranian in Iran: first, he says "Since when have you become so American?" and then he insists that "Iran" is his Iran and not that of the immigrant. Where is the immigrant supposed be from? He should not become American, yet he cannot justly claim to "have" an Iran. The problem, though, is presented as a paradox that the Iranian in Iran cannot overcome. For the immigrant, by contrast, it is somewhat obvious: Iran is still his country, yet he works and lives in a place where he must also speak English. In this skit, the Iranians in Iran appear to blame those in the United States no matter what they do.

Still, in "Melli," there is a constant reference to the continued existence of a true, good, natural Iran, which cannot be reached because of the present government. If only the two men could talk to each other, they would discover that they have much in common. However, the Iranian state, which even appears in the United States, prevents contact between people. Danger associated with the Islamic Republic is not confined to Iran; it lurks in the United States as well. After the skit, a female announcer returns and asks for support for the Leukemia patient, connecting this program with the previous one, "Pars." There are more advertisements, another brief discussion of Clinton's victory, advice from a doctor about acne, advice from a lawyer about immigration laws in the United States, and advice about taxes when buying and selling houses. Finally, there is another music video about a woman wearing a *chador* who glances provocatively at a peasant, the singer. The rural setting makes the woman's *chador* acceptable: here, the *chador* is indicative of folkloric and traditional dress rather than religion. The program then ends with another advertisement for a travel agency.

## "PEYK"

After two other programs, "T.V. of Iran" and "Diyar," which is a subsidiary program produced by "Melli," the program "Peyk" begins. *Peyk*, which means "message," suggests news from Iran. Unlike the other programs, "Peyk" begins with the declaration: "In the name of God." In juxtaposition to the other programs, the declaration indicates that the program has religious orientations. However, the declaration, made in Persian rather than Arabic, separates the program from stereo-types of an Islamic regime controlled by religious leaders who speak Arabic or Persian, with Arabic accents.[21] The introductory scenes and music are also different from the two previous programs described above. Instead of anthems, the voices of a woman reciting and a man singing poetry, accompanied by classical music, provide the background for images of flowers. Flowers are a common motif of Persian classical literature and its symbolic language. As such, their significance deepens as they are shown, with the classical music in the background, in the United States. Both the voice of a woman reciting poetry and Persian classical music, neither of which were on the radio in Iran for several years after the revolution, also separate the program from earlier stereo-types of the regime.[22] That is to say, although the program is more reli-gious than the previous two, it also claims to be authentically Iranian, thus touching on the complex relationship between Iranian nationalism and pan-Islamism, which surfaced during and after the 1978–79 revo-lution.

As the images of flowers end, there are two advertisements for restaurants, and then the news begins. Unlike the previous two pro-grams, the images accompanying the introduction to the news on "Peyk" include some shots of industry, highlighting the successful con-tinuation and development of Iran's economy. The news announcers are two clean-shaven men in ties. Their ties and their lack of beards not only return us to the comment made by the television producer in "Melli" that *pasdaran and hezbollahi* also exist in the United States but also sug-gest that these newscasters are not the stereotyped men of the Islamic Republic. The fact that the two news announcers in this show do not have beards and are wearing ties signifies that the program was designed to attract exile viewers. The format of the news in this program is also more serious than the two previous programs; the newscasters do not smile, they speak matter-of-factly, and there is more description of events in Iran: there is specific news about Tehran University and the Parliament. The more detailed news about events in Iran, unlike the above two programs, presents a vision of Iran as continuing on an every-day level. After the news, a skit begins.

The skit for November 15 is framed around an earlier one, which focused on the initial problems of a newlywed couple. In the previous skit broadcast on November 8, the newlywed wife writes a letter to her mother describing her new life. All the women in this program cover their hair and wear long overcoats. The skit follows the development of the couple's first days together. When the husband asks that the wife make dinner and iron his shirts, she does neither, saying that she does not have time to prepare anything to eat and that if he wants his shirts ironed, he should take them to the laundry. The scene becomes tense, and they argue. Eventually, he says that either she start doing her share or she should return to her father's house—it is her decision. To this ultimatum, she cries and says that she wants to change her ways but that she needs his help. The next morning, when the husband goes to the kitchen, he sees that the table has been set for breakfast and that she is not there. She soon enters with fresh bread and food for the day. He is very pleased, which, she says, makes her happy. As he is about to leave for work, she hands him a letter to her mother to mail. The final scene is her mother reading the letter and crying. In the letter, the daughter blames the mother for not having prepared her for her responsibilities in marriage and life.

According to this skit, the success or failure of the Iranian family rests on mothers. It is their responsibility to teach their daughters how to keep a household happy, clean, and neat. Without this preparation, the Iranian family and, by extension, the Iranian nation will fall apart. On the one hand, the mother, who was raised before the revolution, could be seen to refer to the irresponsible values of that time. On the other hand, the daughter might represent the new, young woman of post-revolutionary Iran. If the daughter had continued in the ways of her mother, her own marriage would have collapsed. But the daughter "comes to her senses" and understands the importance of her gendered responsibilities for saving her marriage and her country. It is through the actions of Iranian women that the nation can reproduce itself successfully. This skit, in juxtaposition to the previous programs, highlights the central role women play in the imagery and the politics of the Iranian nation.

On November 15, the skit begins with the man coming home from work. Before he can relax, the wife sends him out to get fruit and sweets for the expected guests. The scene changes and follows the development of three other couples who must buy the newlyweds gifts. The first couple continually argue, and after walking around the streets of Tehran for hours, they finally choose a blanket. The wife does not like it and is embarrassed to give it to the newlyweds. The husband, instead, wants to buy anything since, he says, it is the thought that counts. They argue all the way to the newlyweds' apartment. The second couple is a wiser, older couple. The husband is a university professor who refuses to be hurried into buying anything, despite his wife's occasional insistences that they buy something soon. As she brings him tea, does the ironing, and smiles at his stubbornness, he reads the newspaper and comments on the death of one of his former students. It is not clear how or where the student died. The professor says that they should think about something that the couple might need. Finally, there is a third couple who is having financial difficulties, and the wife is upset that they do not have enough money for an "elegant" gift. She accuses her husband of not wanting to spend money on her family. The following images are of a series of telephones with a background sound of conversations about who took what gift when and then of hands giving gifts. We return to the older couple, who still has not bought anything. The scene then shifts to the newlyweds' apartment, where, now, there are piles of blankets and thermoses. Clearly, there are too many of the same things, and the couple talks about how they wish that people would either not bring them anything or bring useful gifts. The scene turns to the couple with financial difficulties who are still arguing. The man finally removes a small stack of bills from his coat pocket and gives it to his wife, saying that is all they have, and she is welcome to take what she wants for the gift, but that it is then her responsibility to pay for their living expenses. With this, we return to the newlyweds, who propose unacceptable alternatives to this gift-giving custom, and the skit ends. The skit is a pragmatic statement about unnecessary consumerism; it suggests that although thoughtful gifts are important, ones that are given out of mere obligation are useless. This moralistic and pedagogic skit illustrates the everyday life dilemmas of "ordinary" people. When the skit ends, an image of a waterfall emerges, Santur music is played in the background, and the "Peyk" program ends.

## EVOKING NATIONAL IDENTITY

These three programs, "Pars," "Melli," and "Peyk" illustrate simultaneous visions of Iran and Iranians. In the first program, Iran is seen as an unstable place whose imagined glorious and beautiful past is nonetheless longed for. It is an Iran of "Persians" who live and prosper in the United States. The second program, which is explicitly royalist, envisions an Iran whose ordinary citizens have continued the attitudes and beliefs of the previous era but whose present government is dangerous and threatening. Here the true and rightful leaders continue in exile, without the organizations and powers of the past, but with its images and memories. The last program illustrates an Iran of serious individuals concerned for the wellbeing of the nation. They strive to overcome some of the faults and extravagances of the previous era.

Although these programs evoke different visions of Iranian national identity, they do so in similar ways: by illustrating that the nation has historical roots in a place as well as by presenting the people as subjects of symbolic systems that are performed as living and reproductive traditions.[23] They present images of land and monuments, references to legitimate rule, and everyday signs of performed identification. While the images of land work to reinforce the autochthonous connections of viewers to place and the references to legitimate rule serve as bridges between past glories or abuses of empire and projects for the future, the programs also illustrate everyday practices such that "the scraps, patches, and rages of daily life [are] repeatedly turned into signs of a national culture."[24] As each program defines the nation, it highlights its similarites and differences with other visions. These contending visions, however, are themselves contained within the limits of the oppositions, exposing the shared assumptions of what should be negotiated.

These Persian-language programs broadcast in Washington, D.C., all emphasize the beauty and power of Iran's land. In addition to fields and mountains, the program "Peyk," in particular, focuses on flowers connecting Iranian "culture" of poetry with "nature," the Iranian past with the present. As specific cultural referents, flowers traverse time from a "classical period" through today, continually reproducing. For the most part, however, this land is not untouched but is marked with ancient and modern monuments. While some seem to blend into or even grow from the ground like flowers, most stand as undeniable reminders of human presence on and even domination of the land. These monumental markings are the confirmations that people are connected to the place. For the anti-Islamic Republic programs, this land is marked with monuments dedicated to a claimed past glory, one that ranges from the pre-Islamic Achaemenids to the Pahlavis. While the programs do not explain the land and monuments, since it is assumed that the viewers are, to some degree, aware of their significance, these images serve as reminders of the ancient and recent past as well as the continuation of place. Images of the land, nature, and monuments are not only primordial and continuous, they illustrate that those who are watching the programs originate and belong in Iran.

The programs also make claims about legitimate rule. These claims, which range from a secular republic, a monarchy, to an Islamic republic, act as bridges between the past and the future. They refer to Iran's past, whether to extol the glories of the monarchy or to highlight the abuses of that system, as well as propose projects for the future. Even though it is unlikely that Iranians in the United States will return to Iran, each of the anti-Islamic Republic programs continues to claim that it is the appropriate representative of the nation. Just as the skit on the pro-royalist program "Melli" suggests, if only the Iranian state could be circumvented, Iranians in the United States and in Iran would find that they have much more in common than they expected, especially in their disrespect for the present state. As different views of Iranian history and visions for the future, the programs place themselves in competition with each other. Despite the underlying political leanings of the programs, however, these programs focus on the people as a collective making the political, as such, seem less important in constructing the nation.

In addition to reminders of the past and projects for the future, these programs evoke national identity through the performances of daily activities. The emphasis on the land and its monuments as well as the references to legitimate rule are complimented with enactments of the continuing, reproducing present. These performances of daily life, which point to symbols of identification such as dress codes, language, and music, as well as community interests and concerns, are enacted in the news segments, advertisements, and skits. The skits, for example— which portray issues such as the relationship between Iranians in the United States and those in Iran, the roles of husbands and wives in mar- riage, and the practices of gift-giving—reinforce the continuing nation- people. The programs portray Iranian lifestyles as emblematic of Irani- ans in general, albeit with differences.

On the one hand, these differences are shown to be subsumed, per- haps uncomfortably, under the umbrella of one nation-people. For example, although the programs note the differences between Iranians in Iran and Iranians in the United States, it is as though the fundamen- tal connections remain unbroken. Even language, which has become one of the banners of national identity and which is problematic for the gen- erations of Iranians living in the United States, will somehow be over- come by other even more fundamental connections. On the other hand, the programs maintain their differences through signs of identification, such as head covers, ties, and declarations of faith. These signs of eth- nic, social, religious, and political identification work to define what the nation should and should not be. While these differences define the inclusions and exclusions of national identity, they also share an under- lying discourse of debate: the oppositions and contending images estab- lish the boundaries within which differences are played out.

## NEGOTIATING HERE AND THERE

Evoking nation-ness in these programs is further complicated: in addi- tion to attention to and defining the past, present, and future of the nation, long-distance nationalism must also negotiate the complex rela- tionship between "here" and "there."[25] These programs not only focus on land, legitimate rule, and daily activities but also confront the diffi- culty that the "nation" is divided by thousands of miles. Throughout the music videos, advertisements, news segments, and skits, the programs directly or indirectly touch on the ambiguities of where the nation is. For the diaspora community, while there is a keen awareness that the true land of the nation is there rather than here. Not only do some of the nation-people continue to live, and even thrive, here, but they have no real intention to return.

The relation between here and there becomes more than a difference of actual place: the opposition between the two is full of other meanings, and at times these spatial adverbs connote more than whether the object being talked about, Iran, is physically close to or far from the speaker. These spatial adverbs also suggest rich and poor, repressive and free, and even fake and authentic. The relationship between here and there is also constituted differently at different points. Sometimes "there" becomes more specified, or marked, than "here." Other times, here is more specified. Although here and there are usually separate, sometimes they are even imposed on one another so that there should be no distinction, such as in the advertisement for the grocery store.

The constant play between here and there is evident in the words of the talking head quoted at the beginning of the article. As I noted earlier, what the man says is striking. However, it is striking not only because of the declaration that Iranians must retain their national identities outside Iran, but also because of the ways he uses the words *here* and *foreign*, *they* and *we*. There is something awkward about the phrases, something almost confusing. Analyzing the two sentences highlights how he produces intricate relations among himself, other Iranians outside Iran, and Iran. In the first part of the first sentence, the man says that it does not matter how long "they" are in "a foreign country." Taken alone, this clause is not awkward: the man is speaking of people, excluding himself, who are either temporarily or more permanently residing in a foreign country. In Persian, the term for *foreign*, *khareji*, derives from the Arabic root for *outside*, on the other side of a boundary. Moreover, this 'outside' is an indefinite place, as the expression *a foreign country* does not refer to a specific country. In the second part of the same sentence, however, the man uses the word *here* ("they wouldn't be from here"). The juxtaposition between 'a foreign country' and 'here' is striking, since 'foreign' indicates outside, or on the other side of a boundary, and 'here' refers to a proximal space. It seems that he has made a mistake, but this apparent mistake alerts us to an interesting point. The man is making two parallel moves: first, he is making 'here' foreign, or 'outside' and therefore defining the adverb's opposite, 'there', as not foreign. Second, he is identifying 'here' as *any* foreign country. The awkward use of the spatial adverbs both exemplifies the diasporia experience and illustrates the tensions of long-distance nationalism.

The talking head makes another shift, rendering these phrases even more confusing. In the first sentences, he uses the third-person plural ending indicating 'they', excluding himself from the comment about how many years one could be in a foreign country, 'here'. In itself, this is not too awkward: it is common to say "they are here." This, however, indicates that the speaker is somehow excluded from the group even though they all share the same (physical) space. What is unsettling is that the speaker then switches pronouns and uses 'we', thus including himself in the plurality of belonging to Iran and never losing his national identity. The switch to 'we', is a stark indication of his affiliation with belonging 'there'.

Belonging in and to Iran, to there rather than here, unravels the relationship between nation and state. For the anti-Islamic Republic programs, national identity is equated with the distant land, which is both the source of a supposedly shared culture and the goal of return. However, this supposedly shared culture is marked by factionalism, and the goal of the diaspora is not simply a return to the land. It is a return tied to politics, a return aimed at statehood. While the programs portray a nation continuing to thrive independent of the state, they also make clear that this nation is incomplete and that only a nation with a state would fulfill their nostalgia for Iran. For "Peyk," it is clearly different: the program speaks from the point of view of the state. Nevertheless this program also resorts to appeals to an inclusive Iranianness downplaying the ideology of the state. Here the nation is already fulfilled with a state. The program replaces nostalgia with the realities of Iran as a living and reproducing country. This difference, however, does not mean that "Peyk" does not appeal to national imaginings. Like its counterparts, it participates in the construction of an Iran that is at the same time all-encompassing and exclusive, the ambivalence that allows for and sustains this long-distance nationalism.

## BIBLIOGRAPHY

Abu-Lughod, Lila. 1997. "The Interpretation of Culture(s) After Television." *Representations* 59: 109–34.

———. 1996. "Dramatic Reversals: Political Islam and Egyptian Television." Pp. 269–82 in *Political Islam*, Joel Beinin and Joe Stork, eds. Berkeley: University of California Press.

———. 1995a. "Movie Stars and Islamic Moralism in Egypt." *Social Text* 42: 53–67.

———. 1995b. "The Objects of Soap Opera: Egyptian Television and the Cultural Politics of Modernity." In *Worlds Apart: Modernity through the Prism of the Local*, Daniel Miller, ed. London: Routledge.

———. 1993a. "Finding a Place for Islam: Egyptian Television Serials and the National Interest." *Public Culture* 5, no. 3: 493–513.

———. 1993b. "Islam and Public Culture: The Politics of Egyptian Television Serials." *Middle East Report* 180, 23, no. 1: 25–30.

Adelkhah, Fariba. 1991. "Michael Jackson ne peut absolument rien faire: Les pratiques musicales en Republique Islamique d'Iran." *Cahiers d'études sur la méditerranée orientale et le monde turco-iranien* 11: 23–40.

Adelkhah, Fariba, and Jean-François Bayart. 1991. "Entretien avec Jean During: Epuration et essor de la musique sous la Republique Islamique d'Iran." *Cahiers d'études sur la méditerranée orientale et le monde turco-iranien* 11: 17–21.

Agha, Asif. 1996. "Shema and Superposition in Spatial Deixis." *Anthropological Linguistics* 38, no. 4: 643–82.

Anderson, Benedict. 1994. "Exodus." *Critical Inquiry* 20, no. 2: 314–27.

———. 1993. "Long-Distance Nationalism: World Capitalism and the Rise of Identity Politics." Paper Delivered at the University of Michigan, Ann Arbor.

———. 1991 [1983]. *Imagined Communities: Reflections on the Origin and the Spread of Nationalism*. New York: Verso.

Appadurai, Arjun. 1990. "Disjuncture and Difference in the Global Cultural Economy." *Public Culture* 2, no. 2: 1–24.

Armbrust, Walter. 1996. *Mass Culture and Modernism in Egypt*. Cambridge: Cambridge Universtiy Press.

———. 1992. "The National Vernacular: Folklore and Egyptian Popular Culture." *Michigan Quarterly Review* 31: 525–42.

Bhabha, Homi K., ed. 1990. *Nation and Narration*. New York: Routledge.

Bourdieu, Pierre. 1998 [1996]. *On Television*. New York: New.

Chehabi, Houchang E. 1993. "Staging the Emperor's New Clothes: Dress Codes and Nation-Building under Reza Shah." *Iranian Studies* 26, nos. 3–4: 209–33.

Foucault, Michel. 1972. *The Archaeology of Knowledge*. New York: Pantheon.

Hanks, William F. 1992. "The Indexical Ground of Deictic Reference." In *Rethinking Context: Language as an Interactive Phenomenon*, Alessandro Duranti and Charles Goodwin, eds. Cambridge: Cambridge University Press.

———. 1990. *Referential Practice*. Chicago: University of Chicago Press.

Kelley, Ron, ed. 1993. *Irangeles: Iranians in Los Angeles*. Los Angeles: University of California Press.

Naficy, Hamid. 1993a. "From Broadcasting to Narrowcasting: Middle East Diaspora in Los Angeles." *Middle East Report* 180, 23, no. 1: 31–37.

———. 1993b. *The Making of Exile Cultures: Iranian Television in Los Angeles*. Minneapolis: University of Minnesota Press.

———. 1991. "From Liminality to Incorporation: Iranian Exile Television in the USA." In *Iranian Refugees and Exiles since Khomeini*, Asghar Fathi, ed. Costa Mesa: Mazda Publishers.

Silverstein, Michael. 1976. "Shifters, Linguistic Categories, and Cultural Descriptions." In *Meaning in Anthropology*, Keith H. Basso and Henry A. Selby, eds. Albuquerque: University of New Mexico Press.

# NOTES

1. Melli Television aired in Washington, D.C. November 8, 1992. The original sentence is "Shayad dah sal, bist sal, si sal keshvar-e khareji budand vali mal-e inja nistand. In-e keh ma hoviat-e mun-o, hoviat-e melli-e mun-o hich vajh

az dast nemidim." Note that the announcer changes the place reference in the sentence. He begins the sentence from a view from Iran, people were in "a foreign country," but then switches to say "here," meaning the United States. He also shifts the subject of the sentences from "they" to "we." I will discuss these shifts later in this chapter.

2. See Anderson 1993, p. 16.

3. See Anderson 1991; 1993; 1994; Appadurai 1990; and Bhabha 1990.

4. See Abu-Lughod 1997; 1996; 1995a; 1995b; 1993a; 1993b.

5. See Armbrust in this volume, and also 1996; 1992.

6. See Naficy 1993a; 1993b; 1991.

7. See Naficy 1993a, p. 34.

8. In his critique of French television journalism, Bourdieu similarly argues that despite their political and social differences, television news programs in France form a structured social space, or journalistic field, in which they share a set of assumptions; see Bourdieu 1998, pp. 40–47.

9. See Kelley 1993 for more information on these groups.

10. *Los Angeles Times*, March 19, 1992 H11, and quoted by Hamid Naficy in "From Broadcasting to Narrowcasting," *Middle East Report* (January-February 1993). Mehdi Bozorgmehr, Georges Sabagh, and Claudia Der-Martirosian published their 1986 figures in their article "Beyond Nationality: Religio-Ethnic Diversity," *Irangeles: Iranians in Los Angeles* (1993).

11. See Kelley 1993, p. viii.

12. See Naficy 1993b, p. 64.

13. See ibid.

14. See ibid., p. 74.

15. Of course not all Iranian men who wear or wore ties are royalist, nor are all men who do not supporters of the Islamic Republic. However, depending on the context, ties can be indicators of opposition to or support of particular politics. Abu-Lughod and Armburst also note that styles of dress in Egyptian soap operas and films are indicators of social, political, and religious position; see Abu-Lughod 1993a, p. 499, and 1996, p. 273; and Armbrust 1996, pp. 23–24.

16. See Chehabi 1993.

17. The scene seems to be from postrevolution Iran, since all the women are wearing *chador* (full-length covering), and there is brief image of a religious scholar.

18. Although "Melli" is also the name for the National Front, here one gets the sense of the ideological mix: royalist and nationalist.

19. The original words are "Hala az key vase-ye ma amrikai shodi? Khob dorost harf bezan, ghorbunet beram."

20. Pasdaran are the members of the Revolutionary Guard Corps, a postrevolution military force. Hezbollah literally means "Party of God"; however, here the term loosely refers to a young, bureaucratic class whose members are devoted to the ideology of the Islamic Republic in its most dogmatic form.

21. The program begins with the Persian declaration *be nam-e Khoda* rather than the Arabic version, *bism Allah al-rahman al-rahim*, which means "in the name of God, the most compassionate, the most merciful."

22. For more on music in the Islamic Republic, see Adelkhah 1991 and Adelkhah and Bayart 1991.

23. See Bhabha 1990.

24. See ibid., p. 297.

25. For further discussions on deictics, see Agha 1996; Hanks 1992; 1990; and Silverstein 1976.

# INDEX